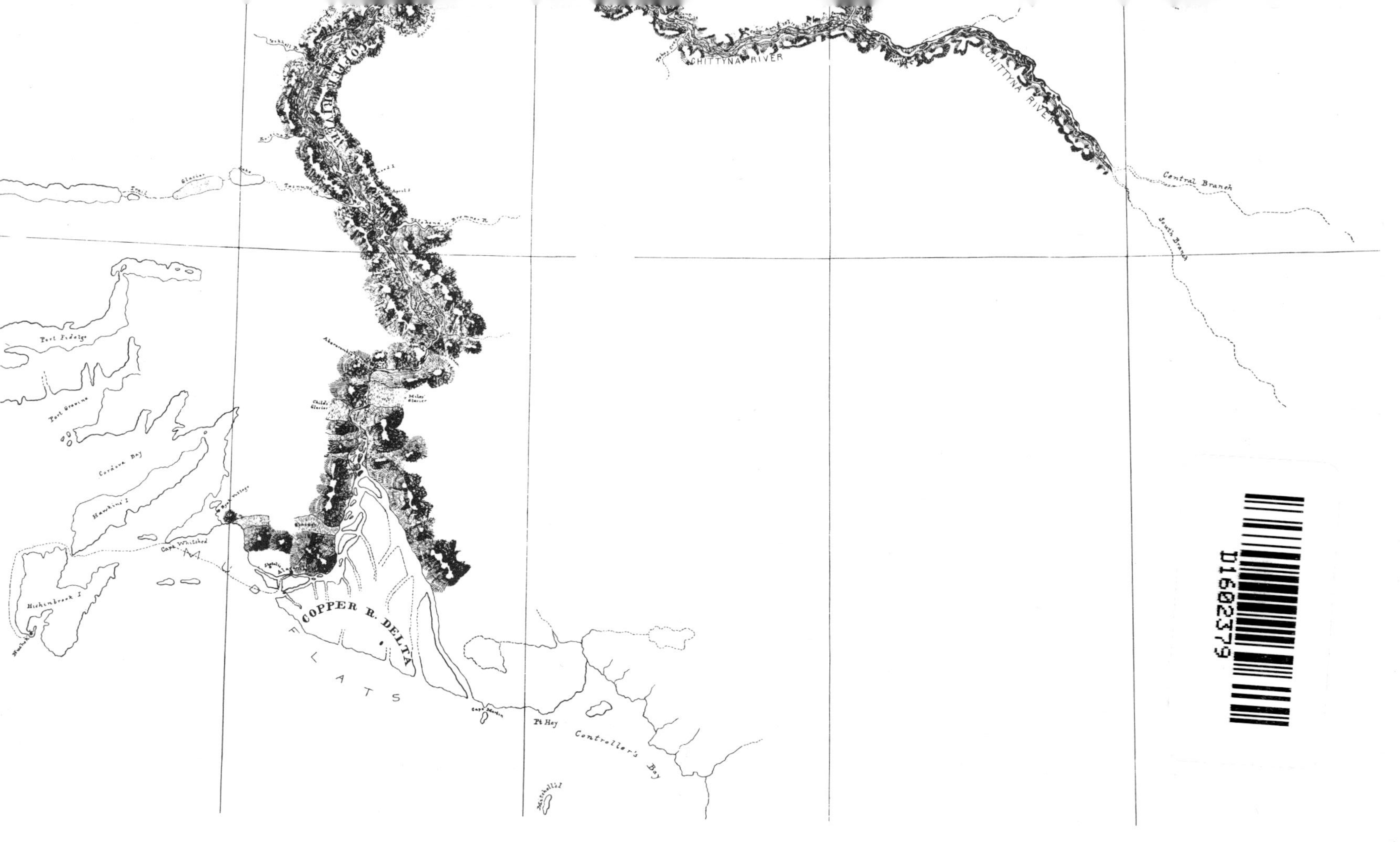
COPPER RIVER
CHITTYNA RIVER
CHITTYNA RIVER
Central Branch
South Branch
Glacier
Trail
Port Fidalgo
Port Gravina
Cordova Bay
Hawkins I
Hichinbrook I
Cape Whitshed
Childs Glacier
Miles Glacier
COPPER R. DELTA
FLATS
Cape Martin
Pt Hey
Controller's Bay
Matchell's I
D1602379

ALLEN

Major General Henry T. Allen. (Signal Corps Photograph No. 73146, National Archives)

HEATH TWICHELL, JR.

ALLEN

The Biography of an Army Officer 1859–1930

RUTGERS UNIVERSITY PRESS
New Brunswick New Jersey

Library of Congress Cataloging in Publication Data

Twichell, Heath, 1934–
Allen: the biography of an Army officer, 1859–1930.

Bibliography: p.
1. Allen, Henry Tureman, 1859–1930. I. Title.
U53.A44T94 355.3′31′0924 [B] 74-12224
ISBN 0-8135-0778-2

Manufactured in the United States of America by Quinn & Boden Company, Inc., Rahway, New Jersey

For Peggy–
Like Dora, a good army wife

Contents

List of Illustrations

A. Photographs

B. Maps

Preface and Acknowledgements

Most readers have probably never heard of Henry T. Allen. I certainly never had until, in doing research for a paper on German disarmament after the First World War, I read two books he wrote about his experiences as commander of the American occupation forces in the Rhineland from 1919 to 1923.[1] Although both books are invaluable sources on the four-power occupation and conditions in Germany during this period, I was equally impressed by what they revealed about their author. I decided to find out more about him.

The only published accounts of Allen's life are contained in two brief biographical sketches,[2] but these were even more intriguing to me. Here was a complex and unusual man, possessing many seemingly contradictory qualities: a haughty aristocrat who never lost his boyish love of fun; a toughened veteran of three wars who devoted himself to the welfare and protection of war-ravaged civilians each time the fighting ended; an urbane sophisticate who obviously relished "collecting" many of the great men of the era as his friends; and a supremely ambitious military professional with a profound understanding of the democratic traditions of his country. He was much else besides: a scholar, a talented linguist, a sportsman, an explorer, a diplomat, an author, and even a politician.

His life began before the Indian frontier had disappeared and the last blank spaces on the maps of American territory were filled in. Before he died the United States had transformed itself, under the imperatives of its manifest destiny but with many a reluctant backward glance, into a first-rank world power with great international responsibilities. During this process of national transformation, Allen took part in nearly every major step involving the participation of the U.S. Army. Although few of the roles he played were individually of outstanding historical importance, collectively they entitle him, in my opinion, to consideration as a significant figure in American history.

While this book is primarily a study of Allen's military career and accomplishments, I have attempted to make it something more than simply a biography. Interwoven with the colorful strands of Allen's life is a paradoxical theme: the growing tendency of the army to become involved in affairs not purely military all the while there has been an increasing amount of professionalization within the organization in an attempt to define, emphasize, and preserve its internal standards and unique ethic. Allen's career is a perfect example of this paradox, but to illustrate it more fully many of the episodes of his life have been portrayed against the wider backdrop of related events in American military history. Only in this way can Allen's ambitions, frustrations, failures, and triumphs be completely understood.

Allen is not an attack or a defense of the man or of the organization in which he served. Nor is it an examination of that fictitious thing, the "military mind." I have simply tried to show what I sincerely believe: that the United States Army, in all its diversity, reflects the strengths and weaknesses and the great purposes and foolish mistakes of the people in it and the nation itself. There is much to praise and much to criticize. I have done both.

Allen's papers, comprising approximately 15,000 items and filling seventy-eight boxes, have been donated by his family to the Library of Congress. Although I have relied heavily on this material, other primary sources and secondary works have been used to ensure that this is my version of Allen's life and not his. I would like to have included more material on Allen's wife Dora, but very little information about her is available, particularly during the later years of their marriage. This is not to say that the letters and diaries he saved were collected with any intent to distort or deceive. The man himself is there in his papers, warts and all.

For the historical and literary flaws in this book, I take full responsibility. The credit for whatever merits it has must be shared with many people, beginning with my dissertation committee at American University in Washington, D.C. I am indebted to Dr. Robert Beisner, the committee chairman, and its members, Drs. Dorothy Gondos, Carl Anthon, and Maurice Matloff, for their helpful guidance and sincere interest in my work. To my former colleagues in the Office of the Chief of Military History, Department of the Army, I owe an immense debt of gratitude. Practically everybody in that office has helped me in some way, but I especially want to thank my two cartographers, Mr. Elliot Dunay and Mr. Howell Brewer, and the readers who have contributed many valuable suggestions for improvement: Mr. Charles MacDonald, Mr. John Albright, Mr. Alfred Beck, and Dr. David Wigdor. I am all the more grateful to these busy gentlemen because the assistance they have given me has been solely at the expense of their off-duty time.

Many other friends have helped. Among them are Dr. Mitchell Kerr, Dr. James Hewes, Dr. Richard Bartlett and The Reverend Donald Smythe, S.J., who have read and criticized portions of my manuscript dealing with their historical specialties. All four have also kindly permitted me to read manuscripts of their own being prepared for publication. The Reverend Richard Downing and Mr. John Albright have served as my translators of Spanish documents, and Mr. David Reber is responsible for many of the excellent photographic reproductions. My sister, Ruth Twichell Cochrane, has been my severest literary critic. The clichés that remain in the text are due to my own stubbornness and not to any slips of her heavy editor's pencil.

Thanks must also go to Allen's family. It was a pleasant privilege to know Colonel Henry T. Allen, Jr., and his brother-in-law and sister, Colonel and Mrs. Joseph W. Viner. They trusted me with family memorabilia and graciously consented to answer my often impertinent questions in numerous lengthy interviews. They, too, read the manuscript. Despite its sometimes unflattering portrayal of their ancestor, they never once attempted to have me soften or change it. Knowing these extraordinary people has deepened my understanding of the human qualities of General Allen. I hope it has added that dimension to my writing.

For my wife, Peggy, who after several years at the typewriter often thinks she is married to Henry T. Allen, no word of thanks will ever be sufficient.

The opinions and insertions in this work are my own and are not to be construed as official or as reflecting the views of the Department of the Army or the Department of Defense.

ALLEN

CHAPTER I

Kentucky Gentry

Sharpsburg, in northeastern Kentucky, is set among the gently rolling limestone hills and bluegrass pastures of Bath County. West of Slate Creek, which bisects the county, is some of the most fertile land in the entire state. Sharpsburg lies in the center of this black soil region. To the east, where the foothills of the Appalachians begin, the land is less good for farming but rich in timber and minerals, including iron ore and the bubbling mineral springs which gave the county its name.[1]

Attracted by this abundance, the first white settlers began to arrive around 1775. Many were Virginians, men of substance and breeding who brought their slaves with them. An early landowner was John Allen, a distinguished lawyer who had once had Aaron Burr for a client and who could trace his family back to the Old World and through four generations in the New. He acquired land in Kentucky around 1785 and moved his family there from Virginia in 1806.[2] When Bath County was established in 1811, Judge John Allen convened the first circuit court near Owingsville, the new county seat.[3]

John Allen's son, Ruben Sanford, was born in Paris, Kentucky, in 1810. In 1832, Sanford Allen married Susannah Shumate of Huguenot immigrant ancestry.[4] A few years later they settled twelve miles northwest of Owingsville in Sharpsburg, a "thriving little community" with "three churches, one tavern, six doctors, four stores, two sawmills, one bagging factory, two wool factories, ten mechanical shops, and one male and one female school." [5] In 1860 the town had a white population of 284.[6]

One of the stores in Sharpsburg was Sanford Allen's. His business letterhead proclaimed him a dealer in "Staple and Fancy Drygoods, Queensware, etc.; Ladies Ties, Gloves and Jewelry a Speciality." [7]

Allen also owned considerable land and livestock, but the store was his primary source of income. Prior to the Civil War, his holdings were valued at $42,600, including eleven slaves, thus ranking him among the dozen wealthiest men in the county.[8] Socially, the Allens' position was as secure as good lineage, good land, and good money could make it.

A block down Main Street from the store stood the comfortable and unpretentious Allen home. Built in Sharpsburg's early days, it was of two-story log construction covered with white clapboard. The thick plastered walls of its low-ceilinged rooms kept it cool in the summer, and six fireplaces warmed it in the winter. The house sat close to the street, but in back there were trees, a large lawn and garden with a rainwater cistern, stables for the horses, and slave cabins.[9] In these pleasant surroundings, Susannah Allen gave birth to her thirteenth child, Henry Tureman Allen, on April 13, 1859.

Henry's father was a serious, God-fearing man who worked hard and lived temperately. But for his black cutaway and stovepipe hat, a daguerreotype of him taken around this time might be a portrait of an Old Testament prophet. His eyes, set in a deeply lined and weathered face, pierce the viewer with a stern and righteous intensity. Susannah Allen's portrait is no less revealing of hard work, firm convictions, and strong personality. Extremely devout, she was influential in the establishment of Sharpsburg's Baptist Church and raised her children in that faith.[10]

In all Susannah Allen bore her husband ten sons and four daughters. The oldest daughter, Mary Jane, had already married and moved away at the time of Henry's birth. Four other children lay buried out by the garden behind the house. At home, besides Henry there remained two girls, Virginia and Eliza, then seventeen and thirteen; and five boys—Julian, fifteen and a clerk in his father's store; John, eleven; Frank, nine; Charles, seven; and Sanford, five. Thomas, the last boy, was born in 1861. The bonds among these children remained close and strong throughout their lives, but Henry's favorites were always Virginia (Jenny), whose special charge he was as an infant, and Tom, his younger brother.[11]

Henry's childhood was secure and protected despite the Civil War. No menfolk of the family went off to fight; Sanford Allen was too old, and Julian, his oldest son, was too young. Although loyalties were divided in this border area, Confederate sympathies predominated. Beginning in 1862, a detachment of Federal troops occupied the courthouse in Owingsville, the hometown of Confederate General

The Allen Home in Sharpsburg as It Looks Today. (Photograph by the Author)

John B. Hood. After that, bands of Confederate guerrillas raided the town several times and fought occasionally in the countryside with Federal cavalry patrols.[12] Once the Union soldiers came to Sharpsburg looking for Henry's father, who was thought to have information on the guerrillas, but he hid for several days in the attic until the troops went away.[13] The war never came any closer. The Emancipation Proclamation cost the Allens their eleven slaves (one of whom was already a runaway in 1860), but the 1870 census recorded five "domestics" and five "hired hands" in the household.[14] The drygoods business continued to flourish, and in 1866 Sanford Allen founded the first bank in Sharpsburg.[15] Five years after the war his estate was valued at $72,000.[16]

Henry or "Hal" grew up in the outdoors with a love for horses and hunting dogs. The men in blue and gray had vanished by the time he was old enough to stray from town on horseback, and he may well have explored the guerrillas' hideouts and ridden along the forest trails where they had skirmished with the cavalry.

This was Daniel Boone country, too. Old men sat and rocked, chewed tobacco, and told about the time "Old Dan'l" rescued the Calloway girls from the Indians up near Moorefield. And once, right after the battle at Blue Lick, he camped for a night under a tree on the Lockridge place, just outside of town. Nearby there were also ancient Indian mounds and fortifications for a boy to explore, half-hidden in thickets of buckeye, pawpaw, and hackberry, and shrouded in the mystery of legend.[17] Flat Creek meandered through the low hills and over limestone outcroppings, forming pools here and there deep enough for swimming and fishing. The groves of black walnut, honey locust, ash, and hickory along its banks provided shade from the summer heat and many a stump or log for sitting and whittling or just thinking.

Sometimes Hal may have helped around the family store. The variety of its merchandise would have been a large wonder to a small boy. No doubt he enjoyed meeting and talking with the customers; good conversation became one of his lifelong pleasures. Hal's liking for talk was matched by his taste for pranks. His favorite childhood story was the time he and Buck, a Negro boy his own age, let Buck's pet bear cub loose in the Negro Methodist church on a drowsy Sunday morning. The service ended abruptly—with a stampede for the recessional.[18] A whipping followed such escapades as inevitably as Judgment Day but without much apparent effect.

Buck was the son of one of the Allens' former slaves. He and Hal

Ruben Sanford Allen, 1810–1874. (Photograph courtesy of Col. Henry T. Allen, Jr.)

were playmates and the best of friends for years. As they grew older, the relationship changed to that of master-servant, but their friendship remained.

The two boys could not always get into mischief together, for Hal had to go to school. Prior to 1872 there was no organized public school system in the county, and classes were held in most communities in any available vacant building or barn and often, in summer, under the shade of a tree.[19] The children of Owingsville and Sharpsburg were more fortunate than most in the county. Owingsville could boast of the Bath Seminary and Normal School, a private academy with several teachers and a broad classical curriculum. In Sharpsburg, Walker Bourne, a cultured early settler from Virginia, taught generations of young gentlemen until his death in 1873 at the age of eighty-three.[20] From Bourne, young Henry Allen learned his three R's and an abiding love of books. He read for the rest of his life, often falling asleep over a book at night. His letters and diaries as an adult are full of references to works of philosophy, science, politics, economics, and history, as well as to classical literature, poetry, and popular novels.

Where Henry went to school after Bourne's death is uncertain, but he may have transferred to the Bath Normal School in Owingsville, where he had relatives with whom he could have stayed. He was fourteen that year, and his parents wanted him to get the best preparation for college. He may also have gone to the Boys' Academy in Georgetown, about forty miles away, near Lexington. The Academy was a preparatory school associated with Georgetown College, a small and very conservative Baptist institution.[21]

Wherever Henry finished secondary school, he began to develop a talent for languages. At either the Bath Normal School or Georgetown Academy he would have had several years of Latin, French, and German. Apparently a few years away at school also made him aware of the limitations of Sharpsburg. Many of its residents had never ventured farther than Owingsville or Mount Sterling. The bucolic isolation of his birthplace was not for Henry.

In 1876, two years after Sanford Allen's death, Henry entered Georgetown College to fulfill his mother's wish that he study for the ministry. Only a few of the ninety or so students then enrolled at Georgetown were destined to become men of the cloth, but such a profession was a logical choice for Henry.[22] Since his older brothers were already managing the family store and the bank, he could never hope to be more than a junior partner. His father had willed him money for his education, plus two thousand dollars in cash.[23] That was

Susannah Shumate Allen, 1815–1885. (Photograph courtesy of Col. and Mrs. Joseph W. Viner)

enough to start his own business or go into farming, but prospects along those lines showed little promise in 1876. The country was in the midst of a major depression after the panic of '73; farm prices had dropped one third in the last ten years, and small bankers and businessmen were also faring badly. What else could an intelligent, ambitious, and personable young man of good family and moderate means do for a living?

After only four months' study at Georgetown, Henry thought of an alternative. He could go to West Point and join the army.

It is easy to imagine Susannah Allen's reaction to this proposal. Grandfather Allen had, of course, gone off to fight the British in the Revolution, but there had been no other soldiers in the family except for Uncle William Allen's stint in the Mexican War.[24] Neither of them had been professional soldiers. Although the schooling at West Point was reputedly good, Henry would have to serve in the army for at least eight years afterward, probably far from home at some dangerous frontier outpost. (Custer's fate that June was no doubt fresh in her mind.) Common soldiers were the worst kind of men: immigrants, drifters who could not make a go of anything else, or even criminals. The pendulum of popular esteem had swung since the Civil War, and "Soldier, will you work?" was the common gibe of the day.[25] True, there was John Hood from Owingsville, a graduate of West Point, a general, and a hero in the War Between the States. And Robert E. Lee was certainly a gentleman. But they had fought for a good cause and lost, and look at them now. Who had been in the White House? General Grant, that awful little man who was a nobody and a failure in civilian life and who cussed and smoked cigars and drank whiskey. No, Susannah Allen did not like the idea of her son in the army at all.

But Henry's will was a match for his mother's. In December, 1876, while home on Christmas vacation, he wrote the Secretary of War and asked for an appointment to West Point.[26]

Although the War Department advised him to obtain a nomination for appointment from his senator or representative, the only nomination available for the next year in the Tenth Congressional District was already promised to one of his cousins in Owingsville, Charles Goodpaster. Henry glumly finished his first year at Georgetown. Then, in June, his prospects for West Point brightened. Cousin Charles, planning to enter the Academy a year later, went with his father for a look at the place and quickly decided that West Point was not for him. After a family consultation, he decided to give up the appointment.[27] If the Tenth District's congressman would agree, Henry could have it.

Henry went to Brooksville and paid a visit to the offices of Clarke and Field, Attorneys at Law, where the Honorable John B. Clarke, Democrat, held forth when he was not away in Washington. Clarke knew of the Allens and was evidently impressed with Henry. Regarding young Allen as "a close student and a very meritorious young man," Clarke wrote a letter of nomination for him to the Secretary of War.[28] It was Henry's first experience with a politician's power to confer favors. He remembered it.

Four days later, on July 9, 1877, the War Department approved the appointment. Within a week, Henry received instructions to report to West Point the following June. Inclosed was a circular that described the examinations he would take and told him what clothing and belongings to bring. His acceptance of the appointment, accompanied by a letter of parental consent, was mailed back to Washington on July 17, 1877. Significantly, Susannah Allen did not sign the letter. Julian, thirty-three, signed it as Henry's guardian.[29]

He had the appointment, conditional on his passing the entrance examinations. Henry had few worries about the physical examination: he was already six feet tall and, at 160 pounds, as lean and quick as one of his hunting dogs. His eyesight and hearing were as sharp as any woodsman's, and he could jump into the saddle from a flat-footed start. But a look at the list of academic subjects and sample questions in the War Department circular produced more concern.

He would be examined in reading, writing and orthography, arithmetic, grammar, geography, and history. Sample questions: "Divide 3380321 by MDCCXCIX and express the quotient by the Roman system of notation." "What was the difference between the Royal, the Chartered and the Proprietary Colonies?" "How many colonies were there originally in Massachusetts and Connecticut? When were they united? How many in Pennsylvania? When were they separated?" [30] There were pages of such questions in the circular. Henry decided he needed more academic preparation than he would get from another year at fundamentalist Georgetown.

In the fall of 1877, he entered Peekskill Military Academy, on the Hudson River just below West Point, where he could better prepare for West Point's science and engineering-oriented curriculum and also learn some military fundamentals. Peekskill offered two different courses, one commercial, the other college preparatory, stressing English and mathematics. To be sure of passing the entrance examinations, Henry took both courses. The following June he received two diplomas certifying that he had successfully completed classes in bookkeeping, commercial arithmetic, penmanship, English grammar, rhetoric, composition, literature, arithmetic, algebra, geometry, geography, general history, natural philosophy, chemistry, and Latin.[31] This heavy course load at Peekskill indicates another of Allen's traits, his capacity for concentrated effort and careful preparation to achieve any goal he set for himself. Throughout his life, he seldom left anything to fate or luck.

During the year at Peekskill, Henry had met some of the other 173 young men who would be competing for the 100 cadetships vacant that June.[32] Despite all his preparation and good family background, Allen had no clear advantage over the majority of the candidates. Contrary to his mother's doubts, most of them were "gentlemen," or at least the sons of gentlemen.[33] Although they came from all parts of the country, many had finished their studies at fine Eastern schools. Like Henry, some also had a year or more of college. Their reasons for entering West Point were varied. For some it offered the best path to a worthwhile career that, with luck, might be capped with military honors and glory. Others undoubtedly saw no further than the halo of glamour surrounding the academy itself, or the chance to get a free education in exchange for a few years of interesting service.

Allen's motives probably included a mixture of all of these. The army undoubtedly attracted him because of his love of horses and the outdoors, but his decision to try for West Point appears to have been more of a reaction to the other possibilities open to him than anything else. Even so, except for the appointment given up by his cousin, Allen might never have entered the academy. In later years he referred to this quirk of fate when he wrote: "Though having been destined and partly educated for the clergy, I fell into a cavalry saddle." [34] Whatever his other motives, West Point offered him a chance for a career of his own, away from the limited horizons of Sharpsburg and Bath County. The place had certainly been a pleasant one in which to grow up, but his future there looked dull. He was ready for a change.

On June 10, 1878, two months past his eighteenth birthday, trunk in hand and heart in mouth, Cadet Candidate Allen left Peekskill for the short ride up to West Point.

CHAPTER II

"Of Bullet Buttons, Plumes, of Ladies' Smiles and Fun"

—West Point Life, anonymous poem [1]

Passing through West Point's South Gate, Henry Allen entered a different world, part college, part army post and part historical shrine. With its massive natural setting, imposing gothic-style buildings, glittering martial display and courtly customs and traditions, the Military Academy could stir the heart of any visitor. In the late afternoon sun there were impressive full-dress parades in front of the granite barracks which faced the Plain, a verdant plateau jutting out high above a great bend in the Hudson River. Beneath the Plain, on shaded Flirtation Walk, cadets strolled with their female admirers who came up in fluttering swarms for the weekend hops and parades. There were cannons and battle flags from bygone wars and heroes' monuments galore. From dawn to dark, bugle calls sounded over the Plain and echoed and re-echoed across the river gorge. Behind this glamorous and romantic facade, however, West Point had other faces not apparent to the casual visitor. The new cadet soon discovered them.

Clutching his letter of appointment, Allen found his way to the Administration Building and reported. An officer gave him a sheaf of forms to fill out and then sent him before the medical examining board. He asked about the academic examinations. Not for ten days yet, he was told. Next, since candidates were not allowed to have any money, he went to the Treasurer's Office to deposit all the funds in his possession. Then, still carrying his trunk, he was escorted by an enlisted orderly to the cadet barracks area and left standing before a door.[2] He knocked. What happened next went something like this:

West Point, *ca.* 1880. *Top:* Cadet Barracks and Officers' Quarters. *Center:* Trophy Point. *Bottom:* View of the Plain and Barracks from Trophy Point. (Photographs from USMA Archives)

"Come in!" commanded a harsh voice. Inside the room two upperclassmen sat at a table. As Allen entered, one jumped up and blocked his way.

"Leave your things in the hall. Don't you know better than to bring them in here? Lay them on the floor and come in and don't be all day about it either. Move lively, I say! Shut the door. Stand there. Come to attention. Put your heels together, turn out your toes, put your hands by your side, palms to the front, fingers closed, little fingers on the seams of the trousers, head up, chin in, shoulders thrown back, chest out, draw in your belly, and keep your eyes on this tack!"

The seated cadet: "What's your name?"

"Allen, sir."

"Put a Mister before it, Dumbjohn. How do you spell it?"

"What's your first name and middle initial?"

"What state are you from?"

"Kentucky."

"Put a 'sir' on every answer, Reb. Don't look at me, keep your eyes on that tack. How many times do you have to be told? About face. Turn around the other way. Don't you know ANYTHING? You'll never get along here, you're too slow. Here's your room number, take your things up there [it was four floors up] and then report to Cadet —— out in the Area. You have two minutes."

Allen turned to go. "Halt, Mr. Dumbjohnny Reb! You forgot to salute and say, 'Yes, sir!' That's better. You now have a minute and a half. . . ." [3]

The next few days passed in a blur of more brusque commands, harsh questions, impossible demands, and contemptuous insults. Nothing the candidates did could please any of these upperclassmen, known as the "Beast Detail." They hovered like eagles above a flock of lambs, ready to pounce on any mistake or sign of weakness, and they seemed to enjoy the sport. At least the splendidly bemedaled and gold-braided officers who supervised the drill and came to inspect rooms were not insulting or contemptuous, but they were just as hard to satisfy. Stern-faced, they rarely said a word to the candidates, who learned of their displeasure only by reading the list of delinquencies and demerits posted daily on the company bulletin board.

The ordeal continued. There seemed to be unending formations to be late for, countless inspections to fail, and volumes of cadet lore and regulations to memorize and recite at the whim of any upperclassman. There was no respite from the hazing and harassment. The candidate was fair game during mealtime, in the privacy of his barracks room, and even when asleep.

Soon, the long-dreaded academic examinations began. Over a period of four days, each candidate was examined orally and in writing by a board of officers. After each day's tests there were more long, sweaty hours of close-order drill. When the examinations finally ended there was nothing to do but wait for the results to be posted and endure more formations, inspections, drill, and hazing.

This was "Beast Barracks," the first of the other "faces" of West Point, and these were the rites of passage that weeded out the weak and unwilling and transformed the youthful civilian into a soldierly plebe. West Point told him, "Take the pressure or quit, and good riddance."

By the end of June, the examination results were posted. Those who had failed or already decided West Point was not for them packed their bags and left. Among the survivors was Henry Allen. With them, he received his first tight-fitting gray uniform, called a "plebe skin," and took the Cadet Oath on July 1, 1878.[4] He was now part of the Corps of Cadets of the United States Military Academy. The rites of Beast Barracks were over; those of plebe year had only begun.

Ahead lay forty-nine weeks almost as bad as the ones just completed, starting with two months of summer camp at Old Fort Clinton before classroom instruction began in September. Next June, when a new crop of cadet candidates began to arrive, Allen could look forward to Recognition Day, when he would shake hands with the upperclassmen and become one of them. Beyond that distant day, however, stretched three more years of academic grind and strict adherence to the rules and regulations. The only other prospect of relief was a summer's leave after the second year, though he might also be able to meet some young women at the hops and take an occasional stroll on Flirtation Walk.

First came summer camp, out on the Plain overlooking the river. For the new plebe, in the company of those upperclassmen not on leave, there was more hazing, always humiliating and sometimes brutal. Although hazing was against regulations, in its milder forms it was often winked at by the tactical officers. Plebes who resisted or objected were challenged to a fight by an upperclassman, picked to insure that the upstart got a good licking.[5] Mostly, though, summer camp consisted of basic instruction in infantry and artillery tactics, and drill and more drill. But for Allen there was also new pride in

Cadet Henry T. Allen. (Photograph courtesy of Col. Henry T. Allen, Jr.)

mastering elementary military skills and a growing sense of belonging to the corps. Once in a while he had a chance in the evenings for a little privacy and relaxation, to write letters home, or to visit around the campfires of plebe friends in the other companies. Here was another West Point: pride in joining the Long Gray Line and new friendships made and strengthened by shared hardships and experiences.

After his year at Peekskill, Allen fitted easily into cadet gray. He was popular with his classmates, who soon called him Hal. Two, in particular, became his close friends. They were Charles G. Treat, a husky Maine-born Midwesterner who was known as "Jim," and Barrington West, an easy-going fellow Kentuckian. West and Allen shared a spartan barracks room.[6] By the end of plebe year Allen had also won the respect of the upperclassmen as well as the tactical officers and instructors. So far, his record was excellent. Among the fifty-one plebes who stuck out the year until Recognition Day, he ranked fifteenth in overall order of merit. He stood fifth in English, tenth in French, and twenty-fifth in mathematics. The "0" at the end of Allen's demerit ledger earned him a tie for first place in Military Discipline with several other plebes, but his disciplinary record was hardly unblemished. He had merely been diligent in working off all accumulated infractions. In June, 1879, he was promoted to cadet corporal, a distinction given to few of his classmates.[7]

Hal had toed the line for a year, but was too full of "spizzerinctum"[8] to remain intimidated for very long. As a more relaxed upperclassman he became a gay blade and a regular hop-goer. A contemporary noted dryly that "he always found spare time to give to the ladies."[9] He also had fun in numerous ways not officially sanctioned and began accumulating demerits at an alarming rate. Some of the milestones in his descending path from disciplinary grace:

Jan. 7, 1880:	Throwing missile in ranks returning from supper.
Nov. 25, 1880:	One hour and fifty minutes late reporting return on permit.
Jan. 13, 1881:	Off Limits.
April 7, 1881:	In bed at inspection by Officer of the Day.
June 10, 1881:	Wearing dancing shoes to examination.
July 6, 1881:	Entering Commandant's Office with one button of pants unbuttoned.
Sept. 1, 1881:	Late reporting at Taps.
April 29, 1882:	Making unnecessary noise while taking hurdles at cavalry drill.[10]

Cadets were always dreaming up elaborate pranks to play on the humorless "Tacs" (tactical officers). The most memorable such occasion of Hal's cadet career occurred on New Year's Eve, 1879, when the corps participated in a thunderous welcome to the New Year. As a yearling, Allen was not one of the ringleaders, who were all first classmen (seniors), but it is a safe bet he was in on the fun. After the hop that night, when the cadet guards had been relieved and taps had sounded, dozens of cadets slipped out of their bunks and took their posts according to a prearranged plan. Precisely at midnight, the reveille gun and numerous cannons on Trophy Point went off. Startled tactical officers in various stages of undress and inebriation converged on the cadet barracks from their quarters, only to be repulsed by a fiery barrage of rockets, cherry bombs, and sputtering firecrackers. No cadet officers appeared to restore order; they had been locked in their rooms. By the time the befuddled Tacs had organized a cadet roll call, all the culprits were present in ranks. Only the innocent few denied a part in the affair. Everyone else kept silence. Since no ringleaders could be found, the entire corps was confined to cadet limits indefinitely. That meant the loss of what few social privileges cadets enjoyed, but it was accepted with silent glee as a small price for a glorious triumph.[11]

With such diversions, Allen's class standing slipped lower each year. By graduation he stood twentieth in a class which had dwindled to thirty-seven members. Only nine classmates stood below him in total number of demerits.[12] Yet, if anything, his popularity had increased, and he remained well regarded by the officers. Being something of a dandy, few of his demerits were for poor personal appearance: "In dress he was more than perfect, beyond what was required or practiced, even among the fastidious of West Point's upperclassmen."[13] He was promoted to cadet first sergeant in his third year and to cadet lieutenant when he became a first classman.[14]

Robert Lee Bullard, thirty-six years later Allen's superior officer in World War I, remembered him at West Point when their positions were reversed.

> For a year I was in the same company with Henry Allen, seeing him daily among his superiors, equals and inferiors in rank. . . . Everywhere he carried himself proudly; he was at ease in every situation. . . . he was a handsome, well-proportioned, well-bred soldier, free and graceful in his movements, clear eyed and confident in voice and manner. . . . He was plainly vain but in such good taste as not to stir in observers the tendency to laugh or jeer that vanity usually moves. In promise, he was another Jeb Stuart.[15]

Bullard described Allen as "the center of any gathering" and always good-humored, even towards plebes. "He was not among those sharp speaking, dominating, exacting cadets who had been placed as drill masters over the plebes to jerk us into shape for military duty." [16]

Here, then, is an early portrait of Henry Allen: handsome and a bit vain about it, poised and confident, a ladies' man, and too high-spirited to let West Point turn him into a military drudge.

Although it may not have made Allen into a martial paragon, West Point left its mark on him. Four years of rigorous academic and military training were bound to inculcate certain attitudes and habits of thought. Something more can be learned about him by a look at how and what he was taught at West Point.

The academic system there in the 1880s had been developed by Sylvanus Thayer, the academy's fifth superintendent, during the years from 1817 to 1833. Thayer had stressed science and engineering in the curriculum and decreed small classes in every subject, in which each man recited and received a grade every day. In theory, this permitted each instructor to give individual attention to the dozen or so cadets in his charge. It also required the cadet to be thoroughly prepared for each day's lessons.[17] Since he was sure to be called on to recite, a cadet could not hide his unpreparedness or inability to understand the material being taught. Barring outright stupidity or a desire to be "found deficient" at examination time and dismissed, the cadet learned what the academy wanted him to learn.

In Thayer's day and for several decades thereafter, West Point enjoyed a sense of intellectual leadership in the field of higher education. Thayer's pedagogic methods were relatively advanced for their time, and he attracted a group of well-qualified soldier-scholars who stayed on at the academy long after he left.[18] To Thayer's intellectual heirs, his methods seemed justified by the results. West Point was rightly proud of its contributions to a nation whose industrial and territorial expansion in the nineteenth century cried out for men with the kind of talents, both technical and military, which it produced. There were successful graduates in significant numbers in a variety of careers besides the army.[19]

This very success was the best argument against change, but by the time Allen entered the academy, forty-five years after Thayer left it, intellectual dry rot had set in. Thayer's heirs inherited his educational principles but not his innovative spirit. The principles hardened into a rigid formula for imparting knowledge, doled out in prescribed daily doses. Elderly professors whose receptivity to fresh intellectual currents was in most cases inversely proportional to their years of tenure dominated the faculty.[20] Most of the younger instructors were themselves products of this educational system. Very few professors or instructors had attended other institutions of higher learning or bothered to obtain advanced degrees in their field.[21] Only the professors had tenure; the officer instructors came from the ranks of the army and returned there after a few years of breathing chalk dust.

While West Point rested on Thayer's laurels, other institutions began to surpass it in educational quality and vigor. Years after leaving the academy, Thayer himself unsuccessfully attempted to persuade the Academic Board to modernize the curriculum and teaching methods. His successors preferred the *status quo*, revering his early accomplishments and ignoring his later advice.[22]

Though minor adjustments had been made from time to time, the curriculum changed almost as little as the academy's granite foundations. Every cadet took the same subjects, and there were no electives. Allen's four-year course of study was laid out like this:

1st Year	2nd Year	3rd Year	4th Year
Mathematics	Mathematics	Natural Philosophy	Engineering
French	French	Chemistry, Mineralogy and Geology	Law
English	Drawing	Drawing	Spanish
Fencing, Bayonet Exercise	Riding	Tactics *	Ordnance and Gunnery
		Riding	Riding [23]

* Also taught each summer.

During the academic year, the cadet's daily routine never varied. Five days a week it was up for reveille at 5:45 A.M. and nothing but study, classroom recitations, drill or parades, and more study until lights out and taps at 10:00 P.M. Saturdays began the same way, but after the weekly inspection at two o'clock the rest of the day was free, providing the cadet was not confined to his room or marching off demerits back and forth in the Area for some gross infraction or too many minor ones. Except for compulsory chapel, Sundays were free for him to enjoy privileges and receive visitors.[24]

Classes were military formations lasting two to three hours each and followed essentially the same rigid format regardless of the subject being taught. After marching to class, the cadets filed into their assigned room and took their places at attention behind their desks or benches. After the section-marcher saluted and reported to the instructor, class began. Some cadets would be assigned topics from the day's lesson and sent to the blackboard to prepare for recitation. While they prepared their equations, figures, or whatever, others were called to recite or answer questions standing, at quivering attention and without benefit of notes, directly in front of the instructor. Each man sat down when he had finished reciting and satisfactorily answered any questions. No extraneous talking was allowed between cadets at any time. When a bugle call signaled the end of the class period, the instructor dismissed his students curtly, and they marched away. Every few weeks cadets were transferred between sections according to their level of ability and progress. Examinations came in January and June, and if the cadet failed one subject he was dismissed from the academy.[25]

Despite the grim seriousness of it all, cadets always managed in subtle and elaborate ways to have a laugh or two at their elders' expense. Most officers, especially the more pompous, incompetent, or stupid ones, unknowingly bore mocking nicknames or became the butt of jokes. A favorite target was Patrice d'Janon, the Professor of Spanish from 1865 to 1882. He was a native of Venezuela, and his Spanish was therefore excellent, if not of Castilian purity. His command of English grammar left much tc be desired, however, though he was too vain to admit it. One year a cadet, in translating from Spanish into English, used the word "snizzen" for the past participle of "to sneeze." Professor d'Janon immediately corrected him, but the cadet stoutly maintained "snizzen" was right. The other cadets in the section backed him up. With perfectly straight faces they insisted to a man that the principal parts of the verb "to sneeze" were "sneeze, snoze, snizzen." Finally convinced, or perhaps prevented by his pride from checking with the Professor of English, the good Señor insisted it be translated that way thereafter.[26] The cadets smirkingly obliged.

French, the other foreign language taught, was partly in the hands of a man of even more doubtful competence. He was Edward A. Wood, a tobacco-chewing Civil War veteran, whose French accent was execrable. It is recorded he always found a convenient excuse to be absent from the post when distinguished French visitors arrived.[27]

By no means all of the faculty were incompetent. Some had studied under Thayer's scholarly protégés and were widely respected in their fields. Such men as Peter S. Michie, Edgar W. Bass, and Samuel E. Tillman were then honored as minor deities in the pantheon of American education. Michie taught engineering and natural philosophy from 1867 to 1901. Bass taught mathematics from 1878 to 1898, and Tillman taught chemistry, mineralogy and geology intermittently from 1870 to 1911.[28] Whatever the caliber of the teacher, the Thayer system of daily recitations in small classes guaranteed some learning, if not much free-roaming classroom give-and-take. And if the cadet's intellectual curiosity was not particularly stimulated, at least he learned methodical study habits and how to organize and express what he learned logically and with precision and confidence—valuable traits in any profession, and vital ones for an army officer. In this respect, the Academic Department reinforced the work of the Tactical Department, whose mission was to teach more warlike skills.

The Tactical Department was headed by the Commandant of Cadets, a very senior lieutenant colonel, and staffed by six to eight other officers and one civilian. The civilian, a permanent member of the staff, taught military gymnastics, swordsmanship, and bayonet. The majors, captains, and lieutenants were picked for their maturity and experience. Some were even Civil War veterans. Besides routine administration, the duties of these officers included instructing and inspecting the cadets and providing living models of military bearing for their emulation. Four of the lieutenants also commanded the cadet companies, each of which had its internal cadet chain of command.[29] Like the academic instructors, the Tacs served a tour of duty at West Point and then returned to their regular army units.

The military training encompassed far more than dress parades, close-order drill, and white-glove inspections. It went on year-round, in the classroom, on the drill field and firing range, and up in the mountains and valleys immediately to the west and south of the main post. During the summer encampments there was a minimum of classroom theory and a maximum of practical application. In the winter months this ratio was reversed. The basic textbooks for all military instruction were the official army-service and drill regulations for the three arms: infantry, artillery, and cavalry. Great reliance was placed on detailed memorization of these regulations and rote practice of the drills they prescribed. Each year more advanced and complex subjects were introduced, while the cadet also increasingly assumed the duties of the officer and noncommissioned officer in preparing, presenting, and supervising instruction for the lower classes.

Cadets learned to ride and were introduced to the finer points of hippology—no mystery to Allen. They also learned the fundamentals of military hygiene, developed their physical stamina and co-ordination, and daily practiced promptness and attention to detail.[30]

The cement for all these academic and military building blocks was discipline, enforced in the classroom and on the drill field under the supervision of the Superintendent, to whom the Commandant and the Professors of the Academic Board were subordinate.[31] This discipline was not so much harsh as strict, impartial and extremely impersonal. A wide gulf separated the officer from the cadet, who could easily get the impression that when he pinned on his gold bars he was supposed to become an Olympian figure, aloof and unapproachable.[32]

After four years the cadet graduated, confident of his ability to exercise command. He had received a solid foundation in the basics of his chosen profession, plus a good background in engineering and science and a thin veneer of the liberal arts. For all its faults, West Point had a realistic, if limited, appreciation of the immediate needs of the small American army of the late nineteenth century.[33] The Academy took little notice, however, of the potential problems created by citizen armies in a mass conflict or of the benefits to be gained by the application of new technology to military equipment and tactics.[34]

Such reflections probably never entered Henry Allen's mind during June Week of 1882 or anyone else's at West Point for that matter. For returning old grads it was a time of sentimental reunions and swapping war stories. For the graduate-to-be, it was a happy last whirl of picnics, hops, parades, and greeting proud relatives and friends. Henry was in his element as he led his classmates and their ladies through the intricate steps of the German, the climax of the graduation hop. Miss Blossom Drum, daughter of the Adjutant General of the Army, was on his arm that night.[35] Three days later he listened to the commencement address by the Commandant of the Infantry and Cavalry School at Fort Leavenworth, who told the class:

> Be not deceived and accept the foolish delusion . . . that the soldier's obligations only begin when summoned to meet a foreign enemy or to put down armed resistance which has overthrown civil power. . . . A soldier is now expected to exert himself within proper limits to preserve and organize peace. He should labor, in unison with the citizen and philanthropist, to impress and extend our civilization. So vast is the field of operations of our small army, and so scattered are the troops, it is possible, if not extremely probable, that in a few short years, whatever may be your age and rank, you may be obliged to administer affairs wherein considerable knowledge of civil matters may be necessary.[36]

Crossing the stage, Henry received his diploma. Then it was farewells, a last look around, and off to New York City for the traditional graduation night celebration at Delmonico's, where classmates gathered for a last fling together before scattering for graduation leave and on to their first posts.[37] Traditional on such occasions was the singing of *Benny Havens, Oh!* Set to the tune of *Wearing of the Green* to honor the man who once sold ale and "spiritous liquors" to cadets who made their way to his cottage outside the gate after taps, it went:

Come, fill your glasses, fellows, and stand up in a row;
To singing sentimentally, we're going for to go;
In the Army there's sobriety, promotion's very slow,
So we'll sing our reminiscences of Benny Havens, oh!

Oh! Benny Havens, oh!, oh! Benny Havens, oh!
We'll sing our reminiscences of Benny Havens, oh!

To the ladies of our Army our cups shall ever flow,
Companions in our exile, our shield 'gainst every woe;
May they see their husbands Generals, with double pay also,
And join us in our choruses at Benny Havens, oh!

(Chorus)

May the Army be augmented, promotion be less slow;
May our country in her hour of need be ready for the foe;
May we find a soldier's resting place beneath a soldier's blow,
With room enough beside our graves for Benny Havens, oh!

(Chorus)

To our kind old Alma Mater, our rockbound Highland home,
We'll cast back many a fond regret, as o'er life's sea we roam,
Until on our last battlefield the lights of heaven shall glow,
We'll never fail to drink to her and Benny Havens, oh![38]

(Chorus)

For Allen and many others at Delmonico's that night, those verses were prophetic. The next day he left New York for home.

Sharpsburg had not changed much, although business conditions had begun to improve and his older brothers were again prospering. For a while Allen probably enjoyed being home again, visiting old friends and relatives and regaling them with stories of his exploits on the Hudson. The town belles were no doubt as taken with Henry as he was with himself. But, as the summer passed slowly, Sharpsburg's attractions again began to pall for him.

In late July he received his commission as a second lieutenant in the 2nd Cavalry Regiment and orders from the War Department to report at the end of September to Fort Keogh, Montana Territory.[39] A cavalry post in Indian country was exactly what he wanted. There had been no more serious trouble with the nearby Sioux and other tribes for the past several years, but one could never tell. In January, 1877, on the Tongue River not far from Fort Keogh, General Nelson A. Miles had won a pitched battle in the bitter cold against Crazy Horse's braves.[40] And in the last few months there had been reports of new trouble along the Milk River in northern Montana, caused by several thousand Cree Indians who were supposed to stay in Canada, but who saw nothing wrong in a visit to an old hunting ground, regardless of its location in relation to the white man's boundaries.[41]

With packing his things and making arrangements to ship his horses and dogs, time passed quickly for Henry. His Negro friend, Buck, volunteered to come along and serve as his "striker," a combination orderly and jack-of-all-trades.[42] The family saw them off for Lexington where they caught a train and headed West.

Allen reported at Fort Keogh on September 30, 1882.[43] His unit, Troop E of the 2nd Cavalry, was in the field as part of a mixed force of six cavalry troops and two infantry companies deployed over several hundred miles of the Yellowstone River Valley to guard the construction and surveying parties of the Northern Pacific Railroad. By 1882, with settlers pouring into the valley, there was little actual danger from marauding Indians, but the presence of the troops served as insurance against any alarms which might demoralize the workmen and slow up construction.[44]

Anxious to get to his troop, he left Fort Keogh the same day and headed further west on the Northern Pacific. The train took him as far as Custer Station. From there he rode out to Fort Custer, reported at regimental headquarters on October 1, and several days later joined Troop E in the field. Captain Eli Huggins, an enlisted veteran of the Civil War commanded the troop. First Lieutenant James Allison was the only other officer in the unit. Within a few days Allen had also met the twenty-eight of Troop E's forty-four soldiers present for duty in the field.[45]

They were a rough and colorful bunch. In most units there were a few who did not care to discuss their pasts and might even be living under an assumed name; some were toughs or troublemakers. There were always a few professional privates, grizzled veterans of the Civil War (or even the Mexican War) with many service chevrons on their arms, but too great a penchant for booze or gambling or both. To relieve the aching monotony of frontier duty almost everyone drank and gambled, especially on payday, but not everybody was a drunk or a gambler. Raw recruits, fresh from farm or urban slum provided many hours of amusement before they were accepted by the older veterans, who went by nicknames like "Brute," "Nigger," "Josh," "Guts," "Tinker Bill," and "Crazy Jim." But such characters were usually in the minority. Most of the soldiers in any unit were just ordinary, decent types from humble backgrounds and with limited ambitions. They did the best they knew how and stayed out of trouble, most of the time. Given the conditions under which he lived both in the field and in the garrison, a soldier could be forgiven an occasional spree at the nearest saloon or "hog ranch," the apt name for the combination groggery and brothel found somewhere near almost every frontier post. As Kipling has said, "Single men in barracks don't grow into plaster saints." [46] In the company of such men some of the stiffness of the new West Pointer must soon have worn off Second Lieutenant Allen.

In December, Troop E returned to Fort Keogh. After ten weeks in the field, Allen could unpack his books and other belongings and settle into bachelor quarters. Built under constant Indian harassment in 1876–77, and named in honor of an officer who had died with Custer, Keogh lacked the solid permanence of the long-established Eastern posts.[47] Situated on the bank of the Yellowstone River, two miles above the mouth of the Tongue, the post consisted of a headquarters building, several drafty two-story barracks, and more than a dozen officers' and noncommissioned officers' quarters of a log or frame construction around a windswept parade ground. Stables and storerooms, a makeshift hospital, a guardhouse, and miscellaneous rickety shacks for teamsters, quartermaster employees, and Indian interpreters practically exhausted the list of facilities. The post limits also enclosed a cemetery and a stockade containing several hundred Indian prisoners.[48] The barracks housed Allen's cavalry troop and eight companies of the 5th Infantry. Lieutenant Colonel Joseph Whistler, Regimental Commander of the 5th Infantry led this mixed force of 395 men.[49]

Though they campaigned together in the field, in garrison the cavalry and infantry soldiers had little use for each other. The horse soldiers regarded their footweary comrades with a mixture of pity and contempt. The infantry heartily reciprocated by referring to the mounted troopers as "sore asses." [50]

Fort Keogh, Montana Territory, *ca.* 1884. (Signal Corps Photograph No. 87188, National Archives)

No such lines were drawn among the twenty-five officers in the garrison. Allen paid the traditional courtesy calls on each family, became acquainted with the other bachelors, had a look around nearby Miles City, and soon felt at home on the post. Within a few days something interesting turned up.

A War Department circular had just been received at Keogh. It asked for an officer volunteer to lead a rescue expedition to an army meteorological station on Ellesmere Island, well above the Arctic Circle. The expedition would try to get through in the summer of 1883 and bring out Lieutenant Adolphus Greely and his party of twenty-four who would be completing a second year of exploration and scientific observations after a relief expedition had failed to reach them the previous summer. Allen volunteered. His local commanders approved and forwarded his application through channels back to Washington. To help his cause, he also wrote personal letters to General W. B. Hazen, the Chief Signal Officer, to Senator J. S. Williams and Representative J. C. S. Blackburn, both of Kentucky. To Williams, a family friend from Mount Sterling, whom he addressed by his Civil War rank of general, Allen wrote:

> If you will use your influence to get me the position I will be under many obligations. . . .
>
> I will promise my utmost attention and diligence in case I get the detail. . . .
>
> I am so anxious for the detail that I will take any position that may be assigned me. . . .[51]

"General" Williams forwarded this letter to the War Department with a favorable recommendation, but Lieutenant E. A. Garlington of the 7th Cavalry got the job. Garlington, U.S.M.A. 1876, was older and more experienced than Allen and had applied sooner.[52]

Allen's application for the Greely relief expedition was revealing in several ways. In a West nearly won, the Indian frontier had already lost its challenge for him. Becoming fascinated by the unknown Arctic, he was willing to endure hardship and danger for an assignment that would take him there. He was also willing to use personal influence to help get what he wanted.[53] For the moment, though, he was stuck at Fort Keogh.

Life there, if not very exciting, should still have been fairly interesting and pleasant for him in the winter and spring of 1883. First, he had to learn the garrison duties of a junior officer and adjust to the daily routine of the post. The cavalry soldier's day began with reveille at 6:00 A.M. and ended with taps and lights out each night at 9:30. In between there were roll calls, meal formations, guard and work details, drill (both mounted and dismounted), target practice, and always, horses to be groomed and cared for. Saturday was spent almost entirely in clean-up work and on Sunday at 9:00 came the weekly inspection. Church was at 10:15.[54] Lieutenant Allen was not required to attend all these formations but other chores such as being Officer of the Guard, inspecting the stables and mess hall, tending to official correspondence, and sitting on an occasional court-martial kept him busy enough most of the time.

Mounted patrols went out occasionally that winter to repair a telegraph line, escort a paymaster, or coax a straying party of Indians back onto their reservation. These assignments must have been challenging enough with only the snow and wind to fight, and though there was always the chance of greater danger, in fact they went routinely.[55]

As the weather warmed again, outdoor target practice and a monthly shooting competition began. Allen consistently scored high.[56] In his spare time, he explored the ninety square miles of the Keogh Reservation. His pack of greyhounds went along to chase the rabbits, coyotes, and antelope from the thickets of cane and willow along the river bank and through the sagebrush and wildflowers on the rolling tableland above.[57] Often he rode out beyond Miles City to visit his brother Tom, who at Henry's persuasion had come out from Kentucky and bought a ranch. Pooling their inheritances to buy more livestock, they became partners in the venture.[58] Allen had other off-duty diversions as well.

Never a stick-in-the-mud, he was a welcome addition to the social circle of the tiny community. He soon became the special favorite of several post families including the Rices, Logans, and Girards. Rice and Logan were company commanders, and Girard was the post surgeon. All three were senior captains. At their quarters and elsewhere, Henry was much in demand for his quick humor, informed conversation, and light touch on the dance floor. He kept himself primed for good talk by subscribing to *The New York Times, Harper's, The Army and Navy Register, The Pioneer Press, The Paris Kentuckian,* and the *Montana Churchman.*[59]

Though he seems to have been popular and well thought of by most in the garrison, he did not always return the esteem. The off-duty conduct of the soldiers at the saloons and "hog ranches" of Miles City may have been understandable, but for those officers who failed to measure up to his own standards Allen had nothing but contempt: "Suffice it to say that from the appearance, speech and manners of some, it could hardly be said that the Army is the 'nest of the Aristocracy.'"[60] Such officers probably regarded him with some justice as a sarcastic young snob. Others and their wives he thought were nice enough but dull.

Late summer of 1883 brought a welcome change of scenery and companions. As a result of his performance on the rifle range Allen received orders to compete in the annual Department of the Missouri shooting matches and departed for Fort Snelling, Minnesota, on September 8. He was gone for the rest of the month.[61] Though he did not make the Department team and the higher level competition back East, the trip had another equally pleasant outcome. After such matches, contestants were customarily granted a number of days' leave without having it charged against their record.[62] Some time that fall, probably right after returning from Fort Snelling, Henry visited Yellowstone National Park with Captain and Mrs. Rice. There were others along, including a pretty "blackeyed young lady of Chicago," Miss Jennie Dora Johnston.[63] The steep and rocky trails of the park were an appropriate place for Henry and Dora to begin their courtship.

Dora was Henry's age and from a family equally as aristocratic but considerably more well-to-do than his. The Johnstons claimed descent from Samuel Johnson, the first president of Columbia College. Dora's father and grandfather, both named William Sage Johnston, had been very successful in business and real estate in Chicago, where for many years they maintained a spacious and elegant family home.[64] After the Civil War, when Dora was five, the Johnstons moved out to Lake Forest, described by a contemporary Chicagoan as a "quiet, retired village with a fine moral and spiritual tone pervading it, one of our most beautiful suburbs."[65]

Dora's father remained active in Chicago business, but he was also a civic leader in Lake Forest, serving as mayor for a time and supporting the construction of parks and churches. In the late 1860's the Johnstons built a new home there which, though less formal in style, rivaled their Chicago mansion in spaciousness and comfort.[66] Dora lived in this house for about ten years. Her mother died in 1875, leaving seven children for her father to raise. Josephine (Effie), Clifford, and Gertrude (Gertie) were older than Dora, and Nina, Mabel, and Roy were younger. There were always plenty of servants, nannies, and governesses to run the house and look after the children, but when Effie married Clarence Dix in 1879 and Clifford was old enough to go

Jennie Dora Johnston. (Photograph courtesy of Col. and Mrs. Joseph W. Viner)

into business, William Johnston moved the rest of his family into smaller quarters. After he died in 1882, Effie's apartment suite in Chicago's Ontario Hotel became "home" for the Johnston children. Always a traveling family, they then used their ample inheritance to gallivant about, visiting cousins in Philadelphia and Boston, summering with friends at the most fashionable spas, and taking an occasional trip to Europe.[67]

In the summer of 1883, a visit to Yellowstone Park must have been *the* fashionable trip for socially prominent Easterners, especially after President Chester A. Arthur went through it in August with a large entourage.[68] The newly completed Northern Pacific Railroad passed close to the park, where the Mammoth Hot Springs Hotel had just been opened. That September several trains left Chicago's Union Station jammed with sightseers eager for the breath-taking ride over the Rockies. Many passengers also took a side trip into the awesome beauties of the park. Most probably Dora came out by train from Chicago at the invitation of the Rices and stopped off at Keogh on the way. The entire party, Henry included, would then have taken the N.P.R.R. on to Livingston, Montana, and from there transferred to a spur line for the sixty-mile ride up the narrow Yellowstone Gorge to the entrance of the park.

Although Dora rode horseback well enough, the raw wilderness was not her natural element, especially when it turned rainy and cold, and some days she could not help being miserable and cross. Loving few things more than to banter with an attractive woman, Henry often rode beside her and tried to cheer her up.[69] Judging from the tone of their later letters, their conversations must have been witty, outspoken, and frequently cutting. No doubt she mocked his self-importance and he teased her for being a tenderfoot. They shared a common interest in books, though Henry's tastes were deeper and more varied. When they returned to Keogh, Dora stayed on for a few days and had more long talks with him.[70] Problems arose, particularly the uncertainty of when, if ever, they would meet again. They parted with promises to write, but more as friends than sweethearts. Henry said he would try to get leave over the Christmas holidays, but it was more than two years before he saw her again.

When Dora left, another long winter loomed ahead at Keogh. No patrol or escort duties were assigned him to break the routine and his request for a leave at Christmas was denied, to Dora's annoyance. Yet he was hardly pining away. In March, after a snippy note from her he wrote:

Dear Little Dora:

I address you as formerly and strange to say do not accuse myself for so doing, notwithstanding you give me nothing at the beginning and much within the body of the letter that seems wholly sarcastic to me. . . . You evidently maintain some interest else you would not have written as much as you did.

After denying her accusation that his own letters were sarcastic, he went on about what fun he was having off duty:

I wish time and again you could be here for my birthday German . . . . I mean to have nice favors and a good supper. . . . Keogh has been remarkably lively for the past two months. We have had a phantom, a masquerade, a German, a Martha Washington, besides the regular Friday hops and private parties. We danced the minuet at the M.W. party. I had quite a nice costume for it though made here. I have had elegant sport chasing this Winter, have in fact caught jack rabbits, coyotes, deer and antelope . . . with my hounds. I have a magnificent pack now 7 in all. . . . We have had an ice skating rink on the parade ground for two or three months.

Realizing the impression this made, he added rather lamely at the end: "Reading and study absorb much of my time notwithstanding what is said above." [71]

Life at Keogh may have been gay, but it was also repetitious and superficial. Henry eventually tired of the same old army shop talk and rehashed post gossip. And with all the eligible young ladies already spoken for or so desperately unattractive as to chill his ardor, Dora had no serious rival on the post. Keogh was much like Sharpsburg—pleasant but not very interesting. Allen was restless again.

In May came good news. The entire 2nd Cavalry Regiment had orders to change stations with the 1st Cavalry. Since the 1st was in Washington Territory, this involved a trip of more than nine hundred miles across the Rockies. Along with the headquarters and several other troops of the 2nd Cavalry, Troop E's new post would be Fort Walla Walla.[72] Even if the routine there proved to be little different than at Keogh, at least the move itself promised to be busy and enjoyable. Troop E was to march west and join the remainder of the regiment in the vicinity of Billings, 164 miles away. The column of mounted men and wagons left on May 19.

The first leg of the trip was hot and dusty by day and cold at night. Resting in the evenings in his comfortably furnished tent with Buck to tend the stove and bring him his meals, Allen started keeping a diary and saving letters for his "archives," a habit hardly ever broken through the rest of his life. Each day as they rode, the Rockies grew clearer on the western horizon. He often roamed far from the column, and once was "taken to task" for chasing antelope with his greyhounds. The miners, ranchers, and Indians he met along the way were interesting to talk with, and he enjoyed showing off his fine thoroughbred horse. Every few days his mail caught up with him. The newspapers brought the "doings of Congress" and the latest from Wall Street. From Miles City Tom wrote that the 3,300 ewes they had jointly purchased had just produced 2,700 lambs. At Billings, on May 28, Henry found a package of goodies waiting from Mrs. Girard.[73] Three days later he wrote Dora:

> We are now nearing the famous Livingston where four of you slept in one bed with Col. Rice as sentinel . . . I wish our Park party was along and especially that part of it that got so tired one day riding along in the mud and rain with no one but her escort.[74]

Near Billings Troop E had met the main column from Fort Custer, and together they marched on to Helena. There, on June 5, Allen learned that his mother was seriously ill, but there was no need for him to come home yet. The trail past Helena climbed steeply to the Continental Divide. By the Hellgate River, two years after graduating from West Point, he ate snow at the "summit of the Rockies." On June 20, near Missoula, the regiment boarded railroad cars and rode down into Washington Territory in relative comfort. After another short march they arrived at Fort Walla Walla on June 30. Its tree-shaded barracks and quarters were a welcome sight.[75]

The townspeople of Walla Walla turned out in gala fashion to greet them. With a population of nearly 7,000 people, the town offered attractions considerably more civilized than those available in Miles City. As soon as Allen could get off, he went to town to see a play and was reprimanded when he returned for wearing civilian clothes on post. He attended reveille, police call, and stables for the first time in his army experience and was also given the "honor" of arranging the firing of the Fourth of July salute and of trying seven court-martial cases. Competition to select a shooting team to represent the post at the Department matches at Fort Vancouver began in August. He tried out and made it.[76] With plenty to do in pleasant surroundings, he did not miss Keogh at all, especially since he had just met a girl in Walla Walla as pretty as Dora. Unfortunately, she already had a suitor of long standing. Allen solved this problem by slipping a piece of limburger cheese into the gentleman's pocket. That may have made him at least one enemy, but the joke was evidently appreciated by the lady.[77] Before he could really stake his claim in Walla Walla, however, he had to leave for the competition at Vancouver.

He did well in the matches and this time made the department team. On August 25, he boarded a steamer headed for three weeks in San Francisco and the Pacific Division competition. There his shooting luck left him, possibly as a result of too many nights spent sampling the city's cosmopolitan pleasures. By September 19 he was back in Vancouver, pockets empty, and trophyless.[78]

On returning he was told that the Department Commander, General Nelson A. Miles, wanted him as aide-de-camp. Miles was a crusty old Indian fighter, already a legend in the army, and the job as his aide was an honor and a great opportunity for Allen. He hurried back to Walla Walla to pick up his things and returned immediately to Vancouver.[79] If the young lieutenant had a rosy mental picture of forthcoming travels in style, meeting lots of famous people, and being at the great general's side in the field should there be another Indian uprising, Miles surprised him. He had other plans for his new aide.

CHAPTER III

Twenty-Five Hundred Miles on an Empty Stomach

Steamer *Ancon*
en route to Alaska
Oct. 8, 1884

Dear Little Dora:

You hardly expected, I imagine, to get a letter from Alaska. . . . This is the eighth day out and we will not reach Sitka for a week longer. From Sitka it will take from three to ten days to reach my destination, which is the mouth of the Copper River. . . .[1]

Allen's first orders from General Miles had been to go find his former aide, Lieutenant W. R. Abercrombie, who had not been heard from since the previous spring, when Miles dispatched him with an exploring party on an expedition up the Copper River.[2]

During the two weeks on the northbound steamer, Allen let his beard grow, wrote letters, and read. Alaska was his "chief theme of study" and he "consumed all or nearly all written concerning it . . . including Schwatka's unpublished report" (of a recent expedition on the Yukon). Typical of his catholic reading tastes, however, were the other books he brought with him. They included Upton's *Armies of Asia and Europe,* four popular novels (two in English, one in French and one in German), *The Koran, Popular Quotations,* a treatise on economics, and a "short scientific work."[3]

Allen landed at Sitka on October 16. From there he intended to charter any available sea-worthy vessel and proceed to Nuchek, on Hinchinbrook Island, the closest harbor to the mouth of the Copper River, fifty miles away across the Gulf of Alaska. At Nuchek he planned to make inquiries for Abercrombie and his men and proceed to the mainland if necessary.

Finding a suitable vessel and a willing crew in Sitka so late in the season was not easy, but he finally succeeded in chartering a small schooner, the *Leo*. The *Leo's* captain could not leave for Nuchek until October 27, so Allen had ten days with nothing to do but look around.[4]

In Sitka, tiny as it was, he discovered a fascinating mixture of several cultures. It had been an Indian village when the Russians arrived in 1799 to establish a trading post. Over the years, they had built log fortifications and blockhouses to guard the harbor. Next to the Indian settlement stood a newer town, looking very much like an outpost in the wilds of Siberia and dominated by an imposing rough-hewn fortress known as "The Castle," once the residence of the governors of Russian America.[5]

Inside the "Castle" Allen found a library to browse in, full of books on Alaska left behind by the last Russian governor. Here was an unexpected chance to learn more about the area. To his dismay, most of the books were in Russian. His inability to converse with the few Russians still living in Sitka added to his frustration. If he wanted to become an expert on Alaska, he would have to learn their language. He decided to begin immediately. However, he did not spend all of his time in Sitka trying to make sense of the Cyrillic alphabet.

For several days he wandered through the Indian settlement, buying trinkets for Dora and observing the native customs, including a funeral ceremony, with intense curiosity. Poking around town, he discovered a Chinese cook in a boarding house who claimed he could produce an authentic Chinese meal. Allen hired him and gave a dinner party for some U.S. Navy officers he had just met. He also met a local character named "Six Finger Jack," who spoke not only Russian but several Indian dialects, and hired him as an interpreter.[6]

Finally, the *Leo* was ready to leave for Nuchek. There, a week later, on November 3, Allen found a dejected and disgusted Abercrombie. The difficult terrain and harsh weather in the Copper River area were apparently too much for him; after going only sixty miles upriver he had given up and returned to Nuchek with his men to await a ship from home.[7]

The return trip was rough and unpleasant. The *Leo's* cabin stank of unwashed bodies and stale cooking. The captain grossly miscalculated the course back to Sitka and the extra days at sea resulted in their missing the government steamer for Portland. Rather than wait another month for its return, Allen and Abercrombie accepted the cap-

Sitka, Alaska Territory, *ca.* 1890. (Signal Corps Photograph No. 91708, National Archives)

tain's offer to take them back himself for $250. This leg of the trip was equally unpleasant. When the two lieutenants were not seasick, they spent most of their time playing cards and talking about politics, girls, and the food they would eat to forget the *Leo's* miserable fare. (Their first meal on landing consisted of oysters and icecream, washed down with cider.) During the voyage, Allen evidently decided to ask for orders to complete Abercrombie's mission upon his return, for his diary is full of tips and advice on exploring techniques from Abercrombie and his men. He made a tentative deal with the captain "to carry a government party to Nuchek from Sitka, if the Commanding Officer, Department of the Columbia desires it, on or before March 1, 1885." By December 16, he was back in Vancouver writing his report. To General Miles he sent a request for permission to resume the exploration of the Copper River.[8]

Previously Henry had promised Dora he would ask for a leave that winter. After procrastinating three weeks, he told her he might not be coming East for many months:

> . . . I am willing to forego almost any benefit . . . for an attempt at exploration of Alaska. There is a prospect now of my going . . . as soon as Feb. . . . I hope to be able to get some valuable information from regions never visited by white men.
>
> The detail will be a flattering one in as much as several officers senior to myself desire it.
>
> Your remark: "You seem to enjoy it the further off from civilization you get" is decidedly uncomplimentary and I will show you if ever I *do* get East that I too enjoy civilization. I have laughed quite a good deal at the expression. . . .[9]

An understanding of what Allen hoped to accomplish in Alaska requires some explanation of the history of its exploration prior to 1885. When the territory was purchased from Russia in 1867, most Americans were ignorant of its resources and geographical characteristics. "Seward's Icebox" was known to be a rich source of fish and furs and of ice for thirsty Californians, and that was about all.[10]

Based on the pioneering exploits of Vitus Bering, James Cook, and others, and the reports, frequently inaccurate, of several generations of trappers and traders, the Russians had a fair knowledge of the coastline, some of the major rivers, and a few other geographical features of the interior. The general course of the Yukon River from its sources to the sea was known, but only one of its tributaries, the Porcupine, had been explored completely. The Kuskokwim had been followed for

1,000 miles from its mouth, though its headwaters had not been reached. All but one of its tributaries, the Holitna, remained uncharted. The Nushagak and Alsek rivers were known, the latter only from the reports of natives. The Copper River, at least below the Tazlina, had been traveled by white men, but no reliable data on its course existed. Lake Iliamna had been discovered but not Lake Clark. On the Arctic coast only the mouths of the Kobuk, Noatak, and Coleville rivers had been plotted. Away from the rivers, and especially north of the Yukon, the map of Russian America contained vast blank spaces.[11]

The first significant inland explorations by Americans began shortly before 1867. Initial failures in laying the Atlantic telegraph cable had caused the Western Union Company to seek an alternate cable route to Europe. A predominantly overland line through Canada, Alaska, and Siberia was considered feasible, though extremely difficult. The company obtained the necessary concessions from foreign governments, and a party under the leadership of a noted naturalist, Robert Kennicott, landed in Alaska in late 1865 to survey and explore the Yukon Basin. Work was hampered from the first by difficulties with equipment and weather and then by the death of Kennicott. Having expended $3,000,000 on the Alaskan survey, Western Union lost all interest in the overland route upon the successful completion of the Atlantic cable in 1866. The remainder of Kennicott's party, under William H. Dall, went ahead on their own with part of the planned survey of the Yukon Basin.[12]

For ten years after 1867, the U.S. Army had responsibility for Alaska. Troops occupied the garrison in Sitka for ten years. Five other widely scattered posts were briefly set up, but in 1877 the army withdrew and full responsibility for the territory passed to the Treasury Department, already in charge of Alaskan commerce. From 1879 to 1884, the Navy and the Treasury Department jointly administered the area. The first civil government was then established, with the capital in Sitka.[13] For seventeen years Alaska had been neglected administratively and passed around like a stepchild.

What commercial services existed in 1885 were largely provided by the Alaska Commercial Company. Over the years it had gained an almost complete monopoly by the gradual extension of its network of trading posts and a supporting system of transport. That conditions in Alaska were harsh and that interest in the area was low are indicated by the 1880 census, which found the non-Indian population to be less than it had been thirteen years before, in the last year of Russian occupation. In 1880, only 215 white men lived in Sitka.[14]

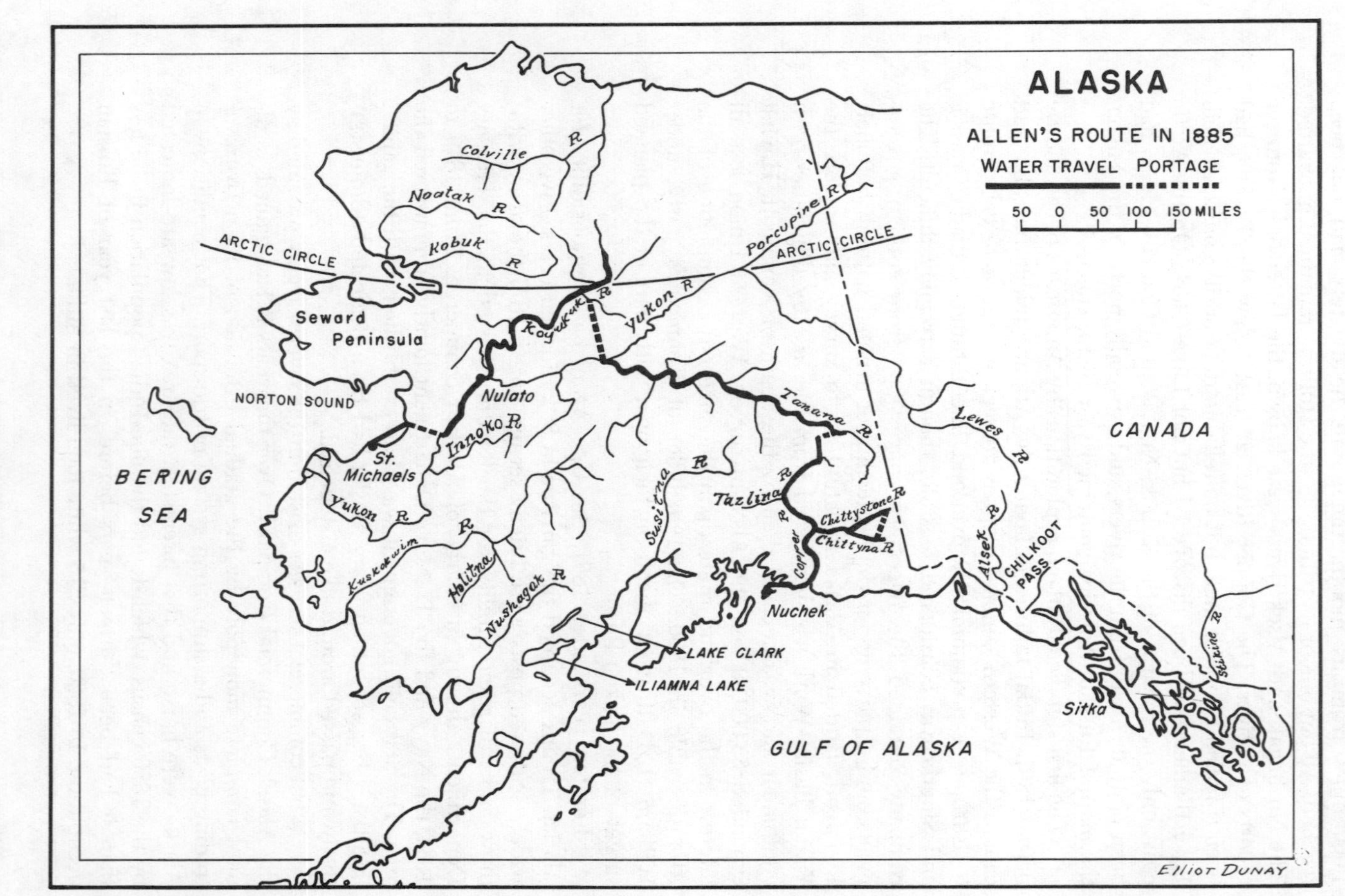
ALASKA
ALLEN'S ROUTE IN 1885
WATER TRAVEL PORTAGE
50 0 50 100 150 MILES
Colville R
Noatak R
Kobuk R
ARCTIC CIRCLE
Porcupine R
ARCTIC CIRCLE
Seward Peninsula
Koyukuk R
Yukon R
NORTON SOUND
Nulato
Innoko R
Tanana R
Lewes R
CANADA
St. Michaels
BERING SEA
Yukon R
Susitna R
Tazlina R
Chittystone R
Copper R
Chittyna R
Alsek R
CHILKOOT PASS
Kuskokwim R
Holitna
Nushagak R
Nuchek
LAKE CLARK
ILIAMNA LAKE
Stikine R
Sitka
GULF OF ALASKA
Elliot Dunay

Reflecting this stagnation, American exploration and mapping of Alaska's nearly 600,000 square miles had been carried out after 1867 in a desultory fashion and with very little government backing. Working on his own with another scientist, George Davidson, Dall continued to gather and compile data intermittently through the next decades on the area's geography, flora, and fauna.[15] In 1869, Captain Charles Raymond became the first U.S. Army officer to lead an expedition into the interior. Since his mission was merely to determine whether a particular Hudson Bay Company trading post on the Yukon was on American soil, little knowledge accrued from his efforts. In 1877, an Army Signal Corps meteorological station was established at St. Michaels. A Russian Alaskan, Ivan Petrof, spent two years on the lower Yukon and Kuskokwim as agent for the Tenth Census. Petrof's report in 1880 formed the basis for the entire Alaskan census and was accompanied by the best map of the territory yet produced, but most of his data on areas with which he was not personally familiar were based on speculation or the reports of untrained observers.[16] Aside from these activities, most of the other "official" expeditions were usually the result of individual initiative, since Congress generally refused to authorize funds for the specific purpose of Alaskan exploration.[17]

In 1883, Lieutenant Frederick Schwatka led a party of seven men overland through the Chilkoot Pass to the Lewes River and thence by boat down the entire length of the Yukon. Although his journey had already been duplicated by others, Schwatka produced the first complete and detailed survey of that river. General Miles deserves the credit for sending him to Alaska in the face of opposition from the War Department. Besides the expense involved, Washington had also objected to Schwatka's proposed route, part of which took him through Canada. On his own responsibility, Miles ordered him to go anyway.[18] Congress later gave its approval of a *fait accompli* by appropriating money to publish Schwatka's official report.[19]

Schwatka's success led General Miles to dispatch Lieutenant Abercrombie up the Copper River in the spring of 1884. That Abercrombie had almost totally failed to accomplish his mission was not known until he and Allen returned to Vancouver together in December.

During the next month, a series of letters and telegrams concerning Allen's request to resume the Copper River exploration passed between Vancouver, San Francisco, and Washington. In his report, Allen had stated he could make the trip with only two soldiers, but

General Miles also asked for an interpreter, a packer, and ten Indian scouts for him, all to be paid for by the War Department.[20] In Washington General Philip H. Sheridan did not share Miles's enthusiasm for such ventures, and he bluntly refused to authorize money or extra men for Allen. He told Miles to "furnish the necessary transportation and subsistence stores," and added testily, "if these conditions are not satisfactory you can indefinitely postpone the expedition." [21]

Despite these restrictions, Miles expanded the expedition in other ways. He gave Allen permission to try to reach the headwaters of the unsurveyed Tanana River and to follow the course of the Tanana to its juncture with the Yukon. He would then follow the Yukon to the sea. His final instructions allowed him to explore even further.

In accordance with Sheridan's orders, Allen started out with only two other men, although he did have permission to hire up to five Indian guides in Alaska if needed. For his companions in this adventure, he selected Sergeant Cady Robertson, a sturdy and dependable N.C.O. from his own unit, and Private Frederick W. Fickett, Signal Corps, whom he had met in Alaska the previous October. Fickett was familiar with Alaskan conditions and was a capable photographer and meteorologist.

Allen was allocated $500 for the purchase of sufficient concentrated rations to last a year and given authority to expend up to $2,000 in government checks to cover the cost of chartering transport, hiring guides, buying additional equipment or provisions, and other incidentals.[22]

His orders, dated January 27, 1885, read in part:

> . . . In view of the fact that so little is known of the interior of Alaska, and the conflicting interest between the white people and Indians of that territory may in the near future result in serious disturbances between the two races, the Department Commander authorizes you to proceed to that Territory for the purpose of obtaining all information which will be valuable and important to the military branch of the Government.
>
> You will . . . ascertain as far as practicable the number, character, and disposition of all natives living in that section of country; how subdivided into tribes and bands; the district of country they inhabit; their relations to each other, and especially their disposition toward the United States Government and . . . the whites who are making their way into that region.
>
> You will further examine their modes of life and their means of communication from one part of the country to the other, and amount and kinds of material of war in their possession and from whence obtained. You will further obtain such information as may be practicable as to the character

of the country of means of using and sustaining a military force. . . . Also ascertain the character of the climate. . . .

Let your researches be thorough, and endeavor to complete as far as practicable all desired information in each portion of the country as you advance into the interior, that your work may be resumed hereafter, if deemed necessary, at any point at which you may be compelled by untoward circumstances to abandon it.

You will endeavor to impress the natives with the friendly disposition of the Government. . . .

In no case will you move in any section of the country where you cannot go without provoking hostilities. . . .

You are not authorized to exercise any control of affairs in that territory. . . .

If you are in all respects fortunate and successful, it is possible for you to ascend the Copper River and descend the Tanana, and return in 1885, and this will be your general instruction; but under the peculiar circumstances which will inevitably surround you, much must be left to your discretion and judgment, and therefore regarding your movements after leaving the Copper River no definite directions can be given to you. . . .

You now have ample funds; they are to be used for the payment of yourself and party; but so long as you have them you will not suffer from hunger or permit your party to.

With best wishes for your success and safe return.[23]

At eleven o'clock in the evening of January 28, the party left Portland for Sitka aboard the government steamship *Idaho.* They took with them two sextants (one a pocket model), an artificial horizon, a "best grade" chronometer, a camera with dry plates and chemicals, two barometers, a psychrometer (hygrometer), prismatic and pocket compasses, a year's supply of food, and miscellaneous items such as medicine and a tent. Each man had a rifle and plenty of ammunition, plus his own bedding and extra clothing.[24] Allen and Fickett carried diaries.

Upon disembarking at Sitka on February 7, Allen found that his plans had already gone awry. The *Leo,* supposedly waiting for him per arrangements made with her captain back in December, had just sailed for San Francisco. Nuchek was 432 miles away across the Gulf of Alaska and no one else in Sitka was willing to risk the trip in that stormy season. Allen decided to borrow a canoe and go across the straits to Kilisnoo to seek help. Three days later he was back in Sitka after a fruitless and exhausting 140 mile round trip. The success of his plan to reach the headwaters of the Copper depended on getting there before March when the ice in the river began to break up and melt. If the ice held, travel upstream would be much easier, but now such a prospect looked bleak indeed.

His last hope was the navy sloop *Pinta,* anchored in Sitka harbor, though the captain had already refused to take him to Nuchek without authority from the Navy Department. This request went back to Portland with the returning *Idaho.* In the meantime, Allen and his two men spent the time practicing with their instruments, packing and repacking their equipment, and acquiring more gear—notably several sleds and three sleeping bags waterproofed with linseed oil and beeswax. At last, the *Idaho* returned with the necessary permission and the party departed on the *Pinta* for Nuchek on March 16.[25]

The *Pinta* hove to a mile offshore from Nuchek late on the evening of March 19, and the three men and all their equipment were rowed ashore. George Holt, the only white man living on the island, met them and reported the ice still holding on the Copper River. After some difficulty, Allen procured two battered rowboats and three native volunteers to make the trip across to the mainland. Having had unfortunate experiences with the Russians, most of the natives were distrustful of white men. The Copper River tribes had a fearsome reputation. No less than eleven white men had been murdered by them since the turn of the century. (A year later, Holt became their twelfth victim.) A warship in the area, however, temporarily inspired respect. "The further we travelled," Allen wrote, "the larger became the size of the *Pinta* and its guns." [26]

They were set to leave Nuchek the next day. At the last minute, a prospector named Peter Johnson decided to accompany them and rejoin his partner, John Bremner, then somewhere up the Copper River. Early on the gray morning of March 20, seven men in two rowboats pushed off from Nuchek into a strong surf and bitter wind.

To get to the mouth of the river took six days of rowing from dawn to dark. Each evening they stopped along the unprotected shoreline. On the second day out a gale began that lasted for nearly two weeks and kept them almost constantly soaked. The temperature, meanwhile, hovered near freezing.

On the evening of March 25 they reached the river's mouth. It proved to be an enormous mud flat on which the boats became stranded. To carry everything to solid land, each man would be forced to walk several miles back and forth through hip-deep ooze. Allen's immediate goal was to find the nearby native village of Alganik, where he hoped to get help unloading the boats and guides for the trip upstream. On his map, the name of the village appeared in bold letters right where he stood, but Alganik itself was nowhere in sight. After wandering in the dark for several hours, he found it. The settlement consisted of two huts, each measuring about twelve by thirteen feet and already overcrowded by the presence of several visiting families from upriver. Too exhausted to worry about amenities, the newcomers moved right in and flopped down wherever they could find a few inches of bare dirt floor. That night Allen slept with twenty-nine Indians and ten dogs.

The arduous task of unloading the boats took up the next two days. The Indians repeatedly quit, throwing their loads down in the mud and walking off. By using threats, cajolery, and barter Allen finally got everything carried ashore. None of the natives wanted to guide him upstream, but he overcame this problem with a little psychology. He had them draw lots for the "privilege" and thus obtained the services of five somewhat reluctant guides. To add to his worries, the ice had begun to break up on the river. Progress would be much slower without the benefit of a smooth surface under the sled runners.

On March 29, the group of four white men and five Indians started north. Two men paddled a canoe while the others pulled sleds along the shore. Their advance was painfully slow. The freezing rain, which had let up briefly, began its steady pouring again and soon turned the ground into a miserably unpleasant mixture of mud and slush. They stumbled and fell on patches of crusted snow not quite strong enough to support a man's weight. No one had any rain cover except a poncho. Allen soon decided to abandon much of the equipment in order to make better speed and left half the ammunition, most of the cooking utensils, and some of the food and extra clothing in a cache only a few miles above Alganik. Even this was not enough. A few hours later the tent and more clothing and food were left behind. He and his men kept only the scientific equipment, their weapons and remaining ammunition, a few trinkets for trading purposes, 150 pounds of flour, 100 pounds of beans, 40 pounds of rice, 2 sides of bacon, 15 pounds of tea, small amounts of beef extract, deviled ham and chocolate, and the clothing they had on their backs. Each man carried a fifty-pound pack. The remaining load was distributed on the sleds and in the canoe. The sleds, though lightened considerably, still required one man to pull and one to push.[27]

The lower valley of the Copper was a half-frozen hell. Full of jagged chunks of ice, the river varied from a rushing torrent between vertical rock walls to multiple braided channels which meandered sluggishly through marshy flats up to fifteen miles wide. Where the shoreline was not rugged cliffs, it was overgrown by dense thickets. Away from the river the terrain was even more difficult. The Indians grew more surly with every mile. One morning they refused to come out of their improvised sleeping shelters. Allen had to drag them out physically and tear the shelters down before they would go on. Indian and white man alike fell often from exhaustion and snow blindness.

Through all this, Allen kept his diary current and he and Fickett made frequent observations and measurements. During the entire expedition, no matter what, Allen plotted their course by sextant, chronometer, and compass several times each day while Fickett recorded temperature, rainfall, relative humidity, and barometric pressure. Fickett also took numerous photographs while on the Copper. Before leaving the river, he sent the exposed plates and the camera back to Nuchek with some natives. Unfortunately, they became curious and opened the package, ruining the plates. Later, on the Tanana, the psychrometer was stolen and the aneroid barometer damaged, so that his meteorological data from that point on were incomplete.[28]

Despite all adversity, Allen kept his wry sense of humor.

> April 8: . . . travelled 13 miles. Found an abandoned native cabin . . . ate a meal of spoiled fish. The natives interpreted the hieroglyphics on the wall . . . surprised we did not understand. Our failure to do so afforded more evidence to them of their superiority over us. . . . We were not aware that this was also a suburb of the far-famed Taral, which we reached the following morning, two and a half miles farther up the river.[29]

At Taral, even more squalid than Alganik, Johnson's partner Bremner, looking like a happy scarecrow, rushed out to greet them. He had been almost out of ammunition and slowly starving. The two prospectors had a private huddle and decided to continue on up the river with Allen. At this point, only 230 pounds of food remained to feed the five white men and their guides until they reached the Yukon, far to the north.

Nevertheless, instead of pushing on right away, Allen decided to use Taral as a base and explore the Chittyna River, a tributary that joined the Copper at that point. Leaving some of the party at Taral to guard the remaining supplies, he headed east up the Chittyna with only four days' supply of food. He intended to live off the land, but Alaska in the early spring is not a place of abundant wildlife. Allen "celebrated" his twenty-sixth birthday, April 13, 1885, by eating rotten moose meat left over by the wolves.[30] Even this tasty fare was not always available, and both white men and natives frequently fainted from hunger. They visited several native villages on the Chittyna and its tributary, the Chittystone, and at each village were welcomed with a feast (by local standards). However, subsequent meals at any given village had to be paid for by barter.

Having surveyed most of the Chittyna Valley, Allen returned to Taral by native boat on May 4. This boat, called a *baidarra,* provided the party with its chief means of transportation for the next month. It was twenty-seven feet long, five feet in the beam, twenty-two inches deep and covered with untanned moose skins. No metal held its wooden frame together, only rawhide strings and willow sprouts. A native chieftain named Nicolai had the *baidarra* built for Allen, and then he too decided to accompany his new friend up the Copper.

They resumed the journey north from Taral on May 6. At this point in its course, the current in the river ran at a rate of from seven to nine miles an hour. The only way progress could be made was by a process called cordelling. Two men stayed in the *baidarra,* one steering and one fending with a pole, while everyone else pulled from the shore on a rope attached to the bow. Since the water temperature was forty-three degrees and there was frequently no footing on the river bank, it was unpleasant and exhausting work.[31]

Understandably, the guides again grew surly and uncooperative. Other difficulties kept cropping up, especially with the tribes with whom they came in contact along the way.

> . . . had we been less dependent on the natives, I should certainly have let them understand that the ablest worker was the chiefest man. . . . On one occasion, when I attempted to snub a lazy chief by making a . . . present to one of his vassals, and a splendid worker, rather than to himself, he pocketed the article and took all the credit for possessing so valuable a worker. These *tyones* [chiefs] barely condescended to consider me their equal and on no occasion would they consider my men as such. They were reluctant to believe that anyone who would pull on the rope of a boat, carry a pack, or take equal foot with his men could be a *tyone.*[32]

Above Taral the Copper River describes a great three-quarter circle, heading first west, then north and east. Inside this bend is a range of mountains, of which at this time only one, Mount Wrangell, was named. As Allen progressed upstream, he plotted the location of the other peaks in the range. He also calculated their height but less accurately. To several he gave the names they bear today: Mounts Sanford, Blackburn, and Drum.[33]

Such flattery might later ease the upward path of Allen's career, but it was of no immediate help to him and his men. Travel up the river got no easier as they approached its headwaters. Often more than a week passed without their seeing another human being. The Indians they did meet were usually as hungry as they were. It was too early in the season to catch salmon, and game was unbelievably scarce. These are entries in Fickett's journal:

May 28—Had a little paste, rotten wormy meat for dinner; rotten goose eggs and a little rice for supper. Each meal about one-fourth of what we needed. We went into camp. Whole party played out.

May 29—Party nearly played out for want of food. Can just crawl, had to stop in middle of PM to make a flapjack for each, and a little beef tea.

May 30—Arrived at an Indian house at 11 AM hungry. Decided to abandon boat. Indian gave us a dinner of boiled meat from which he scraped the maggots by handfuls before cutting it up. It tasted good, maggots and all.[34]

After four more days along the banks of the dwindling Copper, Allen decided not to follow it further east to its source. With two new guides, the party struck out almost due north up the Slana River toward the headwaters of the Tanana. Allen's map, compiled by Dall and Petrof, told him the Copper and Tanana rivers were several hundred miles apart and separated by a high range of mountains. The portage supposedly took thirty days. All of this proved false. They left the Copper on June 4, reached the head of the Slana River the next day, and by a series of easy marches over a low pass (named by Allen for General Miles) in the Alaskan Range, arrived at the Tanana near its source on June 10. The total distance between the two rivers was less than one hundred miles.

The first settlement they came upon near the Tanana was a village Allen called Nandell's. The natives looked poor and scrawny but far better off than those along the Copper. Many of the people of Nandell's had never seen a white man, but they possessed utensils which had obviously come from traders. A few of them even knew parts of the alphabet. Easier times were ahead. The party would be approaching civilization instead of leaving it behind, and the river current now ran in their favor, too. Allen had planned to build a crude raft and simply drift down the Tanana to the Yukon. The natives at Nandell's advised against the raft because of the rapids downstream. Instead, they helped him build another skin-covered boat, much like the one abandoned on the Copper.

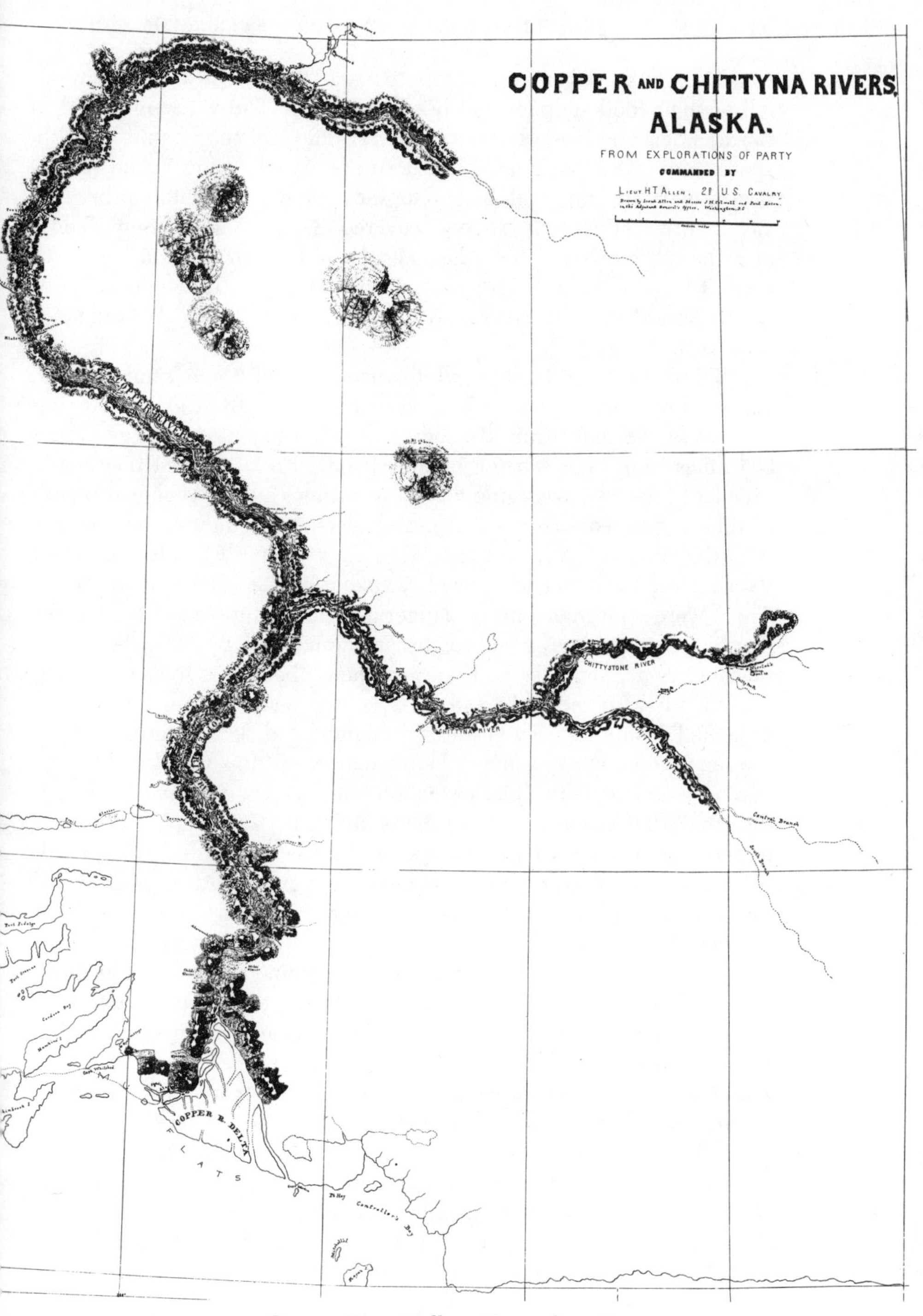

Copper River Valley: Drawn by Allen

Despite these good omens, the party had little cause for optimism. All of their food supplies had been consumed. The white men had to barter pocket knives, shirts, and everything else they could possibly spare to obtain provisions to last until they reached the Yukon. Bremner, the prospector, had begun to show signs of mental instability. Black sores, apparently scurvy, covered Sergeant Robertson's body, and the antiscorbutic that Allen had brought along did not seem to help. To make things even worse, no one at Nandell's would agree to accompany them downriver. A tribe further along would kill them all, they said.[35]

Thus, on June 14, five white men, two of them semi-invalids, started down the uncharted Tanana on their own. By Allen's reckoning they were 566 miles from the mouth of the Tanana at the Yukon and 384 miles from their starting point, Alganik. From the first they made excellent progress, averaging fifty to sixty miles a day. Allen had plenty of time to plot compass azimuths and sextant readings as they drifted with the current, except for two tense days when all hands were busy steering and balancing to prevent capsizing in mile after mile of rapids. There were other moments of danger as well. At the end of the second day on the river, they reached the area inhabited by the tribe which the natives at Nandell's had warned them about. No sooner had the party landed for the night and set up camp when several Indians approached. Using forceful gestures they indicated their chief wanted to see the white men. Wishing to know more about this warlike tribe and hoping to persuade its chief of his intention to pass peaceably through the area, Allen decided to meet the issue boldly. Leaving three men at the boat with instructions to escape on the river if anything happened, Allen and Fickett warily accompanied their guides. After walking for two and one-half hours in the dark along a winding forest trail, they reached the chief's village. The chief, named Kheeltat, welcomed them with a frown but said nothing. Even more ominously, the guides fired several shots into the air. Still, no one spoke as the minutes ticked by. The two white men had now been awake for nearly twenty-hour hours. Despite their anxious plight, both fell asleep, weak from hunger and exhaustion. They were wakened by the firing of more shots. Twenty-six braves and four squaws faced them.

Allen began to explain his purpose by using sign language and a map, but no one seemed interested in that. He soon discovered why. Having treated some of the people at Nandell's with the drugs he carried with him, his reputation as a "medicine man" had preceded him. The chief pointed at Allen's medical kit and then at his own mouth.

The kit contained three kinds of pills: the standard army purgative and antipurgative tablets and quinine. With considerable relief Allen began doling them out; one pill of each kind to the chief, two kinds to his assistants, and only one to the lesser members of the tribe. He and Fickett did not stay around to watch the results of the white man's powerful medicine, but hurried back to the boat with Kheeltat's blessing.[36] The party launched their boat, fast.

By June 21 they had run out of food again and were unable to catch any fish as they drifted along. For three days they lived on nothing but candle tallow, until at last they reached the Yukon. Allen's map showed a trading station at the confluence of the Tanana and the Yukon. They found nothing. A few miles further downstream, at Nuklukyet, they came upon the station—boarded up. Breaking in, they found three dozen hard crackers, three quarts of beans, twenty pounds of flour, and some salt and machine oil. According to the local Indians, a steamboat was expected up the river in ten or twelve days. Until then, the five gaunt explorers would have to live on a slim diet of beans, crackers, and fish fried in machine oil.[37]

The first week in July was the traditional time for the natives to meet the steamboat and engage in some celebration and trade. That the white man happened to have a great holiday on July Fourth was to them merely a happy coincidence, but they were only too glad to add the joys of his celebration to their own. In Allen's words:

> On July 4, the station was indeed thronged with natives all of whom were disposed to be sociable and to help share our small apartments. Once divested of its novelty, their society was not to be envied. . . . To show their patriotism, a grand firing of guns announced July 4, a flag was immediately run up the newly made pole, and a general shouting and dancing indulged in. In their zeal they had begun their salute before midnight of July 3.[38]

On July 11, with the steamboat *Yukon* a week overdue at Nuklukyet, Allen borrowed a canoe and went downriver to meet it and hurry it on. Five days later he returned on the *Yukon* only to find several in the party sicker than ever. Sergeant Robertson's scurvy, in particular, had not responded to more wholesome food. No one would have blamed Allen for calling it quits on the spot. He had accomplished his mission and could well have ridden the steamboat in comfort down the Yukon to the coast and caught the next ship for San Francisco or Portland. Instead, he decided to do some more exploring.

Loath to waste the few remaining weeks of good weather, Allen wanted to see the headwaters of the Koyukuk River, of which only the lower reaches had been mapped. The Koyukuk natives were rumored to be warlike, but by then he was skeptical of such reports. Private Fickett was game, but Johnson and Bremner had had enough. They chose to remain on the Yukon and do some more prospecting. Allen decided to have Robertson go back downriver on the *Yukon* when it returned to Nuklukyet in August and hold the steamboat at Nulato, where the Koyukuk joins the Yukon. If Allen and Fickett had not appeared by August 23, the *Yukon* was to continue down the river and Robertson would wait for them at St. Michaels, on the coast.[39]

After the usual difficulties in hiring guides, they started overland for the Koyukuk on July 28 accompanied by seven Indians and five dogs. Each Indian carried a fifty-pound pack, mostly food, and each dog carried twenty-five pounds more. Allen and Fickett would not starve on this trip. They carried only their weapons and instruments, plus a torn piece of waterproof linen (the remnant of a sleeping bag) and one blanket apiece. Although there was no trail, they made good progress for several days. The brief heat of the Alaskan summer brought out swarms of mosquitos and flies to torture them as they hurried along. Yet, Allen was not satisfied with the pace: "The natives unanimously agreed that six more days would be required to reach the Koyukuk. They were informed that rations would not be issued after the end of the fourth day. They believed it. We reached the river at the end of the fourth day," having covered 120 miles on foot in six and one-half days.[40]

Obtaining another boat, the party traveled north along the river for six days, reaching latitude 67° 16′, well above the Arctic Circle, before turning back at noon on August 9. Allen gave Fickett's name to the northernmost tributary of the Koyukuk.[41] The run down the Koyukuk was pleasant and uneventful, despite unmistakable evidence that the summer was rapidly ending. Allen mapped 556 miles of the Koyukuk as they drifted along, using more than 440 compass bearings and countless sextant observations. They arrived at Nulato on the evening of August 21, only to find that the steamboat had left several hours before. Sergeant Robertson had been unable to persuade its captain to wait. There was nothing else to do but make their way out to the coast on their own.[42]

Allen paid off the guides. One of them, named "Dandy," had become his favorite. Only later did he learn Dandy was a murderer. A Russian trader, who had been mistreating Dandy's mother, got helplessly drunk one night and Dandy crushed his head with an axe, though

Allen, knowing this, said of him, "a more peaceable Indian in appearance does not at present live in the Yukon."[43]

On August 22, Allen and Fickett started down the Yukon in the boat they had used on the Koyukuk. Below Nulato, the Yukon swings south and passes within about 120 miles of St. Michaels, their destination on the coast. Rather than follow the river itself several hundred miles farther south and west and then follow the coast back up to St. Michaels, Allen decided to take an overland shortcut from the point on the river nearest to it. The portage began on August 23, with the help of natives hired on the spot. They reached the coast at Norton Sound on August 27, with Allen still taking observations and measurements every step of the way. Borrowing another boat and hiring some native oarsmen, Allen and Fickett covered the remaining fifty-five miles to St. Michaels in three days. Arriving there on the evening of August 30, 1885, they found Sergeant Robertson waiting. This time their luck held, for the United States revenue cutter *Corwin* was stopping at St. Michaels after having picked up some shipwrecked whalers.[44]

They left St. Michaels aboard the *Corwin* on September 5, bound for San Francisco, with a stop at Oumalaska to pick up coal. All three men had been on the verge of physical collapse, but now with plenty of rest and food, their spirits soared. While they waited at Oumalaska for the coal steamer, Allen browsed in the ship's library, fussed over his scientific data, and brought his diary up to date. One night he went to a dance on the island. Since his partner spoke only Russian, his gallantry was "severely tested," he wrote. He also recorded his decision to ask for permission to go to Russia and learn the language once he completed his report.[45]

The coal steamer arrived on September 30. It brought word of General Miles's transfer to the Department of the Missouri and Allen's relief as his aide. There was also news from home. Susannah Allen had died in Sharpsburg on March 30, 1885, while her son was somewhere on the Copper River. Her last words were for him: "Meet me in heaven."[46]

Allen docked in San Francisco on October 12 to find himself a celebrity. "The reporters were very vigilant and of course the usual trash appeared in the papers the following morning. They are only sufficiently educated to appreciate only incidents, stories, etc." The local geographical society asked him to stay a while and give a talk, but since he was anticipating orders to go to Washington to make his

The Alaskan Explorer at St. Michaels, September, 1885. (Photograph courtesy of Col. Henry T. Allen, Jr.)

report and wanted to spend some time at home en route, he departed almost immediately.[47]

Shortly after reaching Vancouver he received a warm letter of congratulations from General Miles,[48] but no word from Dora awaited him. Perhaps he expected none after she had shown such bitterness and disappointment the previous winter over his going to Alaska. He waited two weeks before sending her a note that expressed far more than the mere geographical distance between them:

Dear Miss Dora:

I trust that this finds you well and happy and I assure you it carries the best wishes of an old friend.

Hal Allen [49]

When she answered, he learned she was in Philadelphia visiting friends. There, after Henry had reached Washington in early December, they met again. It was two years and two months since they had last seen each other. Their brief reunion restored the *status quo ante.* Henry's next letter from Washington was addressed to "Dear Little Dora" and signed "yours affectionately." It was full of details about his plunge into Washington society, including the calls he had made accompanied by Mrs. Drum to the homes of cabinet members. Perhaps to make Dora jealous he mentioned escorting the daughter of Chief Justice Morrison R. Waite to several affairs. As for going out to Chicago for the Christmas holidays, he was sorry, but he had to get started on his report even though official Washington's interest in Alaska did not match his own. "Really," he said, "I can't understand why everybody says, 'take your time, don't be in a hurry' just as though life were eternal." [50]

Before beginning the report Allen had a complete physical check-up. His weight was almost back to normal, but he still suffered from "nervous exhaustion" and the doctor recommended no more than three hours of work a day.[51]

The report took him several months to write and contained not only a narrative description of the entire expedition, but also much of scientific value. From his data, Allen prepared detailed maps of the Copper, Tanana, and Koyukuk rivers and several of their tributaries, as well as a general map of Alaska which incorporated this information and other miscellaneous observations. He made no claim to extreme accuracy in view of the speed with which he had moved and the adverse conditions under which the observations had been made. Nevertheless, with the exception of the "Mt. Tillman" mistake, a comparison of his maps with modern ones leads to the conclusion his performance as a surveyor was quite creditable.[52] In less than seven months and under the most grueling hardships he had traveled more than 2,500 miles and mapped the valleys of three large and previously unsurveyed rivers totaling more than 1,500 miles in length. He named many features of the terrain and included panoramic sketches of some of the more important ones. In addition, the report contained an estimated census of the number of Indians living in each valley, as well as descriptions of their customs, sketches of their weapons and modes of transportation, and many other details. There were knowledgeable comments on Alaskan plants and wildlife, with descriptions of unfamiliar species. Allen also included geological and mineralogical information, with indications of the probable location of deposits of copper and other minerals. He even compiled a brief dictionary of the language of the Indians of the Copper River.

Private Fickett's report formed an annex to Allen's and added meteorological data and comments on the soil and Alaska's potential for certain crops.

Finally, Allen was careful to answer the military and sociopolitical questions which were the main justification for his expedition in the first place. As for the conduct of military operations in Alaska, he could speak from first-hand experience that they would be extremely difficult. In contrast to what he had been led to believe by previous reports, he found the natives along his route peaceable but poor and sickly and in need of government help, especially those in the lower Yukon valley. His comments on them were both wise and humane:

> I know of no place in the possession of the United States where charity could with more justice be dispensed than among these people.
>
> Their continual intercourse with Russians and whites for fifty years has had its effects in altering their customs, though it is not evident that the association has been beneficial to them. . . .
>
> Their poverty-stricken, humiliated condition is taken advantage of by the traders who demand from them much greater prices . . . than are obtained from the bolder and more independent natives . . . farther up the river. . . .
>
> The question of an industrial education . . . now supposed to be best for Indian children, for the Yukon River natives is certainly a subject for consideration. . . . What industry can be taught children living in such an inhospitable climate as theirs? . . . The primary object of the education should be to teach them more feasible methods of living. . . . Without the

further development of their country, or financial assistance, I cannot see that the benefits of an industrial education would in any manner be for their welfare.[53]

Allen submitted his report to the War Department in April, 1885, but it was not published until 1887. It created little stir in the United States, though both the Royal Geographic Society in London and the Geographic Society of Bremen wanted to publish it.[54] The judgment of Allen's foreign contemporaries as to the difficulty and importance of his work is confirmed by a modern scholar who has written, "It was an incredible accomplishment that deserves to be ranked with the great explorations of North America." [55]

While preparing the report, Allen had considerable difficulty obtaining translations from Russian source materials on Alaska available in Washington. The State Department's Russian translator was practically incompetent, and no one else could help him. In May, he took a long-contemplated step and asked Adjutant General Drum for permission to go to Europe on detached duty for nine months to study Russian. He had already made limited progress in the language, he said, and added:

> In the libraries of the State Department and of Congress there are many [Russian] records of much value, but which are effectively sealed to the Army at large. . . . They are supposed to contain much valuable information concerning our Alaskan territory and I am specially desirous of mastering the language sufficiently well to make not discreditable translations from these as well as other Russian works.[56]

General Drum informed him the Secretary of War had reluctantly denied his request, "in view of the very long period you have been absent from your company." [57] Allen paid his farewell calls, packed his bags, and prepared to head back to Walla Walla. On the way he planned to stop in Chicago to see Dora and meet her brothers and sisters.

CHAPTER IV

Companions in Exile

Dora's family was not particularly impressed by Henry. With his brash self-confidence, colorful tales of the Arctic wilds and luxuriant Alaskan-grown beard, he appeared to be a gentleman turned frontier roughneck. Worse yet, his eyes, red and heavy-lidded from constant reading, made them suspect he was also a heavy drinker.[1] Henry was equally unimpressed. He found Dora's brothers and sisters rude, selfish, and quarrelsome and never changed his opinion of them.[2] He saw faults in Dora, too, but hers were minor by comparison.

He and Dora spent about a week together in Lake Forest, "spooning" when they could escape the family and talking seriously about their future. They were definitely in love now, but if Henry proposed marriage, Dora was not ready to accept. Very little was settled between them before he had to leave for Walla Walla.

Their letters over the next few months make clear the reasons for her hesitation. For one, in Dora's eyes, Henry seemed unconcerned with her interests and feelings. Perhaps her own ego was nearly as big as his, but she can hardly be blamed for her mounting annoyance at receiving a series of letters, all as self-centered as this first one after his return to Walla Walla:

Dear Little Dora:

After a delightful journey, . . . a "warm welcome" awaited me and the band serenaded beginning with "Home Again." . . .

I am disappointed not finding a single word from the one of all that would give me most pleasure. . . .

I have donned my uniform and feel already quite at home in it, yet I shall struggle not to fall in the ways usually trod by garrison officers. There was a hop and how flat it was! It requires a struggle for an undiplomatic person like myself not to show my utter unappreciation of the things that seem to interest many. There are some very nice people here, but they have remained too long in the same channels. Doubtless I am spoiled and will possibly find it all more congenial in the course of time. . . . The soldiers here are apparently extremely glad to see me and I appreciate it much.

Lovingly yours,
Hal A.[3]

When his conceit provoked a scolding reply, he was temporarily contrite:

I can't imagine you cross with anyone except me for I think you naturally very amiable. . . . I am indeed interested in anything that appeals to you.

But then, in the same letter, he went blithely on with his boasting:

. . . I find that my early riding is proving a stimulus to some of my confreres. They do not possess sufficient *abandon* for my cavalry ideas.

Washington is not the only place where invitations are extended to unknown, never-before-seen guests. One of the *élite* has sent me an invitation for a picnic. . . .[4]

When she tried the tactic of not answering some of his letters, he responded sarcastically:

I had almost become persuaded that you were ill, so long have you delayed writing. . . . I have received but two letters whilst this is my *fourth* to you. Olivette [apparently a mutual friend] is now in the town and I was seriously thinking of transferring my affections, especially after her sweet smiles given a few days since. . . .[5]

Yet, despite his taunts, he loved her deeply and pleaded for her love and trust in return:

. . . Can you imagine with what reluctance I left you, what pain I have since felt, and what greater sweeter pain to think that you grieved some. How often have I thought of you since then and what feelings I would have expressed to you long ere this had your letters seemed more responsive.

You are the only woman that I have ever spoken to in this manner and for this reason I have been called "cold and calculating." . . . Have I not told you that I love you and have you not indirectly, at least, promised to be mine? Yet you have no confidence in me who am willing to trust you to the extreme. . . .[6]

Something else about Henry made Dora uneasy. From his reading had come the conviction that no denomination held exclusive custody of religious truth. While en route to Alaska he had written her, "I have ordered Renan's *Life of Jesus* sent to you, but fear you will not indorse his views." [7] She did not. Renan's theological relativism offended her own earnest Presbyterian beliefs. This issue, too, remained unsettled during Henry's stay in Chicago. Later she wrote him, "I fear your unbelief is greater than your love." [8] To which he replied:

> To my mind the two ideas are entirely unantagonistic and I cannot conceive how you can put them in antithesis. You may doubt the former but you can not the love of your devoted—Hal.[9]

Finally, there was his obsession with Alaska. Before leaving Washington, Allen had asked his friends in Congress to introduce a bill authorizing another expedition with the understanding he would lead it. Dora asked him to give up such schemes. With little chance to excel in the dull routine of garrison life, he was looking for a faster way to build a reputation and could not see why his going to Alaska should stand in the way of their marriage:

> Would you have me refuse any channel that leads to distinction, that helps bring honor to you simply because it entailed hardships to me and possibly privations to you? I would be only too willing and glad to form indissoluble bonds before entering on such an undertaking. . . .[10]

They had been planning a reunion at Christmastime, but toward the end of September he told her it was going to be difficult for him to get away because of the shortage of officers in his unit. He could do it "by pulling strings, yet this measure ought not to be resorted to except under unusual conditions." Then, a week later, she learned he had been selected to command Troop "L" at Fort Coeur d'Alêne in Idaho Territory. He would be going up, he said, to relieve a captain who was going on leave, "the duration of which I do not know . . . it means a detail of several months during which time it will probably be impossible to get away." [11]

Despite such disappointments and her continuing misgivings, Dora decided Henry was her man. She gradually let him know she was willing to trust his judgment about their future. No wedding date had been set, and in fact she had not even said "yes" yet, but neither did she object when he suggested a European honeymoon "in case the [Alaskan] appropriation fails." [12]

There matters rested while they waited for Congress to convene in December, each hoping for a different outcome. Allen got settled at Coeur d'Alêne. To improve his chances of obtaining leave to go to Europe he began to spend several hours a day studying Russian. Now confident of Dora's love, he was full of himself again:

> I am not sure that I would be specially improved here were I to continue attending roll calls, drills etc. for a natural generation, on the other hand my chances for the blissful abodes of the eternal hereafter would certainly be curtailed. . . .

In the same letter he told Dora about taking the post commander, "Gen'l" Carlin, out deer hunting. The old gentleman was evidently no sportsman. Allen mocked his forgetfulness in not bringing along any ammunition and his lack of knowledge about guns: "He may have anticipated riding up and striking the beautiful animals with the heavy muzzle." [13]

December passed with no word from Washington on the Alaskan bill. Dora and Henry exchanged Christmas presents and tried to make plans. If the bill did not pass, they would be married as soon as possible. And, if he could obtain permission to study in Russia, their honeymoon would be in Europe. But, if the bill did pass, she was not promising anything. Henry pleaded with her:

> Sweetheart, it pains me to write to you my convictions concerning this matter, but being fully persuaded that the methods I have chosen, . . . are best for our mutual good, I venture. . . . It opens to me a chance of securing reputation and what higher goal can a man strive for? . . .[14]

In January, the suspense was over:

> I received a letter . . . from the member [Senator Beck of Kentucky] who has been fathering the bill and he says [it] will never pass the committee, much less reach the House for consideration. Now dearest, are you happy? I am not specially so, except in so far as it gives you happiness. . . .[15]

Dora exploded:

> My Dearest Henry T.
>
> . . . I am highly complimented that the disappointment is such that you see no profit or pleasure, in being obliged, to give up your trip and

remain here. If you feel that way my dear Henry you certainly had better not take the trouble to come on or ask for a leave (except on your own account) as it may not add to your happiness, and it would be a pity to put you to so much inconvenience, just for mine. You may not have noticed it, but you have not expressed a single wish to see me . . . for the last three or four months. I may be cold in actions but "still waters run deep," and I am very sensitive about a great many things. I really think you are more wrapped up in your plans, expeditions, etc. than you are aware of. I hope you are well and I know you are happy. . . . I pray for you every night—and am sure I shall be answered sometime.

Most devotedly yours,
Dora [16]

Within a few weeks tempers cooled and they began making plans again. But more difficulties arose. Allen learned he could not put in for six-months' leave until mid-April. Then, when he did submit his request, Washington disapproved it, ostensibly because of the shortage of officers in the regiment, though he suspected someone in the War Department simply felt he was asking for more consideration than a second lieutenant deserved.[17] He asked Dora to be patient; he would try again. Her reaction can be imagined. She had already written, "I have not quite decided whether I shall insist on your leaving the army." [18] He had treated this as a great joke, and now when she repeated her doubts about the "stony path" of army life, he answered:

. . . if I were a young lady, I would not show such poor taste as to select an army officer. . . . All officers are modelled on the same block verbally and physically, thereby differing from any other class of professional men. There is another consideration, which is their poverty connected with most extravagant tastes. . . .[19]

He soon apologized for not taking her more seriously:

. . . It is my hope that you may see as little of the rough side of army life as possible. . . . I am glad that you do know so little of garrison life, if you knew more I feel confident I would like you less. For some reason I have never had any *penchant* for girls *tout à fait* with garrison life. . . .

. . . I think there is promise of a brilliant future for capable persons in the army and hence I prefer it to any other occupation.

The daily routine does not interest me, nor do I care for the gold lace or the parade. I would prefer New York to any other place to live, were I content to lead a life of pleasure. . . .[20]

In May, he applied for and received two months' leave, to start on the fifteenth. When he could personally exert some influence in Washington on his own behalf he intended to have the leave extended to six months or longer and obtain permission to go abroad.[21] Once again, however, something prevented his coming East. When an increasingly impatient and exasperated Dora sent a telegram asking when she could expect him, he had to tell her his commanding officer refused to let him go yet. He wanted Allen to survey the St. Joseph River before he left. The colonel relented slightly when Allen told him he was soon to be married, but still insisted that he stay until the only other officer in his troop returned from several weeks of temporary duty at another post.[22]

Allen finally left for Chicago on May 31. Even the weather conspired against him. Spring rains and flooding mountain streams washed out several bridges and delayed his train for thirty-six hours. On the way he stopped at Keogh for two days to see his brother Tom and his old friends the Rices and tell them of his engagement. The news surprised Tom but not Mrs. Rice. From the army wives' superefficient grapevine, she had known about it for months. Henry arrived in Chicago on June 8 and moved into a hotel. Dora stayed at the Ontario with her sister, Mrs. Dix.[23] Together again after almost a year, the couple made their final plans.

The wedding was set for July. Where they would spend their honeymoon, however, remained undecided until Allen arrived in Washington three weeks later. There he wangled a six-months' extension of his leave and permission to go abroad. The order was signed by his host, Adjutant General Richard C. Drum.[24] Jumping channels this way may have made Allen some enemies out West, but at this point he did not care. Besides, an assignment at West Point on his return from overseas was being discussed at the War Department. Of Mrs. Drum's reaction to the marriage of her favorite young bachelor, Henry wrote his fiancée:

> . . . Mrs. Drum, after looking at your picture, became very meditative and came to me and kissed me saying she was satisfied and felt you would make me a good wife. She also said that she did not know whether ambition or love would rule me, but that now I must sacrifice everything to you. . . .[25]

On a blistering hot day in Chicago, July 12, 1887, Dora Johnston and Henry Allen were married. The simple Episcopal ceremony took place in the Dix apartment. Dora's sisters were bridesmaids and a West

Point friend of Henry's, John Biddle, was best man. Sixty guests were present at the reception. Immediately afterward, accompanied by Dora's sisters, the couple left for a few days in Bar Harbor, Maine.[26] From there they went to New York and sailed, alone, for Europe. Although Dora had wanted some of her family to accompany them abroad, Henry was understandably lukewarm to the idea and teased her about being afraid to be alone with him ("beauty and the beast") until she relented.[27]

They docked in Bremen on August 13 and traveled by train to Vienna via Hamburg, Cologne, Wiesbaden, Schlangenbad, and Frankfort, spending two or three days sightseeing in each city along the way. They went for drives, visited art galleries and museums, attended an outdoor concert and a circus, and took a cruise up the Rhine. After ten days in Vienna, they left for St. Petersburg, arriving on September 15.[28]

St. Petersburg was built on water, the "Venice of the North." Through its center ran the broad Neva River, emptying the cold gray waters of Lake Ladoga, not far to the northeast, into the Gulf of Finland. Two hundred years before, the area had been marshland, but Peter the Great had been determined to have his new capital and his "Window on the West." To get what he wanted, he used up vast amounts of money, thousands of tons of stone, and hundreds of human lives. Like Venice, Peter's city of islands, canals, and bridges had beautiful baroque public buildings and palaces in pastel shades of blue, green, red, and yellow. (He had imported Italian architects to build most of them.) It was a strange, artificial creation. The people on the streets might be stolid local peasants or exotic Tartars or Cossacks from thousands of miles farther east, but the Russian nobility who flocked to the Czar's court spoke French, aped the manners and dress of their European cousins, and spent as little time as possible on the estates which financed their finery, their trips abroad, and their mistresses.[29] No capital of Europe glittered more or cared less.

Dora was unhappy in St. Petersburg. So far, the honeymoon had not been all roses and caviar. The combination of two strong personalities made for frequent ugly spats, and the strain of constant travel and changing climate probably did not help much. The weather was cold and rainy when they arrived, and winter began early that year.[30]

Soon after they moved into the Hôtel d'Europe, Allen hired a young Russian man with whom he daily practiced conversation.[31] He took Dora sightseeing occasionally and to the ballet and opera in the evenings, but most days she had her own language lessons (French and Russian) in the mornings and made calls alone or went out shopping with her maid in the afternoons. An entry in her diary for October 20 is typical: ". . . had a good time and came home at six to find Henry still buried in his Russian." Frequent headaches, backaches, and cramps did not improve her disposition. Neither of them yet realized it, but she was pregnant. The fights continued. During a "scuffle on Thanksgiving Day . . . Henry demolished a lamp. . . . Henry and I still are a trifle out. . . . He has the mistaken idea that I am obstinate. . . ." [32]

Allen's leave expired on January 31, 1888. In November, he wrote General Drum an official letter asking for another six-month extension, in a duty status if possible, and on leave if not, in order to complete his Russian studies.[33] On December 7, he received a cablegram from the War Department denying his request and he and Dora began to pack and pay farewell calls on friends. Four days later another cable arrived granting six more months of leave. Dora did not share his elation.[34]

Christmas at the Hôtel d'Europe was quiet and a little lonely, though with Dora's pregnancy now unmistakable and her continuing bouts of illness, Henry had become much more solicitous and tender. Both were happier.[35] A cable and a letter from the War Department soon upset everything. "In view of the absence of so many lieutenants of your regiment," he was told, "the Secretary of War desires that you . . . return . . . and rejoin your regiment as soon as you conveniently can." Someone at the War Department, reacting to a request from Allen's commanding officer at Fort Coeur d'Alêne for another officer to replace him, finally decided that Henry had been on a "boondoggle" long enough.[36]

In desperation Allen immediately wrote letters to Senator Beck and Chief Justice Morrison Waite and asked them to use their influence with Secretary of War William C. Endicott to have him appointed Military Attaché in St. Petersburg. Both gentlemen made this request for Allen, but Endicott said "no." [37] In late February Henry and Dora left St. Petersburg. They planned to sail from France after a stop in Paris to visit the Dixes, who were then touring the continent. The long train ride was terribly hard on Dora. By the time they got to Paris she was under sedation and in no condition to travel farther. Henry had to leave her in Paris. The Dixes agreed to stay with her until the baby came and she was well enough to travel.[38] By early April Allen was back in Washington, staying briefly with the Drums while checking at the War Department on the possibility of a West Point detail. General

Drum seemed agreeable to such an assignment, but General Philip Sheridan insisted Allen return to his unit.

On the way West he stopped in Chicago to see the rest of Dora's family and check on her financial affairs. Both errands proved unpleasant. Clifford, Gertie, and Nina Johnston seemed to go out of their way to be insulting. And when Allen got to the bank, he found Dora's account down to almost nothing. The annual income from her share of the family's real estate holdings had not been enough to support their extravagances in Europe.[39]

By April 12, depressed and worried, he was back at Fort Sherman (Coeur d'Alêne's new name):

My own darling little Spoon,

I hope this finds you with plenty of strength and courage for daily I grow more solicitous concerning you. Not one word have I heard since leaving you March 23rd, the night that almost broke my heart. . . . I am almost blue—a state that you know is quite foreign to my nature.

I will at an early date begin to lay a wire connecting me with West Point for next year. At the expiration of four years there I would be ready to entertain propositions looking toward civilian life. By that time we could have entirely disposed of our indebtedness and you would have seen army life, both West and East. . . .[40]

Two weeks later, Clarence Dix cabled from Paris: "Your daughter came this morning, hard time but doing fairly well." [41] Allen learned the news while at breakfast in the officers' mess and rushed off through a driving thunderstorm to the telegraph office to cable Dora's family in Chicago, his brother Frank, and Mrs. Drum. Then he sat down and wrote his wife:

Well! the *cochon* is a girl, a fact I should have known before from its great "kicking" ability. I shall continue to be anxious until you write to me and tell me all . . . what does "fairly well" mean? I'm half crazy to see you. . . .

Now, Spoon, you probably would like to know what my views are for a name. . . . Let her have your name . . . which will also perpetuate your mother's name, Jennie Johnston Allen, or some form of the first name such as Jane or Jeannie. . . .

. . . I hope the *cochon* resembles you and especially your lovely bright eyes, pretty mouth and winning ways. . . .

Is the *cochon* old enough to have a kiss sent to it? I feel something like the small boy with a new brother or sister. "Don't know nothing 'bout babies." [42]

After three weeks he received several brief, unsatisfactory notes from Clarence that only increased his anxiety. Dora's first letter reached Fort Sherman May 27. She was weak and thin and pale, she said, and the baby was ugly. Would he still love them both? He reassured her and joked about his "poor innocent" daughter having his features.[43] Her next letter mentioned the name she had chosen, Valerie. Her disregard of his explicit wishes provoked a long, angry tirade. Calling Valerie an "absurd name," he accused his wife of "shallowness of mind" and asked if she was ashamed of her own name or of others in the family. "The pedigrees of American families," he said, "are none too long or descriptive at best and the most we can do is preserve by name a memory of past ancestors." Her stubbornness in this matter was "unwomanly" and caused him to fear she was again becoming "as set in your ideas as when we married." Trusting there would "never be occasion to speak further concerning . . . these invented names," he concluded:

> I am willing to give you all my love, and as much devotion as a man can from the depths of his heart, but I demand something in return. You know that in my feelings to you it is everything or nothing. This you don't understand and I can't explain it myself; I simply know that even a small injury from you is appalling to me and annoys me beyond measure. . . . If you value our happiness, please don't do it. . . . A wife's ideas should be subordinated to her husband who if he loves her will never be able to do all he desires for her comfort and happiness.[44]

No sooner had he mailed this than he began to apologize for losing his temper. He was sorry, but still sure she would see the strength of his arguments and change her mind.[45]

From June 10 to July 6, Allen's unit went on field maneuvers along with the cavalry and infantry detachments from Fort Spokane and Fort Walla Walla. The force of 500 men, "small by European standards," assembled in the mountains near the Canadian border, eighty miles northwest of Fort Sherman, and spent several weeks marching and countermarching against an imaginary enemy. Though Allen underwent some long days (and a few nights) in the saddle on scouting missions to the front and flanks, the ponderous movements of the main body, tied to the slow pace of the infantry, gave him plenty of time in camp to relax and enjoy life.[46] Sitting in the evenings on the cot in his lamp-lit tent in the midst of a forest of tall pines with a bonfire crackling cheerfully nearby, Henry described for Dora how well an officer could live "in the field" if he had an extra income and the tastes of a gentleman. He and the other lieutenant in the troop shared three tents, a Chinese cook, and two strikers, and their larder trunk contained "wine, beer, and all sorts of canned vegetables." Several of the other officers in the camp were surprised and envious of such luxuries when Allen invited them to dine. "Today we gave a dinner party," he gloated, "and these dinners are not to be scorned." Their guests had "soup, nice roast, chicken, salad, three or four vegetables, dessert, cheese, biscuit, coffee and claret and champagne," all served by the attentive Buck on a field table covered with a fine linen cloth.[47]

Such pleasures notwithstanding, Allen had begun to think seriously about getting out of the army and entering Kentucky politics. Bitter at the enforced separation from Dora, he wrote, "When I think of all the pleasures we have enjoyed together and how we might now be doing the same . . . it makes me think 'Damn the Army!' "[48] A month earlier he had written to ask General Miles for his advice on running for Congress. Miles was encouraging: "In my judgment, if you were elected . . . it would open to you a much wider field than your present position."[49]

Having also sounded out his friends at home, Henry broached the subject with Dora, but only after making his decision:

> I might as well tell you now that they inform me from Kentucky that I could carry seven of the twelve counties this fall. . . . It would be a great feather in your old boy's cap to go to Congress at his age. Politics are expensive however and that is a decided consideration in these days. . . . I have decided . . . to let the matter lie over until two years hence. . . .[50]

Even with his own entry into politics postponed, he kept up with political affairs through the Eastern newspapers. One night in camp, shortly before the Republican Convention that summer, Allen's ardent support of Benjamin Harrison's candidacy had this result:

> Last night we were having a demonstration which I started in favor of Harrison. . . . We burned down several large trees and I set off fifteen gallons of kerosene. All very pretty but I am short about one half a moustache. What remains, however, is able to dispense with curling irons.

As an afterthought, he added:

> I believe I told you that I know the Harrisons quite well. Mrs. H. is the woman who volunteered to furnish me with [in]*fluence* before I left

Washington. It is hardly possible her husband can be elected so we'll probably not have the occasion to demand as much as a foreign mission.[51]

Besides politics, Henry had many other things on his mind, the most important of which was to get Dora home as soon as possible. She did not seem to be in any hurry. In mid-June she and the baby and a French wet nurse left Paris and went to Baden-Baden with Effie and Clarence Dix. From there she first wrote she still did not feel strong enough to make the ocean voyage. Then, she said the Dixes were not planning to come home until late September, and she could not find other suitable traveling companions to sail with sooner. The prospect of not seeing her until October made Henry frantic. But, with five or six weeks between every letter and its reply, it was impossible to carry on any sort of connected discussion of their plans.[52]

Returning to Fort Sherman from maneuvers in early July, he was momentarily cheered by a note in which she told him, "I love you now with my whole heart and consider myself blessed when I make you happy and contented. . . ." Perhaps he assumed from this she had received his letter about a proper name for the baby and decided to please him:

> Darling Jeannie I miss you all the time and long to hold you in my arms. . . . How often I think of our spoony times . . . and wish above all things that we had never had the slightest disagreement. I am prepared to never take issue with you again for I know you now have more confidence in your old love-sick boy than ever before.[53]

Her next letter came as a shock. She had not changed her mind at all about the name. This touched off another harsh polemic on family pedigrees and wifely obedience, written on their first anniversary. In addition, her stubbornness about the name reminded him of another infuriating Johnston family trait, their careless extravagance. He scolded her for being overdrawn:

> . . . I see I'll have to be with you to keep you from going off à la Johnston. It would be the climax of absurdity to rush headlong into debt all because there was probably a legacy sufficient to cover the indebtedness. . . . There will be numerous uses for your "legacy" all of which will in the end be more conducive to your happiness than an extravagant use of it now. . . .
>
> . . . you must not think that I am at all miserly, for I am not and want you to have everything that is necessary to make you both comfortable.

As for me, present expenses are quite light, but I have kept well down to bedrock by paying some of the debts. . . . I could run them as long as I choose, but I don't think it best or right.[54]

Several days later, the first photograph of his two-month-old daughter arrived. It put him in a better mood again:

. . . she looks like a mouse in a basket of feathers, the predominating features being her eyes. Her heavy eyelids indicate she is a strong drinker, but as to resemblance to you or to myself, I can see no more than exists between an egg and a chicken.[55]

On July 20, Allen received a telegram from the War Department ordering him to report by September 1 for duty with the Department of Modern Languages at West Point. His ebullience fully restored by this good news, he immediately cabled it to Dora, and then, in case the cable went astray, wrote her a letter as well. He was "delighted," and especially for her sake, that she could "come directly from Europe to such a charming station." The assignment would solve all their "troubles," for now, knowing "exactly what to expect and *how long* to expect it," they could plan their future. After four years at West Point he hoped to resign and "go to Congress." Meanwhile, life would be pleasant:

. . . Darling, this is one of the best details in the Army. . . . The telegram came direct from Gen'l Drum so you can imagine the interest in that direction. . . .

Well, Old Spoonie, won't we have some delightfully charming times together, you and me and our Valuable Valentine Val. . . . I love you for your letter this morning, Darling, and kiss you many times.

Your Heathen Harry[56]

Despite Henry's apparent new mellowness, Dora's persistence in showing those "Johnston traits" still irritated him. Almost anything set him off, even her complaints about how homely and cranky the baby was:

I can't see that she is such a deuced ugly baby. . . . I do hope she may resemble you, but I do object to her possessing a Johnston disposition untrammeled in its indifference to other members of the universe. To look like me and to be selfish, indifferent and erratic would be too much for any girl. You can't begin too soon in teaching her to be generous towards and thoughtful of others and also that there is a relation between cause and effect in the simplest details of hourly life. . . . Spoon even you can hardly imagine my aversion to the disposition I have been describing, but thank God I have married the flower of the family.[57]

The baby's name remained a source of friction. He told her he would "sacrifice my feelings of love to those of principle" if she continued to oppose him on this subject.[58] In the end, he won. The baby was named Jeanette.

Allen departed for West Point on August 6. He stopped briefly in Miles City and saw his brother Tom, who was "happy as a clam over the prospects for the stock business," though he told Henry it would be several years before they made any money.[59] The next stop on the trip East was Kentucky. With his brother Frank, Henry went to the Republican congressional convention, where he lost his illusions about politics:

[It was] one of the most disgusting affairs a gentleman can be called to witness. Think of my going through it as a principal two or four years hence. It is certainly like wading through the filth of pig pens to reach the parlor, passing through political impurities to reach Congress. I feel as though I had been wallowing in Democracy wrapped in the grand old banner of Jeffersonian victory!! [60]

He reported for duty at West Point on August 28, still a second lieutenant more than six years after graduation. Dora, Jeanette, and the nursemaid docked in New York the next day. They stayed in the West Point Hotel until their quarters were ready.[61]

There are no letters or diaries to tell us about their reunion after those five difficult months. Given the differences so evident in their letters, a period of strained readjustment was probably inevitable before they settled down to enjoy the calm and orderly life at West Point. Allen's duties were light. Teaching French only four hours a day,[62] he had time to spend with his wife and daughter at home or to take them on carriage drives around the post. Shopping and theater trips to New York were an easy hour away by train. With friends and classmates stationed on the post, the evening social life was varied and stimulating. Other friends often came up for weekend visits. The Allens' roomy old quarters of stone and brick, well staffed with servants and overfurnished in the best Victorian taste (with Russian accents), made entertaining no trouble at all. The severity of the formal high-ceilinged rooms was softened by the glow of well-used fireplaces and the laugh-

Allen as an Instructor at West Point. (Photograph courtesy of Col. Henry T. Allen, Jr.)

ter of children and guests.[63] In May and June of 1889, the family took a New England seaside vacation at Manchester and Narragansett. Later that summer Allen taught his daughter to ride, "strapped on the saddle by her feet," while he led the horse by a halter.[64] It is doubtful whether the Allens saved much money while at West Point, even though Henry was promoted to first lieutenant after his first year there, but altogether it must have been a very pleasant tour. Their second child, Henry, Jr. (Harry), was born in the West Point Hospital on August 11, 1889.

One episode may have threatened Dora's happiness. In December, 1888, General Miles, then commanding the Division of the Pacific, asked if Allen was interested in another exploring trip to Alaska. He was, but nothing came of it. General John Schofield in the War Department opposed the project.[65] A year later, a different opportunity came Allen's way.

The War Department had begun selecting the first American military attachés for permanent duty in London, Paris, Vienna, Berlin, and St. Petersburg. They would be assigned to the newly created Military Information Division in the Adjutant General's office.[66] Allen applied for the post at St. Petersburg.

He took care that his application should not be shunted aside in the War Department. First, he asked for help from his Kentucky friends in Congress, Senators Beck and Joseph C. S. Blackburn and Representative William C. P. Breckenridge. He also wrote and offered his services directly to the newly appointed Minister to Russia, Charles Emory Smith, whom he had never met. Smith, the politically influential editor of the Philadelphia *Press*, had not yet left for Russia. In Philadelphia he received a series of letters and visits from mutual friends, all recommending Allen. Impressed, Smith asked for him through the Secretary of State.[67] The final note in Allen's masterful orchestration of influence was supplied by General Drum, recently retired, but still a power in Washington. He wrote the Secretary of War:

> . . . I beg, most respectfully to commend the name of this competent and industrious young officer to your consideration; believing that so far as our military interests are concerned, no better selection could be made.[68]

Secretary of War Redfield Proctor hemmed and hawed for a few days because of Allen's rank and age. He would have preferred a more senior officer in view of "the difficulties that have attended the detail of officers of low rank at the courts of foreign countries." [69] However, no one else could match Allen's combination of qualifications, not the least of which were an outside source of income and friends in high places. Even so, his language ability was probably the decisive factor. Secretary Proctor gave him the job.[70]

In April, having sold most of their household goods at West Point and shipped their horses and dogs back to Kentucky with the ever-faithful Buck, the Allen family set off for Europe. It was a difficult trip for Dora with Jeanette a rambunctious two-year-old and Harry only nine months, but both children made the trip well. By mid-May the Allens were ensconced once more in the Hôtel d'Europe.[71]

Allen's duties as military attaché were rather vaguely defined, his letter of instructions stating only that he was to "perform such service," under the supervision of the United States Minister, "as may be assigned to you from time to time by the Secretary of War." [72] In the first few weeks he spent most of his time making official and social calls, renewing old acquaintances, and developing new contacts in the military and diplomatic community.

The purpose of the attaché system, long in use in Europe if not by the United States, was to facilitate the open exchange of military information between countries and, thereby, it was hoped, prevent dangerous miscalculations based on mutually inaccurate assessments of the military capabilities and intentions of each. Secure in its isolation, however, the United States's intent in having military attachés at this time seems to have been primarily to obtain technical information useful in improving the weapons, tactics, and organization of its own forces. The essence of Allen's job was thus to gather information about Russian military affairs. Political, social, and economic matters were of secondary interest to the War Department and only as they related to Russia's general military efficiency. In addition, he was expected to report any information about other nations gleaned from his contacts with the other foreign officers and diplomats accredited to the court of the Czar. How to obtain such information was left to his own discretion, but he was in no sense to be a spy. Nevertheless, the *modus operandi* of any military attaché was such that he occasionally learned things his official hosts would have preferred to conceal. Such situations called for a great deal of tact and discretion to avoid embarrassment to all concerned.[73]

The Allens' life in Russia soon settled into a pattern. Diplomatic and social activity at court was at a minimum during the summer months and the St. Petersburg climate uncomfortably muggy, so each June Allen moved his family out to a rented *dacha* in the countryside where they stayed until late September or October. In the summer of 1890 they had a place on Lake Ladoga at Schouvalova, half an hour's ride from the city. In 1891, 1892, and 1894, they took a *dacha* on the Gulf of Finland, the first year near Viborg, seventy miles away, and the last two at Terrioki, much nearer St. Petersburg. From each place Allen was able to commute to the city by train, but since there was not much to do at the legation he spent most of the time with his family. These long, lazy summers in the fresh air and sunshine were idyllic for the children. There were sand and water to play in, ducks and sea-gulls to feed, trees to climb, hammocks to swing in, and a horse-drawn carriage to take them on leisurely rides with their parents in the late afternoon. Jeanette and Harry (dubbed "Johnny" and "Pal") soon had a new sister to play with. Daria Gertrude Allen was born on March 30, 1892, and quickly nicknamed "Dasha." The children always had nannies to look after them. Mary, the girl the Allens brought with them from West Point, left with many farewell tears in 1891. A succession of Swiss, French, German, and Russian women, none of whom spoke English, followed her. French became the language of the household and the children practically forgot their mother tongue. Jeanette and Harry, in particular, had difficulty understanding their cousins when their parents took them home to America for a visit in the summer of 1893.[74]

Each fall the family returned to their apartment on the Quai de la Coeur, down the street from the legation. After the summer doldrums Allen had more work to do. Besides the continuing round of official calls to make there were libraries, archives, and bookstores to visit in search of information, and periodic inspection trips to nearby military installations and schools. Since he was the only American member of the legation staff who spoke Russian, French, and German fluently, he was invaluable to the three ministers under whom he served. Each of these gentlemen, Charles E. Smith, Andrew D. White, and Clifton R. Breckenridge, frequently took him along on their own official calls to act as a kind of combination advisor-interpreter. Translating documents and writing filled up the rest of each working day.[75] In addition to his routine periodic reports for the Military Information Division, Allen also received occasional requests for information or assistance from other Federal departments or private individuals.[76] He sent a dispatch (pouch) or a letter to the War Department on an average of once every two weeks. The contents of this dispatch, sent on August 25, 1890, were representative of most:

Data on Areas and Populations, Russia (general) and St. Petersburg
Garrison Changes and New Russian Army Organization, 1888–89
Data on Russian Breech Loading Guns w/drawings (Confidential)
Data on Field Guns, Cartridges, Projectiles w/drawings (Confidential)
Location and Designation of Troops in Russia, 1890
Maps of European and Asiatic Russia (Military Districts)
Data on Rangefinders and Gunpowder (Experimental Items) [77]

Even with Henry busy, Dora seemed reasonably happy in St. Petersburg this time, for a while at least. During the fall of 1890, the Dixes came to stay for six weeks, followed for two months after Christmas by Dora's cousin, Charles Hanks, with his wife and young son. The Dixes, who apparently spent more time in Europe than in Chicago, returned for several more long visits over the next four years, both in St. Petersburg and Terrioki. Not only did Dora often have relatives to keep her company, but she and Henry seldom had an empty engagement calendar. In the evenings they either entertained at home or went out to dinner parties, usually followed by a ball, an opera, or the ballet. Such a life was expected of them, and, besides, there was no better place to pick up the latest military information than in drawing-room conversations after too much good food and wine. Fortunately, on their combined income they were able to move fairly comfortably through this rarified social atmosphere. All of the other attachés at the court far outranked Allen,[78] but this did not seem to make either him or Dora feel socially inferior.

Nevertheless, it was far from one long gay whirl. Dora hated the interminable, bitter winters. Their two-bedroom apartment, though elegant, was drafty and damp. The first winter Jeanette and Harry were so ill with fevers and bronchitis they nearly died before Allen could obtain leave in March to take them to the milder climate of Venice. Dora and the children spent the next two months with the Hankses at resorts in Italy, Switzerland, France, and Germany. When the Hankses left for home Allen took another leave and brought his family back to Viborg, by way of a cruise through the Baltic.

Dora remained in St. Petersburg the entire winter of 1891–92 in order to have her third baby. Luckily, that winter the two older children remained healthy except for minor colds, and there were no complications when she delivered Dasha. Still, she was convinced that the winter climate and crowded apartment were unhealthy. The next winter she would have taken the children to France and Italy if Dasha had been old enough to travel and if Henry had not promised to ask for a long leave to take them all back to the United States in April.

Henry and Dora at St. Petersburg. (Photograph courtesy of Col. Henry T. Allen, Jr.)

Henry returned from this leave after four months, but Dora and the children did not come back to Russia for more than a year. Instead, when he sailed from New York in July, 1893, she remained behind and spent several months with the Hankses at Narragansett Pier. In October she went to France with the Dixes.[79] Henry tried to get her to return to St. Petersburg by Christmas, but she refused and spent the winter at Monte Carlo and Hyeres. Even had she been willing to go back for Christmas she could not, for she and the children were soon very sick again, first with influenza and then diphtheria. She pleaded with him to take leave and join them, but he said he was too busy to get away.[80] That was true, perhaps, but he was also having a good time by himself. That fall the Emperor's Huntsman, Colonel Alexander Dietz, invited Allen for two weeks of hunting at his estate 300 miles from St. Petersburg. Employing as many as 300 serfs as beaters each day, Allen and the other guests hunted wolves or game birds in the marshes and brakes of Dietz's vast holdings.[81] The evening banquets frequently ended in all-night revelry:

> . . . This is the day of our gala dinner. Mrs. Ponamareff, her daughter and son-in-law, the Malakoffs, the young lady visitor (the gypsy singer whose name I don't know), the Uncle Ponamareff . . . Alexander Dietz, Vladimir Dietz, Gen'l Grunwaldt (Comdg Chevalier Guards), Prince Golystin and myself. . . . It was a five course dinner and the guitar of young P with the singing of the young lady offered a spicy accompaniment to the coffee and cigarettes. There was drunk in all 5 bot[tles] champagne, 4 bots beer, 2½ cognac, 2½ madeira, 1 red wine, 4 white wine, ¾ whiskey and 4 large samovars of water. What is more, Alex. Dietz and myself drank very little, as did one or two of the ladies. . . . It was really one of the greatest drinking bouts I ever saw and greatly encouraged by the ladies.[82]

In January of 1894, since Dora still refused to return to St. Petersburg, Henry applied for a transfer to the attaché post in Paris. While they waited for the War Department to act on his request, he saw no reason to deny himself the pleasures of the winter social season:

> Tonight . . . the Marie Theater was literally packed. Nearly all the Imperial Family . . . was there. Visited in several loges. . . . Reached [illegible] at 11:30 and the dance was in full swing. . . . Danced the mazurka with Princess Gagarin whose husband was stationed at Tashkent. She is quite an intelligent little blond who interests herself in much besides the frivolities of a society woman. . . . We supped at 2:30 this morning and I arrived home at 4:00 A.M.[83]

The Allen Children: Harry, Dasha, and Jeanette (Taken in Venice, 1894).
(Photograph courtesy of Col. and Mrs. Joseph W. Viner)

Such a life as a "geographical bachelor" could hardly have been conducive to marital fidelity. Charming, handsome, and virile at thirty-four, Allen was obviously a great favorite with the ladies. He even received love notes from a few of his more ardent admirers.[84] Under the circumstances it would not have been surprising if he had an affair or two, though there is a great deal of evidence to the contrary. His duties required him to mix socially as well as officially with the elite of St. Petersburg, and it was natural for him to meet many ladies and good sense for him to cultivate them as useful sources of information. All the other attachés did exactly the same thing. No doubt some of them had discreet affairs, but the penalty for the scandal of exposure was to be called home in disgrace. For a man as conscious of his career and his future as Henry Allen, that would have been a very high price to pay. There is more direct proof of his ability to resist such temptations as well as of his outstanding overall performance as attaché. Shortly before leaving his post in 1894, Andrew D. White wrote to Clifton R. Breckenridge, his successor as minister, about Allen:

> . . . a man of the highest character, of fine manners, pleasant address, acquainted with everybody, liked by everybody, whose acquaintance is worth having in the circles in which the legation has to do, speaking easily in French, German and Russian and having moreover good sound sense and perfect loyalty to the interests of the United States here, he has been to me and would be especially to a newly arrived minister invaluable if not indispensable. . . . His high moral, intellectual and social qualities have attached me strongly to him.[85]

Finally, Henry made no attempt to hide his numerous tête-à-têtes with other women from Dora. Perhaps he was also protecting himself in advance from gossip and trying to make her jealous enough to come home. His candor only made her angry and suspicious, though she finally agreed to return in the spring of 1894 after the War Department refused to transfer him to Paris. Their diaries for the last summer at Terrioki are not pleasant to read.

In September, orders came from Washington for Allen to return to the United States. Since White was also leaving that fall, he protested Allen's orders on the ground he should remain long enough to help Breckenridge get settled in his job. The War Department consented to leave Allen in St. Petersburg until the following April.[86]

He advised Breckenridge on all manner of things and went everywhere with him on his round of introductory calls. Allen had admired and respected Smith and White, but he was ashamed of the new minister. A man of "limited views," having no income except his salary, plainly attired, and speaking only English (and that, "poorly"), Breckenridge made a bad impression on Allen, who wrote, "It is really scandalous to have a man who does not know his own language." His manners were no better. At the Emperor's New Year's reception, Breckenridge "leaned upon a chair while talking to the Empress." [87]

With his tour coming to an end after more than four years, Allen grew reflective about his experiences and impressions in Russia. He had no illusions about the reactionary regime of Alexander III, just ended, or about the corrupt life at court. He commented unfavorably on every major czarist policy except one, the expansion of the railroad system. All the others—Pan-Slavism, persecution of the Jews, suspicion and exclusiveness toward foreigners, the limits placed on education, suppression of peasant and urban unrest in the face of famine, higher tariffs, and increases in military expenditures—he felt were wrong, though he also understood their historical origins and the difficulty of breaking deep-seated traditions and habits of thought.[88]

Nor did he have many illusions about the value of his own accomplishments as attaché: "From the military point of view there is very little here of special importance if the great efforts to improve the artillery be excepted." [89] As early as December, 1890, at the time of the Indian scare with the Sioux Ghost Dance sect, he had been restless enough in St. Petersburg to ask to be reassigned to his regiment in order not to miss a chance to participate in an Indian campaign.[90] After four more years of playing the diplomat and writing reports, Allen was even hungrier for a life of action, though he doubted he would get it at his next duty station. "Still, I feel that sooner or later I shall play a prominent part in the States. By nature I am better fitted for a man of action than for a writer, yet I do not despair of doing something in a literary way before my end arrives." [91]

His accomplishments "in a literary way" were already considerable. The publication of his report on the Alaskan Expedition had brought him a silver medal from the Russian government and honorary membership in the geographic societies of several nations. Much of his writing in Russia was unofficial. He wrote or translated articles on aspects of the Russian Army for several of the military journals recently established in the United States.[92] For several years he also worked at translating a history of the Crimean War, though there is no evidence it was ever published. His wolf-hunting experiences in Russia led to an article on that sport for a book entitled *Hunting in Many Lands*, published by the Boone and Crockett Club.[93] More importantly, the article brought Allen into contact with the book's editor, Theodore Roosevelt. Having asked Allen to write the piece, T.R. sent him a complimentary note with some friendly suggestions for improving his literary style when he submitted it in the summer of 1894.[94] The two men, sharing common interests and alike in many ways, met in Washington the following July and began a lifelong friendship.

The Allens left Russia on April 24, 1895, after a last-minute transportation mix-up. They had to charter a private train from St. Petersburg in order to catch the only steamer for Stockholm.[95] Allen had obtained permission to visit Sweden for a month on the way home to collect information on that nation's military system and had spent the last six months learning Swedish. In Sweden he visited troop units, military schools, and arms and munitions factories and had several audiences with the King and Crown Prince to discuss military affairs. Allen left the country impressed by the friendly informality and democratic ideas of its ruling class.[96]

When he arrived in Washington in mid-June, his first interview was with Major John B. Babcock, Chief of the Military Information Division. Babcock complimented him on his work in Russia but said many of his reports were "too political." MID was more interested in technical intelligence.[97] Babcock assigned him to temporary duty with the Division until he finished his report on the Swedish Army and the War Department decided where to send him next. In the meantime, since there was no need to swelter in Washington while writing the report, Henry took Dora and the children to the New England shore for the summer, but not before paying calls on his old friends Miles, Smith, and White. He also had lunch several times with Roosevelt.[98]

Allen had just finished the report in September when word came from Sharpsburg that Tom, broken in health from the failure of his ranch, was home and apparently dying of typhoid fever.[99] All of the Allen brothers and sisters gathered for the vigil and took their turns by his bedside. When Tom began to improve, Henry returned to Washington. Since General Miles had recently assumed command of the army, Allen was optimistic as to what his new assignment would be.[100]

His orders were for Fort Riley, Kansas. Miles could not help him. He had tried to have Allen assigned to his staff in the War Department, but Secretary of War Daniel S. Lamont would not hear of it. Lieutenant Allen was to be assigned to troop duty.[101] No one could argue the fact that he had not had much of it recently. Perhaps the rather plaintive comments on Allen's efficiency reports by a succession of regimental commanders influenced Lamont's decision. When asked for his evaluation of Allen's performance and abilities, all one colonel could do was state: "As Lieutenant Allen has been detached from his Regiment almost continuously since 1884, his more complete record is in the Adjutant General's Office." [102]

Fort Riley was a green oasis of lawns and parade grounds and huge old cottonwood trees in the valley of the Kansas River. From the tops of the barren sandstone bluffs that overlooked the post, the dry, treeless prairie rolled away in all directions with hardly a farmhouse or windmill to catch the eye. The quarters on officers' row were comfortable but plain, each constructed of native stone with a wooden veranda. Before Dora and the children arrived in November, Henry had their things from Russia unpacked and was already at work in his new job as commanding officer of Troop A, 2nd Cavalry. Although he admitted to being rusty at drilling troops after a lapse of seven years, he found no more challenge or enjoyment in it than before. Within a few months he became the squadron adjutant, a position that gave him more time to indulge his tastes in hunting and riding. With three fine horses just purchased in Kentucky and his pack of four greyhounds, five foxhounds, and five wolfhounds (the latter brought from Russia), he was the undisputed new leader of the post's sporting set. He organized a polo club and was elected master of the hounds of the riding club. Otherwise, the daily routine and social life differed little from those at Keogh and Sherman. The children grew healthy and roamed all over the post in perfect safety, though young Harry, age six and too long overprotected by his mother, was occasionally bullied unmercifully by some of the rougher "army brats." The family stayed at Riley for nearly two years, except for a short excursion to Colorado to escape the worst of the summer heat and several trips East to visit relatives and hire replacements for the nannies who were always quitting or being fired by the hard-to-please Dora.[103]

In May, 1897, a letter arrived from Adjutant General George D. Ruggles, asking Allen if he would like another attaché assignment. Andrew D. White had just been appointed Ambassador to Germany by President McKinley and had asked to have Allen with him in Berlin. Within three weeks the Allens were packed and on their way.[104]

No sooner had they moved into temporary summer quarters in a suburb of Berlin when Allen had to leave. General Miles was also in Europe that summer, having gone over to observe the war between Greece and Turkey and attend the summer maneuvers of the major European powers.[105] In July, Allen joined Miles's entourage in Berlin and accompanied him to Sweden and Russia, renewing many old friendships along the way. The party returned to Germany in time to witness the maneuvers in September between the Bavarian and Prussian Armies.[106] Six weeks of daily contact with Miles was more than enough to change Allen's opinion of him. Long ago he had written of the general:

> I would rather serve under him than any general officer. I admire his ambition and progressive methods; neither would he hesitate to dare a danger provided the goal were an honorable one.[107]

Now, from close up, his clay feet showed. To Allen he seemed conceited, ill-informed, and opinionated, though there was still no doubt of his courage and natural intelligence.[108]

After Miles left, Allen barely had time to get his family settled in their new apartment on Berlin's Regentenstrasse and to start on the mounting pile of paperwork on his desk before he was off again, this time to Sweden as temporary attaché for King Oscar's twenty-fifth jubilee. By October, 1897, however, he had settled down to the familiar routine; collecting information and materials, making calls and inspection visits; talking to the right people at the right parties, translating, writing reports, and, as always, reading. Once again he was the lowest ranking attaché.[109]

In March, 1898, one month after the *Maine* blew up in Havana harbor, Allen submitted an application volunteering for troop duty. He may not have been certain war was imminent, but he did not intend to miss another chance at combat by being in the wrong place if it did come. Miles answered his request with a personal letter, telling him the most valuable service he could perform was to stay where he was and collect information about Spanish intentions and capabilities.[110] Let Allen's State Department colleagues do that; he wanted to get into the fighting that now seemed almost certain. In the last three weeks before war was declared he wrote pleading letters to Miles and anyone else he thought could help him, including General Wesley Merritt, just below Miles in the War Department, and Colonel Abraham Arnold, the senior cavalry officer at Fort Riley.[111] With the war two weeks old and no answer from any of them, Allen played his trump card. On May 8, he wrote Charles E. Smith, then McKinley's Postmaster General, confidante, and chief dispenser of patronage. He told Smith he would accept anything, "any position at all," and begged him to bring his request to

Military Attachés at the Kaiser's court. Allen is second from right in back row. (Photograph courtesy of Col. Henry T. Allen, Jr.)

the attention of the President or Secretary of War. Eight days later came the Secretary's telegram: "Report in person at this office without delay."[112]

Dora stayed in Berlin until the children finished school while her husband went happily off to war. "He was gone," she wrote, "before we had time to turn around."[113]

CHAPTER V

The Iron *Comandante*

It was a "splendid little war"—for some. At the end of July, 1898, Dora Allen saw her husband again. Off Staten Island she stood on the deck of a tug alongside a troopship bringing the sick and wounded back from Cuba.

> . . . after a while he came out on the upper deck and my heart almost stopped beating. . . . Poor man, he had been ill with yellow fever and typhoid. . . . An abscess had formed on the left side of his face; he had lost about 53 pounds and altogether was about the most pitiful object I had seen for some time. . . .[1]

Nine weeks earlier, Allen had landed in New York from Germany, caught the first train for Washington, and gone straight to the War Department. He joined the milling crowd in Adjutant General Henry C. Corbin's office late on Friday afternoon, May 27. Someone told him General Miles had recommended him for a volunteer commission as a major and a position on his staff. Before accepting, Allen decided to call on Postmaster General Smith to see what other vacancies might be available, preferably something closer to the fight. Smith promised to take him to see President McKinley as soon as possible.[2]

Meanwhile, Allen looked about him with a critical eye. Washington was seething with personal and political friction. With his eyes on a lieutenant-generalcy in command of a well-prepared invasion of Puerto Rico, Miles told Allen that Secretary of War Russell Alger was "crazy" in his haste to invade Cuba and that Alger, Corbin, and McKinley cared only about the political side of the war. From a visit with Senator William Lindsay of Kentucky and dinner with Smith, Allen heard the other side of the story. Lindsay described Miles as being "very vain and fond of adulation" and implied that he had alienated every politician in Washington.[3]

While the great men of the day fought over the larger issues of the war, their underlings squabbled as bitterly over personal spoils. No novice at it himself, Allen was nonetheless shocked at the blatant way both regular officers and civilians used personal influence to obtain commissions and choice assignments, regardless of their professional qualifications. Someone took the opening on Miles's staff right out from under Allen's nose before he could see the President. Miles left for Florida three days later. Allen need not have worried. On June 2, he went to the White House with Smith, "who evidently scored" with McKinley. Twelve hours later Allen was on the train for Tampa with orders to join the only squadron of his regiment in the invasion force. As a thirty-nine-year-old first lieutenant he was to be given command of Troop "D" of the 2nd Cavalry. Later he also received a major's commission in the Volunteers, but that did not matter as much as the chance, after sixteen years of service, to lead men in combat.[4] Troop "D" consisted of three officers, sixty-nine men, and sixty-seven horses. Allen took command of it on June 7, aboard the transport *Matteawan* in Tampa harbor, where the convoy to carry the 16,000-man expeditionary corps to Cuba was slowly assembling. Under the command of General William R. Shafter, the invasion force consisted of two infantry divisions, a cavalry division, a battalion of engineers, a signal detachment, four batteries of light artillery and two of heavy artillery.[5]

The miserably inadequate planning and preparation that attended almost all aspects of the invasion of Cuba in 1898 is a story already told.[6] For Allen and his men, sweltering for a week aboard the crowded transport in the harbor in the midst of swirling chaos and rumors, it meant bad food and short, missing, or misplaced supplies. Word came that the Spanish fleet had been sighted en route to Cuba.[7] After one false start, the convoy finally assembled and sailed out of Tampa Bay. Because of the lack of transport space, all of the horses of the cavalry division except those in Allen's squadron had to be left behind. The convoy anchored off Santiago on June 19, but in the confusion Allen's squadron took five more days to get unloaded and ashore. Each of its four troops landed in Cuba after losing four or five horses from the heat of the ill-ventilated transport hold or in the half-mile swim from the ship to Cuban soil. Since no one had made provision for a better way to get the horses ashore, they were simply pushed off the deck and into the water.[8]

The 1st Squadron, the only mounted cavalry in the invasion force, was placed under General Shafter's direct command. Since Shafter could not do much that would be tactically decisive with 300 mounted troops because of the nearly impenetrable undergrowth and the few good roads around Santiago, he used them instead "in escorting wagon and pack trains and in furnishing escorts for light [artillery] batteries in battle, and orderlies for [his] own and division headquarters." [9] Although Shafter officially commended the squadron for this work and praised its officers by name, Allen was disappointed at missing a chance for greater glory. "It has always been a source of regret," he later wrote, "that we could not have had the experience and sensation of a charge against anything." [10]

In the course of its escort and scouting duties, however, Troop "D" did hear the crack of Spanish bullets passing close. On June 30, Shafter assigned Allen to work with General Henry W. Lawton's 2nd Division on the right flank in the vicinity of El Caney. There, horses on both sides of Allen were shot and his orderly wounded in the temple.[11] Within three days the outer ring of Santiago's defenses fell. A lull began while the besieged Spanish commander, General José Toral, considered Shafter's unconditional surrender terms.[12]

While Toral agonized, Shafter maintained the siege. At first the Spanish refused to surrender. Civilians began pouring out of Santiago when it looked as if the fighting would resume. They were permitted to go to refugee camps hastily set up in towns to the rear of American lines, though most settlements were already crowded with people displaced by the earlier fighting. One of these camps was at El Caney, four miles northeast of Santiago. In peacetime no more than 500 people lived in the village. Now it held 20,000. For almost a week responsibility for the town and its refugees passed from unit to unit. Each day conditions got worse. Men fought like animals for the little available food. American attempts to get voluntary co-operation in enforcing sanitary measures were largely ignored. On July 10, Allen had just finished taking eleven wagon-loads of supplies to El Caney when he was ordered to return with his unit and take "full charge." [13]

For a week, as "mayor" of El Caney, he had little with which to fight mounting hunger, disease, and panic except his own wits. The quartermaster could spare him only 5,000 rations each day. Allen had four times that number to feed. Medicine was equally scarce. To help him set priorities and keep order, he organized an advisory body consisting of the English, French, and German consuls from Santiago and an executive committee made up of five influential Cubans. A "police department" (a chief and two assistants) and a "medical department" (one surgeon), all Cubans, rounded out Allen's impromptu civil government. They had "plenty of good will," he said, but they were "literally overpowered by the enormity of the situation." [14] Adding to his problems, the defiant Spaniards lobbed an occasional shell in the general direction of the American lines. Some sailed too far and exploded around El Caney. Allen's own men, busy with food distribution and essential repair and construction work, began to drop from the "acclimatizing fever." Only Toral's surrender, on July 16, prevented a desperate situation from becoming a tragic one. By the next morning all the refugees had returned home. All were weak and most were sick, but none had died under Allen's charge.[15] Soon he too came down with the fever and was evacuated. Allen called the duty at El Caney "the most harrowing and disagreeable I have ever undertaken." [16] It was far from what he had anticipated when he kissed Dora goodby in Berlin. Nor did he expect to be sent home from Cuba on a hospital ship.

Weak and delirious, he had to be carried off the ship to Dora's waiting carriage. She drove him from the dock to the army hospital at Fort Wadsworth on Staten Island.[17] It took a month there and four months of sick leave before he was ready again for duty. That fall his promotion to regular army captain came through, but the War Department delayed his return to Berlin as attaché pending the reorganization of the army. Instead, in December, he went to Atlanta to become Adjutant General of the Department of the Gulf.[18] He stayed in Atlanta less than five months. Ambassador White held his job open, and the Allens were back in Germany by the end of May, 1899.[19]

Even as he returned to Berlin, Allen saw a better chance to advance his career opening in the recently annexed Philippines, where for the past four months American troops had been fighting to put down insurrection. Although he could not have his orders changed before he left, all through the summer and fall he and his friends kept up a barrage of letters to the men who could give him what he wanted, from the President on down. Allen first wrote to General Lawton, with whom he had worked in Cuba. Lawton had already gone to the Philippines.

> . . . I long to see active service in the Philippines and therefore take the liberty of appealing to you with the hope that you may see fit in some way to aid me. Many persons would say that it is foolish to give up such an important post as Berlin, but after due consideration I feel that it is best in this case to follow my impulses. Specially is this true now that I am thoroughly healthy and strong in every respect, and that active service does not occur often in a lifetime. . . .

> It seems from unofficial sources, that there will be a necessity to call out some volunteers, and it is with these as a field officer that I would like to serve. . . . I promise you a good account of myself. . . .[20]

General Miles wrote in Allen's behalf to President McKinley,[21] but even the recommendation of the ranking army general did not seem to help. Three days after Miles's appeal, Adjutant General Corbin wrote Allen that the President had appointed only three volunteer colonels and one lieutenant colonel from the cavalry. McKinley "felt this was the full quota that the cavalry arm of the service was entitled to," said Corbin, adding apologetically: "The fact that there were so few places and so many good men made it difficult to determine who should be appointed." [22]

Allen turned again to his civilian friends for help. The Governor of Kentucky wrote the War Department he would muster the Second Kentucky Regiment providing Allen received command of it.[23] Theodore Roosevelt, Governor of New York after his heroics in Cuba, enthusiastically endorsed this plan. "You . . . could do just what [Leonard] Wood and I did [with the Rough Riders]," he wrote Allen, "and you could get an ideal body of fighting men." Roosevelt, too, promised to see what he could do for Allen in Washington.[24]

The War Department (or the President) finally relented under the accumulating weight of such letters. Told he would be relieved as attaché and given another volunteer commission upon completion of the fall maneuvers of the Austrian and German armies,[25] Allen fretted and stewed through each day. Even a hunting party on Prince Hohenlohe's estate failed to improve his mood. By comparison with what he could be doing in the Philippines, everything else seemed dull and pointless. He began to suspect Adjutant General Corbin, whom he had long regarded as a friend, of playing a "double role" and putting him off with vague promises.[26] By mid-October, with the maneuvers long over and no further word from Washington, Allen was convinced of it. Perhaps it was only a coincidence, but, on October 26, two weeks after former President and Mrs. Harrison were guests of the Allens' at a steeplechase at Carlshorst, Allen received orders to join the 43rd Volunteer Infantry Regiment at Fort Ethan Allen in Vermont. The regiment was scheduled to sail in three weeks for the Philippines. He did not get everything he wanted. Having asked to be a colonel in the Volunteers, he had to settle for another major's commission.[27] At least he had been given a second chance to distinguish himself in combat.

The insurrection in the Philippines in 1899 was the outgrowth of a native rebellion that began long before the Americans replaced the Spanish as colonial masters of the islands. It started, mildly enough, as an attempt by a few well-educated Filipinos in the last third of the nineteenth century to win more of a share in their own government and to curb the power of the corrupt Spanish friars. By 1896, in the face of increasing Spanish intransigence and repression, including the execution of José Rizal, a moderate leader, an organized rebellion broke out. A secret society known as the *Katipunan* (Sons of the Nation) was formed and soon came under the forceful and able leadership of Emilio Aguinaldo. Its members took to the hills and conducted sporadic guerrilla warfare. The Spanish retaliated with military measures, in themselves largely ineffective, and with mass arrests, beatings, and torture. Imprisonment, execution, or deportation was the fate of any Filipino suspected of sympathy for the movement. In 1897, the Spanish home government put pressure on its officials in Manila to come to terms with the rebels so that troops in the Philippines could be released and sent to deal with an even more serious rebellion in Cuba. Accordingly, the colonial governor made a pact with Aguinaldo. Its terms amounted to a Spanish agreement to allow Filipinos the same political and legal rights as Spaniards and to pay an indemnity to the insurgents to cover their losses in confiscated property and care for the widows and orphans of those executed. In exchange, the insurgent leaders agreed to stop fighting and go into exile. Aguinaldo established himself in Hong Kong in the expectation that the Spanish would keep their part of the bargain. The indemnity was paid, but the bad faith of the Spanish on the other terms had become evident by the day Admiral George Dewey sailed into Manila Bay and destroyed their fleet. The insurgents, their grievances still unsatisfied, immediately assumed that America's defeat of Spain meant Philippine independence.[28] Certain actions by Dewey and his superiors in Washington initially did little to correct this impression.

Deadlock followed Dewey's smashing victory of May 1, 1898. He controlled Manila harbor and the sea approaches, but the Spanish still held that city and other fortified areas throughout the islands. Aguinaldo, brought back from Hong Kong on Dewey's orders, rallied his followers and besieged Manila by land. Other insurgent bands, many only nominally under Aguinaldo's control, went on an anti-Spanish rampage throughout the archipelago. The Americans initially lacked the troops to force the Manila garrison to surrender, but they refused to give the insurgents the honor of doing it. Dewey also feared the results in Manila of their thirst for Spanish blood.[29]

During the next three months, as the deadlock continued, an expeditionary force arrived from the United States and assembled outside Manila. On August 13 the city's garrison capitulated after a brief bombardment and a limited attack by American troops. At almost the same time, the United States and Spanish governments signed a protocol in Washington ending hostilities.[30] Pending the negotiation of a peace treaty, however, no one could say for certain to whom the Philippines belonged.

The next few months were tense and awkward. Having assisted in the siege of Manila, the insurgents were in a strong position. American troops in the Philippines at this time numbered about 11,000 men, while Aguinaldo's forces in the Manila area were estimated at 12,000. The latter were fairly well supplied with arms and ammunition, either captured from the Spanish or purchased out of the indemnity funds. The Americans held only Manila and Cavite; the rest of Luzon was more or less controlled by the insurgents. Elsewhere in the islands the Spanish tried to maintain *de facto* government.[31]

Meanwhile an angry debate arose in the United States as to whether the Philippines should be retained as a colony, a prospect new to American political traditions and repugnant to many for a variety of other reasons as well.[32] Well publicized in the islands and known to the insurgent leaders, the debate gave them all the more assurance that Filipino independence would soon be recognized. In anticipation, they set up a provisional republic with its capital at Malolos, northeast of Manila, and began drafting a constitution.[33] As 1898 ended with no indication that recognition would be forthcoming, the insurgents grew increasingly restless, and their relations with American officials in Manila cooled. In December the peace treaty was signed. For an indemnity of $20,000,000, Spain ceded the Philippines to the United States. When United States intentions to assume control of the islands became clear a month later, most insurgents concluded that independence could only be won by more fighting. A few of the more moderate still felt they could negotiate a fair settlement since the Americans seemed more sympathetic to their goals than the Spanish had been. However, any chance for moderation died in a crossfire of bullets outside Manila on the night of February 4, 1899. Uncertain of insurgent intentions, American troops opened fire on one of Aguinaldo's patrols that ventured too near.[34] This incident reignited the insurrection. The fires of rebellion burned for several more years.

By February, there were about 21,000 American troops in and around Manila, of whom 9,000 were volunteers whose enlistments were soon to expire. Such a force was inadequate for both defense of the city and extended operations in the field, especially in view of Aguinaldo's growing strength, rumored at 40,000 around Manila alone. Congress authorized an increase in the size of the regular army and also an extra force of 35,000 volunteers to suppress the insurrection. U.S. Army strength in the islands reached its peak of 71,528 in 1900.[35]

Allen asked for duty in the Philippines against this background of renewed fighting and military build-up. This time Dora was packed and ready to leave Berlin when her husband received his orders. From New York he went immediately to Fort Ethan Allen and she left for Boston to stay with relatives. A few days later Dora brought the children back to New York to see their father board the transport *Meade*. It sailed out of the harbor with 1,400 other men of the 43rd Volunteer Infantry early on the morning of November 16, 1899.[36]

The trip, via Gibraltar and the Suez Canal, took six weeks. Allen divided his time between brushing up on his Spanish, rusty eighteen years out of West Point, and writing an article on the "Proposed Reorganization for Our Central Staff," later published in one of the service journals as part of the general post-mortem on the organizational deficiencies of the War Department made glaringly obvious by the Spanish American War.[37] For exercise he walked the deck with his pet terrier, "Wallace Wakem," none too flatteringly named after a brother-in-law. On New Year's Eve, 1899, the *Meade* dropped anchor in Manila Bay, and by January 5 all three battalions of the 43rd were in camp outside the city, eager to do some "scrapping." Allen took command of the 425 men of the 3rd Battalion and put them through final preparations for combat.[38]

In the preceding eleven months, the U.S. Army had gained control of most of central Luzon as well as the island's important population centers and lines of communication. Aguinaldo's remaining forces were widely scattered and difficult for him to keep in touch with, pursued as he was from hideout to hideout. Growing short of weapons and ammunition, the insurgents avoided pitched battles whenever possible and relied increasingly on unconventional tactics. In the close quarter of an ambush, a bolo knife could be almost as effective as a rifle. For the army, it seemed like a return to the days of the Indian campaigns, only here the terrain favored the enemy.[39]

Although the total land area of the Philippines is approximately 114,400 square miles, with a population estimated at over 7,600,000 at the time American occupation began, only eleven of the more than 7,000 islands in the archipelago are larger than 1,000 square miles in size. Luzon and Mindanao, roughly equal in area, are the two largest, having between them almost seventy per cent of the land. Their geography and climate are typical of most. In the interior are heavily wooded mountains, interspersed with numerous lakes and rolling upland prairies. Fast-flowing rivers and streams abound. Surrounding the mountains are fertile lowlands. Along the coast, the beaches and headlands are interrupted by large swamps and stands of mangrove and nipa palm. The climate in the lowlands is warm, humid, and unhealthy for the unacclimated white man.

Adding to the difficulties of terrain and climate in 1899 was the fact that the Spanish had done little to develop the islands. Schools, churches, and hospitals had been built in all the major towns, and there were many prosperous plantations, but connecting roads and railroads were poor or nonexistent. Coastal travel was often easiest by boat. Many of the interior sections were almost inaccessible.[40] In all, it was not an ideal area for military operations. The fighting had already become bitter and costly to both sides. In the months following Allen's arrival it grew more so. The insurgents were far from beaten, even on Luzon. On the other islands, where they had been quick to take advantage of the vacuum left by the departure of Spanish troops and officials and the shortage of Americans to replace them, insurgent control had hardly been challenged.[41] The newly arrived 43rd Infantry Regiment was one of the units scheduled to make this challenge. The regiment was the major unit in an expedition under the command of Brigadier General William Kobbé, whose orders were to occupy important coastal towns and conduct operations against the insurgents on Samar and Leyte in the Visayas, the group of islands immediately south of Luzon.

One of Aguinaldo's chief subordinates, a fiercely mustachioed half-Chinese, half-Tagalog general named Vincente Lucban, had "governed" Samar and Leyte for almost a year. His first act had been to kill all the Spanish friars and replace them with native priests loyal to himself. Through them and backed by his army, he had held sway over the hapless Visayans, levying high taxes and promising them the defeat of the Americans and *Independencia* in return.[42] General Kobbé directed the 43rd's commander, Colonel Arthur Murray, to begin the campaign against Lucban by landing at two points on the west coast of Samar. Colonel Murray selected the 2nd Battalion to land at Calbayog on January 26. Even though the insurgents set fire to the town, the battalion went ashore against very light resistance. Catbalogan,

Samar's capital and Lucban's headquarters, was next. Allen's 3rd Battalion had the mission.[43]

From the sea Samar looked like a bright green helmet, with a rounded mass of central hills rising abruptly from a narrow lip of beaches and lowlands. In some places the ocean had eaten away the lip, and cliffs rose directly from the surf. Almost all the towns lay directly on the coast, ports for the island's principal export crop, hemp. Inland, though the highest elevation was only 2,789 feet, the hills were rugged, steep, and matted with undergrowth beneath a dense canopy of taller trees. The valleys, cut by rushing streams fed by an annual rainfall of over 100 inches, were twisting corridors of humid jungle seldom wide enough to be cultivated. Roads between the coastal towns were scarcely more than trails; in the interior, even trails were hard to find. One officer called Samar "an evil looking humpbacked island." [44] An insurgent leader as ruthless and tenacious as Lucban operating in this environment added the final ingredient for a difficult and protracted guerrilla war.

When Kobbé's flotilla of three gunboats and four transports anchored off Catbalogan, a white flag went up over the town. With two other officers Allen rowed ashore to demand the surrender of Lucban and his forces. If he complied, all his men would be freed after giving up their weapons, and he would be paroled upon taking an oath of loyalty to the United States. If he refused, war would come to Samar.

The white flag was a stall for time. One of Lucban's underlings met the Americans on the beach. Allen asked to see Lucban. Frederick Palmer, a correspondent with Allen from *Collier's Weekly*, recorded the conversation:

"I don't know where he is. He sent me to say that he had nothing to say, and he didn't care to talk to you. He proposes to fight."

"Then why did you put up this flag?" Allen asked.

"We didn't know but *you* wanted to do something," came the reply.

"Oh, we shall. Good morning," said Allen politely as he turned to leave.[45]

Rather than surrender Catbalogan, Lucban burned it. Before Allen had returned to Kobbé's ship he could hear and smell the fires behind him. As insurgent cannon balls splashed around the transports, the men of the 43rd climbed into launches and headed for the beach through drifting smoke and the crack of musket fire. Three hours later Catbalogan was in Allen's hands. His troops spent the rest of the day putting out fires. Casualties were light on both sides. The Americans

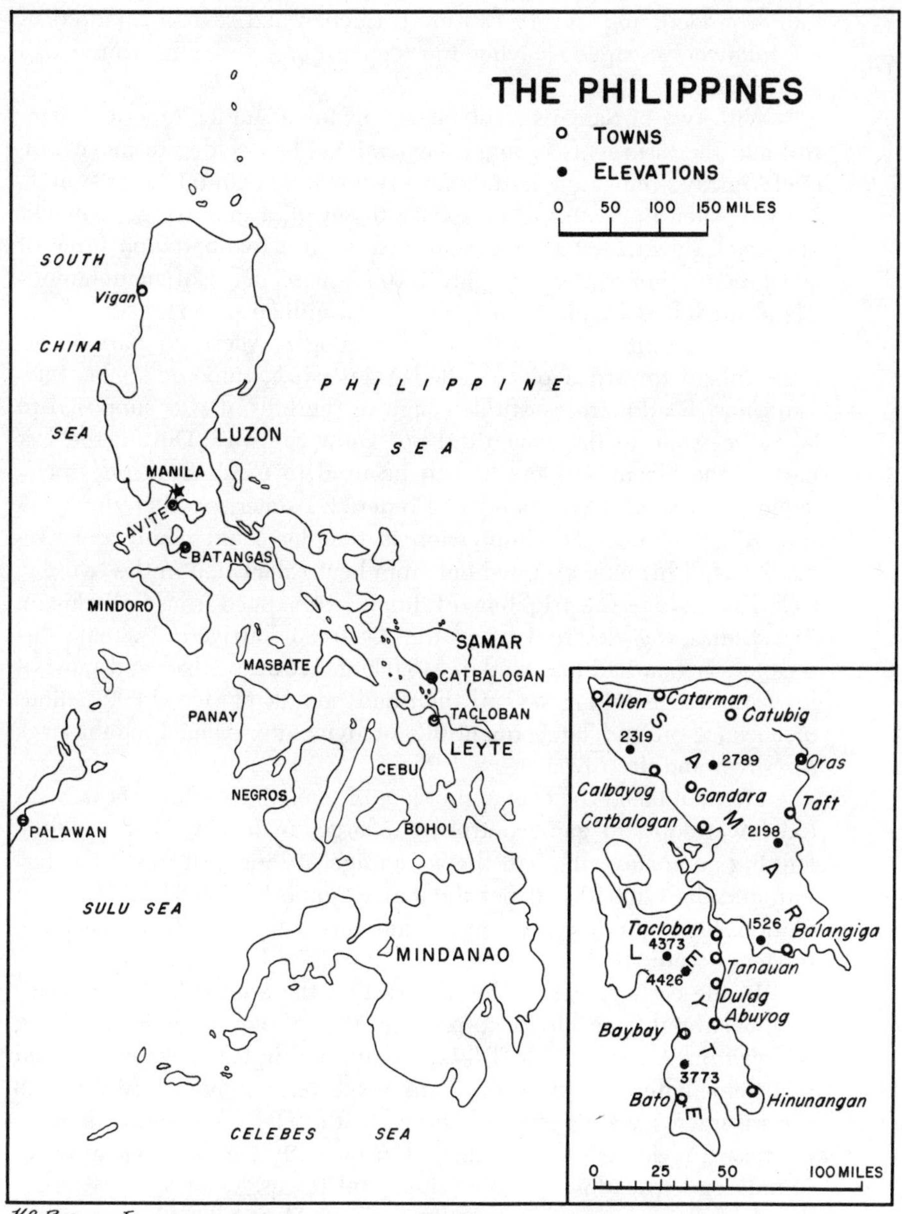

The Philippines: Enlarged Inset of Leyte and Samar

lost one killed and two wounded, while there were five Filipinos killed, four wounded, and twenty captured. Lucban and several hundred of his followers escaped, leaving fourteen cannon and numerous small arms behind.[46]

With two of Samar's most important towns under American control and the insurgents in flight, General Kobbé decided to move Colonel Murray's remaining battalion to Leyte and begin operations there. He left Allen in command on Samar to set up a military government and track down Lucban, no mean task with a two-battalion force of 900 green volunteers on roughly 5,000 square miles of mountainous island inhabited by almost a quarter of a million people.[47]

The day after the landing at Catbalogan Allen led part of his force inland toward a place called Maestranza, rumored to be Lucban's new headquarters. Hidden high in the hills, it was supposed to be inaccessible to those who did not know the way. During the last part of the ascent, ladders had to be used to climb from one rocky ledge to the next. Correspondent Frederick Palmer, panting along beside Allen, wrote: "My impression is that he could climb a waterfall." [48] Half his men dropped out from heat exhaustion in the two-day trek. Except for a few frightened Filipinos kidnapped from Catbalogan, Maestranza was deserted when the Americans arrived. To make his escape, Lucban had to abandon $18,000 in Mexican silver and most of his supplies, including several thousand pounds of rice, 1,000 gallons of coconut oil and large quantities of dynamite. Allen brought back the silver and destroyed the rest.[49]

He then faced the classic problem of guerrilla warfare: how, with too few troops, to gain control of a large, undeveloped area while fighting an enemy who had the advantage of familiarity with the terrain and the sympathy, if not the active support, of much of the population. Since there was no magic answer to this problem, many approaches were tried.

In the early stages of the insurrection the army adopted a policy of almost total benevolence to prove to the Filipinos they had nothing to fear from American rule. Prisoners captured in battle were disarmed and immediately released. Civilians suspected of giving assistance to the insurgents were rarely interfered with. The army began a well-conceived civic action campaign, starting with a massive clean-up of Manila and spreading to other cities and towns.[50]

Such measures worked, up to a point. Most Filipinos seemed to accept American sovereignty as at least an improvement over Spanish rule and a better alternative than more years of fighting and the possible return of terror and repression. By May, 1900, the military and political situation looked good to General Elwell S. Otis, commander of the Division of the Philippines since September, 1899. Believing the insurrection nearly over, he asked to be relieved.[51] General Arthur MacArthur took his place.

Otis, who seldom left his office and never visited his troops under fire, was too optimistic. The insurgents may have been scattered and disorganized, but their morale was unbroken and most of their leaders were still at large. Many Filipinos secretly supported them, either out of conviction or fear, while publicly declaring their loyalty to the Americans. Until Otis' policies were changed by MacArthur in December, 1900, there was no effective way to prevent the guerrillas from taking or getting whatever they needed from the rest of their countrymen.[52]

Prior to late 1900 some insurgents had voluntarily surrendered, but those who did not surrender were not to be won over by fair treatment and good works. They and their civilian sympathizers regarded the army's reluctance to use tough measures more as a sign of weakness and indecision than of humanitarian scruples. The rising clamor of the anti-imperialist movement in the United States gave them hope for a change in American policy that even McKinley's re-election (with Roosevelt, an ardent expansionist, as his running mate) failed to dash.[53] The insurgents' reading of the forces at work in their favor in the United States may have been too optimistic, but an explanation of their motives for fighting on, written by the rebel leader on Leyte to Major Gilmore of the 43rd Infantry, nevertheless contained some haunting perceptions:

> . . . we all know the superiority in every way of the great nation of . . . America and the opposition we are showing . . . is not with the object of defeating it, but to convince them of our reason and right in order that they may do us justice. We all know also that the American nation is not willing to fight against the Filipinos, and that they are convinced that independence should be given to us, but the imperialists in America are opposed to it, in order to keep in status quo the Filipino affair, and we also know that by expending so many millions of dollars in this way, provoked by the imperialists, . . . the nation will give up the idea of retaining the archipelago, to avoid that a rebellion may break out in America, beside the danger of getting into trouble with other nations.[54]

As the insurrection dragged into 1901, the fighting became more and more barbaric. Both sides increasingly committed atrocities. On the American side, these were the acts of a relatively few individuals acting on their own heated impulses and not the result of any officially sanctioned campaign of terror. MacArthur's new approach, tough as it was, could in no way be interpreted as condoning atrocities. He based his policies on the Army's General Order 100, which dated from the Civil War and contained basically humane and internationally accepted rules of conduct toward both combatants and noncombatants in a theater of war. American officers in the Philippines were well aware of these rules.[55] Yet, perhaps inevitably, serious violations occurred. The "water cure," forcing a man to drink water until his stomach became bloated and then squeezing or jumping on it until he vomited, was a fairly common way of getting a prisoner to talk. More than one Filipino died of the "cure." Unarmed captives were sometimes shot in cold blood. Word of such incidents eventually spread and became common knowledge in the United States.[56]

Against a background of increasing public indignation, led by many of the same men, such as Carl Schurz and Charles Francis Adams, who had opposed annexation in the first place, the Secretary of War ordered courts-martial in those cases where an investigation supported the allegations.

Schurz and Adams had an unexpected ally in the person of General Miles, who, by 1902, was at odds with the administration on many points, including the annexation and subjugation of the Philippines. Miles felt this was a violation of the Constitution and an inexcusable waste of American lives and money, but his influence on Philippine policy was as minimal as it had been on the Cuban campaign. In August, 1902, Secretary of War Elihu Root finally granted Miles's request to visit the Philippines. Root's motive was to get him out of Washington while the War Department was being reorganized (something else Miles objected to) and keep him occupied until he could be retired for age in 1903. Root miscalculated the amount of trouble Miles could make in the Philippines. Once there he heard enough stories from Filipinos to convince him prisoners were indeed being mistreated. Without consulting the War Department he issued an order to stop it. Both Washington and the commander in Manila reacted strongly to the implications of this, and the White House countermanded the order. Through the press Root claimed Miles had jumped to conclusions; Miles insisted his order was justified. The net result was more pressure on the army and the Administration to proceed with the still pending investigations and courts-martial.[57]

Some of the alleged perpetrators were never brought to trial or were found not guilty for lack of evidence or witnesses. Others received relatively light sentences. For example, Major Edwin F. Glenn of the 5th Infantry was relieved of command for a month and fined $50 for using the water cure on Samar in November, 1900. Lieutenant Preston Brown, 2nd Infantry, was charged with murdering an unarmed, unresisting prisoner on Luzon in December, 1900, and convicted of manslaughter. President Roosevelt later commuted Brown's sentence of imprisonment and dismissal from the service to a reduction in rank and pay.[58]

If the army's record in the Philippines was stained by the acts of a few brutal and irresponsible men, on the insurgent side even more atrocities were committed, including some at the instigation of leaders who could not easily plead ignorance of the rules of warfare. Lucban, for one, made no effort to check the bloody excesses of his followers. Many of the insurgent atrocities were committed against Filipino "collaborators,"[59] but Americans were the victims of the grisliest one of all. It happened on Samar.

In September, 1901, most of the garrison at Balangiga were butchered as they sat down to breakfast. A group of Lucban's men who had come in several days before and pretended to surrender carried out the surprise attack. These "prisoners" had been well treated and then released, given bolos, and put to work around the garrison and the nearby town. Of the seventy-four American officers and men at Balangiga, fifty-two were killed and almost all of the rest wounded. The assault was led by the local *presidente*, supposedly a trustworthy official, and even the village priest was a party to the plot. An army relief expedition which arrived the next day with boat-mounted Gatling guns blazing found the horribly mutilated bodies of their comrades. Kerosene had been poured over the garrison commander's head and set afire as he lay wounded. He was still roasting. Another officer's face had been laid open from ear to ear with a bolo and the great gash filled with his breakfast jam. Another man's belly had been neatly cut open and filled with flour and dried codfish. The wounds of the dead and dying were covered with thousands of stinging ants.[60]

The Americans on Samar went after those responsible for the massacre with a bitter vengeance. Reinforcements, commanded by Brigadier General Jacob H. Smith, were sent to the island. Before they landed, Smith gave the now infamous instructions to one of his battalion commanders: "I want no prisoners. . . . I wish you to kill and burn. The more you kill and burn, the better you will please me. . . . The interior of Samar must be made a howling wilderness."[61]

Fortunately, Smith's instructions were neither condoned by his superiors nor taken literally by most of his subordinates, although two of them were later tried and acquitted on the dubious grounds of "justified military reprisal" for the firing-squad execution of eleven native bearers whose dereliction had allegedly led to some American deaths. Smith himself was court-martialled in 1902 and convicted of "conduct to the prejudice of good order and military discipline." President Roosevelt retired him from active service.[62] Even if most American officers in the Philippines understood and accepted the necessity for General Smith's punishment, many shared the anger and frustration which prompted the intemperate violence of his orders. Some undoubtedly sympathized with him. Allen did not. Long before "Jakey" Smith's court-martial, Allen expressed contempt for his mentality and methods in a letter to William Howard Taft: "In Leyte General Jakey has done his best to make an insurgent situation in order that he might be able to say that he pacified it." Allen went on to quote some of Smith's vicious and bitter profanity about the "niggers." [63]

The relatively gentle methods of General Otis had been futile in dealing with a popular rebellion. The much harsher ones advocated by officers such as Smith, Glenn, and Brown could not be tolerated and, in any case, would have proven equally self-defeating in the long run. Better methods existed. They were embodied in General MacArthur's new policies, spelled out in a proclamation to the Filipino people in December, 1900, and in subsequent implementing orders. MacArthur had several good reasons for delaying until December his proclamation and the renewed offensive that accompanied it. By then he would have the maximum number of troops available and the rainy season would be over. More importantly, perhaps, he too was waiting to see who won the 1900 election, although he based his plans on the assumption of McKinley's victory.

As commander of an occupying army engaged in combat, MacArthur acknowledged his responsibility to provide protection to the civilian population so long as it obeyed his orders. Anyone giving aid and comfort to the insurgents or having knowledge of those who did without reporting it was henceforth subject to detention and trial by the military authorities. Insurgent reprisals against those who cooperated with the Americans would be treated as crimes; assassination was murder and not a legitimate act of war. Captured insurgents would be imprisoned for the duration of hostilities, but those who voluntarily surrendered would still be disarmed and set free. Prominent or popular agitators would be deported. Men who posed as peaceful citizens by day and fought as guerrillas by night lost their right to be treated as prisoners of war if captured. And, finally, all Filipino newspapers were warned of the consequences of publishing inflammatory or seditious articles.[64]

Beginning in 1901, MacArthur's new policies, widely applied, had the effect of gradually isolating the insurgents from the rest of the population, both physically and morally, and were probably the most important contributing factor in the virtual collapse of the insurrection eighteen months later. Nevertheless, these policies succeeded only because they were applied in a favorable atmosphere created by many other factors. Among them were the obvious good will of the Americans as evidenced by their civic works, health and educational programs; the generally humane treatment of those rebels who were captured or surrendered; American willingness to let Filipinos form a political party and participate in government; the continuation of military pressure against the remaining insurgents and their inability to replenish their supplies; the surrender of Aguinaldo; and the general war-weariness of the Filipinos.[65]

One historian of the insurrection strongly implies that Allen should receive the credit for being the first American in the Philippines to work out and apply most of the methods later adopted by MacArthur for the islands as a whole.[66] Since many officers faced the same problems as Allen, it is hard to believe at least a few others were not also thinking and acting along the same lines as he, especially since the precedent and authority for the measures he took already existed in General Order 100. However, an examination of the reports for the last six months of 1900 of all the commanders of military districts and subdistricts throughout the islands shows that Allen's gave the clearest descriptions of such methods and strong evidence they worked. His reports were also among the few that included detailed information on methods of restoring normal political and economic conditions.[67] It is reasonable to assume General MacArthur knew of these reports. Another officer neatly summarized Allen's technique as "treating the good man very well indeed and the bad man very harshly, . . . the *curacha* [dance] or the *carcel* [jail] . . . and no middle ground."[68] Although Allen was later to apply these methods with greater success on Leyte, he developed them first on Samar.

Less than a month after the landing at Catbalogan in January, 1900, Allen became Military Governor of Samar. The title hardly corresponded with the reality. He had merely sent out a dozen small probing expeditions and garrisoned a few towns, mainly in the region extending in an arc between Catbalogan and Calbayog. Patrols began moving regularly around and between each occupied town. During February Lucban avoided combat, and Allen was too busy putting together a framework of military government to press him very hard as long as he stayed outside the radius of American control. Inside that area, Allen published proclamations and held meetings in each community, explaining his policies and telling the people what he expected of them. His ability to speak Spanish was an immense help in earning the respect and eventual loyalty of most of the officials and upper-class elements.[69]

However, the quickly promised co-operation of local officials was hard to depend on at first. Lucban's threat to kill those who co-operated carried far more weight than Allen's threat that they would lose their jobs if they did not. Allen eventually jailed some *presidentes* and *alcaldes* who tried to please both sides, but a few preferred jail to any other kind of American protection against the insurgent chief's kidnappers and assassins.[70] Although some of Lucban's officers had surrendered, the pacification of even a part of Samar was an illusion as long as he was free.

Beginning in March, Allen's patrols spread out farther from the garrisoned towns, and several larger expeditions crisscrossed the island. Units going out in force seldom found any insurgents, though they often stumbled onto their hastily deserted camps, but anything less than a platoon could usually count on being ambushed. That month the insurgents lost more than 100 men to four Americans killed and twelve wounded.[71]

Pacification of Samar may have looked easy on a map (especially since its interior had never been charted), but it was turning out differently on the ground. Lucban had plenty of supporters and places to hide. The Americans controlled as far as they could see to shoot. The overland expeditions, while producing more insurgent than American casualties, were hard on Allen's soldiers. Five days in the hills were enough to wear out a man's boots and his body. And when he came back it was not to a few days of rest but to guard duty and work details around the garrison. Allen asked General Kobbé for more troops. To Dora he wrote, "the guerrilla warfare . . . is apt to continue for a very long time."[72] Instead of giving him more troops, Kobbé took some away; more urgently needed elsewhere, one of Allen's eight companies left in March, another in May. Allen's solution was to ask for authority to organize natives of proven loyalty into a company of scouts. Division Headquarters in Manila reluctantly granted permission since a number of companies of native scouts had already been organized on Luzon and Negros, but several months passed on Samar before enough scouts were recruited and trained to make any difference.[73]

In the meantime, the thinning out of Allen's forces emboldened Lucban. April opened with a rash of attacks and acts of terror. Six hundred insurgents overran the newly established thirty-one-man garrison in the interior at Catubig and almost wiped it out. The nineteen Americans killed and four wounded there cost Lucban 150 of his own men. Two hundred and ten more insurgents died and twenty were captured in thirteen other engagements during April.[74] Despite the slaughter, Lucban's grip on the island remained unbroken. Allen began to realize that the only way to defeat him was to combine continued military pressure with stricter measures to discourage his civilian supporters. In March he had written General Kobbé, "I propose to use very mild measures with good natives, but deadly stringent ones with others, especially Tagalogs." [75] On April 25, Allen put this plan into effect with a proclamation in Spanish, "*Habitantes de Samar.*" To the people of Samar, he said:

> . . . The time has come for you to decide what is best for you; you have been governed for more than a year by a group of Tagalogs, people foreign to your province . . . having no love for it. [They] . . . deceive you with false news . . . of victories . . . [and] impose immense sacrifices upon you. . . .

Allen then contrasted the base motives of these "cowardly Tagalogs" with those of the Americans who wanted "the people to be truly sovereign" and who had come to Samar not to enrich themselves, but "to give you a government of honor and dignity, . . . to open the ports of these islands to commerce, . . . to bring here the advancements of the sciences and the arts, [and] to develop agriculture and industry to the level they have reached in America."

As governor, Allen was well aware of the economic paralysis besetting the island, "the fault of those bandits who attack the towns. . . . you must understand that all the evil they do is to yourselves."

He ended the proclamation with a promise and a threat. Although he would "treat with kindness and benevolence all who repent of their actions . . . and submit," if the towns continued "in their inertia and indifference" to what was happening and to deprecate his "well-intentioned offers," he was also determined "to pursue without rest and firmly punish" all those who directly or indirectly disturbed "the tranquility of the province."

> I hope you will not oblige me to [use fear and terror] . . . , and I do not want to; war only causes the ruin of peoples. . . . You . . . are the ones who will lose the most. . . . Do not be fools, separate yourselves from those who deceive you. If you abandon them, if they do not find aid and sympathizers in the towns of Samar, . . . we can soon do away with these animals who only want the ruin of the province. So help me and trust me and I will do all I can. . . .[76]

After this, Allen's troops kept up the pressure on Lucban by vigorous patrolling, but losses on both sides dropped sharply. In June, for the first time in five months, no Americans died on Samar. Since January, casualties had been thirty-one killed, twenty-nine wounded and two captured.[77] Lucban lay low, rebuilding his forces and waiting to see what the public reaction to Allen's proclamation would be. As long as Allen remained on the island he backed his words with actions, but he was not there much longer.

By June, with Samar quiet if not under complete control, Allen asked for three weeks off to go to Manila and take a competitive examination for promotion to regular army major. Several vacancies existed in the Adjutant General's and Inspector General's corps. Although Allen's branch was cavalry and his most recent experience was with infantry combat, he felt confident of his ability to pass the test. He did, but to his chagrin failed to score high enough on some of the more abstruse administrative subjects to qualify for promotion.[78] Since his commission as a major in the volunteers was temporary, his real status in the army was still that of a captain. That the army was full of captains his own age was small consolation; enough of the better ones had already been promoted to make him feel he was falling behind. Although Colonel Murray had recently recommended him for a brevet promotion to regular army major, nothing had come of it.[79]

In July, 1900, another unit took responsibility for Samar, and Allen and his men rejoined Colonel Murray and the rest of the 43rd Infantry on Leyte. With Allen came the newly organized company of native scouts.

Having initially just one battalion to work with on Leyte, Murray had chosen to garrison only a few key coastal towns in order to conduct field operations in strength. The result had been greater insurgent losses than on Samar, but little effective control of any part of the island. Even the lightly garrisoned towns were not secure from insurgent attacks and reprisals.[80]

Geographically, Leyte resembled Samar except that it was only about half as large and long and narrow in shape. In addition, though the mountains that formed Leyte's spine were up to 1,500 feet higher than those on Samar, relatively more land was under cultivation, supporting a denser and more prosperous population. The "Lucban" of Leyte was a Tagalog named Ambrose Moxica. As wily and elusive as Lucban, his immediate superior in the insurgent hierarchy, Moxica appears to have been a more intelligent and capable military organizer. In its own way, his guerrilla organization was as complex and sophisticated as Murray's regiment and far better adapted for survival in the jungle. At the beginning of 1900 Moxica had about 500 officers and men on Leyte. They were organized into a battalion consisting of a headquarters, an artillery company, three companies of infantry, one section each of marine infantry, "flying" (roving) guerrillas, and bolomen, plus a hospital and a court-martial section. In addition, Moxica had a small personal staff of his own, including two "politico-military" officers to handle liaison with civil officials and make propaganda.[81] Murray had no one on his staff whose duties fitted that description.

Although Moxica's "artillery" consisted of a few clumsy old brass cannons (and even some wooden ones) and not all of the infantry had modern rifles, his original force was formidable enough before the Americans got to Leyte. Allen described how Moxica expanded and motivated it afterward:

> The regular officers were authorized to organize bolero [bolo] companies. . . . and so successful were they in this work that practically every able-bodied man . . . became a member of a bolero company. [The new junior officers] . . . were often natives who had never worn a pair of shoes . . . too often selected for their criminal tendencies, and flattered by their new titles they were willing to attempt anything demanded by their superiors.
>
> It is difficult to understand the success with which these Tagalog officials have fired the Visayans for the noble cause of independence, except by admitting that they were ready for a revolt against Western government, as they had learned it, whether administered by Spaniards, Americans, or any other civilized nation.[82]

In July, with the entire regiment again at his disposal, Murray divided Leyte into three subdistricts, one for each of his battalions. The first subdistrict, commanded by Major Lincoln C. Andrews, covered the northeast portion of the island. Andrews' headquarters was collocated with Murray's at Tacloban, the province capital. From Baybay, Major John C. Gilmore commanded the third subdistrict on the western coast of Leyte. Allen had the rest of the island for his second subdistrict, though for the time being he ignored the thinly populated and inaccessible southern portion. He set up his headquarters at Dulag on July 7 and began the work of getting his subdistrict firmly under control. Five of the largest towns were immediately garrisoned and soon thereafter connected with Dulag by a telegraph line. As on Samar, patrols then moved continuously around each garrison. While this was being done, larger expeditions headed into Moxica's territory. Allen led several himself.[83]

The first time out, he took 100 troops on a fruitless two-weeks' march across to the western coast and back. Only forty made it both ways over the mountains with him. The rest all managed to straggle in to safety, victims only of the heat and steep slopes.[84] Thereafter, Allen picked his men more carefully. He also began to use the native scouts. Before the next expedition a motley assemblage of soldiers stood in front of Allen's headquarters; the Americans bronzed and bearded under their campaign hats and dressed for speed and comfort and not spit and polish; the scouts half as tall and a darker shade of brown, wearing anything from loincloths to army castoffs and carrying rifles their own height. Allen did some amazing things with them.

One of his more successful "hikes," as he liked to call them, took place in the mountains of Leyte between August 27 and September 3, 1900. With a force of about 200 men (half of it the scout company commanded by First Lieutenant Lorenzo G. Gasser), and in the "most inclement weather," Allen marched more than 100 miles over the ruggedest of mountain trails and captured:

> . . . the Chief Purveyor of the Insurgent Army, three captains of boleros, one a close friend of the Insurgent General Moxica, another the ex-president of Burauen, 143 bolomen, . . . the archives of the insurgent army of Leyte, . . . the side arms of General Moxica and staff with six chests of their personal effects, the medical supply depot of the insurgents, 5000 pesos, 8 rifles, 1 shotgun, 8 revolvers, 250 rounds of ammunition, a number of bolos and daggers, a large supply of rice and other provisions and burned four insurgent barracks. . . .

Only three men were wounded in this entire operation: one insurgent, one American sergeant, and one Leyte scout.[85]

Although Moxica continued to elude everyone, several expeditions in September resulted in the capture of 219 more insurgents and an increasing number of surrenders in Allen's subdistrict. Among the documents captured in Moxica's camp on August 30 was a letter from his second in command, Lieutenant Colonel Bañez, compromising the two leading officials of the town of Abuyog. Both had previously taken the American oath of allegiance. Allen's reaction was swift and firm. Using scouts, he increased the size of the town's garrison and then jailed the two men, appointed new officials, and replaced the entire police force. In his next report Allen could say with dry satisfaction, "presumably this fact hastened Bañez's surrender, since which time he has labored to ameliorate the lot of his Abuyog relations and sympathizers." [86]

Most of Allen's fellow officers still objected to the idea of using native troops to supplement Americans for both garrison duty and field operations, but he was proving it could be done. What had begun on Samar as a dubious experiment could not be scoffed at so easily on Leyte. Allen called attention to his use of native soldiers in an official report:

> . . . It is not my intention to suggest that these scouts are on the whole nearly equal to American soldiers, though in ferreting out insurgents and criminals and in understanding motive and method of the natives . . . they are of inestimable value. With a careful selection of recruits and good thorough military training they produce an effective military police body at about one third the cost (or less) of Americans. This must eventually have importance in our Philippine policy.

He went on to say that because of a slow and careful recruiting policy, "there has never been the slightest suspicion of treachery on the part of any member of the company." Having taken from April until October to fill the company's quota of 100 men (exclusive of Lieutenant Gasser and six American noncommissioned officers), Allen's plan was to put "two or three squads in each town garrisoned by our soldiers" and, later, even larger detachments "in towns that were burned by insurgents and are now being rebuilt." [87]

By September of 1900, life seemed to be returning to normal in Allen's subdistrict. People who had fled their homes in the midst of the earlier fighting felt safe enough to return and rebuild. Insurgent raids and reprisals grew increasingly rare. Most of Allen's troops kept after Moxica, but no Filipino townsman forgot that Americans were around. Allen was shrewd enough to turn this potential source of friction into a highly visible asset. Soldiers not only patrolled the roads but repaired them so that traffic and produce could move more easily from town to town and down to the ports. His troops supervised or helped with the construction or improvement of all sorts of facilities for the common benefit, form sewer systems to docks. Schools began to reopen in the subdistrict, helped by a donation of Spanish-English books and dictionaries solicited by Allen himself through the *New York Sun.*[88]

Also in September, the town of Dulag held its annual fiesta in honor of its patron saint. No incidents of any kind marred the festivities, despite an influx of several thousand people. More than 3,000 attended two Masses. Americans and Filipinos enjoyed three days of parades, band concerts, dances, and sporting events. One American company even put on a minstrel show. On the last night of the celebration, Allen entertained the officials from all the towns in the subdistrict at a Chinese dinner eaten with chopsticks.[89] Speaking Spanish and learning Visayan, he was at his polished best, but his guests knew what other qualities lay beneath that urbane and gracious exterior. He had become known on Leyte as the "Iron *Comandante.*" [90] The title pleased him.

At the end of September, he volunteered for duty in China with the American expeditionary force sent in during the Boxer Rebellion. As far as he could see, the insurrection had collapsed on Leyte and there was little left for him to do.[91] Colonel Murray disagreed, and Allen stayed where he was.

October and November were quiet months. The work of patrolling and rebuilding went on. Living up to one of the connotations of his nickname, Allen led several more grueling mountain "hikes." There was no sign of Moxica and not much insurgent activity of any kind. Allen began to relax a little for the first time in almost a year. He decided to move his headquarters from Dulag to the larger and more pleasantly situated town of Tanauan. A comfortably light and airy building overlooking its harbor became his new office. His letters to Dora, still in Boston, told her the worst was over. He was healthy and safe and in great spirits. Just being able to ride again gave him the most pleasure. "I can still spring into the saddle from the ground," he wrote. At Thanksgiving he organized a field day for his men and participated himself, winning a pony race. He even had enough free time to write about his recent experiences for *Outing Magazine* and *The National Geographic,* though neither article was ever published.[92] A few problems still worried him, particularly Moxica's whereabouts and the apparent stalling of his own career, but, all in all, the future looked hopeful. The recent election victory of McKinley and Roosevelt was a blow to insurgent hopes. Whatever Moxica's next move, he could hardly undo the solid progress of the past five months, progress so obvious Allen's superiors could not fail to recognize it. In fact, Colonel Murray was getting ready to recommend him for another brevet promotion. If that came through, it would at last put him on the road toward the goal he had set for himself and had confided to Dora the previous spring: "health permitting" to remain in the Philippines long enough "to get command of the entire Archipelago." [93]

As December opened, the Americans on Leyte had a rude shock. Lucban left Samar to join forces with Moxica and announced his presence with a characteristically bombastic proclamation. It began:

> FELLOW CITIZENS OF LEYTE: The moment has arrived when you must demonstrate with greater energy than ever your valor and patriotism. The time is at hand when these oaths and words of fidelity given to our country under the sacred folds of our flag should be executed by you. . . . We must resort to arms, because engraved upon your faithful Filipino hearts is the cry, Liberty or death! Independence or extermination! . . .[94]

No general uprising followed Lucban's proclamation, though it caused some anxious moments at first. Reports came in that officials in some of the ungarrisoned towns had openly declared themselves for the rebels, but there was little evidence of ordinary citizens once more fleeing their homes and heading for the hills. Several American patrols were attacked, the first time that had happened in many weeks. In reality, this was the beginning of the death spasm of the insurgency on Leyte. The convulsions lasted five more months.

They were hectic months for Allen, whose duties gradually expanded until he was responsible for control of the entire island. On December 5, because Major Andrews was on sick-leave, Colonel Murray added Andrews' battalion and subdistrict to Allen's command. During the next three weeks Allen sent out twenty-four major expeditions, ranging in size from one platoon to several companies and led two of the larger operations himself. Although Allen's own subdistrict remained relatively quiet, it was a different story in Andrews' area. In the mountains northwest of Tacloban almost every expedition found an enemy willing to stand and fight. By the end of the month the insurgents had lost more than 100 men killed and captured. With MacArthur's new policies in effect, most of the civil officials who had switched sides once too often were rounded up and jailed, and Allen had additional strong powers, including the authority to impose newspaper censorship and to deport agitators.[95] But since Lucban and Moxica boasted of thousands of followers, 100 more or less did not seem to make much difference. Another year of bloodshed began.

In January Allen took temporary command of the regiment while Colonel Murray went to Manila.[96] Before Murray left, he and Allen decided to move forces into the southern part of the island, the one area where American control had not yet been attempted. Expecting resistance, Allen loaded 120 American troops and native scouts aboard two steamers and headed south from Tacloban on January 8. The first stop was Hinunangan. No insurgents opened fire as the ships approached, and, although the townspeople temporarily fled, they soon returned with cautious smiles of welcome. The force proceeded on around the coast, landing at a different place each day with the same results. Pushing inland, the troops found only a few small, long-deserted guerrilla camps. Within a week, there was little left except the routine work of appointing officials, administering oaths, and otherwise organizing an area that comprised almost one-sixth of the island. Leaving the expedition under the command of Lieutenant Gasser (who accomplished the rest of the mission in five weeks without firing a shot), Allen returned to Tacloban.[97] In northern and central Leyte the rest of his troops were still grinding away at the insurgents and finding fights with little difficulty. Insurgent losses for January and February were much like December's. American losses were less each month.[98]

By the end of February it had become pathetically one-sided. Never well supplied with arms and ammunition, the insurgents were finally running out completely. Even food and medicine could no longer be easily obtained. Although Moxica still refused to admit defeat, his "army" began to melt away. In March more than 2,000 of his followers surrendered.[99] Lucban slunk back to Samar, where he held out for another year. News of Aguinaldo's capture and taking of the oath of allegiance reached Moxica a few days after he abandoned his last mountain hideout as it was being overrun. That did it. On April 18, 1901, he surrendered. Almost 1,500 of his men followed his example, bringing in with them a large number of bolos, but only three revolvers, four rifles, one shotgun, and 100 rounds of ammunition—pitiful evidence of Moxica's weakness. He estimated that about seventy of his rifles remained in the hands of those who chose to stay on in the hills, die-hard rebels or criminals facing prosecution.[100] In time, they became almost indistinguishable from the common bandits who had always infested the Philippines. The insurrection on Leyte seemed to be over.

At the end of May, the 43rd Volunteer Infantry Regiment loaded on a transport and sailed for the United States. Allen was not aboard. On April 22, 1901, the Philippine Commission, headed by William Howard Taft, had appointed him Military Governor of Leyte.[101]

Allen had been recommended for the position by Brigadier General R. P. Hughes, commander of the Department of the Visayas, but he accepted it somewhat reluctantly. He would have preferred to lead the five battalions of native troops being organized in the department, but only if the troops were considered a regiment and he could get the higher rank that went with such a command.[102] Another possibility was a civil position in Taft's new administration. Allen heard from a mutual friend that Vice President Roosevelt had recommended him for such a job.[103] Neither possibility had materialized by the time Allen had to make his decision whether to go home with the 43rd or to stay in the Philippines. He chose to stay and take what he could get, but he regarded his appointment as governor of Leyte as an interim position during the period of transition from military to civil rule. Once Taft took over from MacArthur as governor of the Philippines Allen would see what other opportunities might be offered him.[104] He was sure enough of a good assignment in the islands to write Dora to come out with the children, even if he could not yet tell her where they would live.

The children were "wild to go," but Dora had doubts at first.[105] The last year and a half had probably been the hardest of her life. Ill much of the time, living from month to month with the Hankses in Boston with her belongings never completely unpacked, constantly worried about Henry's health and safety, and concerned over young Harry's homesickness and scholastic difficulties in private school, she was understandably anxious to have her husband home and hesitant about traipsing off to another exotic foreign land. In fourteen years of marriage, she had moved more times than she could count and lived mostly in hotels and rented apartments. The closest thing to a real home the children had ever known were the quarters at West Point and Fort Riley, and each of those tours had lasted less than two years. Longing for some stability and permanence in her life, she asked in her diary: "Oh, when will we have a home and have the family all together?" [106] In the end, like a good army wife, she obeyed her husband's call. She and the children sailed from San Francisco for Manila in late August.

By then, Allen had a new assignment that promised to fulfill both his hopes and hers. On July 31, 1901, the Philippine Commission, in office since July 4, selected him from several candidates recommended by General Adna R. Chaffee to organize and head the Philippine Constabulary on the basis of his success on Leyte and his ability to work with native troops.[107] To his delight, the job combined a civil position with the pay and prerogatives of a brigadier general (though not the rank), and it gave him command of a "small army," to be composed of Filipinos led by American officers.[108] For Dora it meant the prospect of a pleasant social life as part of Manila's elite and, more importantly, the hope of settling down in one place for at least a few years.

CHAPTER VI

Always Outnumbered; Never Outfought

—Motto of the Philippine Constabulary [1]

With the inauguration of William Howard Taft as governor on July 4, 1901, civil government replaced military rule in the Philippines. Taft and the other four members of his presidentially appointed Philippine Commission had received a cold welcome from General MacArthur, who did not believe the time had arrived to put control of the islands in civilian hands. More than two years of fighting *insurrectos* had convinced him of the desire of most Filipinos for independence, but he was there to carry out the orders of his government that they be pacified and assimilated. MacArthur had predicted this might take ten more years of fighting. To his mind anything less than total military control of the islands in the meantime was an invitation to disaster. Taft assured him he would continue to have "full military powers." "That would be all right," the general replied, "if I had not been exercising so much more power before you came." [2]

Taft's benevolent attitude toward the Filipinos was well known. Though he certainly did not oppose the desire of American businessmen to make profits in the Philippines, he had said the United States was holding the islands primarily to improve the welfare of the Filipinos. This, of course, also made them better customers. But Taft was no cynic; he was sincere when he referred to the Filipinos as our "little brown brothers." The soldiers facing death out in the jungles had an answer to this: "He may be a brother of Big Bill Taft, but he ain't no brother of mine!" [3]

On the day of the inauguration MacArthur was replaced as Commander of the Division of the Philippines by General Adna R. Chaffee, whose views on civil government were believed to be more compatible with Taft's (and those of the Secretary of War and the President).[4] Both Chaffee and Taft took their orders from the War Department. Chaffee assumed command of 43,000 army troops scattered over 500 posts in the Philippines.[5] In September he began turning over administrative control of the islands to Taft and his commission. The civil government assumed full responsibility for maintaining law and order in twenty-four provinces. Only after a formal request for assistance by the governor himself would the army again conduct field operations in these areas. As yet unpacified and thus remaining temporarily under military rule were the provinces of Batangas and Laguna on Luzon, the islands of Samar, Cebu, and Bohol, and all of Mindanao and the Sulu Archipelago.[6]

From July to September of 1901, the civil government completed its internal organization. One of its new bureaus was the Philippine Constabulary, created on July 18, 1901, by Act No. 175 of the Philippine Commission.[7] The constabulary was the brainchild of Luke E. Wright, Taft's Vice-Governor and Secretary of Commerce and Police, who saw the need for an insular police force whose purview would be the maintenance of public order beyond the capabilities or jurisdiction of the often inefficient native municipal police. The constabulary would also operate in areas or against illegal activities not requiring the intervention of the army, whose organization made it unsuited for police work and whose operations tended to be expensive and cumbersome.[8]

Wright's general scheme was to create a force of approximately 5,000 "peace officers" by enlisting no more than 150 natives from each province. Over them would be the Chief of Constabulary, four assistant chiefs, and, for each province, up to four provincial inspectors. In emergencies the chief would have authority to combine the forces of two or more provinces. Provincial inspectors were to have the additional duty of "thorough and frequent inspections of the municipal police." The purpose of the constabulary was "to prevent and suppress brigandage, insurrection, unlawful assemblies and breaches of the peace. . . ."[9]

The constabulary would have had plenty to do even if its job had been only to clean up the smashed pieces of the insurrection left behind by the army. But this was not its primary mission. The elimination of insurrection was the army's main reason for remaining in the Philippines. The suppression of brigandage and other kinds of public disorder should have been the corollary responsibility of the constabulary. By mid-1901, however, it was becoming difficult to tell which Filipinos still resisting American authority were *insurrectos* and which were common bandits.

The insurgency had never been well organized. The strength of Aguinaldo's forces in each locality waxed and waned according to the degree of American military pressure and the amount of support from the population. Numerous small guerrilla bands had operated independently of him, and others put themselves under his command only from time to time. Many had ignored his recent appeal to lay down their arms and fought on. But some Filipinos were not really fighting for the cause of *Independencia.* The Philippines had long been infested with bandit gangs, bands of anti-Catholic religious fanatics, and uncivilized mountain tribes who preyed on the Spanish and their own countrymen with equal rapacity. The Spanish had never been able to stop the depredations of these groups, and it was natural for many of them to join the later insurrection against the Americans when it suited their purposes. In the different islands, these bandits and fanatics went by different names: ladrones, *tulisanes, pulajanes,* or *babaylanes.* In Spanish times the number of *tulisanes* in Cavite Province had made travel hazardous even near Manila. The Spaniards called Cavite the *madre de tulisanes* (mother of bandits).[10]

Reflecting the power of the Church on Filipino minds, many outlaws gave themselves fanciful religious titles, often claiming to be the reincarnation of some biblical figure. At one time after the Americans came, there were no less than three who claimed to be "Jesus Christ," one "God Almighty," and several the "Virgin Mary" serving in various provincial jails. Several bandit leaders styled themselves "Pope" and claimed to be immune from bullets, passing their immunity to their followers by giving them magic charms to wear. If a man so protected fell in battle, the gullible natives were told he would be resurrected in three days. "Pope" Filipe Salvador, one of the worst of these outlaws professing religious inspiration, operated in the vicinity of Manila at the head of a band calling itself the *Santa Yglesia* (Holy Church). A deserter from Aguinaldo's army, Salvador plundered and burned for ten years before he was finally captured by the constabulary, tried, and hanged.[11] Like Salvador, many of the other *insurrectos* turned to banditry when they lost hope of defeating the Americans, although they continued to use the slogans of the insurrection to mask their real colors.

It was against such groups—a mixed bag of true revolutionaries, bloodthirsty cutthroats, and armed religious fanatics—that both the army and the constabulary had to fight. The somewhat arbitrary division of peace-keeping responsibility for "unpacified" and "pacified" provinces between the two organizations was an administrative attempt to avoid jurisdictional disputes between them. It was only partially successful. Because fugitive bands, whatever their stripe, paid no attention to provincial boundaries, the question of who had primary responsibility for going after them remained a source of friction between the army and constabulary for many years.[12]

When Allen became Chief of the Constabulary in July, 1901, he faced a unique set of problems for which no precedent existed in American military experience. He could draw from the lessons the army had learned with the Philippine scouts in matters of recruiting, training and leadership, but, except for the fact that both the scouts and the constabulary had American officers, the two forces had little else in common. The former, organized into 100-man companies equipped and supplied through existing army channels, shared their garrisons with larger numbers of American troops and were employed conventionally alongside regular army units. About 5,000 scouts had been slowly raised over the past two years using the full resources available to the army. Despite a careful process of selection, training, and deployment, when not closely supervised the scouts had a reputation for both unreliability under fire and cruelty to their fellow Filipinos.[13]

Quickly, Allen had to put a native force of the same size in the field using the limited facilities and funds of a newly established civilian government and with nothing more than token help from the army. He had to deploy this force in small detachments to hundreds of scattered posts, most of them far from the steadying presence of American troops.

Four other regular army captains were detailed to the constabulary with Allen to begin the job. They were good, experienced men, but the army could spare no more like them.[14] These five officers were in an anomalous position. Although their duties were essentially military, they were officials of the civil government and completely under civilian control and supervision. Allen's pay and prerogatives were equivalent to a brigadier general's, while each of his four assistant chiefs received those of a colonel. But, as far as the army was concerned, they were all still captains. Initially, in deference to the army, the constabulary did not use military titles at all. In addition to the chief and assistant chiefs, there were only inspectors of various grades.[15]

Since no more regulars were available to help him, Allen had to recruit all the junior officers needed to command each detachment and to serve as provincial inspectors and staff. He had no difficulty finding them. By the end of June, 1902, when the constabulary had been in existence eleven months, he had selected 193 officers. Most were ex-lieutenants and sergeants from the volunteer regiments leaving the Philippines who stayed on when their units were shipped home and mustered out. These men could have been lured only by the prospect of more adventure, for they accepted a cut from what their army pay had been when they signed up for a two-year hitch in the constabulary with an annual salary of from $800 to $1,400, depending on the position. Allen also took on a few men who had seen service in a foreign army. Some later came in with only a background of military schooling in the United States. He put them all through a special training program and then sent them out to the provinces to organize and train their native detachments.[16]

Every man who wanted to become a constabulary officer went for an interview with Allen. The applicant entered the constabulary headquarters in Manila and was shown into his office, a high-ceilinged room with its paneled walls covered with bolos, spears, shields, and other trophies of war. The tall, shuttered windows at Allen's back dimmed the blazing sunlight outside. He sat, immaculate and formal, behind an immense, uncluttered desk.[17] Coolly fixing his visitor with eyes the color of wood smoke, he would ask a series of pointed questions, probing the applicant's motives for joining the constabulary and for defects in his character. The last question was always, "Do you drink?" Although Allen was no teetotaler, his tone implied that addiction to the bottle was incompatible with the danger and lonely responsibilities a constabulary officer would face. Not many drunkards passed this unnerving sobriety test. One who did looked Allen in the eye and answered, "I drink all I want, and at any time I want. But . . . drunk or sober, I can fight like Hell!" Allen hired him.[18]

In the rush to organize the constabulary some doubtful characters were thus enlisted, but the overall quality of Allen's officers was exceptionally high. The exploits of many of them would be almost unbelievable were they not recorded in official reports and confirmed by witnesses.

There was Captain Harrison O. Fletcher, who first made a name for himself by subduing the mutinous crew of a ship anchored offshore near his isolated constabulary post. Most of the crew had been killed and several passengers wounded in the mutiny. With two of his men, Fletcher rowed out to the ship, boarded it unobserved, killed two of the surprised mutineers, and captured the rest, thirty-four in all.[19] One night five months later, in January, 1903, he was ambushed while riding from his post to the next town. In his own words:

> Well, it didn't amount to much. I . . . had only gone a short distance, when thirty ladrones jumped me. . . . four of them got in their work with their bolos before I could draw my weapons, but I turned loose on them and by the time I emptied my revolver and carbine they had all disappeared except five unfortunates who were lying dead on the ground. I caught one hombre and took him back with me as a souvenir.[20]

Fletcher returned to town to have his bolo wounds dressed and then immediately picked up his detachment, pursued the rest of the gang, and killed six more in the next few hours.[21]

Then there was Inspector Henry Knauber, a native of Germany and veteran of many army campaigns in the Philippines. A band of eight *tulisanes* attacked him en route to a troubled area of Cavite Province. Knauber's horse was shot from under him in the first volley and he and his two enlisted companions met the bolo rush that immediately followed in a hand-to-hand fight in shoulder-high grass. His report to Allen read simply:

> Eight outlaws killed, three rifles, one revolver, several bolos and one trumpet captured. Constabulary casualties: one horse killed.[22]

Another constabulary officer in the same mold was John R. White. Already a veteran of the British, German, and American armies, White was soon a legend in the Philippines. Sent to Negros in early 1902 to "put out the last flames of insurrection," [23] he led a hand-picked force of nineteen men against the mountain fortress of "Papa" Isio, guarded by 200 of his followers. Three days of climbing brought White within 100 yards of the redoubt before he and his men were spotted and pinned down by a combination of rifle fire, spears, arrows, and plummeting rocks and boulders, some of the latter weighing as much as two tons. Unable to persuade his men to charge through this terrifying barrage, White finally got up and, taunting them to follow, calmly walked through it himself. He and six of his men were wounded, but they stormed over Papa Isio's trenches and captured and burned his camp.[24]

The most legendary of all constabulary fighters was Captain Cary I. Crockett (naturally enough a descendant of Davy) whose bullet and bolo scars numbered only slightly fewer than his battle feats. Once, gravely wounded himself, he actually had to be pulled out from beneath a pile of his dead and dying adversaries.[25] On another occasion, he and Allen, nineteen years his senior, shared the honors for beating off an ambush and bolo attack.[26]

Among the Filipino enlisted men were some just as tough and fearless. (Strictly speaking, these men were "constables," but to Allen they were soldiers.) None of the officers just mentioned would have lived through their constabulary tours if the men they led had ever let them down in a desperate situation. Although the salary of a junior officer was low by Western standards, the pay of his troops was generous in Filipino eyes. Besides, there was great prestige in wearing a uniform and working for the Americans. More than enough native volunteers came forward to fill the constabulary's ranks, and Allen's subordinates could afford to be selective. Every constabulary recruit had to have recommendations from at least two prominent men in his community as to his loyalty and trustworthiness,[27] but once in a while this rule was waived to enlist a particularly promising prospect. One eager volunteer who could not get the required recommendations was told half-jokingly he could prove his loyalty by bringing in the head of the local ladrone chief. Several weeks later he walked into the nearest constabulary post carrying not only the chief's head but those of several of his gang. He was hired on the spot.[28]

As a precaution against overenthusiastic and indiscriminate indulgence in such practices, constabulary detachments were normally employed in their home community where each enlisted man was known. This policy was in sharp contrast to the Spanish practice under the constabulary's predecessor, the civil guard. To make the guard as ruthless as possible, the Spaniards deliberately employed its members far from their own homes in areas inhabited by their traditional tribal enemies.[29] Social pressure and discipline made good soldiers out of most Filipinos, but Allen knew the most effective measure of all—leadership.

> The Filipinos, like all people, will fight when properly paid, fed, and disciplined, but above all when properly led. This is the keynote to an entirely successful use of Filipinos as soldiers. . . . It is therefore of the utmost importance that high-grade officers, thoroughly courageous, upright, sober, intelligent, and energetic, be placed over them. It is folly to assign as officers men unfit for duty with American soldiers. . . .[30]

By December of 1901, with more than 2,000 men enlisted and inspectors at work in all but six provinces, the constabulary was approaching fifty per cent of its authorized level. Even with half of his force yet to be organized Allen was already so confident of success he predicted that two-thirds of the American troops in the Philippines could soon go home:

> In my opinion, 15,000 American soldiers will suffice for the Philippines one year from this date. This seems to many a radically small estimate, but . . . I am willing to stake my reputation on that number.[31]

Six months later Allen commanded 193 officers, 5,317 men, and a network of 202 constabulary posts. Over the next five years the size of his "army" varied according to the degree of threat to law and order and his political fortunes with the civil government and the army hierarchy in the Philippines, but it never totaled less than 5,000. The peak years of constabulary activity were from 1903 to 1905, and during this time its strength rose to an average of almost 300 officers and 6,900 men.[32]

As a quasi-military organization, the constabulary aroused a mixture of scorn, resentment, and amusement in the regular army. Here was a raw and untested native force presuming to take over part of the army's mission. Several years of successful campaigning by Allen's men eventually overcame most of this negative attitude,[33] but many difficulties were put in his way. An example of this was the matter of weapons for his troops. In 1901, 1,372 army rifles had been set aside for constabulary use, but the army objected to arming any Filipinos not under its direct supervision with weapons as good as its own for fear they would then fall into the wrong hands. General Chaffee explained his position to the Adjutant General in Washington:

> Great efforts have been made by my two predecessors to bring about a disarming of the people of these islands. . . . Even now it is self evident, that 50, 100, or 200 men, with hostile intent, armed with rifle or carbine, constitute a force that takes thousands of troops and months of time to overcome.[34]

There was perhaps some justification for Chaffee's reluctance until the constabulary had proved itself, but six years passed before it had adequate weapons. Initially, Allen's men had pistols or obsolete, single-shot, black-powder shotguns with which to fight guerrillas and bandits armed with high-powered, smokeless, repeating rifles captured from the Spanish or stolen from army warehouses where they lay in cosmoline preservative, unused. By 1902, most of the constabulary were armed with single-shot Springfield rifles having no bayonet. Allen kept agitating for something better by pointing to the many occasions when his men had been rushed at close quarters by superior numbers and had suffered needless casualties because they were practically unarmed after having fired their first shot. Not without continuing opposition from Chaffee's successors, the Ordnance Bureau in Washington finally agreed in 1906 to equip the constabulary with the six-shot Krag-Jörgensen rifle recently discarded by the army as its standard weapon.[35]

If the constabulary's weapons were a cause of friction, its "uniforms" were the source of much army amusement. They were supposed to be of native cloth, khaki in color but of a different shade than the army's, and with scarlet piping and distinctly different insignias of rank.[36] Allen devised this uniform and it was worn punctiliously around his headquarters, but out in the *pueblos* and *barrios,* far from a constabulary supply commissary, it was sometimes a different story. A detachment about to go out on patrol often looked very much like the outlaw band it was chasing. John R. White described his first command:

> . . . uniforms were . . . made by local tailors after a general pattern to suit personal preferences; leggins the *soldados* had none; some were shod and some went barefoot; some wore blue flannel shirts, others cañamo [linen] blouses; hats and caps were of various kinds. . . .
>
> . . . Ammunition was carried in pockets or homemade belts of light duck; haversacks, also homemade, were stuffed to overflowing with all sorts of non-uniform articles. Cooking utensils dangled from shoulders or belts; and in the latter, bolos were stuck with a rakish, brigandish effect. The one really uniform article of equipment was a scarlet blanket which each man carried in a roll over his shoulder. Altogether they looked as pretty a bunch of ladrones as could well be imagined and it was to be hoped that if we met any Regulars or Scouts they would see me first—otherwise they would surely open fire on my detachment.[37]

A typical constabulary mission by just such a rag-tag detachment as White's has been described by W. Cameron Forbes in his book, *The Philippine Islands.* Their enemy was "Captain" Yping and his bandit gang who had been plundering and terrorizing the natives in the rich lowlands of Negros from a stronghold in the mountains back of the town of Isabela. What follows is a paraphrase of Forbes's romantic account of an adventure.

The lieutenant inspects his men in front of the low, whitewashed constabulary headquarters, and out of the village they march, up a dusty road past cultivated fields and clusters of thatched huts. Soon the road becomes a path and then a trail as they enter the hush of the tropical forest. They will spend at least a week under the gloom of the jungle's dense canopy, out of contact with any source of help. After two days of following the trail as it winds up into the hills, they leave it and strike off cross-country. After another day of climbing they reach Yping's lair, a rocky cleft in a mountain peak. But before they can get close enough to open fire, a sentinel sees them and fires a warning shot. There is only one way to attack—straight ahead into the mouth of the canyon over a series of trenches. The constabulary is outnumbered, perhaps three to one, perhaps more, as they mix with the bandits in hand-to-hand combat. In a few minutes it is all over. Bodies sprawl grotesquely in the trenches. A wounded soldier lies dying from a musket wound in his chest, inflicted at point-blank range by Yping himself. But Yping lies beside him with a small blue hole in his forehead and the back of his head blown off. With his revolver, the lieutenant has saved the government the expense of a trial and execution.

Some of Yping's men have managed to escape in the melee, but without their loot. Back of the trenches are a dozen huts containing the accumulation of years of raiding. Here is a large mirror from a rich man's hacienda; there is a sack of pesos that not long ago represented the monthly earnings of a Chinese merchant. As the soldiers search the huts the pile grows higher; sacks of sugar, bolts of yard goods, jewelry, and, most importantly, the rifles and other weapons with which these bandits have terrorized the lowlanders.

The soldiers bury their dead and nurse the wounded. It is too late to start back that day, so the living enjoy Yping's posthumous hospitality. That night they roast his fattest pigs and chickens over a blazing fire and cook his corn and sweet potatoes in the embers. Songs, played on a captured guitar, are sung around the campfire, and each man brags about his part in the fight. The officer sits nearby, pleased with the day's work and hoping it has finally put a stop to brigandage in his part of the province. Sentinels are posted, and the rest of the detachment sleep on comfortable pallets in the huts. They start back at first light, burning everything left behind.

A week or so later a brief notice is printed in the Manila papers:

> Lieutenant —— and a detachment of twelve Constabulary met Yping's band in superior force in the mountains back of Isabela, killing seven bandits, including Yping, and capturing four rifles, two muskets with many bolos. Two Constabulary soldiers were killed and two wounded.[38]

Despite the heroics of Allen's men in hundreds of similar encounters, Allen himself was often a controversial and unpopular figure as

Chief of the Philippine Constabulary. His relatively liberal attitudes toward Filipinos, his actions and methods in organizing the constabulary, his belief in the workability of civil government, and his outspoken opposition to certain army policies, not to mention his overweening ambition, all cost Allen dearly, particularly among his army contemporaries and superiors. Perhaps most unforgivable in their eyes was his "disloyalty," as one of the army's own, to its own view of its proper role in the islands. Though Taft and Wright had no cause to complain of Allen's loyalty or even of his achievements, his methods sometimes annoyed them too.

In a real sense, the friction between the constabulary and the army was only a reflection of the mutual coolness between most army leaders in the Philippines and their counterparts in the civil government. General Chaffee may have been more circumspect about voicing his opinions than his predecessor, but for more than a year he and other senior officers in the Philippines shared MacArthur's doubts as to the wisdom of the early transfer to civilian rule.[39] For his part, Taft tended to underestimate many of the problems he faced, and sometimes airily dismissed army warnings about new insurgent build-ups and charges about the constabulary's failure to deal with them as attempts to undermine his administration.[40] Nevertheless, Taft and Chaffee were friends and respected each other; they merely saw the threat to internal stability with different eyes. The army was unhappy about its loss of total control of the islands, but if its appraisal of the continuing instability of the military situation was much more pessimistic than that of the civilians, it was also somewhat more accurate. On the other hand, the officials of the civil government had good cause to suspect self-serving motives behind the army's dire warnings and predictions. In addition, after President Roosevelt's Amnesty Proclamation officially declaring the end of the insurrection on July 4, 1902, they were doubtless under pressure from Washington to avoid any use of army troops that could be interpreted as an admission that the fires of insurrection still smoldered.[41]

Allen became the lightning rod for civil-military disputes on the subject of Philippine pacification. The wonder is that he came out of this highly charged situation with any friends at all, civilian or military. Whenever the constabulary got into difficulty, particularly in 1902–03 and again in 1905, there were calls for his head. That he stayed on until 1907 was an indication that, for all the controversy around him, his accomplishments were genuine.

Perhaps at the bottom of Allen's unpopularity in army circles were his attitudes toward Filipinos, individually and as a people. He had more confidence than most army officers in the native aptitude for self-government, although he felt some American supervision would be necessary until the general level of education could be raised and an experienced body of civil servants had been trained. All of this might take many years, but he did not doubt that eventually Filipinos could and should rule themselves. He urged self-rule at the municipal level as early as January, 1901, in his reports from Leyte.[42] Of the necessity for recognizing native aspirations, Allen wrote a close friend of Taft's a year later:

> . . . to arrive at the best method of administering . . . these islands, it is necessary to study the situation through Philippine eyes as well as through American eyes. After all, they have ambitions and aspirations which cannot be ruthlessly trampled on without costing us much blood and treasure . . . [and] that is not well understood out here.[43]

In an overly familiar "Dear Colonel" letter to President Roosevelt, two months after McKinley's assassination, Allen again emphasized his faith in Filipino political ability, adding only a word of caution about their flamboyant and emotional approach to politics. "They impress me as embryo politicians of the French style," he said; "at intriguing they are masters." In the same letter Allen apologized for his disrespect and never forgot his manners again with T.R.[44]

Allen may have been privately condescending about certain native tendencies, but he treated educated Filipinos of the upper class as his equals in every respect, mingling with them socially as both guest and host and corresponding with many native officials in a friendly and dignified way.[45] Nor was he too proud to be seen at native fiestas, rubbing shoulders with Filipinos of every class. On such occasions he often danced with the pretty, dark-skinned señoritas who spoke no English (and sometimes, not even Spanish). If his letters to Dora referred to these partners as "little Brownies,"[46] at least the epithet was milder than the one habitually used by many other Americans. As we have seen, Allen so disapproved of General "Jakey" Smith's long outburst about the "—— —— niggers" he reported it word for word to Taft, saying, "From this you have an idea of the man who is charged with the administration of military affairs on Leyte." In another letter to Taft more than two years later, Allen told him he wanted no "nigger haters" in the constabulary.[47] Allen's moderate racial views put him in the minority among the senior officers of his day.[48] And his related belief in Filipino ability for self-rule undercut army contentions that it should maintain a sizable force to keep order in the islands for years to come.[49] Although these issues may have been at the heart of many of Allen's differences with army leaders in the Philippines, they were not the immediate ones that brought him into direct confrontation with Major General Chaffee and his successors, Generals George W. Davis, James F. Wade, and Henry C. Corbin.

The first and most persistent issue on which Allen was at odds with the military has already been mentioned: the matter of better weapons for the constabulary. His position on another question, that of how many regular troops would be needed in the Philippines once the constabulary reached its full strength, endeared him even less to the army. In contrast to Allen's optimistic prediction in December of 1901 that only 15,000 regulars (plus 5,000 scouts and 5,000 constabulary) would be needed within a year, at least one officer, Major General Lloyd Wheaton, commanding the Department of North Philippines, gloomily estimated that 50,000 regulars should remain until at least 1906.[50] The actual figures for the end of 1902 were 22,000 regulars, 5,000 scouts, and 6,000 constabulary.[51] However, Allen's nearly accurate prophecy may have been self-fulfilling rather than a true reflection of the needs of the situation. Supremely confident of the future success of his new organization, he was telling his civilian superiors what they wanted to hear. Taft used Allen's figures and not the army's as the basis for his recommendations to the War Department as to how many troops should remain.[52]

Perhaps partly as a result of army hostility to the constabulary, Allen soon became convinced that some Americans in military and business circles did not want to see the civil government succeed. Naming names, he kept Taft informed of efforts by certain individuals in Manila (none of them of high rank) to discredit his regime.[53] As further proof, he sent Taft clippings of hostile articles in the *Army and Navy Journal,* the unofficial mouthpiece of the military establishment. Taft, who either took a less conspiratorial view of such criticism or had more confidence than Allen in Washington's support of his policies, returned one of these articles to him with the comment, "I am not greatly excited by the views of the *Army and Navy Journal.*" [54]

The solution to the friction between the military and civilian representatives of the American government in the Philippines was, in Allen's opinion, the subordination of the military to the civilians. To Senator Albert J. Beveridge he wrote:

. . . knowing the genius and traditions of the American people and its utter indisposition to stand for a Military Government for any length of time I am prepared to say that the Chief Executive of these islands should be the head of the government, both Civil and Military.[55]

One of the factors that may have influenced Allen to make this recommendation was his desire to put the army's scouts to better use under his own command. When it became apparent the army would not be subordinated to the civil government in the Philippines. Allen went about getting control of the scouts more directly. In the spring of 1902 he proposed putting them under the command of the chief of the constabulary. Six months later, he went so far as to write a memorandum outlining the features of the legislation necessary to enact this proposal into law and submitted it to both Vice-Governor Wright and Adjutant General Corbin.[56]

Allen's arguments were logical and politically expedient. The constabulary might need help and it would be less expensive and politically explosive to furnish it with a maximum of native troops and a minimum of American. Besides, since native troops had no problems with the language and knew the local customs and terrain, they were better at tracking down ladrones. Finally, since the constabulary was specifically organized for this kind of work, it could use the scout companies more efficiently than if the army tried to do the same thing.[57] General Chaffee objected to this idea, but Luke Wright, Acting Civil Governor while the ailing Taft took a seven-months' leave of absence, agreed with Allen's logic.[58] The Philippine Commission asked the War Department to request the necessary legislation from Congress. Further, to overcome army objections to turning command of the scouts over to a junior army officer, the commission proposed that the chief of constabulary be made a brigadier general.[59]

In the fall of 1902, while army leaders contemplated having to swallow this bitter pill, the constabulary began to run into embarrassing difficulties. Following President Roosevelt's amnesty proclamation, most army units withdrew from active campaigning and sat back in their garrisons to watch the constabulary take over responsibility for maintaining law and order. Except on Mindanao against the recalcitrant Moros, no American soldier fired a shot in combat for the next seven months.[60] Despite Allen's earlier confidence, coping with banditry everywhere at once was too much for his men to handle. There were renewed outbreaks of lawlessness and ladronism in almost every province, and particularly serious incidents around Manila and on Leyte.[61] Always the optimist and fiercely proud of his little brown soldiers, Allen kept insisting they couldn't "chin it" if given enough time and support.[62] The Philippine Commission increased the constabulary's authorized strength by more than 1,500, but Allen needed more help than that.

The "Scout Law," as Allen's proposal to combine the scouts and constabulary became known, was one answer to the problem, since it would immediately add 5,000 troops to his command. But some in the army saw other solutions more to their liking. Either the civil government should admit its inability to keep the peace in the Philippines and call out the regulars in strength to do the job or, alternatively, put an officer in command of the constabulary tough enough to do what Allen had allegedly failed to do. In its issue of November 15, 1902, the *Army and Navy Journal* hinted strongly at the first solution in an article critical of the constabulary's failure to stop ladronism around Manila.[63] When the Scout Law seemed certain of passage (albeit with modifications in the army's favor), the second argument surfaced. Since the civil governor would have to go through the formality of nominating an officer to assume the newly created rank of Brigadier General and Chief of Constabulary, the English-language *Manila American* and its Spanish echo, *El Renacimiento,* demanded a replacement for Allen. Their man would assure "the immediate and effective extinction of banditry and . . . the conservation of peace." He was Major Edwin F. Glenn of the 5th Infantry. The *Renacimiento* went on to say of his "nomination":

> [It gave] all Americans . . . great satisfaction . . . because they have confidence in the integrity, aptitude and courage of Glenn, who unquestionably combines, more than any other officer in the Army, the qualities necessary to command the constabulary.[64]

That Glenn was already under charges and soon to be court-martialled and convicted of administering the "water cure" on Samar in 1901 speaks volumes about what kind of a constabulary his backers wanted, although it is impossible now to tell how highly placed they were or how seriously they pushed Glenn's "candidacy."[65]

On January 30, 1903, Congress passed the Scout Law. It authorized the temporary assignment of scout companies to the constabulary "when detailed for that purpose by the commanding general upon the request of the civil governor." The act further stipulated that such units were "to be under the command for tactical purposes of the chief and assistant chiefs of the Philippine Constabulary, who are officers of the United States Army." [66] Despite a partial army victory in blocking the permanent transfer of all scouts to Allen's command, the provisions of the measure still rankled. Chaffee's successor in Manila, General George W. Davis, complained indignantly about the "political considerations" that would prevent his officers from leading into action "the troops of their command whom they had organized, instructed for years, brought to a high state of efficiency, and whose material wants, under other leadership, they must still supply." [67]

Secretary of Commerce and Police Luke E. Wright answered General Davis in his next annual report by calmly restating all of Allen's original arguments and pointing out that, since the Scout Law conferred "the rank of brigadier general and colonel, respectively, to the chief and assistant chiefs of the constabulary," a temporary detail of Philippine scouts for service under these constabulary officers when the public interest demanded it was in no way a reflection on General Davis and his subordinates. To Wright, it was "simply a temporary transfer of command from one Regular Army officer to another." [68]

So Allen had his general's star at last. But it was a somewhat hollow triumph. By stipulation of the Scout Law the rank went with the position he held and not permanently to him. Nevertheless, for more than four years he relished the power and prestige that came with the star. At times until mid-1905, he commanded as many as thirty-five of the army's fifty scout companies and never less than half of them.[69] This gave him a force of over 10,000 men, almost two-thirds as many soldiers as the two-star army commander of the Division of the Philippines. In addition, instead of sitting idly in garrison like most of their army counterparts, Allen's troops were a fighting force and a good one. With the help of the scouts, the constabulary gradually managed to suppress disorder in most of the areas that had been threatened in the fall of 1902. From 1903 to early 1905, white troops were employed only five times at the request of the civil government, always for relatively short periods of time, and in no more than battalion strength.[70] Except for Mindanao, the pacification of the Philippines was now almost completely Allen's show.

And how he enjoyed life! He and Dora and the children lived in a cool and spacious four-bedroom house in Manila's suburbs with a stable in back and surrounded by "a fine garden filled with tropical plants." They had two Chinese cooks, a staff of servants, and a carriage with footmen. In the evenings when cooler breezes came in from the bay, Allen would put on his best white uniform and take the family

Chief of Philippine Constabulary. (Photograph courtesy of Col. Henry T. Allen, Jr.)

for a drive along the Lunetta, Manila's waterfront equivalent of New York's fashionable Fifth Avenue.[71] All of the other American and native elite of Manila society were there too, the men nodding gravely to each other and the women and children smiling and waving. When the Manila heat grew too unbearable, the family could always retreat to their cottage next door to the Tafts at the American "summer colony" in the mountains at Baguio. Jeanette, then fifteen, Harry, fourteen, and Dasha, eleven, were especially enchanted with the trinkets, pet monkeys and birds their father brought them from his travels on inspection trips all over the islands. For two years Dora enjoyed the Philippines as much as her children, but in 1903 she contracted a painful skin disease after an operation and had to spend months in bed.[72]

As long as Allen's health continued good he was willing to stay in the tropics, but the vindication of his promotion had left a bittersweet aftertaste. Growing tired of fighting friend and foe alike and feeling he had finally placed the constabulary in a strong position, he began to look around for a less controversial job. If possible he wanted an assignment that would convert his temporary general's star into a permanent one.

In June, 1903, he wrote the President and asked for the governorship of the newly created Moro Province on Mindanao,[73] but the job was given to Major General Leonard Wood, who already commanded the troops on the island. Believing Wood's tour as military governor would be temporary (it was not; he stayed three years), Allen then asked to succeed him, with the permanent regular army rank of brigadier general. This time, instead of a direct approach, he went back to his old tactic of writing influential friends and asking them to write the President. One who did so was Andrew D. White. Roosevelt sent White's letter asking this favor for Allen to the Army Chief of Staff, Lieutenant General Samuel B. M. Young, for comment. General Young's objections to the proposal may be taken as a compendium of the attitudes of most senior officers about Henry T. Allen, Brigadier General and Chief of Constabulary (Captain, U.S. Army).

Young insisted that the dual position of Governor of the Moro Province and Commanding General of the Department of Mindanao was in "every sense an appropriate command for a Major General." He could not bring himself "to the view that an officer of the subordinate rank of captain, . . . even though holding the temporary grade of brigadier general, should be assigned thereto." He went on to say that Allen's rank had been "specially conferred" by Act of Congress to promote the "efficiency and development" of the constabulary, and that to use that rank as "the basis of an assignment to other and different duties would be in violation of the spirit if not the letter of . . . the legislation." Further, Young was positive there were many other officers senior to Allen whose qualifications for the position equaled those "it is claimed he possesses." "To pass them over," said the Chief of Staff, "in favor of an officer of subordinate rank . . . would be construed as a reflection upon them . . . and prove detrimental to the best interests of the service." [74]

Even before General Young sent this answer to the President, he received a different request directly from Allen, asking for permission to travel to Korea, Manchuria, and China that fall as an official observer in the "advent of troubles in that region." As if to convince Roosevelt that Allen was nothing but a restless malcontent, Young added a paragraph about this request to his comments on White's letter and concluded with: "I replied . . . that he should remain in his present assignment as Chief of Constabulary, for the performance of the important duties of which he was given a special rank." [75]

Doubtless to Young's further annoyance, Allen simply requested leave from his duties in the Philippines and managed to be on the Asian mainland anyway when the "troubles in that region" began. Having put the children and the still-ailing Dora on a ship for home, he landed at Chemlupo, Korea, on February 8, 1904, the day the Russo-Japanese War began. After an exchange of telegrams between Seoul, Washington, and Manila, he then succeeded in having himself appointed attaché to the legation in Seoul for a period of three months with the status of an official observer in the war.[76]

To his great disappointment, he did not manage to see very much. The Japanese refused to permit any foreign military observers to have a close look at what was going on at the front and were especially suspicious of Allen because of his knowledge of Russian and acquaintance with some of the generals on the other side. In addition, a permanent team of ten American military observers, including Captain John J. Pershing, soon arrived on the scene. On April 1, Allen received a telegram from Manila ordering him to return. Although he had prepared numerous reports for inclusion in the dispatches of the U.S. Minister in Seoul and had also written others for Taft, Secretary of War since his return from the Philippines that January, Allen accomplished little in his two months in Korea.[77] And, in the meantime, a constabulary detachment stationed at Vigan on northern Luzon had mutinied.

A bandit leader and ex-*insurrecto* named Artemio Ricarte (known as "The Viper") instigated the mutiny. One of his officers in the days of the rebellion was a man named Nicolas Calvo, who had since become a constabulary private. Ricarte sent Calvo a letter suggesting he and his friends at Vigan might find banditry more rewarding than life in the constabulary. Calvo showed this letter to several friends, and together they began to work on their comrades to join the conspiracy. On the night of February 7, 1904, they shot up the town, stole all the guns, supplies, and money they could carry, freed the prisoners in the local jail and disappeared into the hills. A quickly assembled force of constabulary, scouts, and regular army cavalry pursued them. Within a week all but three of the renegades had surrendered or been captured. Calvo and two other ringleaders were sentenced to death by a Filipino court, and twelve others got forty years in prison.[78]

The Vigan mutiny was an isolated incident, but it provided more ammunition for detractors of the constabulary, who had warned all along that it would turn out to be undisciplined and unreliable. Perhaps inevitably, in view of the speed with which Allen had put his force together, there had been complaints against constabulary enlisted men for corruption, mistreatment of native civilians, and other misdemeanors. Allen saw to it each charge was carefully investigated, and punishment, when justified, was swift and severe. Frequently, however, the allegations proved to be false, trumped up by elements among the population in league with one gang of ladrones or another, or by Filipino businessmen whose smuggling operations and other illegal activities were threatened by constabulary vigilance.[79] Overall, the constabulary's disciplinary record was, in fact, excellent. A better measure of the high average quality of Allen's native soldiers than the well-publicized escapades of a few of them was the constabulary's desertion rate. During Allen's six years as chief it averaged only seven-tenths of one per cent, nine times lower than the army rate for the same period.[80]

It was a similar story with Allen's officers. In the first year he had weeded out most of the few obviously weak and unstable ones who got past his initial interview, but not before some of them had given the constabulary a bad name, at least among those who were waiting to say, "I told you so." In addition, after August, 1902, Allen required all his officers to pass a rigorous examination, similar to the army's promotion tests, to prove their professional qualifications.[81] Nevertheless, he continued to be embarrassed occasionally by the actions of some misfit.

The most painful such incident happened in 1904. A captain and a lieutenant, both awaiting trial for previous acts of misconduct, absconded with several thousand pesos in constabulary funds and tried to flee the islands in a commandeered boat. Forced at gunpoint to sail into a severe tropical storm, the unwilling native crew took their revenge when one officer dozed off while on guard over his sleeping comrade. They rushed the pair, killing the lieutenant and severely wounding the captain before he could reach for his revolver. Moments later, four natives lay dead on the deck, and the rest of the crew had jumped overboard. Alone in the storm, the captain managed to beach the craft on the nearest island, bury the stolen money, and take off into the hills. He was soon captured by a constabulary patrol, tried, and sentenced to seventeen years in prison.[82]

By 1904, in spite of the full-time assistance of more than 3,000 scouts, and part-time help from the rest of the army, the constabulary still had not completely pacified its areas of responsibility. Grumbling and complaints of the late-1902 variety began to be heard again. Cavite Province on Luzon and the islands of Leyte and Samar were Allen's major remaining headaches. As always, he insisted his troops could do the job, given enough time and support. He managed to hang on to responsibility for Cavite and Leyte, but "Bloody Samar" was another matter.[83]

Samar was taken over by the constabulary in mid-1902 after General Smith had revenged Balangiga and Lucban had been captured. After that, one of Lucban's former officers, "Pope" Pablo by name, quietly began to raise another army in the interior. Using his impressive title, and freely handing out *antingantings* (magic charms) to guarantee invincibility and immortality, he recruited his followers, called *pulajanes*, from the ignorant hill people of the island. Pablo motivated his men with a combination of mystical fanaticism and down-to-earth economic grievances. They were to avenge themselves on the unbelieving lowlanders and the heathen Americans, who were allegedly cheating them by paying low prices for their crops and selling them at a huge profit.[84] For two years Pablo bided his time, making only a few small raids to get weapons and other supplies. Constabulary patrols sent to the interior to eliminate the source of these annoyances found nothing. In the spring of 1904, after he had been joined by another ex-insurgent leader, Enrique Dagohob, Pablo was ready.

The first sign of the trouble to come had been an attack on a constabulary patrol in February. In that action 500 of Pablo's *pulajanes* killed the American patrol leader and several soldiers and captured their rifles. In July and August, Dagohob's and Pablo's forces swept out of the mountains in northern Samar and began burning villages and killing natives who would not join their movement. Several more detachments of scouts and constabulary were hit and nearly wiped out. In August, Allen sent Captain Cary Crockett to Samar with a company of reinforcements. It was not enough.[85] The civil government adopted a policy of reconcentration in the most threatened region and set up two large camps for the population at Catbalogan and in the Gandara Valley. Thereafter, any native found outside of these camps was considered a *pulajan.* Simultaneously, more reinforcements came in. By late fall, Captain Alexander L. Dade, Allen's ranking subordinate on the island, commanded a force of over 1,900 constabulary and scouts. Still, the *pulajanes* kept overrunning isolated posts and making off with large numbers of rifles and quantities of ammunition. Each success enhanced their prestige and increased Dade's problems in obtaining co-operation and information from the rest of the population.[86] Allen could not reinforce him further for fear of weakening the security of other areas.

Pressure to "clean up Samar" began to build on Governor Wright. Having just denied charges concerning the bad state of affairs in the Philippines, including a statement that "whole districts are in the hands of ladrones," by Roosevelt's Democratic opponent for the presidency, Alton B. Parker, Wright may have hesitated to request large-scale army assistance because of the possible political repercussions at home.[87] However, in December, with Roosevelt safely re-elected, Wright took a cautious first step toward using the army on Samar. In a telegram to Allen he implied it might be desirable to have the army garrison some of the island's larger towns, thus freeing more constabulary and scouts to scour the interior.

Allen had recently taken personal command of all his forces on Samar, and he could see for himself the wisdom of such a step. On December 31, he requested enough American soldiers to garrison four towns. Using the several thousand native troops under his own command he planned to set up new garrisons deep in the interior and conduct operations between these points and the coastal areas.[88] These tactics resulted in many hot and weary chases but few engagements, none of them decisive. The army began to assist in an unobtrusive way. In mid-February, a battalion of infantry regulars supposedly on a mapping expedition "happened" to link up in the Gandara Valley with a force of several hundred constabulary and scouts led by Allen. Together they searched for the 2,000 *pulajanes* reported entrenched in the area. They found nothing, yet small patrols over the same ground invariably encountered an ambush.[89] That same month a newspaper correspondent from Manila wrote:

> There is no law in Samar today—beyond the will of the pulajanes. The American authority extends as far as the sentinels around the few military posts and no further. Outside, all is anarchy and bloodshed. There is no question of putting down an outbreak but rather one of reconquering the greater part of the island.[90]

Two weeks later Allen accompanied Crockett on an expedition to the northeast coast of Samar. With about 200 scouts and constabulary they landed at Gamay Bay and pushed inland toward a *pulajan* fortress, several hours' march away. After a little more than an hour, the head of the column walked into a trap. Hundreds of bolomen rose out of the tall grass on both sides of the trail and charged, screaming "*tad, tad*" (hack to pieces). Crockett, in the lead, was immediately wounded in the arm, but managed to keep control of his men and direct the fire of their single-shot Springfield rifles. Most of them had no time to reload before the bolomen were in their midst, swinging their long blades with deadly effect. Fortunately, a few of the constabulary had repeating-action riot guns, and their extra firepower was decisive. Not far behind Crockett stood Allen, silver stars glinting on the high collar of his dress uniform. As the bolo rush swept toward him, he "got into it with both feet" and his "pumping Winchester also" and killed three *pulajan* officers, easily identified by their gaudy costumes. Leaderless, the bolomen fled. Leaving a small party to tend the wounded, Allen and Crockett continued on to their objective only to find the *pulajanes* had evacuated and destroyed it.[91]

March, April, and May went by with more of the same kind of fighting and no end in sight. In April, the civil government put a new governor on Samar with authority to command all troops on the island,[92] but problems of control and divided responsibility for field operations continued to create friction between the army and the constabulary. This and Allen's reluctant recognition of the impossibility of rapid suppression of the *pulajanes* with his own forces finally led him to request through Governor Wright that the army take full responsibility for the more turbulent eastern half of the island.[93]

Since the previous November the senior army commander in the Philippines had been Major General Henry C. Corbin, once Allen's "friend" in the Adjutant General's Office. Corbin had been increasingly doubtful of Allen's ability to handle the uprising on Samar,[94] and it no doubt gave him great satisfaction to order Brigadier General William H. Carter, commander of the Department of the Visayas, to take charge of all troops in the island's eastern zone. Having to ask for help was a blow to Allen's pride. He betrayed his bitterness in a letter to Wright on Corbin's and Carter's prospects for success:

> Carter now has a free hand in East Samar; let us see the speed with which he captures leaders and guns. . . . He will now be given a fair chance to learn that capturing and running down criminal bands in Samar requires time and is more difficult than criticism.[95]

Within a week, however, an army expedition in northeastern Samar carried off a surprise attack on one of Dagohob's camps, killing him and ninety of his followers. Another high ranking *pulajan* officer, Antonio Anugar, was killed in August, leaving only "Pope" Pablo among the well-known leaders to rally the movement. Once again Pablo disappeared from sight to try to rebuild his forces, but most of his followers had lost their original enthusiasm. There were sporadic outbreaks of *pulajan* activity on Samar over the next few years, including the massacre of most of a constabulary detachment in March of 1906, but, when Pablo was killed eight months after that incident, the army's work was almost finished. In June, 1907, two years after giving it up, the constabulary reassumed full responsibility for law and order on Samar. Seven thousand *pulajanes* had been killed in the meantime.[96] Although only a few small bands remained, it took the constabulary another four years to track them all down, not for lack of trying but because of Samar's difficult and forbidding terrain.

When the army had to come to Allen's rescue on Samar, criticism of the constabulary by both Americans and Filipinos reached another peak and took on the appearance of an organized campaign. "Philippine Constabulary a Failure," headlined the *Army and Navy Journal.* Similar hostile articles appeared almost simultaneously in several Manila papers. All the old charges and arguments were revived: the constabulary was inefficient, undisciplined, riddled with undesirables, too easy on the native criminal element, and ought to be disbanded.[97] Clearly, the army felt it could do the job better. Allen said as much in his annual report for 1905, adding several other reasons for the constabulary's unpopularity. Among these were "the desire of certain Filipino elements to have the constabulary put under the provincial governors, the . . . earnest wish of those who are desirous of cutting down insular expenses; and above all, the general plan . . . by Manila politicians to depreciate the government." [98]

Though he had no real proof, Allen suspected that the newspaper attacks were directed against him personally as much as against the organization he commanded and that General Corbin was behind this campaign, at least on the American side.[99] Since it appears Corbin had long regarded Allen as an overly ambitious upstart, there may have been some basis for his suspicions. Nevertheless, from Corbin's perspective there was a simpler way of solving the army-constabulary feud than by firing Allen or disbanding his forces. "It would be in the line of greater efficiency, harmony and economy," he wrote in his own annual report for 1905, "if the division commander [himself] were a member of the [Philippine] Commission. . . . This would put all military forces—army, scouts, and constabulary—under one directing head, and result in more unison of action than has at times happened." [100]

In the fall of 1905, in the aftermath of the Samar debacle, the constabulary was reorganized and cut in strength from more than 7,000 to just over 5,000 men. Much to the army's satisfaction, all the scouts were put back under its control, although Washington ignored General Corbin's more far-reaching proposals.[101] Allen stayed in Manila long enough to oversee the beginning of the reorganization and then, during the painful process of carrying it out, left for the United States on a long and well-deserved leave. He had not seen Dora and the children for almost two years. Except for a brief trip to Japan with them in the summer of 1902 and his few months in Korea in 1904, he had not been away from his duties in the Philippines for five years.

While home he divided his time between visiting with the family, seeing his brothers and sisters, checking on business investments in Kentucky, and looking after his interests in Washington.[102] In that city he succeeded in accomplishing at least one of his objectives, obtaining an appointment to West Point for his son. If Harry passed the entrance examinations he would enter the academy in 1909. Allen also tried again to have his general's rank made permanent, but, despite several talks with Taft and Roosevelt, he could get nothing out of them except hints it was time he thought about giving up the constabulary and vague assurances that his permanent promotion would be considered in due course.[103] With his future status still unsettled, Allen returned to Manila in June, 1906, nine months after he had left.

In the fall he took the examination for promotion to regular army major and passed it, but the prospect of having to revert to that rank instead of captain was small satisfaction. Rather than face the humiliation he began to consider retirement.[104] His pride soon received another blow. Taft wrote that he would be relieved in the Philippines the following spring and assigned to command the detail of troops in Yellowstone Park.[105] To go from the command of as many as 10,000 soldiers and the responsibility for law and order in almost 100,000 square miles of the Philippines to directing two troops of cavalry, perhaps 100 men, in a 3,300-square-mile tourist attraction in a remote corner of the United States was quite a comedown. Allen decided to make one last effort to keep his general's star.

He wrote to Major General J. Franklin Bell, the newly appointed Chief of Staff of the Army. Allen considered Bell an old friend. They had served together in Cuba and in the early years in the Philippines. Bell was familiar with Allen's work, both on Leyte with the 43rd Infantry and as Chief of Constabulary. He said to Bell, "I have always refrained from talking with you about my personal advancement, but I am going to do it now in the hope that you will consider the matter in an entirely judicial way, leaving friendship entirely aside." Then he asked:

> Has the work required in the organization and administration of the Constabulary been sufficient to demonstrate that the head of it has the capacity necessary in a general officer, and have the results been of sufficient importance and magnitude . . . to justify the President and Secretary before the country and the Army in giving the head of the organization special recognition?
>
> Now Bell, please consider well this matter, and give me fully your views—just as though you were not Chief of Staff.[106]

Before giving Allen a reply, Bell undoubtedly summarized in his own mind the record on which Allen based his plea. He knew why Allen had often been controversial and unpopular as head of the constabulary. But, if he had been ambitious, he had never been unprincipled, and he had fought for what he sincerely believed was right. Although Allen's ambition, or more charitably, his overoptimism, had led him to attempt more with the constabulary than it was at times capable of, no one could deny his organization had been an overall success. Beginning in late 1901, it had progressively taken over the burden of the fighting from the army. Despite the setbacks requiring further army help, the constabulary had accomplished its primary mission: to bring domestic stability to the Philippines once the backbone of the insurrection was broken. A few simple statistics illustrate the army's declining role and the magnitude of the constabulary's achievement.

Deaths in Action vs. Average Strength [107]

	U.S. Army		Constabulary	
Time Period	Avg. Strength	Deaths	Avg. Strength	Deaths
1898	14,000	27	0 (until mid-1901)	0
1899–1901	51,000	752	2,600 (end 1901)	6
1902–1906	17,000	239	6,400	971

During the first six years of its existence, while suffering nearly 1,000 casualties, the constabulary was responsible for the deaths of 3,153 *insurrectos* and ladrones and the capture or surrender of 10,755 more, along with 5,341 firearms.[108] However, the constabulary had been much more than simply a force of bandit fighters. Its other contributions in bringing peace and stability to the Philippines need to be mentioned to round out the picture of its accomplishments. General Bell was certainly aware of these, too.

The constabulary's more routine police duties included collecting intelligence information, furnishing escorts to civilian officials in dangerous areas, guarding jails, escorting prisoners, and patrolling highways and back-country districts. Any job that required small parties of armed men intimately acquainted with local conditions was the constabulary's assignment. Its responsibilities for supervision of the municipal police have already been noted. Frequent inspections by constabulary officers did much to improve their efficiency, honesty, and treatment of their fellow Filipinos. In those early years the constabulary performed service on behalf of almost every other branch of the civil government as well. Throughout the islands it maintained supply stores open to all Americans serving in any official capacity, military or civilian. In 1902, it took over the insular telegraph and telephone service from the army, trained native operators, expanded the number of lines, and ran the whole system until 1906, when the Bureau of Posts assumed charge of it. The constabulary was also responsible for the control and regulation of firearms in the hands of civilians. It established a medical service that treated its own personnel, prisoners, and civilians alike, and assisted the Bureau of Health and Agriculture in enforcing quarantines and combating epidemics. Finally, the constabulary succeeded in suppressing the practice of head-hunting among the primitive peoples of northern Luzon. It did all these things at no expense to the American taxpayer. Insular revenues paid the $250 annual cost of each constabulary soldier; the Federal Government spent four times that amount on his American counterpart stationed in the islands.[109] More than any other man, Allen deserved the credit for this impressive list of accomplishments.

Nevertheless, Allen could not have picked a worse time to ask for special consideration. Just four months earlier John J. Pershing had been jumped from captain to general-officer rank following his brilliant campaign against the Lake Lanao Moros on Mindanao. Precedents existed for such a disregard of rank and seniority in the promotions of both Bell himself and Leonard Wood under similar circumstances back in 1901, but that was at the height of the insurrection. Coming five years later, Pershing's promotion caused a much greater furor in army circles, and, because his father-in-law was Chairman of the Senate Military Affairs Committee, there were inevitable charges of influence.[110]

In February, 1907, General Bell answered Allen's letter and began by saying he had sounded out the Secretary of War on the subject of Allen's promotion. Taft had "not the slightest intention" of promoting him, said Bell, nor in his own opinion did Allen deserve such recognition:

> . . . although many men have been appointed brigadier general with less excuse I cannot bring myself to recommend your appointment, for the simple reason that I am opposed to the appointment of men as young as yourself. . . . [Allen was then forty-seven. Bell had been promoted to brigadier general at the age of forty-five.]
>
> . . . a desire to tell the truth would entirely preclude my throwing any bouquets to you based on any spirit of cooperation which you ever displayed in my work in the Islands. It is impossible for me to forget the embarrassment caused my operations in Batangas and Laguna by your failure to permit my cooperation with you in Cavite and by your permitting . . . Wright to kick me so unceremoniously out of Tayabas before my operations were completed there.

Bell went on to mention as another old grievance Allen's failure to discipline a subordinate after having promised him he would do so. Then he added:

> . . . I several times tried to give you some good advice . . . but my advice always dropped off you like water off a duck's back. . . . I finally came to a conclusion, which I have never since found reason for modifying, namely, that your hide was too thick to be pierced by advice from your friends.

. . . I shall always be willing to do anything I reasonably can for you . . . but the army does not consider [what you ask] is right and reasonable. . . . Whether rightly or wrongly army officers as a rule consider that you have been fortunate, not unfortunate. . . . I have been very frank, but I am not inspired by unfriendliness. I have a kind of feeling that if I had expressed myself less frankly you would never be able to realize that I mean what I say.[111]

Allen could hardly believe his eyes. Stiffly, he thanked Bell for his "brutally frank" reply and then defended the actions Bell objected to by saying he had merely been following the orders of his civilian superiors. He denied that army sentiment opposed his promotion; he knew at least a dozen senior officers who were in favor of it, including Leonard Wood. Allen closed with a protestation of friendship and admiration:

Why in the name of God should I have wanted to thwart a man whom I specially liked and admired? . . . If you keep up that feeling which I again assure [you] is wrongly founded, I shall certainly believe that you are vindictive.[112]

Bell's answer to this contained some phrases which should have sounded hauntingly familiar to Allen, but probably did not. Nineteen years before he had used almost the same words in a letter to Dora complaining about the faults of her family.[113] Bell said to him now:

I never cherish resentment, . . . and when you reach a state of mind enabling you to recognize wherein you have failed to show me that consideration which was due, and acknowledge it, I am perfectly positive that any grievance on that account will have entirely disappeared.

I have at least one consolation . . . in knowing that I have succeeded at last in arousing you to an appreciation that there is some virtue in giving consideration to what effect your own acts may have upon the feelings of your friends and comrades.[114]

Thus, Allen's last hope for permanent recognition for his magnificent achievements in the Philippines foundered on the rock of a personal relationship gone sour. With Bell on his side, Allen might have persuaded the amiable Taft to change his mind; with Bell an enemy, Allen's cause was hopeless. Convinced of his own rightness and intent on going his own way, he had been too blind to the feelings of others, forgetting that these, as well as his undeniable accomplishments, might have a future bearing on his career. Even with Bell's long-nursed grudge out in the open, Allen made no attempt to apologize. Those who knew him well could not have been surprised at such arrogance and pride. As a brigadier general he had had far more opportunities to display these qualities than as a captain or lieutenant. General officers are not expected to be meek and humble, but even a little humility was not in Allen's make-up. Unfortunately for him, within a few weeks after he left the Philippines on April 15, 1907, he took off his general's star.[115] The next ten years of his career were a struggle to get it back.

CHAPTER VII

Promotion's Very Slow

As a rule the sense of justice, fair play and right to equal opportunities is . . . strongly developed in the American. . . . The army is no exception to this rule. [But:]

Do young men selecting the army as a career enjoy *a right to equal opportunity* on a parity with those who go into . . . other professions or business where advancement depends almost solely on individual efforts and merit?

Is it *fair play* to yoke vigorous, wholesome specimens of manhood with the weak and non-progressive and say that, regardless of qualifications and endeavors, their advancement must be pace and pace?

Is it *justice* to men who possess superior attainments and who distinguish themselves in their chosen work to refuse them such recognition as would be their right in other walks of life?

And finally is it a good business procedure for the Government to tolerate a system wherein such restrictions obtain? [1]

The continuing frustrations of Allen's ambitions that had earlier prompted this attack on the system of promotion by seniority (which he called "promotion by senility" among his friends), did not prevent him from thoroughly enjoying his last weeks as a brigadier general on the transport home from the Philippines. Sleeping in the best stateroom aboard and dining at the captain's table, he noted with amusement an old cavalry colonel's resentment and confusion at not knowing whether to address him as "general" or "major." In the ship's library Allen found plenty of books to suit his tastes: J. R. Seeley's *Expansion of England, England in Egypt* by G. M. Towle, plus six other works (in three languages) dealing with British, French, and American colonial policy or military strategy and tactics. After a pleasant, restful month spent catching up on his reading, playing bridge, and writing a short piece for the *Cavalry Journal* on the need for a chief of cavalry, he landed in San Francisco.[2]

Nine days later, on May 24, 1907, Allen was reunited with his family in Washington. In the next two weeks he paid calls on Chief of Staff Bell, Secretary of War Taft, and President Roosevelt. The first session with the irascible Bell ended in a "scrap" as soon as Allen brought up the sore subject of their previous correspondence. There was no moving Bell. Allen was now a major. His detail in command of the troops in Yellowstone National Park was set. His comment on the Chief of Staff, made shortly thereafter, may not have been entirely unbiased: "Bell fails to impress as a man of breadth of vision or sufficiently even temperament for his position." The meeting with Taft was friendlier but no less disappointing. When Allen hinted he would like to be appointed Park Superintendent also, Taft told him the Interior Department had just selected retired Army Chief of Staff Samuel B. M. Young to fill the position. Allen asked if he could remain in the East long enough to see Jeanette graduate from high school in Connecticut. Taft readily consented to this. Perhaps as a gesture to Allen's damaged pride, he also agreed to let him wear his general's star until he reported to Fort Yellowstone on July 1, although officially he had already been a major for more than a month.

During the interview with Roosevelt, Allen made no mention of his shattered hopes for promotion. Instead he gave the President an informal report on conditions in the Philippines and the status of the constabulary. They talked of the growing Japanese threat to American interests in the islands and of their mutual admiration of Leonard Wood, then commanding in Manila. Roosevelt said he would like to see the Philippines granted independence in five or six years. On that optimistic but impersonal note the meeting ended.[3] Having completed his last duty as Chief of Constabulary, Allen left the White House to prepare for the trip that would take him back to obscurity.

On June 26, the Allen family set out from Washington for Fort Yellowstone. Three days later, as the train rattled past Fort Keogh, memories of a similar ride almost twenty-four years earlier in the first days of their courtship surrounded Henry and Dora. At Gardiner, Montana, on the northern edge of the park, they watched the crates containing most of their twenty-year accumulation of household treasures being transferred from the baggage car to a waiting line of army wagons. Then, climbing aboard a stagecoach, they headed into the park toward more old memories.[4] The scenery was just as beautiful and awesome as they remembered, and the ride perhaps a little smoother, but the army post that was to be their new home had not existed in 1883.

Five miles up the road from the station, Fort Yellowstone sat on a sheltered plateau adjacent to the Mammoth Hot Springs at an elevation of about six thousand feet. The post had been built in 1891 to replace the dilapidated temporary buildings hastily thrown up nearby in 1886, when the army first began to patrol the park. As the stagecoach neared the post, the Allens had a glimpse of their quarters, an enormous two-story, sixteen-room frame house. Three others like it made up the "officers' row." Four sets of much smaller noncommissioned officers' quarters, two troop barracks, a headquarters, hospital, guardhouse, and the usual stables and storerooms were clustered among the pine trees on one side of the parade ground.[5] Diagonally opposite the post, across the parade ground and the main road that ran along the edge of the tiny reservation, stood the same posh tourist hotel, the Mammoth, where Henry and Dora had stayed during their first visit to the park. There they stayed again until their quarters were vacated by Henry's predecessor. While they waited for him to leave, Allen took his three children on a horseback tour of the park.[6] On July 14, 1907, he assumed command of the four cavalry troops then at Fort Yellowstone and the five officers and 129 men present for duty.[7]

The day after his arrival, Allen had a conference with General Young, the new park superintendent.[8] Their talk was doubtless brief and formal, given the coolness between them stemming from Allen's earlier attempts to have himself promoted while Young had been Chief of Staff.[9] Young may have wanted to define their official relationship and see that Allen understood his own responsibilities and the duties of his men.

As superintendent, Young was the senior government official at Yellowstone and responsible for the park's upkeep and protection. Since 1886, however, the War Department had provided the Interior Department with one or more troops of cavalry to assist in the latter task. In fact, from that date until Young became superintendent in May, 1907, each successive commander of these soldiers had also been acting superintendent of the park, no civilian officials having been appointed to fill the post during those years. Young had held both positions himself in 1897 as a colonel in the 3rd Cavalry.[10]

From June through September, when the hotels were open and transportation services running, the soldiers had the job of protecting the natural wonders of the park from acts of vandalism by initial-

Fort Yellowstone, *ca.* 1897. (Signal Corps Photograph No. 92-F-85-1, National Archives)

carving or souvenir-hunting tourists. Another duty was to visit all the camp sites and enforce the fire regulations. Occasionally when they overlooked a careless camper the troops also had to put out a forest fire. During the winter months, their main task was to protect Yellowstone's abundant game from poachers. Over the years, the army had set up an effective system of entrance check points, outposts, and patrols covering every accessible part of the park.[11]

For the men it was pleasant, uneventful duty in beautiful surroundings. In the brief, cool summers the well-watered valleys and lush green plateaus beneath the towering peaks must have been close to every cavalryman's idea of heaven for himself and his horse. In the winter, as much as twenty feet of snow fell, and the thermometer often remained below zero for weeks, but the mountains blocked the wind and the soldiers stayed warm in their barracks or cabin outposts except when they had to put on their skis or snowshoes and go out on patrol.[12] Nevertheless, the park's isolation, the long winters, and the lack of the variety of earthy pleasures that soldiers at other posts enjoyed made for morale problems. Desertions were common.[13]

Since 1886 the army had, in effect, run the park. Now, Young and Allen were in an awkward position. Though a retired general, Young, as a civilian official, had no military authority over Allen and thus no control over his men. Yet they were in the park for the purpose of enabling the superintendent to fulfill his responsibilities for protecting it. Such an arrangement would only be satisfactory as long as the two men agreed on matters involving the use of the troops. If any serious disagreement arose it could only be settled in Washington at the level of the Departments of Interior and War. Young was understandably unhappy about his lack of control over the park's "police force." He also objected to the War Department's policy of rotating the units at Yellowstone every few years. No sooner did one unit learn its way around then it left and a new one moved in. To supplement the usually understrength garrison, units from other posts were sometimes sent in on temporary duty during the summer months. They knew even less about the park. Young had six or seven experienced civilian scouts under his own control who helped guide the army men until they learned their own way, but he soon saw a better solution to the problem. He wanted to replace the soldiers entirely with permanent civilian guards.[14]

From his own experiences with the Philippine Constabulary, Allen sympathized somewhat with Young's position. He tried to keep Young happy by acceding to most of his requests and suggestions, but on the issue of civilian guards they split. From what Allen had seen of the stubborn independence and unreliability of Young's handful of civilian scouts, he concluded more like them would be no improvement at all. He had his own solution. On August 11, after an inspection of all his men at their stations in the park, he wrote Chief of Staff Bell and asked for a full strength squadron (400 men) to be stationed at Yellowstone the year around.[15] Allen's request was probably more than justified by the area his men had to cover and the ever-growing number of visitors to the park, but Young may also have seen in it a potential increase in Allen's authority *vis-à-vis* his own and a clever move to block his plan to bring in rangers. Once Fort Yellowstone expanded to accommodate permanently that many soldiers, the War Department would be that much more reluctant to abandon its investment.

Despite their disagreement on this point, relations between the two men remained fairly cordial during the rest of 1907. They often rode together on inspection trips, and Young, a widower, dined frequently at the Allens' quarters. At sixty-eight he was a bit too old to join the polo club Allen organized, but as an old cavalryman he lent it his enthusiastic support. And by late fall, after the President and Secretary of the Interior had disapproved the idea of civilian guards, he appeared to accept the decision gracefully and publicly seconded Allen's request for more troops.[16]

General Young was not the only guest at the Allens' table. High-ranking visitors to the park expected special treatment and they got it: private camping facilities, soldiers to act as orderlies, packers, and cooks,[17] and, if they were Allen's friends or important enough, an invitation to dine at Quarters Number One. General Bell and Secretary Taft were among the Allens' guests that August.[18] A Chinese cook, lured to the park from Billings, Montana, by promises of high pay, arrived just in time to help Dora prepare for Taft's visit. On the morning of the big day the cook stepped into the Allens' back yard and came face to face over the garbage cans with a large and hungry bear. That was more wilderness than he had bargained for. He announced he was quitting, but Dora hid his trunk before he got back to his room. The meal that night was a sumptuous feast. Taft, who loved to eat, was ecstatic in his praise. (At 350 pounds, he weighed exactly twice what Allen did.) For the final course, the cook brought in a large frosted cake and set it before Dora. On it, in curlicued letters of colored sugar were the words: "Goodbye, Mrs. Allen. I Leave Tomorrow."[19]

With things at the park going Allen's way everywhere except in his own kitchen, he could look forward to a long and pleasantly uneventful winter with few military duties and lots of time to spend with his family. The first snow fell on September 29. Soon he and Harry and Dasha (Jeanette had entered Bryn Mawr) were learning to ski together. Although the post was practically snowbound much of the time, the mail got through regularly. Corresponding with Leonard Wood, soon to leave his post in the Philippines to take command of the Department of the East in the United States, and William Crozier, Chief of Ordnance in the War Department, Allen exchanged ideas on the need to modernize the cavalry and drummed up support for his plan to revise the promotion system.[20] The man to whom he wrote most often, however, was General Bell, who least appreciated such attention.

Bell had persuaded Taft to approve Allen's request for more troops, but they had not been immediately forthcoming. When only a few recruits had arrived by October, Allen complained to the Chief of Staff in a personal letter. For good measure he threw in a request for more officers and asked for funds to expand his quarters so that when "you big fellows come out" he could entertain in grander style. This drew an irritable reminder from Bell that Fort Yellowstone stood far down on the list of priorities. He had many more important matters on his mind.[21] In the spring, when Allen nudged him again about improving and expanding Fort Yellowstone and also implied the War Department was moving too slowly toward eliminating unfit officers, Bell fumed:

> You certainly are the most damned persistent cuss I ever saw. Notwithstanding I have told you I have no time for your personal letters you persist in sending them, and I am sorry I am not able to reward your persistence (which sometimes does some good) by approving your projects.[22]

Bell was not going to build a "mansion for a major to live in." That might give important visitors to the park the wrong idea about how the army spent what little money it had. He closed by telling Allen to "keep his shirt on" about changing the promotion system. The Chief of Staff could not afford to antagonize the rest of the army until several other important pending measures became law.[23] Allen's persistence on one point was finally rewarded, however. In May of 1908, two more troops of cavalry arrived from Fort D. A. Russell, Wyoming, giving Fort Yellowstone the full squadron Allen had asked for the previous August.[24]

In the meantime, he had temporarily become acting superintendent of the park. On February 15, General Young took a four months' leave of absence to marry and go East for his honeymoon. His bride was the widow of Mr. Cyrus Huntley, who had been the president of the company that held a near-monopoly on the hotel and transportation concessions in the park. His partner and successor as president of the company and of the powerful Yellowstone National Park Association as well was a man named Harry Child. Mrs. Child and the new Mrs. Young were sisters. Child was the sort of robber-baron entrepreneur who would stop at nothing to increase his advantage over a competitor. Among his good friends were President Roosevelt and Senator Thomas H. Carter of Montana.[25]

Since its establishment in 1872, the park had been the scene of continual inroads by private commercial interests. Opposed to these encroachments, not always successfully, were some officials in the Interior Department and a few conservation-minded members of Congress who felt an obligation to preserve the park as much as possible in its natural state. Of course, certain facilities were necessary for the safety and convenience of visitors, but men like Child never knew when to stop. Congress was constantly besieged with bills to authorize the extension of railroad lines into the park, or to set aside more land for roads, hotels, and so on.[26] General Young's marriage to Child's sister-in-law could only have strengthened Child's hand in the pursuit of his various schemes for making money in the park. One of his objectives in 1907–08 appears to have been the expansion of the hotel adjacent to Fort Yellowstone. General Young was too strong a personality to have been completely in Child's pocket (around the park he was known as "Czar" Young), but it is evident the two men co-operated to their mutual advantage.[27] Allen soon felt they were "gunning" for him.[28] What probably brought them together against him was a revival of the old issue of military versus civilian guards and Allen's opposition to Child's hotel expansion project.

The details of Child's hotel plan are only obliquely referred to in Allen's papers and are hazy in the minds of those still living who knew of it, but it seems he wanted to add a wing on the hotel in a location Allen opposed because it would involve tearing down one of the army's buildings. Unused to being thwarted, the powerful Child rejected Allen's suggestion for another site. As the battle lines were being drawn, something happened that put Allen on the defensive with Young as well.[29]

On August 24, 1908, there occurred one of the most spectacular crimes in the history of the park. On that morning a stocky, bearded man held up seventeen stagecoaches in a row in a canyon a few miles east of Old Faithful and made off with a total of $2,094.20 in money and jewelry from the startled tourist passengers. His method was ridiculously simple. The coaches were in a convoy of twenty-five vehicles, escorted in front by a small detachment of mounted troopers. Because of the blinding dust each coach stayed at least 100 yards behind the one in front. The robber picked the narrowest part of the canyon and let the cavalry and first eight coaches go by. From the ninth he ordered a young man to dismount and gave him a sack to hold while, at gunpoint, he relieved the other occupants of their valuables. With his hostage "bagman" beside him, he repeated the process as each of the remaining coaches rumbled up. By the time word of what had happened filtered up to the front of the column, the robber had escaped. He was pursued by several of the civilian scouts who knew the park and the surrounding area as no one else did, but he was never caught.[30]

The only way such a robbery could have been prevented would have been to put an armed soldier on every stagecoach in the park, an obviously impractical solution even with the four troops of cavalry at Allen's disposal. Nevertheless, the incident gave Young and Child the opening they needed. Remaining outwardly friendly to Allen, they pressed their advantage behind his back. He began to hear rumors of charges being made in Washington: the policing of the park was unsatisfactory; his discipline was slipshod; the soldiers were lazy incompetents who never bothered to learn their way around the park's myriad trails and who drank on duty, were rude to visitors, and poached game themselves.[31] There was probably an element of truth in some of this, for the troops were only of average quality, and their duties often prevented close supervision by their officers and N.C.O.s. Most of the soldiers *were* new and unfamiliar with the park, and many of them were disgruntled at being so far from "civilization." Of the 400 men under Allen's command at the time of the robbery, 337 had arrived as recruits in the last ten months. Of these, sixty-nine had already deserted. Still, Allen had been satisfied on the whole with the conduct of his men, and he was not an officer to tolerate slipshod performance. The previous December General Young had complimented his progress toward making his detachment a model of courtesy and efficiency. And now, without specific charges against himself or his men to act on, Allen was helpless to take corrective action or prepare a defense.[32] On October 19, the axe fell.

A telegram came from Washington informing him that he and his men were to be relieved by another unit the following month. No explanation was given by the War Department and none was requested of him. A few days later Allen received a sympathetic letter from his old friend and classmate Jim Treat, who had been in the Chief of Staff's office on the day the decision was made. It came straight from the President, Treat said. He relayed General Bell's personal advice not to protest the order but to obey it, and, if he wanted an investigation of the whole affair, to ask for it later.[33] By the time Treat's letter arrived, Allen had already sent telegrams to General Bell, Secretary of War Luke Wright (Taft's successor when the latter resigned to campaign for the 1908 election), Secretary of the Interior James R. Garfield, and President Roosevelt's private secretary, William Loeb, a mutual friend of Allen's, Young's, Child's, and Senator Carter's. Each message asked for a reconsideration of the decision and stated that a letter with Allen's side of the story would follow.[34] Loeb's reply had an ominous ring: "Strongly advise you in your own interests not to make effort to secure revocation." [35]

Allen's protests, however, evidently had some effect on the President. He fired General Young, too. By the end of November, both men had left the park.[36] This eased the sting of Allen's own relief and put it in the light of the outcome of an unfortunate conflict of personalities rather than any dereliction of duty on his part, but the fear that others would interpret it differently nagged at him. He wrote to Secretary Wright and asked his opinion whether the incident had hurt his chances for "special promotion" once Taft became President. Wright was noncommital on whether Taft might act on Allen's behalf but he reassured him: "I do not think your change of station ought to or will in the least affect your chances, as I do not believe that anyone regarded you as negligent or inattentive to your duties." [37]

Allen had a choice of several new assignments, none of them very desirable. In early December he and half his squadron arrived at Fort Huachuca, Arizona, and took over the post from the units of the 5th Cavalry who were being sent to Hawaii. The remainder of the troops from Yellowstone went to Fort Apache.[38]

Of Allen's year and a half in "exile" at Fort Huachuca there is not much to be said. Dora and Dasha went with him and lived in Quarters Number One, the nine-room, one-and-one-half-story adobe house set aside for the post commander. Harry had gone off to private school near Boston to prepare for the West Point entrance examinations and Jeanette was still at Bryn Mawr.

Located in the arid southeastern corner of Arizona fifteen miles from the Mexican border, the seventy square miles of the Huachuca reservation were a fine place for cavalry training and target practice (and snakes and gila monsters) but not much else. In recent years the post had been allowed to run down because of lack of money for construction and repairs. Its only connection with the outside world was a daily buckboard run to the railroad station, seven dusty miles away.[39] For his family's sake, Allen put the best face he could on such an assignment. Dasha recalls he used to say: "Think of it as our having a large country estate, all to ourselves," [40] but underneath he must have been bitter. Even the honor of an official trip to Washington to ride in Taft's inaugural parade [41] could only have reminded him how far he had slipped since those heady days near the pinnacle of power in the Philippines.

After the inauguration he took three months of leave and stayed near Washington, making only brief trips to Kentucky on family business and up the East Coast to visit Jeanette and Harry in school. One day, late in May, while Allen was playing polo on the grounds of the Washington Monument, President Taft chanced to ride by on Constitution Avenue. Recognizing his former Chief of Constabulary, he stopped and invited him to dinner at the White House. Later that afternoon a friend on the General Staff told Allen there were rumors Taft wanted him on duty in Washington. The President said nothing about it to him that night at dinner, and no one high up at the War Department seemed to know exactly when he was to come or in what capacity, but the tone of the letter telling Dora all this was positively jubilant.[42] His hopes for the future suddenly bright again, he decided to cut short his leave and return to Fort Huachuca and wait. The news of Harry's failure to pass the West Point physical examination dampened Allen's high spirits as he left Washington, but even that disappointment was tempered by his son's acceptance at Harvard.[43]

The months at Huachuca went by very slowly. In the evenings Allen worked at breaking and training a fine horse to be shipped to President Taft at his request. Polo every afternoon after duty enlivened the routine of training, parades, and inspections, but it all must have seemed flat and dull compared with what he might soon be doing.[44] In late November he was assured of salvation.

In the space of a week Allen received two letters telling him he was to be on the General Staff. The first came from General Wood, a leading contender to replace General Bell as Chief of Staff.[45] The second came from General Arthur Murray, Allen's former commanding officer in the 43rd Volunteers on Leyte, who had since become Chief

Polo at Fort Huachuca. (Photograph courtesy of Col. Henry T. Allen, Jr.)

of Artillery in the War Department. Murray told Allen his new assignment had nothing to do with his hoped-for brigadiership. It had come, Murray said, only because he and Wood "recognized your special ability [as a staff officer]." But Murray went on:

I certainly don't think it will do you any harm to play around the throne and get into the running here. Bell goes out soon and Wood or somebody else will step in and your chances for preferment may materially improve.[46]

Wood's appointment as Chief of Staff two weeks later was greeted in military and political circles with a strongly mixed reaction. He had risen to fame with his friend Theodore Roosevelt in the Spanish-American War (he, and not T.R., had actually commanded the "Rough Riders"), and his achievements thereafter as a military administrator in Cuba and the Philippines had been widely acknowledged as superlative. But Wood was a flamboyant maverick in the military system. The New York *Evening Post* expressed the view of traditionalists in and out of uniform who resented the army's highest position being given to an officer who had not touched every rung of the ladder on his way to the top. The *Post* described Wood as a man

. . . who attended neither West Point, nor any other military school in or outside of the Army; who was until eleven years ago in the active practice of medicine and surgery; who never drilled a company in his life; whose experience as a regimental commander lasted about two months in 1898. Many officers will not fail to say, with a good deal of force that if a man of this education and experience is entitled to practically the leadership of the Army, all the laborious studying of the modern officer is needless.[47]

Wood, like Bell, had been promoted from captain to brigadier general in 1901, over the heads of nearly a thousand more senior regulars. Unlike Bell, he did not object to similar recognition being given other outstanding junior officers. Wood had known Allen since the days of the Santiago campaign and had followed his career and achievements since then with interest. He "heartily approved" of Allen's ideas on changing the promotion system and from their correspondence and Allen's articles in the various service journals knew him to be a thoughtful advocate of army reform.[48] Wood had tried to help Allen keep his star when he left the Philippines in 1907. Now he was in a position to help him again by putting him in the limelight on the General Staff. He did the same for a number of other like-thinking, progressive-minded officers. Wood's biographer called this able, energetic, and ambitious group his "ardent spirits." [49]

Major General Wood moved into the Chief of Staff's baronial office in the War Department in July, 1910. In September, Major Allen reported to him. At fifty-one, Allen was a year older than Wood. The gulf of rank that separated them must have seemed to Allen more uncrossable with each passing year. Unless another lucky break came soon he would probably never be a general again. In two years he would have thirty years of service and be eligible for retirement. He could hang on for a few years after that, but at the ordinary pace of promotion a colonelcy was about all he could expect. That none of his West Point classmates were doing much better was scant comfort. Of the other thirty-six members of the Class of 1882, only half were still on active duty. None of them was a general either. Fourteen had already retired, and four more were dead, including his former roommate, Barrington West. Jim Treat, his best friend in the class, had done well (he had been Commandant of Cadets at the Point from 1901 to 1905 and was currently a student at the War College), but even he had only recently been promoted to lieutenant colonel.[50] A four-year detail "to play around the throne" thus represented Allen's best and perhaps last chance for that lucky promotion break.

Wood put Allen to work on cavalry problems. His duties included supervising the testing of new equipment, formations, and tactics, the purchase of better horses, and the inspection of mounted units and maneuvers at posts all over the country. He also kept track of cavalry developments in foreign armies.[51] This was hardly as glamorous as working on strategic plans or mobilization problems but just as essential. No other office in the War Department concerned itself with purely cavalry matters. Although there had long been Chiefs of Artillery, Engineers, Ordnance, and Signal Corps along with the Offices of the Adjutant General, Inspector General, Surgeon General, and the like, Congress had never authorized a chief of cavalry or a chief of infantry. The unrepresented branches had recently begun a campaign in their professional journals to publicize this lack and build pressure to rectify it.[52] Instead of waiting years for Congress to act, however, General Wood created two new *de facto* chiefs by informally giving two of his more senior assistants responsibility for overseeing the affairs of their particular branches. Though never the most senior cavalry officer on Wood's staff, Allen was "Acting Chief of Cavalry" for most of his War Department tour. With his infantry counterpart, Colonel Joseph W. Duncan, he shared an office directly across the hall from Wood's.[53]

Allen's job may have seemed mundane at times, but he had his share of exposure to the limelight, both professionally and socially.

From time to time he accompanied Wood when the latter went to the White House for a conference or was called to appear before a congressional committee. On several occasions Allen prepared to testify on behalf of army legislation that was meeting tough opposition on the Hill, but he never was called upon to do so. Wood also took him along on inspection trips outside of Washington. Sharing a train compartment they had many hours of serious conversation about the problems of army modernization and national preparedness.[54]

In July, 1911, Henry and Dora and Dasha moved from their apartment on Connecticut Avenue across the Potomac to Fort Myer. Their huge red-brick quarters were next to those of General and Mrs. Wood. After that, the two men often had private talks as they rode together in the early morning on the bluffs overlooking the river and the city.[55] By then Washingtonians were becoming accustomed to the sight of Wood's distinguished-looking assistant riding horseback. He played polo on the monument grounds, organized and rode in various horse shows around town, and spent many a weekend fox hunting on the estates of his friends in Maryland and northern Virginia.[56]

In August, 1912, after two years of working for Wood and five as a major, Allen became a lieutenant colonel. That brought him one step closer to getting his star back, but time was running out. President Taft, the one man who could jump him over the heads of the fifty cavalry colonels and lieutenant colonels who still outranked him, would almost certainly leave office the following March. Since 1909, Taft and Roosevelt's once close friendship had gradually turned into a bitter personal and political feud, and the Republican Party was badly split. If the Democrats won in 1912, few of Allen's political friends and patrons would still be in a position to help him. From Taft on down they were almost all Republicans. There was another difficulty. By law Allen had to leave the General Staff for at least six months after his promotion to lieutenant colonel. Wood promised to bring him back as soon as he legally could, but that still meant being away from his desk at the War Department at the most critical time in his career.

Anticipating these problems, Allen had begun to lay the groundwork for another bid for a brigadiership as early as February of 1912. He could only hope the President's loyalty and friendship would outweigh his current political troubles. To a friend, Allen said of Taft, "I feel, perhaps wrongly, that he owes me a great deal. Without the Constabulary, Civil Government [in the Philippines] could not have existed." [57] In April, after having received a promise of support for his nomination from several senators, including Elihu Root, Allen sent a formal application for special promotion to the White House, accompanying it with a résumé of his service record and numerous letters of recommendation.[58]

Taft held his reply until after the election, seven months later. According to Allen, the President then said he wanted to make him a general before he left office, but felt "there might be some trouble" because he was only a lieutenant colonel.[59] The memory of the furor over Pershing's promotion six years earlier and the desire to avoid another like it undoubtedly influenced Taft's answer. In fact, by coincidence, the controversy over Pershing's meteoric rise had been revived again in 1912 when it appeared for a while that he was being considered for the superintendent's position at West Point.[60] However, the trouble Taft feared over Allen's nomination probably had more to do with his own political weakness and still more with the hatred of General Wood that festered in the heart of many a politician and army officer. By 1912, Wood and the entire General Staff had become the center of one of the most bitter personal power struggles Washington had seen in years. Wood's temperament, his activist conceptions of the role of the United States as a world power, and his strong convictions about the need for army reform from the War Department on down, all guaranteed that his tenure would be a controversial one. Allen, though personally little involved in Wood's battles, had sat in his corner for the past two years—close enough to be spattered with the blood of the principals and to feel the hatred of Wood's foes. How deep that hatred was and what it meant for Allen's promotion chances can only be understood by a look at what Wood was trying to accomplish as Chief of Staff.

In contrast to conventional-minded army colleagues who saw no threat to American supremacy in the Western Hemisphere and could imagine no reason for large-scale military involvement beyond it, Wood believed the United States would almost inevitably be drawn into a future conflict among the other great powers. But, while the legions of Europe were growing to ominous proportions, the American army remained stagnant and sadly unprepared. Wood was not eager for war; he simply saw it as his duty to give the country an instrument which could effectively fight those wars that could not be avoided.[61] Before he could embark on any program of army reform and modernization, however, he first had to strengthen and consolidate his own position in the War Department.

Both the position of Chief of Staff and the entity known as the General Staff had been the creation of the logical and orderly mind of Elihu Root, who had been aghast at the paperwork snarl he found when he became Secretary of War in 1899. He inherited a Gordian knot of red tape whose strands had been drawn ever tighter by the weight of bureaucratic inertia, the tug of tradition, and the pulling and hauling of generations of generals and politicians, each with his own vision of what was right and best for the army. Each of the bureau chiefs in the War Department ran his own satrapy, all too often ignoring not only the requirement for staff co-ordination but the desires of the Commanding General and the needs of the army as a whole.[62]

It took Root more than three years to change any of this, but in February, 1903, after long and determined opposition from General Miles, the bureau chiefs, and their political allies, Congress passed the General Staff Act. The act abolished the position of Commanding General and replaced it with a chief of staff to the President in his role as Commander in Chief. The Chief of Staff was to supervise not only the line of the army but also most of the bureaus and staff agencies that formerly had reported directly to the Secretary of War. To assist the Chief of Staff the act set up a corps of forty-four officers who were to devote themselves to long-range planning for the defense of the United States. They were also given co-ordinating responsibilities among the various other offices of the War Department. Although these reforms were a good beginning, the act had some serious flaws. It permitted several of the bureau chiefs to retain their enclaves of personal power outside the direct supervision of the Chief of Staff. In addition, the vaguely defined responsibilities of the chief's forty-four freewheeling assistants were an invitation for them to meddle in the very kind of routine administration and short-range operational problems they were supposed to avoid.[63]

Between 1903 and 1910 the War Department had time to digest and assimilate Root's reforms, but few additional changes were made. Most of the bureau heads fell sullenly into line under the Chief of Staff, but those few who had kept their autonomy strengthened their positions, helped by the unwillingness or inability of successive chiefs and secretaries to challenge them.[64]

This was the state of affairs facing Wood when he entered the War Department. He also found piles of paperwork on his desk, much of it of no consequence but requiring a decision or signature from him nevertheless. Most of these papers set forth at voluminous length the results of some study by one of the numerous staff committees. Wood soon abolished the lengthy memoranda and reorganized the General Staff's committee system into four working groups, the Mobile Army, Militia, Coast Artillery, and War College divisions. Each was headed by an assistant with authority to act for Wood "in unimportant routine cases" and instructions to prepare reports without recording every minute step of the mental processes involved. The first three divisions dealt with the aspects of modernization and mobilization planning indicated by their titles. The War College Division would co-ordinate the work of the three other divisions and, in conjunction with the War College (another legacy of the Root era), be responsible for overall war planning.[65] Allen's Cavalry Section came under the Mobile Army Division.

With the internal workings of the General Staff arranged to suit him and with the backing of Secretary of War Henry L. Stimson, Wood embarked on the more serious reforms he had in mind. No matter which way he turned, however, he met opposition from those who had vested interests in the *status quo*.

He wanted to close down many of the tiny "hitching post" forts and consolidate all units on the larger remaining posts, where they could be more easily trained and supervised, cheaply supplied, and quickly mobilized. The virtues of this proposal were undeniable, but Wood, like others before and after him, met strong opposition from Congress as soon as his plan was translated into specifics. Wyoming's Fort D. A. Russell, in the home state of Senator Francis E. Warren, Chairman of the Senate Military Affairs Committee, was one example. Senator Warren reacted to Wood's proposal to close Fort Russell as if no greater catastrophe could befall the economic well-being and military security of his constituents.[66] Practically every other sleepy little post also had a protector in Congress, and Wood had that many more enemies.

Wood and Stimson stirred up more controversy with their plan to create an army reserve under Federal control. Wood had little faith in and less authority over the poorly organized and patronage-ridden state militia and disliked the idea of volunteer units, the other traditional American solution to raising large numbers of troops in wartime. To him the most logical alternative was to shorten the current three-year term of enlistment in the Regular Army and require men who had completed their active service to remain on reserve status for a number of years thereafter. This brought howls from those in the army who insisted it took two years just to train a soldier, although Wood claimed and later proved that the training could be done in six months. In addition, the more rapid personnel turnover the plan entailed would increase annual costs for training and supplies and add the expense of the reservists' pay, all of which dismayed most members of Congress. They, and the governors of their home states, also objected to any measure that reduced the Federal Government's need to rely on the state militia in times of emergency. Finally, many Americans were suspicious of the reserve scheme simply because it smacked of European militarism and created, in effect, a large standing army in disguise.[67]

Wood made his bitterest and most implacable enemy, however, within the War Department itself. His opponent was Adjutant General Fred C. Ainsworth, the only officer in the army powerful enough to challenge him. Most of Wood's other enemies ranged themselves on Ainsworth's side. What should have been a rational debate on important issues of national policy became instead a quagmire of personal animosity. Ironically, both Wood and Ainsworth had begun their army careers as doctors. In their two-year battle they forgot the part of their Hippocratic oath pledging them to be "just and generous" to fellow members of the medical profession.

Ainsworth had been in the War Department for twenty years. His contempt for the newfangled general-staff concept was total. "The General Stuff," he called it and sneeringly referred to Wood's corps of assistants as "enthusiastic young officers with what they are pleased to call 'advanced ideas.' "[68]

Over the years Ainsworth had carefully cultivated a reputation for efficiency and administrative infallibility. He knew, almost literally, the contents and location of every piece of paper in every office in his domain. By refusing to sign any document that bore unpleasant tidings for the recipient (in such cases either a subordinate signed or it was carried up to the civilian undersecretary), he had also become known as the man to see in the War Department if you wanted quick and favorable action. He had gotten his start by taking over the Bureau of Pensions and Records and giving it such a thorough revamping it took only twenty-four hours instead of six months to get an answer on a claim. This reform, of course, earned him the gratitude of every politician who had ever promised to see what he could do about a constituent's pension check.[69]

Ainsworth had persuaded Secretary Root the General Staff should not concern itself with the kind of paperwork his bureau specialized in. As a result, the Bureau of Pensions and Records was one of the few military offices exempted from the supervisory control of the Chief of

Staff by the General Staff Act. During Taft's tenure as Secretary of War, Ainsworth had maneuvered himself into the position of Adjutant General and consolidated that office along with his former fiefdom. Under the law, the Adjutant General was subordinate to the Chief of Staff, but Ainsworth imperiously ignored this fact and continued to act as independently as ever.[70]

Wood's predecessors had tolerated Ainsworth's insubordination with varying degrees of exasperation, but the new Chief of Staff would not. Although the two doctors were old friends, the friendship ended within a few days after they began to share a "practice" in the War Department. Ainsworth gave Wood a list of officers on which he recommended those he should keep on the General Staff and those he should replace. Wood sensed an ulterior motive behind this helpful advice and pointedly kept the men Ainsworth did not like.[71] From then on it was open war between them. Ainsworth was the conservative, the supreme bureaucrat, apprehensive of change, and opposing, above all, the concentration of too much power in the hands of one army officer. In his struggle with Wood he had tradition on his side, powerful friends in Congress, and the support of many older officers. Wood, the reformer, had caught the passion for efficiency of the Progressive Age. He also had a better appreciation than Ainsworth of the nation's military weakness. On his side, he had the law that said Ainsworth was his subordinate. As long as Wood also kept the support of Secretary Stimson and the President, he could not lose. But Ainsworth was a proud and stubborn man "with a taste for marching into the guns."[72]

For more than a year the outcome of their struggle remained in doubt. With Stimson's approval, Wood submitted a proposal to Congress that would have consolidated Ainsworth's office and the Inspector General's Department with the General Staff. Ainsworth's political allies modified the plan in such a way that he and not Wood would emerge with a promotion to lieutenant general and control of the new organization. Stimson and Wood managed to block that move. But when they tried to get a bill to reduce the term of enlistment for soldiers from three years to two and set up a reserve under Federal control, counterproposals to raise the enlistment to five years quickly appeared. After the mid-term election of 1910 the Democrats controlled the House of Representatives and were only too glad to embarrass Taft's administration. In testifying for his bill before the House Committee on Military Affairs, Wood faced a hostile majority on the committee. Ainsworth, on the other hand, was called to testify and permitted to indulge his gift for irony and sarcasm against Wood's "harebrained" scheme. He and many other officers felt it would produce an untrained army and an expensive and unnecessary reserve.[73] Stimson and Wood had all they could do merely to keep the term of enlistment from being lengthened.

Wood finally triumphed over Ainsworth on an issue at the very center of the latter's bureaucratic territory. As an outgrowth of a presidentially directed study of government efficiency, the War Department had set up the Board on Business Methods, headed by Ainsworth. One of the board's purposes was to find ways of reducing the army's paperwork. Suggestions from the line and staff were solicited. Many proposals came in to abolish the muster roll, a particularly time-consuming piece of paper to fill out, which came under the purview of the Adjutant General's Office. Ainsworth saw no need for a disruptive change in his smoothly running system. Wood, however, thought the proposal had merit and persuaded Secretary Stimson to approve it. Ainsworth was asked for his comments. He ignored the request. Again Wood prodded him. No response. After a third request from Wood, Ainsworth lashed back with a bitter and vituperative memorandum. It quivered with indignation against the "incompetent amateurs" who dared to presume they knew how to run his business better than he did. The Adjutant General went further. He impugned the motives of the Chief of Staff and the Secretary of War by implying the whole affair was a "subterfuge" such as "would be scorned by honorable men in any of the relations of private life."[74]

Subterfuge or not, Wood had his enemy cornered. He showed the memorandum to Stimson and recommended Ainsworth be disciplined for his intemperate and insubordinate language. On February 15, 1912, Ainsworth received an order relieving him from duty. Stimson began to prepare court-martial charges. Rather than face a trial Ainsworth asked to be allowed to retire. Chuckling, Taft approved his request.[75]

Wood had won a personal victory, but it cost him and Stimson most of their other cherished reforms. Ainsworth still had friends in Congress, and they set out to "get" Wood. Early in 1912, James Hay, the Democratic Chairman of the House Military Affairs Committee, made a deal with his Republican counterpart in the Senate, Francis Warren. Hay promised to block the closing of any army posts if Warren would support an anti-Wood rider on the next army appropriation bill. When the bill reached the President it contained a number of provisions objectionable to Wood and Stimson, but two were the direct outcome of this shabby bipartisan agreement. The first forbade any changes in existing army posts until the matter could be studied by a special commission whose conservative-minded members were specified by name. The second provision stated that after March 5, 1913, no officer could serve as Chief of Staff unless he had spent at least ten years in the line as an officer in the grades below brigadier general. Senator Root, a backer of Wood's, pointed out that the bill "could not better accomplish its purpose if it read that after the 5th of March no man whose initials are L. W. shall be chief of staff." [76]

Washington held its breath to see if Taft would veto the army's appropriation for the coming year because of these two obnoxious riders. The betting was against Wood's survival. At that very moment Taft's and Roosevelt's forces were about to begin battling for the presidential nomination at the Republican Convention in Chicago. Rumor had it that Senator Warren would swing the delegates he controlled over to Roosevelt if Taft vetoed the bill. If Taft stuck by Wood, one of Roosevelt's favorites, he would be risking his own political future. But stick by him he did. On June 17, 1912, the day before the convention began, he signed the veto message written for him by Stimson.[77]

All this political intrigue was going on when Allen submitted his request for promotion. Taft had other things on his mind that summer and fall. Although he won his party's nomination, he then faced a three-way race as a result of Roosevelt's decision to form his own "Bull Moose" party. With Taft campaigning as much against the renegade Roosevelt as against Woodrow Wilson, the Democrats won easily. Taft ran a poor third. As a lame-duck president facing a congress in the same position, he could have been forgiven if he had forgotten Allen entirely in the press of more important last-minute business. Although he seems to have given his old friend's promotion serious consideration, he need not have bothered. There were enough bitter men in both parties, who, having failed to get rid of Wood, at least would try to see to it no protégé of his got any special recognition.[78] Since Taft's days of power were numbered and his influence was shattered by an ignominious defeat, he had no leverage to use in Allen's behalf.

In January of 1913, still on leave from the General Staff, Allen returned to Washington at Wood's request to begin organizing and co-ordinating President Wilson's inaugural parade. Wood was to be Grand Marshal of the parade and made Allen his "Chief of Staff." With a reason to be in the capital he could better lobby for his own promotion. But as the busy days slipped by the only word that came from the White House was not encouraging. To a mutual friend Taft said, "Tell Allen not to worry; I will look after his interests after I am out." [79] On March 4, Allen rode at Wood's side down Pennsylvania

Avenue at the head of the long column of troops and blaring brass bands. He still wore the silver oak leaves of a lieutenant colonel on the epaulets of his dress uniform. As he passed the reviewing stand and saluted his old and new commanders in chief, there was bitterness in his heart.[80] Unable or unwilling to understand the dilemma of Taft's position, Allen never forgave him. Not even personal letters of explanation from Taft and Stimson after they left office could make him believe he had not been the victim of a cheap "trick." [81] Both men told him the same thing. His record fully entitled him to the promotion he sought, and he had been one of three officers considered for the only vacancy then open in the cavalry. The two other officers had been very senior colonels. Although Allen's qualifications equaled theirs, his nomination had not been sent in because of his lesser rank. Taft stated the other reason more indirectly: ". . . we [he and Stimson] concluded that the attitude of the Senate was so hostile . . . it would be doubtful if confirmation would follow." [82]

Allen's last year on the General Staff was quiet and personally uneventful. He already knew he would be returning to the line to join a cavalry regiment at the end of August, 1914. In the meantime he stayed in the background and organized a cavalry summer-training camp at Winchester, Virginia. He also worked on plans to relocate certain cavalry units, part of his chief's latest attempt at army reform on a tack less against the prevailing winds of congressional opposition.[83]

In the spring of 1911, when the War Department had tried to send a division to the Mexican border, ostensibly for maneuvers but actually in response to the outbreak of revolution south of the Rio Grande, it had taken hundreds of orders from Washington and three months to get all the units together. Even then most of the regiments were at half strength. In mid-1912, the War Department began to rearrange the stationing of companies, battalions, and regiments. Without eliminating any posts or raising the specter of a large standing army Wood and Stimson thus achieved one of their major goals: the capability for more rapid mobilization of the divisions of which these units were component parts. Each of four geographical regions of the country was to have a properly balanced mixture of the units necessary to make up one division. The War College worked out plans to assemble them with the minimum waste of transportation and loss of time. By 1913, Wood had the satisfaction of knowing he could bring together a full-strength division in a matter of weeks with just one order.[84] Several times in the next year that order almost had to be given as the disorders in Mexico spread and Mexican-American relations deteriorated, helped along by Wilson's fumbling diplomacy and his refusal to recognize the revolutionary regime of Victoriano Huerta. In fact, in April, 1913, with the President's approval, Wood ordered Brigadier General Pershing to assemble and take command of a cavalry brigade near the border at El Paso, Texas. Wilson was only too willing to use force or the threat of it against Huerta, but he saw little need for his Chief of Staff's brand of across-the-board preparedness.[85]

His four-year tenure ended, Wood left office on April 22, 1914, to return to Governor's Island, New York, and his former position as commander of the Department of the East. If he now had far less influence, he also had more freedom to speak for his unfinished reforms.[86]

Allen's own departure from the General Staff was set for the end of August. He planned to take a three months' leave before reporting to Fort Oglethorpe, Georgia, where he would become the second in command of the 11th Cavalry Regiment. Dora and Dasha would go with him, but the two older children were grown and on their own. That January, Jeanette had married Lieutenant Frank Andrews, a handsome cavalry officer and a West Pointer, Class of 1906. They had met at Fort Yellowstone in 1907 and were now stationed at Fort Ethan Allen, Vermont. Harry, graduated from Harvard in 1913 as a mining engineer, was about to leave for Kentucky and take a job with a coal mining company.[87]

Around noon on August 4, Major General William W. Wotherspoon, Wood's successor as Chief of Staff, called Allen into his office.[88] The headlines that morning read:

WAR BETWEEN POWERS OF EUROPE NOW RAGES
ON LAND AND SEA AND IN THE AIR

ENGLAND STILL HOLDS ALOOF, ALTHOUGH HER
ATTITUDE GROWS MORE MENACING

CONGRESS AND PRESIDENT PROVIDE FOR NEEDS
OF ALL AMERICANS ABROAD.[89]

CHAPTER VIII

Alarums and Excursions

Lieutenant Colonel Allen reported to General Wotherspoon. The Chief of Staff came to the point immediately. There were more than fifty thousand Americans—tourists, expatriates and businessmen—caught in the European war zone. Some were in actual physical danger, and many were having difficulty reaching safe or neutral areas because of the currency and travel restrictions imposed by the belligerent powers. Cables asking for help from these stranded and frightened individuals were pouring into the State Department from all parts of Europe. A relief commission consisting of State Department, War Department, Red Cross, and civilian banking representatives was going to Europe immediately to arrange for the safe conduct of those who wanted to come home. Since no officers above the rank of colonel could leave the country because of the tense situation on the Mexican border, did Allen want to go to Europe as the senior military officer in the commission? General Wotherspoon gave him three minutes to decide. Allen took less time than that.[1]

His son helped him pack by collecting a suitcase full of books on the European powers from the navy library, along with some maps and a "few manuals . . . for brushing up on long unused languages." Harry pleaded with his father to let him come along as an aide, but Allen said no.[2]

On the morning of August 6, 1914, he reported to Assistant Secretary of War Henry Breckenridge abroad the cruiser *Tennessee*, getting up steam at the Brooklyn Navy Yard. Before it sailed late that evening some order and purpose were beginning to emerge from the noisy, milling confusion in the commission's crowded suite of hastily commandeered officers' wardrooms. Breckenridge was the senior government official on board. His State Department opposite number was Minister Henry P. Dodge. Ernest P. Bicknell, Director General of Civilian Relief, represented the Red Cross. Five prominent bankers and two Treasury Department agents were on hand to advise on the intricacies of international finance. Congress had quickly appropriated $2,500,000 for the expedition, of which $1,500,000 was in the ship's hold in the form of gold bullion to help lubricate the machinery of repatriation. The bankers brought aboard an additional $3,000,000 in gold. Also officially attached to the commission were several newspaper correspondents. Under him Allen had twenty army officers with attaché experience or language proficiency and a number of War Department clerks and other specialists.[3]

Before the *Tennessee* reached England, Breckenridge, Allen, and Dodge had decided on a plan of action. The War Department contingent would split into three groups, one to enter Russia via the Scandinavian countries, another to visit the capitals of the Central Powers after landing in neutral Holland, and the third to go directly from England to France. Accompanying each group of officers would be men from the other government and private agencies represented on the relief commission. How they would be greeted in each country and what specific problems they would face in arranging for the repatriation of thousands of individuals no one knew for certain, but Breckenridge and Dodge briefed everyone on the general procedures to be followed. They were to assist American diplomatic personnel already on the scene in each country by helping to interview and process applicants for visas and financial assistance. Those whose funds or credit were exhausted would be lent enough gold to pay their passage home. The treasury officials carefully outlined the disbursing and accounting methods to be used.

During the voyage Allen gave a talk on the historical background of the war and "the strength and organization of the contending nations." Each day the latest bulletins from the ship's cable room were passed around. Allen thought the news from Europe "appalling." On the evening of August 17, the *Tennessee* docked at Falmouth and the key members of the commission set out for London by train with $400,000 in gold.[4]

In London they found a semiofficial committee of American residents already organized and sending people home on British and neutral ships from ports in England and the European side of the channel. The committee's chairman was a prominent young American engineer named Herbert Hoover. Deciding to work through this organization in England rather than to set up another, Breckenridge attached several officers to Hoover's staff and deposited the $400,000 to his account in a London bank. Over the next three days the leaders of the relief commission held a series of conferences at the American Embassy to plot their future course. Most United States citizens in France seemed to be making their way to the coast without too much difficulty, but many thousands more were still unable to leave Central and Eastern Europe. On August 20, Breckenridge dispatched his three teams of officers to the continent. He and Allen went with the largest group, which headed for Berlin and Vienna. Dodge decided to go too. The *Tennessee* dropped anchor off the Dutch coast the next day.[5]

Leaving two army captains and $50,000 in gold at the U.S. Embassy at The Hague, where 2,000 of their fellow citizens were waiting for help, the remaining nineteen Americans arrived in Berlin on August 23 after a sleepless overnight train ride in a crowded coach.[6] Allen commented on the mood of the German capital:

> [The recent German victories] have caused much contentment among the people, but there is absolutely no unusual demonstration to indicate such victories. . . . Germany is evidently fully cognizant that she is fighting for her life. Evidently the German authorities are using every effort to create an American sympathy for their undertaking. . . .
>
> The Germans are intensely bitter toward England and Russia—much more so than toward France. . . .[7]

At the Ministries of War and Foreign Affairs Allen met several officials who were friends from his attaché tour in Berlin fifteen years before. From his talks with them he learned the Germans had enough ammunition and supplies to sustain an army of 5,000,000 men.

The scene at the American Embassy was one of tense confusion. The embassy personnel, "worn nearly to a frazzle" by the throngs of people clamoring for help, were glad to see the relief commission arrive. Many of the American citizens who jammed the building or stood in long lines outside spoke no English and had neither letters of credit nor travelers' checks. Breckenridge put half his party and several hundred thousand dollars in gold at the disposal of the ambassador.[8]

With the remainder of their group, Allen, Breckenridge, and Dodge departed on August 25 for Vienna, where they were met the next day by Ambassador Frederic C. Penfield, "one of the most extraordinary egoists" Allen had ever seen. His bombast, "rarely surpassed in comic operas," was evidently equaled by his inefficiency. The embassy had "done nothing toward systematizing the [relief] work," wrote Allen, and was "apparently incapable of handling the situation except in the dilatory diplomatic way." Breckenridge's men took over "the whole affair." [9]

Despite reports in the Vienna press of a great victory in Poland against the Russians, Allen had "grave doubts" about the fighting capacity of the Austro-Hungarian Empire. From the number of wounded streaming into the capital from Serbia, he suspected the Austrian army had just suffered a "terrible repulse" on that front, but no Austrian official would confirm it. Even the Foreign Minister, Count Leopold von Berchtold, a friend since their days together in St. Petersburg, would only say there was nothing new to report from Serbia "except that there is nothing new." [10]

From Vienna, the three Americans went down the Danube to check on the work of the members of the commission who had gone ahead to help at the embassy in Budapest. In two days, Allen and his companions made their usual calls on high government officials and looked around the city as much as they could. Once again, he was struck by the number of wounded soldiers he saw.[11] Leaving Budapest on August 29, the three men headed for France, traveling by way of the Austrian Tyrol and Switzerland. Allen carried a seventy-pound valise containing $15,000 in gold handcuffed to his wrist. The remainder of the $300,000 brought into Germany a week before was already helping thousands of Americans in Berlin, Vienna, and Budapest pay for train and boat tickets. At the Austrian border, Allen was almost arrested. Having forgotten his army overcoat in the rush to leave Washington, he was wearing a British officer's model purchased in London.[12]

On entering France Allen discovered that the news he had read in Berlin and Vienna of continual German advances was not exaggerated. The French and British armies were indeed staggering in retreat. In Paris, where the rumble of the battle to stem the onrushing German right wing could be heard faintly in the distance, disorder and confusion reigned. Refugees clogged the streets and railroad stations. The French government had evacuated the city and set up in Bordeaux. To Allen every minor French functionary left behind seemed slightly drunk and more than a little hysterical. The American Embassy still appeared to be running smoothly. Despite tremendous pressures, Ambassador Myron T. Herrick had somehow managed the repatriation of most of the Americans in France while simultaneously taking over the affairs of the departed German and Austrian ambassadors.[13]

By September 6, with little for them to do in Paris, Allen and several other officers on the commission decided to borrow an automobile and visit the front. For the next eight days they drove through the French and British sectors north and east of the city, stopping briefly at the headquarters of Generals Foch and Joffre and traveling as many as 200 miles a day over shell-pitted roads lined with more refugees and, often, the rotting corpses of soldiers and animals. In the trenches, first aid stations, and dugout command posts at the front Allen talked to dozens of junior officers and their men, grimy and hollow-eyed from lack of sleep. The colonels and generals he met farther to the rear seemed nearly as battle-worn. "All had an air so different from maneuver time that one look at the expression of half a dozen soldiers told a war story."[14] As Allen watched, these weary and bedraggled men dug in their heels, stopped the German advance, and went over to the attack for the first time in a month. What he was seeing at first hand was one of the most decisive battles in history, the Battle of the Marne.

During their travels Allen and Breckenridge had discussed the possibility of Allen's remaining in Europe as a military observer once the relief commission finished its work. Breckenridge had already received permission from the War Department to place several of the junior officers who had come over on the *Tennessee* with the British and French armies as observers. Allen volunteered for the same duty with the Russians although, by law, having served four years on the General Staff he was supposed to return to duty with troops. Breckenridge felt Allen's qualifications for the observer post were so obvious that the law should be waived in his case. On September 9, he cabled a request to this effect to Secretary of War Lindley M. Garrison.[15]

When Allen returned to Paris from the front he read Secretary Garrison's reply. Instead of going to Russia he was to come home with Breckenridge and report on what he had seen thus far. Disappointed but not surprised, he left Paris for London on September 18.[16]

On arriving in England Allen learned that the commission would be finished and ready to leave in about two weeks. Before sailing he had time to inspect the huge British training camps at Aldershot and Salisbury Plain and to meet a number of diplomatic and military experts and talk about what the war portended.[17] He and Breckenridge had a particularly revealing interview with the Secretary of State for War, Lord Kitchener. Kitchener was "not deceiving himself" as to

Britain's military weakness. The 200,000 men sent over to France "had already eaten up all the supplies England possessed." Their losses had been "very heavy," and the replacements being trained at Aldershot would not be ready for battle until the following spring. In the meantime there were not even enough arms or uniforms to equip them. "It was a crime," he said, "for a nation not to have reserve supplies." [18]

Their work successfully completed, Allen and Breckenridge booked a stateroom together on the *Lusitania* and sailed homeward on October 3. (One hundred and twenty-five thousand Americans had actually been repatriated, more than twice the original estimate.)[19] Six days later Allen was back in Washington, polishing the final draft of his report. Simultaneously, he tried in vain to persuade his superiors to send some experienced senior officers to Europe as observers. To him it seemed as if almost everyone in the War Department had his head in the sand. In disgust, he wrote to Leonard Wood:

> . . . It is a crime for us not to have some first class men in each of the countries. . . . Staff schools and war colleges are as nothing compared to the allopathic doses that one may now get in applied military art by profiting by what is now taking place. The United States is the one great country whose representatives are personae gratae to all the belligerents. I have talked with the Secretary, who is not keen, with Wotherspoon, who feels that he has done about all he can, and with [General Hugh L.] Scott [Wotherspoon's successor-to-be], who says he can do nothing. Breckenridge is very keen about the matter. Now is a moment when the masterful hand of Wood is missed. Being in Scott's room, I am trying to get him to study and ponder over the European situation, with a view to improving ours.[20]

Allen submitted his report to Secretary Garrison on October 21, 1914. In twenty-one typewritten pages, he reviewed the military organization, strategy, strengths, and weaknesses of each of the major powers, discussed their reserve and mobilization systems and level of preparedness prior to the war, commented on the actual or potential impact of advances in technology, predicted certain inevitable results of the war regardless of which side won, and drew from all this what he believed were the lessons for the United States. Allen's discussion of reserves, mobilization, and preparedness echoed the unpopular ideas of his friends Wood and Roosevelt. He contrasted the problems of England, "criminally unprepared for the present struggle," with "the rapidity and smoothness" of the mobilizations of the continental powers, particularly Germany. Whereas the latter nation's preparation for war had "probably never been equaled for thoroughness in the history of the world," and no other army had such a well-balanced and well-supplied organization, mobilization would not be complete for another two years in England. Because of "the suddenness with which wars fall upon a people and the absolute necessity of having *trained* men to increase the peace strength up to war strength," Allen felt the United States needed a European-style reserve system. As Wood had done three years earlier, he recommended shortening enlistments in the active army and adding a five-year period in the reserves to every soldier's obligation. Predicting that Germany would survive despite the "enormously superior numbers" of her enemies, he said: "Preparation does not *necessarily* prevent war, but it *often* does prevent it, and still oftener it prevents invasion and annihilation." [21]

Then, after commenting unfavorably on the ruggedness and reliability of the U.S. Army's standard model machine gun as compared with the makes (all the inventions of Americans) in use in Europe, Allen went on to discuss the significance of the increased role of several other kinds of machines in this war. Having seen the "terrible slaughter" on the battlefield of the Marne resulting from the massing of indirect (not line-of-sight) artillery fire, he confessed to a "change of heart" in his opinion of its effectiveness. Declaring, "It is practically impossible for any large armed force to make headway against another having great superiority in artillery," he urged "a great increase" in that arm for the U.S. Army. He had also changed his mind about the military usefulness of the airplane and the dirigible. Instead of being "limited chiefly . . . to the service of information," he said, "the potentiality of these machines as offensive weapons will be recognized by all nations." He went so far as to predict "an expedition of Zeppelins from Germany against England" and praised the recent congressional action establishing an "embryo Aviation Corps" as "a wise measure." [22] As for the use of trucks by the armies of Europe, Allen said this:

> Probably next to the development in indirect artillery fire and in air craft, the most noteworthy advance in war appliances is the use of the motor truck. . . . They were seen everywhere in the rear of the . . . French and English forces and often times 50 to 100 . . . in one train moving along the road at about 15 to 20 miles per hour. . . . By their great carrying capacity . . . , rate of speed, and mobility [trucks] are simply wonderful in carrying supplies. . . . It has been said that our roads are so inferior to the roads in Europe that we have nothing to learn from that practice. That is a radical mistake. . . . In my opinion we should seek a greater development in the domain of motor vehicles. . . .[23]

As if all this was not enough for the Secretary of War to ponder, Allen added more observations and some unsettling predictions:

> The Hapsburg Empire has been losing in war power since the wars of Frederick the Great. As a whole it cannot be considered a highly progressive State, and its army is simply a true exponent of the country. Whatever happens . . . in this war, great losses in territory must be included in Austro-Hungary's lot.
>
> In view of the possible danger, even though remote, from the Orient, it seems unfortunate that the Allies considered it necessary to use colored troops. [They] . . . are doing wonderful fighting and are supporting their losses with marked fortitude. The superiority of the white man will probably, as a result of this war, disappear from their minds. . . .
>
> The use of the colored man will only advance . . . a struggle between the West and the East—in due course of time. . . . England has seen fit to allow her ally, Japan, to occupy the principal station of the Carolines, thus making her our near neighbor in the Philippines.[24]

Allen concluded his report by stating that none of the "principal nations" involved in the war could be destroyed. "The same people with their racial antipathies and their religious prejudices will continue to exist," he said. Moreover, it was difficult for him to believe "that any great questions connected with these matters" would be solved or that the vanquished would be reconciled with the victors. He then used this pessimistic analysis to refute the argument advanced by others in the War Department that the nation could afford to defer "reasonable war preparations" until the fighting had ended in Europe. Another war was almost certain to follow. To assume that only a German victory in the present war might require any strengthening of America's defenses was to Allen "unwise." Even if the United States had little to fear from the triumph of Germany's European enemies, that outcome would inevitably increase the power of their Asiatic ally, Japan—and Japan was already a threat to American interests in the Pacific.[25]

Secretary Garrison kept Allen's report for several months before returning it to the War College Division—without comment.[26] Allen was only one of many persons high and low, inside and outside the War Department, telling him what should be done. Others were making the same kind of recommendations as Allen, most notably Wood, Stimson, and Roosevelt.[27] But such counsel had to be balanced against President Wilson's admonition to the nation to remain "neutral in thought as in deed" and the advice of caution coming from many senior officers in the War Department. General Wotherspoon, an old soldier in every sense of the word, was retiring as Chief of Staff in less than a month. General Scott, his successor, was another relic of the Indian-fighting army, although possessed of more energy and imagination than Wotherspoon. Scott put what energy he had to work on a proposal to strengthen the coastal defenses of the United States by building large-caliber guns and mounting them on railway carriages. If the invasion of the North American continent was an unlikely outcome of a war in Europe, Scott's idea was at least a modest step in the direction of preparedness. Since it implied no belligerent intentions on the part of the United States, Scott felt the plan should have been palatable to the Administration. Even so, he found a "strange apathy" to it in the War Department. "I got absolutely no support," he wrote. "It was declared impractical and unnecessary."[28]

The War College continued to draft elaborate schemes for mobilization and the creation of a reserve system, but these plans were exercises in futility without the will or the money to implement them. Both were lacking in Washingon. As for the new machines of war whose revolutionary impact was being demonstrated so effectively across the Atlantic, the greybeards in the Ordnance and Quartermaster departments were in no hurry to equip the U.S. Army with them. They dimly recognized the potential of masses of artillery, airplanes, and trucks (although many cavalrymen still snorted at the idea the latter could ever replace the horse in cross-country movement), but such things cost more money than Congress would ever appropriate in peacetime. What was needed was more testing and improvement of these machines. Then, if the need for mass production arose, the army could be equipped with the very latest models. Secretary Garrison did lean far enough toward preparedness to push, unsuccessfully, for his Continental Army Plan, a bill to more than double the size of the army and set up a reserve under Federal control. Aside from that, until 1916 at least, it was pretty much business as usual in the War Department.[29] For all the good it did, Allen might as well have never written his report. On the other hand, given the prevailing mood of the country, the more conservative advice of officers senior to Allen, and, above all, the determinedly neutral policy of President Wilson, Secretary Garrison can hardly be blamed for pigeonholing the disquieting opinions and recommendations of a lowly lieutenant colonel.

As his last duty in Washington, Allen gave a talk to the students and staff of the Army War College entitled: "Observations on the Present European Struggle and the Lessons It Teaches Ourselves." In it he said essentially what he had written for the Secretary of War.[30] If some in Allen's audience agreed with what he had to say, they were as powerless as he to do anything about it.

The following day, October 29, 1914, he left for Kentucky to visit Harry and check on the opening of a coal mine in which he and his brothers had become partners. He had three months of leave coming before he had to report to the 11th Cavalry at Fort Oglethorpe, Georgia. Dora, meanwhile, went to Fort Ethan Allen to be with Jeanette when her first baby came in December. Dasha, whose increasing frailness and pallor worried her parents considerably, went off to the milder climate of Asheville, North Carolina, for a tuberculosis check-up and treatment. Much improved in appearance and spirits she joined her parents at Fort Oglethorpe in February, 1915.[31]

The entire 11th Cavalry Regiment had recently returned from duty in a cold and dingy mining area of Colorado where they had been sent the previous May to help put down disorders arising out of a coal strike.[32] The troopers were glad to be through with this unpleasant experience and sleeping in warm barracks again. Those who had left wives or sweethearts on the post or in nearby Chattanooga were doubly glad to be home. Among the returning bachelor officers there was a race to pay court to the newly arrived colonel's daughter. The winner was a young lieutenant who had been with the regiment since his graduation from West Point in 1913.

His name was Joe Viner. Short, dark, gruff in manner and physically tough, but withal a gentleman and a gentle man, Joe became a regular visitor at the Allens' quarters. Within a few months he and Dasha were engaged to be married.[33]

Viner got along well with his prospective father-in-law, as did most of the other officers in the regiment. The Regimental Commander, Colonel James Lockett, did not. Both he and Allen were West Pointers (Lockett was graduated in 1879), but they had little else in common. Except for two brief tours in the Philippines between 1900 and 1910, Lockett had never been out of the United States. All of his thirty-six years as an officer had been spent with troops. In combat he had shown courage, but otherwise his record was that of an unimaginative plodder. He read no books, had no influential friends and no interest in politics or society, and he hated Allen's guts.[34]

Lockett's lackluster performance in command of the regiment during its months in Colorado was typical. In early May, 1914, when Secretary Garrison began to look around for a unit to reinforce the small contingent of regulars already at the Colorado mines, the 11th Cavalry was all he could spare. Every other unit of similar size might have been needed elsewhere at any moment because of the simultaneous and much more serious crisis with Mexico. Garrison described Lockett to President Wilson as "a level-headed man and as good an officer as we can get under the circumstances."[35] Even this faint praise may have been too generous, for Lockett took the wrong train and arrived in Colorado the day after his troops did, although he had started from Oglethorpe before they left. The Secretary of War kept a tight telegraphic rein on him thereafter. With this high-level supervision and the help of able subordinates Lockett got the job done in Colorado.[36]

At Oglethorpe he was soon eclipsed by his ambitious new second in command. Lockett had never bothered to ask the mayor of Chattanooga to the post for a visit or to see a parade. Allen had him to dinner at his quarters. The mayor responded with an invitation for Allen to speak on the European war and the need for American preparedness before the local manufacturers' association. He was well received and asked to give more talks on the subject. In late 1915 and early 1916, he spoke to several other groups in the Chattanooga-Knoxville area.[37]

Allen also corresponded with Leonard Wood and Theodore Roosevelt about the preparedness movement the two men were organizing. T.R. was up to his old Rough Rider tricks. In the event of a war he wanted to organize a division of volunteers. This time, he promised Allen a share of the glory:

> . . . at present it looks as if those at the head of our national affairs could not be kicked into fighting; still it is always possible that trouble will come. In that event I wish you as Senior Brigade Commander, because I wish to have that Division in such shape that if anything happens to me . . . you can at once take charge . . . and get the best work possible out of it. . . . I shall feel entirely at ease if I am obliged to leave the Division to your care. Naturally I hope . . . I shall not have to leave it to you, except by myself going up and not going out. But . . . there is always a chance, not only of the ordinary disasters of the field, but, in a government like ours, of a man's not being allowed to go to the front.[38]

In their letters, Wood and Allen discussed less romantic and more immediately practical projects. Both agreed the training area at Olgethorpe was large enough to accommodate another cavalry regiment should any new ones be organized. Allen told Wood the 11th Cavalry was not being kept busy enough. With only a monthly practice-ride of fifteen miles, target practice twice a year, and an occasional rehearsal for loading each unit onto railroad cars, the troopers seldom worked up a sweat. Allen suggested they could be put to fuller use by conducting summer training for state militia units or groups of businessmen like those who had volunteered at Wood's and Roosevelt's call to undergo six weeks of basic training at an army camp in Plattsburg, New York. Wood approved both of Allen's ideas. In August, 1915, a unit of cavalry militia trained at Fort Oglethorpe. Allen used some men from the 11th as instructors and commanded this "Joint Camp of Instruction." By early 1916, plans were well underway to repeat the "Plattsburg experiment" at Fort Oglethorpe that summer.[39]

Allen had Lockett's approval for these projects, though they were not the colonel's idea. He gritted his teeth and went along with this cavalier disruption of the post's somnolent routine, but he let his resentment show on Allen's efficiency reports. At the end of 1915, after acknowledging his subordinate's competence and resourcefulness, Lockett added: "Possibly a bit too hot headed and impatient." [40] Six months later, in another report, Lockett scored a bullseye: "A very virile, energetic, intelligent officer who never loses sight of his own interests," he said of Allen. On the next entry on the form, personal animosity slightly spoiled his aim. In response to the question, "For what class of duty is he best suited in event of the outbreak of war?" Lockett put down, "On duty at some General's Headquarters as an aide." [41] By the time these words branding Allen as a social-climbing dilettante were written, he had proven once again he could also be a tough and untiring leader of men.

At 4:10 A.M. on March 9, 1916, a bullet stopped the clock in the railroad station at Columbus, New Mexico.[42] A raid by the Mexican revolutionary and bandit leader Francisco (Pancho) Villa surprised the sleeping border town and its garrison of the 13th Cavalry. Villa's force, estimated at 500 men, burned and looted for several hours before they were driven off and pursued briefly into Mexico by the initially disorganized soldiers. The morning sun rose on the bodies of sixty-seven Mexicans and sixteen Americans dead in the streets of Columbus.[43]

The raid was Villa's most recent depredation against American lives and property on both sides of the border. His motives are still the subject of some debate, but they can be explained in part by a simple desire for vengeance. There were certain individuals in Columbus who, Villa felt, had cheated him in business dealings. He also held a grudge against the nation that had recently recognized the *de facto* government of his archrival, Venustiano Carranza. In addition, Villa needed the supplies obtainable in Columbus denied him since the imposition of an American arms embargo. It is possible he was also playing a deeper game by trying to provoke the Americans into an invasion that would discredit and humiliate Carranza in the eyes of his people. By fanning the flames of popular hatred of the Yankees and posing as the one leader capable of repelling them, Villa may have hoped to overthrow Carranza.[44]

On the same day as the Columbus raid, President Wilson approved the request of Major General Frederick Funston, commanding the Southern Department, to send an expedition into Mexico after Villa. Funston's plan called for two columns of cavalry to cross the border, one at Columbus and the other from Culbertson's Ranch, seventy-five miles farther west. Once in Mexico they would pursue Villa, using the road network between the Sierra Madre Range and the Mexican Northwestern Railroad, both of which ran in a generally north-south direction. Infantry, artillery, and other support units would follow. Brigadier General John J. Pershing, commander of the district around El Paso, was chosen to lead this force of 10,000 men, designated as the Punitive Expedition of the United States Army. Three of the four cavalry regiments to be under his command were already on border duty and quickly available. The fourth was the 11th Cavalry.[45]

At Fort Oglethorpe, the regiment received its marching orders at 1:00 A.M. on March 12. The first railroad cars arrived for loading at the post depot ten hours later, and the first of seven trains bound for Columbus departed at 5:45 that same afternoon. Colonel Lockett rode out on the first train. Allen followed him by four hours on the second. On board were three of his own polo ponies, more spirited than the government's mounts, for his personal use on the expedition. Joe Viner left with the 2nd Squadron early the next morning. Two of Dasha's horses went with him. By 9:30 A.M. on March 13, thirty-two officers and 905 men, with all their horses and field equipment, were on their way to the Mexican border and, perhaps, to war. Dora Allen and Dasha Viner stood on the platform with the other women on the post and saw their husbands off, waving until the trains disappeared into the distance. War or not, such farewells were a familiar experience for Dora after twenty-eight years of marriage to Henry Allen. For Dasha, a bride of four months, it was her initiation as an army wife.[46]

By the time the last of the 11th had reached Columbus near midnight on March 16, the leading elements of Pershing's two columns were already inside Mexico, having crossed the border thirty-six hours earlier. As soon as Lockett arrived, Pershing elevated him to command the eastern column, consisting of a provisional brigade made up of two regiments, the 13th, already on the march, and the 11th. Under Colonel George H. Sands, an officer recently attached to the regiment, the 11th Cavalry entered Mexico on the morning of March 17 with Allen's 1st Squadron in the lead.[47]

Had he chosen to, Carranza could have regarded the entry of American troops as an act of war. Washington claimed to have his sanction for the expedition, but this was not strictly true. The Mexican government had expressed its regret for the "lamentable occurrence at Columbus" and requested permission for its own forces to cross the border into United States territory "in order to exterminate the horde led by Francisco Villa." Reciprocal privileges were promised to the Americans *"if the raid effected at Columbus should . . . be repeated. . . ."*[48] (Italics added.) On March 13, Washington agreed to the Mexican request, adding that it understood the reciprocal agreement was then in force and action could be taken under it "without further interchange of views."[49]

On the same day the Mexican government published a proclamation giving the gist of this agreement and directing its officials in the northern provinces to co-operate with the American army.[50] But, by March 18, with 5,000 United States troops already concentrating at Colonia Dublan, 100 miles due south of Columbus, Carranza had some second thoughts: "the consent . . . in regard to the crossing of armed troops over our frontier line is being erroneously understood by taking it for granted that . . . a military expedition in pursuit of Villa has been permitted. . . ."[51]

Carranza subsequently repudiated the reciprocal agreement entirely and made a number of threatening gestures aimed at forcing the expedition's withdrawal. Some bloodshed resulted, but neither government really wanted to fight. Both stopped short of the kind of confrontation in which the choice was either war or humiliation. In fact, so long as Carranza appeared not to welcome the expedition, it might work to his advantage by eliminating a rival or dispersing his forces. Wilson also stood to gain from the satisfaction of the American public that at last something forceful was being done to protect the long-terrorized residents of the border area.[52]

Restricted in his freedom of action, Pershing thus faced a very delicate situation. Against a background of confused and contradictory diplomatic maneuvering, he had to try to capture Villa without further antagonizing his fellow countrymen. Many of the people of Chihuahua, Villa's home territory, had always been his supporters in the struggle for power with Carranza, Huerta, and Zapata. Others were at least willing to take Villa's side against the American invaders.[53] A hostile population was only one of Pershing's problems. The terrain ahead of him was equally forbidding and largely unmapped.

Four-fifths of the state of Chihuahua is a desertlike plateau. The only forage for animals is the thin grass that springs up in the summer rainy season but lies dormant the rest of the year. Cut by innumerable ravines, the soil ranges in consistency from gravel to fine silt, making it hard going for horses. The ravines run in fresh torrents from June through August, but dwindle to stagnant and poisonous alkali pools when the rains stop. The Sierra Madre Range, which covers the western part of the province and rises to elevations of 10,000 feet, is scarcely more hospitable. Water and forage are more plentiful in the mountains, but some areas are almost inaccessible to men on horseback. Travel through the narrow, rocky canyons is slow and difficult and, for a military force, an open invitation to ambush. For obvious reasons, the Sierra Madre had always been Villa's refuge.[54]

On March 17, Pershing arrived at Colonia Dublan with the western column (the 7th and 10th Cavalry regiments) and set up camp outside the town. According to local reports, Villa was at San Miguel de Babicora, fifty miles to the south, recruiting men and collecting horses and supplies to make up for his losses at Columbus. Pershing immediately dispatched three mounted detachments along parallel routes to cut off Villa's escape. On March 21, the first of the three columns reached the San Miguel area only to find Villa had not been within miles of the place. The commander of this detachment, Colonel William C. Brown of the 10th Cavalry, decided to continue south to San José de Babicora. There he was soon joined by Major Ellwood E. Evans with the second column of the 10th Cavalry. On March 23, Colonel Brown learned of a recent fight between Villa's band and the *Carranzista* garrison at Namquipa. Its commander told Brown that Villa was probably now a few miles farther east. Brown asked the Mexican officer to send out scouting parties to locate Villa and offered to attack him once this was done. The Mexican agreed to the bargain. By March 27, however, no reconnaissance had been made, so the Americans went looking for Villa on their own. Informants told them their quarry was holed up at the Santa Catarina Ranch. Brown had the ranch surrounded the next morning, but Villa was not there. The third of Pershing's columns from Colonia Dublan did make contact with part of Villa's forces at Guerrero on March 29, killing at least thirty bandits and dispersing the rest, but Villa himself, rumored to be

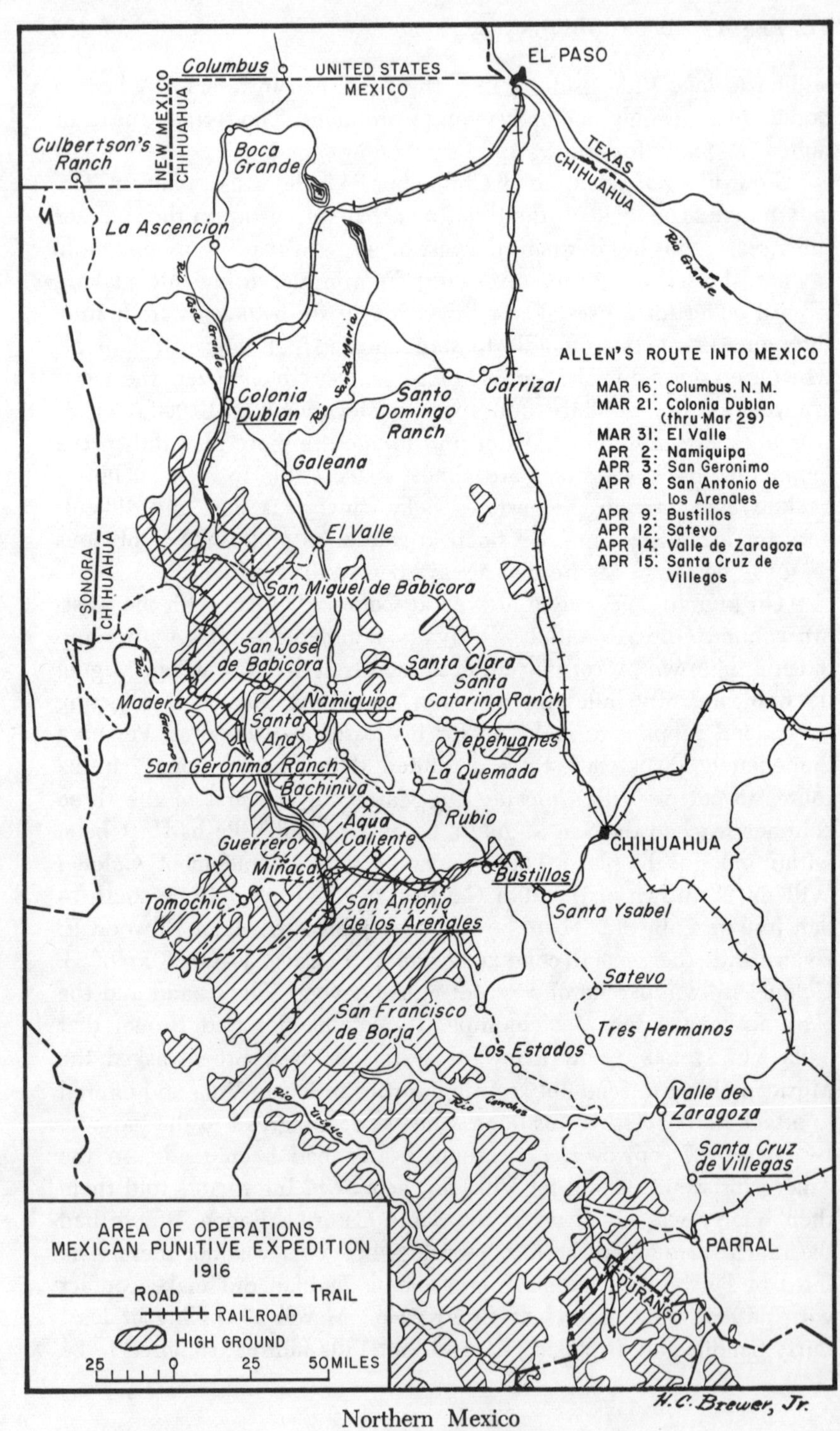

Northern Mexico

wounded and traveling with a small escort, had apparently moved south a few days before.[55]

These experiences were typical of the entire expedition. Villa was everywhere—and nowhere. As Pershing's columns seemed alternately hot on his trail and to have lost the scent entirely, the mystery of his whereabouts drew this satiric report from an American newspaper:

> Since General Pershing was sent out to capture him, Villa has been mortally wounded in the leg and died in a lonely cave. He was assassinated by one of his own band and his grave was identified by a Carranza follower who hoped for a suitable reward from President Wilson. Villa was likewise killed in a brawl at a ranch house where he was engaged in the gentle diversion of burning men and women at the stake. He was also shot on a wild ride and his body cremated. Yet through all these experiences which, it must be confessed, would have impaired the health of any ordinary man, Villa has not only retained the vital spark of life but has renewed his youth and strength. He seems all the better for his vacation, strenuous though it must have been.[56]

While Brown, Dodd, and Evans chased a will-o'-the-wisp, Lockett's provisional brigade arrived at Colonia Dublan. During the last week of March, Pershing sent four more columns south from Colonia Dublan to join in the hunt. By early April, having found no trace of Villa within 100 miles of Namquipa, Pershing concluded his quarry had probably decided to stay hidden in the Sierra Madre and move as fast as possible toward Durango Province, bordering Chihuahua on the south. There was a limit beyond which Pershing could not go without outrunning his supply lines, not to mention risking a Mexican declaration of war. Both dangers increased with every mile. The only way to beat Villa to the Durango line was to use small, fast-moving detachments. From his scattered units Pershing chose the four officers he wanted to command these flying columns: Colonel Brown, Major Frank Tompkins of the 13th Cavalry, and Major Robert L. Howze and Lieutenant Colonel Henry T. Allen of the 11th Cavalry. They handpicked their men and animals.[57] Howze selected Lieutenant Viner as one of the officers he wanted with him.[58]

As they moved ever deeper into Mexico, the four columns spread out in a roughly diamond-shaped formation: Tompkins in the lead, Brown to his left rear a day's march behind, Howze to his right rear at an equal distance, and Allen between them, three days behind Tompkins. Pershing tried to keep in touch with all four officers by using his automobile, an open Dodge touring car, as a mobile command post. But he and they moved so fast Pershing was often out of touch with everyone, bumping along over dusty and unmarked roads. The Signal Corps wire-laying teams could not keep up, and Pershing's radios in the Dodge had a range of only twenty-five miles. He had no staff officers with him, only his aide (a brash young lieutenant named George S. Patton), a cook, and four enlisted bodyguards. For scouting and courier service, Pershing had planned to depend on the eight biplanes assigned to the expedition from the thirteen craft of the First Aero Squadron, the entire military aviation force of the United States. Within a month, all eight underpowered planes had crashed or were out of commission.[59] If these failures of the newest military technology left Pershing to command by the seat of his pants, at least that seat had an automobile cushion under it. Brown, Tompkins, Howze, Allen, and their men were less comfortable.

Allen's column consisted of 108 mounted men, a Mormon missionary interpreter, two *vaqueros* as guides, a pack train of eighty-six mules, and a black burro named Peter. Peter was probably the most important member of the caravan, for he supplied Allen's men with their means for living off the land. Nicknamed the "First American Bank of Mexico," Peter carried on his back 500 dollars in silver.[60] In hastily scribbled pencil notes sent back by courier, Henry told Dora how it was with them:

> [Last night] we had a severe snowstorm with rain; and just now it is hot; this morning we crossed a mountain over the roughest road I have ever seen. . . . Our hands and faces are dreadfully chapped. . . . Everybody and everything is covered with dust.[61]
>
> All of us are peeling . . . dirty and unshaven. . . . However thus far I have left behind only 2 men from sickness. As my medico and his one hospital man were not sufficiently mobile for my purposes I left them behind and have made myself the medico. . . . My column has not even a skillet. All our cooking is done in individual mess kits or in tins that bacon is taken from. . . . Going to bed is a simple proposition. We simply take off our boots and some take off only their spurs. We have had ice every night.[62]
>
> We have now covered over 500 miles and a great deal of it has been on foot to save the horses. Of course the horses have suffered dreadfully and now the men's shoes are about done for. . . . The supplies in a country like this are of course meagre and the grass for our stock very short. We are expecting some supplies today from the rear. . . .[63]
>
> Fresh meat and insufficiently boiled beans caused considerable indigestion and stomach trouble for a while, but everyone is about well now. My health continues excellent.[64]

As the columns began to converge on the town of Parral near the Durango line, the hunger and fatigue of horses and men became secondary problems. They were increasingly harassed by sniper fire, and more than one *Carranzista* official along the way strongly hinted that a further advance would be opposed with force.[65] Major Tompkins reached Parral first, on April 12.

Hoping to obtain provisions and fresh information on Villa's movements, Tompkins found instead a town of 20,000 seething with hatred of the Americanos and a trap laid for him by the commander of the local garrison. That officer promised to lead Tompkins to a campsite near the town where the supplies he needed would be delivered. As they rode together out to the camp, Tompkins realized his danger. By then it was too late. A civilian mob followed the column and soon opened fire on the rear guard. On a hill just ahead were deployed several hundred Carranza soldiers. Turning to the Mexican at his side, Tompkins angrily asked for an explanation. Shrugging his shoulders, the officer denied all responsibility for what was happening and turned his horse back toward town. A few minutes later he sent out a messenger with a demand for the Americans to withdraw immediately. Tompkins replied he would leave as soon as the promised supplies arrived. Instead of returning to Parral, the messenger joined the troops blocking Tompkins' advance. As soon as he rode up they opened fire on the Americans. At the same time, the mob began closing in on both flanks. Outnumbered and almost surrounded, Tompkins' force of about 100 men began to retreat, fighting a rear-guard action for several hours until it reached a defensible position late in the afternoon near Santa Cruz de Villegas, eighteen miles to the north. In the running battle two Americans were killed and six wounded. Tompkins, one of the wounded, estimated his men had killed at least forty Mexicans.[66]

Colonel Brown's detachment rode into Santa Cruz a few hours later, and Howze came in the next day. Riding hard, Allen arrived at 6:00 A.M. on April 15. He and his men had been on the march for seventeen consecutive days and covered the last fifty-five miles to Santa Cruz nonstop in twenty-two hours.[67] Allen had just spent his fifty-seventh birthday in the saddle.

Pershing now had a force of over 600 men and 900 animals concentrated deep inside Mexico. There had been no more shooting since the evening of April 12, but militarily his position was untenable. The diplomatic repercussions of the Parral encounter could well lead to war, and here was part of his command at the end of an impossibly long supply line.[68]

A week before Pershing entered Mexico and almost seventeen months after Allen had recommended the use of trucks to haul supplies in his report to the Secretary of War, the U.S. Army had no organized system of motor transport. A fleet of trucks of various makes had been hastily assembled at Columbus for Pershing's use, but the army had no drivers, no mechanics, and no one who knew how to plan and organize a convoy. Hired civilians drove and maintained the trucks. Inevitably, there were breakdowns on the dusty and rutted Mexican roads. Spare parts were something else no one had thought about. As a result, though most of the trucks somehow stayed in operation, horses and wagons still did much of the hauling.[69] Aside from the vulnerability of a supply line running all the way from Columbus to Santa Cruz de Villegas, Pershing simply lacked the transport to keep his troops supplied at such a distance.

On April 12, the men at Santa Cruz began to withdraw to the north. By early May all of the more southerly outposts had been abandoned, and Namquipa became the main base of operations. In the next two months, while Mexican-American relations continued to worsen, Pershing's patrols had a number of minor skirmishes with the remnants of Villa's forces, but no more was seen or heard of their leader. The last major battle of the expedition came on June 21 at Carrizal. As at Parral, the fight resulted from the opposition of *Carranzista* forces to the movement of American troops in any direction except north. There were forty-eight Americans killed, wounded, or captured in this engagement, and it brought the two governments to the very brink of war. Pershing received orders to withdraw to Colonia Dublan and hold his command in readiness for the worst. Shortly thereafter, in July, 1916, a joint Mexican-American Commission was appointed to try to reach a negotiated solution to the impasse.[70] While the diplomats talked, the troops waited at Colonia Dublan.

In the period of reorganization following the withdrawal from Parral, Pershing brought Allen up to his staff. Much to Allen's distress, he became Inspector General of the expedition. He preferred to remain in the field with his men and suspected (correctly) the staff assignment was Pershing's way of telling him he was getting too old.[71] With bandits still to chase and war with Mexico a distinct possibility, nothing could have been less interesting to Allen than traveling around to the various units, sticking his nose in latrines and mess tents, checking on the status of discipline, training, and maintenance, investigating reports of misconduct, and writing dull reports about it all.[72]

Pershing felt Allen deserved a rest after the race to Parral, and he needed an experienced officer to look after the hundreds of minor details, which, if left unsupervised to go wrong, might seriously impair the efficiency of his command, but he soon changed his mind about putting Allen out to pasture. Allen held the staff job from April 30 to June 21, 1916.[73] During that time he and Pershing saw each other almost daily. They had been casual acquaintances for years. Never having served together, however, neither knew what kind of man the other really was.[74]

Superficially, they were much alike: cool, impersonal, precisely articulate, impatient, disdainful of mediocrity. Both had strong wills and tempers to match. Each knew the other to be ambitious. But Pershing, a brigadier general at fifty-six with ten years in grade, could hardly have seen Allen as a competitor to himself. Although the quirks of fate that had kept Allen from remaining a general back in 1907 still rankled, he kept his resentment concealed. There was irony in their present relationship. Except for the fuss over Pershing's promotion from captain to general in 1906, Allen might well have kept his star and his date of rank of 1903. Pershing had been sélected to lead the Punitive Expedition because of his reputation for level-headedness and the fact that he already commanded the troops in the vicinity of Columbus, but the deciding factor was probably his six years in command of large numbers of troops in the Philippines, more field experience than any other officer of equivalent rank.[75] Allen could claim just as many years of experience, with five times as many men under his command. Only his troops had not been Americans, and he was no longer a general.

No doubt a mutual awareness of this irony kept the two men from becoming close friends, but there were other reasons, too. Beneath the surface they were very different people. Since the death of Pershing's wife and three of their four children in a fire in their quarters less than a year before, he had become a humorless machine of a man.[76] The iron in Allen went deep, but not that far. He had a lighthearted streak in him, an impetuousness, and love of fun, good company, and new adventure that he had never lost since his bachelor days. Polo, hunting, bridge, stimulating talk, and an endless variety of books had always been his favorite diversions. He did not care if some of his more dour associates thought him frivolous because of it. As long as he could also lead men for a thousand miles over desert and mountain, no one could question his toughness.

Nobody ever called Pershing frivolous, though he had once had a zest for life almost equal to Allen's. All of Pershing's enormous energy and considerable intelligence was now focused on one thing: his work. The light in his tent often burned into the gray hours of early morning.[77] But he and Allen found they could work together in harmony. They grew to respect and perhaps even admire each other even though it was never a warm relationship.[78] On Allen's efficiency report for 1916, under Lockett's sneering remarks, Pershing described his Inspector General as "an able, energetic and loyal officer," best suited in time of war for duty "in command of cavalry or as a general staff officer." [79]

In May, word came from the War Department that Allen would be promoted to full colonel on July 1 as a result of the army expansion recently approved by Congress. On June 21, Pershing put him in temporary command of both the 11th Cavalry and the camp at Colonia Dublan.[80] Colonels Lockett and Sands, neither of whom had particularly distinguished himself in Mexico, were both leaving the expedition. Sands, whose stomach ulcer could only tolerate oatmeal, was retiring for disability.[81] Lockett drifted for the next three years from one petty assignment to the next, in charge of a series of examining stations, recruit depots, and training camps.[82]

Pershing told Allen he wanted to keep him with the 11th, but in mid-August the War Department assigned him to command the 13th Cavalry.[83] For the remainder of 1916, as the war clouds faded in the Mexican sky and grew darker eastward over the Atlantic, life at Colonia Dublan settled into an almost peaceful routine. The camp took on the appearance of any post in the American Southwest, complete with rows of new adobe structures (under temporary canvas roofs) laid out with military precision. The cavalry still patrolled around the camp and along the line of communications back to the rear base at Columbus, but there were no more encounters with either Villa's forces or Carranza's. To keep the troops active Pershing began a vigorous training program.[84]

Command of the 13th Cavalry kept Allen busy. Nevertheless, he had plenty of time for all his favorite diversions as well as that constant preoccupation, worrying about his promotion to general.

In June, with his colonelcy assured, he had sent telegrams to his private military and political "Who's Who" saying: "Will greatly appreciate your assistance in securing higher fighting command." [85] During the summer every recipient except one responded with promises to do all he could to help.[86] Only the note from Theodore Roosevelt was not encouraging, though not for any lack of his regard for Allen. From his political limbo at Oyster Bay, T.R. sounded almost pathetic:

"I wish I could help you, but I can't. . . . I have no influence with the powers that be." [87]

While Allen's monomania on the subject of promotion had not diminished in the slightest, his letters to the family showed more fatherly concern and tenderness than ever before. Above all, he wanted to see his wife and children happy. To Dora he wrote:

> Just now our children need money as much as they ever will. . . . We must turn over everything in time and why not do something now for them and ourselves that spells enjoyment.
>
> Don't try to live too economically. Remember who you are!! It seems to me that while you are young enough to *enjoy* that you should profit by the occasion.[88]

He thanked her for all the thoughtful little gifts she sent him to make his adobe-walled tent more comfortable and his mess table the envy of the camp. She worried that Jeanette was spoiling their granddaughter. He teased her not to be an anxious grandmother. "Don't butt in," he said. They talked of their hopes for Harry's future. He was then taking the training course at Plattsburg, and perhaps he might be able to pass the physical examination for a commission and join the army after all. Nothing would please his father more.[89]

As for Joe Viner, Allen proudly predicted a successful army career for his son-in-law. Joe had done well with Major Howze and distinguished himself in several encounters with the *Villistas* after that. Recently he had had his hands full commanding the army's only remaining detachment of Indian Scouts, Apache veterans of General Miles's campaign against Geronimo thirty years earlier. Ably assisted by First Sergeant Chicken, Sergeant Chow Big, and Corporals Big Sharley and B-25, Viner kept the scouts in line—most of the time. One who bore watching was Sergeant Hell Yet-Suey. "Wearing dust goggles, shaking his shoulder length hair and baring his teeth," he could frighten any Mexican prisoner into giving information, but he was prone to use less subtle means. Another problem was Charley Shipp, the tribal judge, who spent most of his time in the guardhouse as a buck private from too much indulgence in tequila.[90]

After his stint with the Apache Scouts, Lieutenant Viner became the Adjutant of the 11th Cavalry. The assignment nearly ruined his promising career. Toward the end of the expedition, General Frederick Funston left his headquarters to inspect the regiment and watch it pass in review at a mounted parade. Pershing accompanied him. As adjutant, Viner took the reports of the assembled squadrons, reported in turn to the regimental commander, and then joined the staff to await the arrival of the reviewing party. Viner's horse was a handsome white stallion, recently purchased from a local rancher to replace one of Dasha's ponies that had gone hopelessly lame on the march back from Parral. Army policy, of course, prohibited stallions in cavalry units. Joe's new horse had thus been immediately gelded. Viner performed the operation himself, assisted by the new regimental vet, fresh from veterinary school. What neither of these young officers realized was that this animal was that rare equine phenomenon, a horse with three testicles. Two were removed and the animal had recovered nicely, with nobody in the regiment the wiser as to his remaining masculine capability at the time of the parade in Funston's honor. It happened that the General's mare was in heat. The predictable occurred. As Funston and Pershing rode out to the place of honor for the review, Viner's horse gave a loud whinny, charged, and mounted Funston's mare. The diminutive general fought successfully to retain his seat, but with considerable damage to his dignity and composure. Several minutes elapsed before aides could separate the wildly plunging and pawing pair. In the meantime the regimental formation dissolved into a formless mass as riders let go their reins and held their sides in helpless laughter. Order of sorts was eventually restored, but the pass in review was ragged-looking indeed. Pershing's near apoplexy subsided into a cold fury. An abashed Lieutenant Viner stood before him that night to receive a merciless dressing down and to be dismissed with the words, "I *never* want to see you again, lieutenant." Pershing later confessed to Allen that he had nearly drawn his saber and chased Viner off the parade field and that only the fact that Joe was Allen's son-in-law had prevented his court-martial.[91]

Eleven months of high drama thus ended on a farcical note as the Mexican and American governments finally moved toward an agreement on the tangled issues behind the intervention. On February 5, 1917, after Mexico assumed full responsibility for future border incidents, the last troops of the Punitive Expedition left Mexican soil and diplomatic relations between the two countries were re-established.[92]

In one sense, the expedition was a total failure. Villa was, after all, still at large, and the memory of Pershing's campaign in Mexico would poison relations between the two countries for years to come. But, for the United States, at least, there were some positive results. The majority of the American people and their leaders began to realize what a few men had been saying all along: the army was almost fatally unprepared to fight a war, any war. For the army itself, the campaign was a romantic farewell to the days and ways of the Indian frontier and a timely chance to test new leaders, new methods, and new equipment.[93]

Two months after Pershing's return from Mexico, the United States declared war on Germany. Goaded by that nation's resumption of unrestricted submarine warfare and the subsequent loss of American ships and lives, President Wilson asked his countrymen to put aside neutrality in thought and deed and prepare for the "months of fiery trial and sacrifice" that lay ahead.[94]

When that call came, Colonel Henry T. Allen still commanded the 13th Cavalry, then stationed at Camp Stewart, Texas, near El Paso. Pershing had just sent a recommendation for his promotion to brigadier general to the War Department.[95]

CHAPTER IX

Leader of the "Tough 'Ombres"

In the month following America's declaration of war on Germany, the War Department worked overtime to draft and present to Congress the mobilization measures necessary to put the nation on a wartime footing. Until this complex machinery could be set up, there was little for those in the army outside Washington to do except continue training, follow the news from the capital and abroad, wait, and wonder what the coming months might bring.

At Camp Stewart, Colonel Henry T. Allen was as impatient and curious as any of his colleagues. Army rumor had it Pershing was being sent to Europe to confer with the Allied military leaders. That probably meant higher command for him when the time came. Another persistent report was that, despite War Department opposition, Theodore Roosevelt's friends in Congress were going to see to it he had a chance to organize his volunteer division. Which of these two stars to hitch his wagon to must have cost Allen many a restless night. When he could stand the uncertainty no longer he sent a telegram to Pershing in Washington:

> Depending on you to advise me relative to Roosevelt's forces and your command. Prefer service with you but wish to be loyal to former. Will be satisfied with your adjustment.[1]

Pershing's answer came back two days later, as he prepared to leave for Europe. He sent it just before the final vote in Congress on the War Department's mobilization bill, which included a congressionally added rider authorizing not one but four volunteer divisions. Disdaining any comment about "Roosevelt's forces," Pershing answered the other half of Allen's question directly:

> As to commanding a force in France, of course nothing has been decided. Therefore, there is nothing to talk about. I have no doubt that troops will go over eventually and should I go, I should be glad to have you with me. I am not only saying this to you, but to others as well, where it will do some good.[2]

If Allen had any lingering doubts about throwing in his lot with Pershing, the actions of the War Department soon dispelled them. No volunteer divisions would be raised despite their authorization by Congress. Roosevelt's admirers were quick to accuse the Administration of petty malice in refusing to give their hero another chance for glory, but there were more important reasons for the demise of the hoary wartime tradition of volunteer units. To his credit, old General Scott had had the wisdom to say to Secretary of War Newton D. Baker:

> This is an unwitting proposition to continue the same old mistakes we have made in all our previous wars by raising a political army. . . . Mr. Roosevelt's request cuts directly across our policy of conscription which we must insist upon in order to win the war. . . .
>
> Mr. Roosevelt proposes . . . to milk the regular army of all its best officers for his one division, to form of the preferred stock the Rough Riders of this war, leaving the great army of millions to be less well instructed and on an inferior status. . . . Mr. Roosevelt has not given this the consideration it deserves. He is very honest about it but he is not a trained soldier in any respect, although he thinks he is, and if sent over in command, would do as he himself considers best . . . , and you would have small control over him.[3]

Roosevelt thus remained in his limbo, bitter, frustrated, and failing in health, while Pershing's star increased in brightness and multiplied fourfold in number. Allen went right up with him.

After ten years of frustration, on May 15, 1917, he became a brigadier general again. Less than three months later he was a major general. Although Pershing's recommendation certainly must have been a factor, what had finally helped Allen far more than army connections or political influence was the fate that brought a war and an enormously expanded army. Many of his contemporaries who were still physically and mentally fit also became generals that summer, among them his old friends Charles G. Treat and Clarence R. Edwards. On the promotion list as well was Edwin F. Glenn, convicted of administering the water cure on Samar seventeen years earlier.[4]

On August 25, Allen took command of the 90th Division at Camp Travis, a partly completed cantonment area on the outskirts of San Antonio, Texas. When he arrived, the division consisted of a small cadre of regular army officers and noncoms and a stack of War Department training regulations and tables of organization.[5]

In April, 1917, the United States had an army of 213,557 men on active duty. Of this number, 80,446 were National Guardsmen temporarily under Federal control, many as a result of a partial mobilization the previous year in response to the danger of war with Mexico.[6] The National Defense Act of 1916 had been passed by Congress at the height of the Mexican crisis. The law provided for a modest increase in the size of the Regular Army over a period of five years, the "federalization" of the state militias into the National Guard, and the creation of an Officers' Reserve Corps. It also gave broad economic mobilization powers to the President.[7] All of this had been a great step toward national preparedness, but after April 6, 1917, it was hardly enough.

On May 18, Congress supplemented the National Defense Act by passing the Selective Service Act. With numerous later amendments, these two bills were the basis on which the United States then proceeded to raise, equip, train, and partially deploy an army of 3,685,458 men in eighteen months. The Selective Service Act immediately empowered the President to fill the Regular Army to its authorized strength, call all National Guardsmen into Federal service, and raise by draft an additional force of a million men, although this limit was later removed.[8]

The number of American combat divisions needed in Europe and the more basic question of how many actually could be raised in time to do any good were the subjects of continual study in the War Department. In the summer of 1917, army planners settled on an initial figure of thirty.[9] Some were designated as regular army divisions and filled up, insofar as possible, with officers and men already in the Regular Army. State militiamen formed the nucleus of each national guard division. The remaining troops needed by these two types of units were to come from the ranks of those who enlisted or were drafted. In addition, a number of national army divisions were being organized from scratch. Allen's new command was a national army division. Except for its cadre, it would be made up entirely of draftees—more than 20,000 of them.[10]

Fresh from various training camps in the Southwest, most of the newly commissioned junior officers had reported to Camp Travis by the end of August. The majority of the infantry lieutenants were Texans, but those in the other branches came from practically every state in the Union. On September 5, the first contingent of 360 recruits arrived. Within a month the division had reached a strength of nearly 25,000 men, almost all from Texas and Oklahoma. The regional pride of its members gave the 90th an unmatched *esprit*. "Together they represented the spirit, the aggressiveness, the manhood of the great Southwest," said the division's historian.[11] The letters "T-O," superimposed, later became the division's shoulder patch, the letters symbolizing the home states of most of its members and the words, "Tough 'Ombres," which is what they called themselves. As a further mark of distinction, Allen required his men to salute in a special way, with an exaggerated snap of the head and eyes as the right hand came up sharply to the temple. Instantly identifying the man who rendered it as a "Tough 'Ombre," the salute became famous throughout the American Expeditionary Forces (A.E.F.).[12]

Despite serious equipment shortages, Allen's division began its training. For the recruits, living in unfinished barracks, dressed in blue coveralls instead of regulation uniforms, wearing heavy boots on sockless feet, and carrying an unfamiliar rifle or a wooden replica, the first months at Travis were devoted to learning the basics of a soldier's life. The officers and noncoms conducted and supervised this instruction and went to school themselves in the evenings and on weekends to learn the more advanced elements of their profession.[13] During this period Allen sent Pershing a note of congratulations on his recent elevation to four-star rank, adding an informal report on how the 90th was shaping up:

> I am putting some punch into this Division right now by starting at the top. Yesterday I had every officer . . . , including four brigadiers, do the [physical] exercises. . . .
>
> Matters are progressing well and my convictions as to making an exceptionally fine division of this command are deeply grounded. It will be a homogeneous command, homogeneously trained for fighting. I have always loved the military game and now that it is being scientifically handled and the people everywhere are backing us up, it is simply engrossing. . . .
>
> The delay in getting arms and equipment is the only fly in the ointment. I fear my good friend Crozier [Chief of Ordnance] has fallen down on the small arms, not to speak of artillery. . . .[14]

In late November, Allen received orders to report to Europe for an inspection tour of the western front. A ripple of excitement passed through Camp Travis. The War Department's policy was to give senior commanders a firsthand look at the fighting prior to bringing their units over.[15] As long as the rest of the division's equipment arrived and the training progressed on schedule, it would be ready for embarkation shortly after Allen's scheduled return in March. With these thoughts in mind, he left Texas on November 22 for New York.[16]

On the way he stopped for a day in Atlanta, Georgia, to see his son, stationed at Camp Gordon as a lieutenant. Harry, his father noted with great satisfaction, looked very "breedy" in uniform. In Washington, Allen paid a call on Acting Chief of Staff John Biddle, his best man in 1887, and spent several days with Jeanette and Frank Andrews. They now had two children, neither of whom Allen had ever seen. Hurrying on to New York, he learned his ship would be delayed for several days before sailing, so he also had time for a brief visit with the Viners at West Point, where Dasha had recently given birth to twin boys. After his fall from Pershing's grace, Joe had been assigned to the Point to teach mathematics, but he was now itching to get off to war.[17]

Allen almost missed going to war himself. His ship sailed several hours ahead of schedule. Arriving too late at the pier, he had to charter a private yacht to catch up with it. Feeling sheepish, he climbed aboard the liner *George Washington* just as it passed the Narrows. For the rest of the voyage he took a lot of good-natured ribbing from the other four generals on the ship. All were going to Europe for the same purpose as Allen. One of the four was J. Franklin Bell, commanding the 77th National Army Division and still a friend despite all their disagreements over the years. After more than a decade, he was once again Allen's equal in rank instead of his superior. As the ship zigzagged at high speed through a rough and submarine-infested sea, the five generals put in long hours together studying maps and battle reports and comparing notes about training and equipment problems. The national army division commanders all seemed to have the same complaint: their units had the lowest priority on equipment and were the first to be levied for men when replacements were needed to fill up regular army or national guard units.[18] Allen's 90th had lost relatively few of its original members so far, but what had just happened to Bell's division was a good example of the problem. In the previous month, 5,000 partially trained men had been transferred out of the 77th and replaced by brand-new recruits.[19]

When the conversation touched on the larger events and issues of the war, Allen was incredulous at how ill-informed some of his companions were:

> One . . . informed me . . . he had never heard of the bombardment of London by Zeppelins, nor of the destruction of Louvain, nor of the report on Belgian atrocities by Lord Bryce.[20]

On December 20, the *George Washington* docked at Brest. Two days later the five generals were in Paris. After a brief interview with Pershing on Christmas Eve, they went first to Croix du Bac in the British sector. In eleven days Allen inspected every imaginable type of unit, fortification, and training and logistical facility. He came away impressed by both the British army's great technical ability to provide its soldiers with the gadgetry of war and its utter lack of imagination in employing either men or gadgets. He witnessed a practice maneuver in which the troops first moved across terrain offering no cover or concealment and then assaulted a strongly fortified dummy position head-on. He ascribed such stupidity to the tendency of British commanders to deny their subordinates any flexibility of maneuver and to insist that their orders, issued in minute detail, be carried out to the letter.[21]

Leaving the British sector, Allen paused briefly in Paris, and then spent ten days with the French at Noyon and Clastres. He found their technical solutions to the problems of living and fighting in the trenches as ingenious as the British, and the French commanders only slightly less rigid in mentality. If there was a difference between the two armies, it was in the atmosphere of stolid efficiency at Croix du Bac and the air of indomitable insouciance Allen sensed around Clastres. After wandering all one morning through miles of slimy, water-filled trenches whose walls towered over his head, he stopped in at the front-line command post of a French battalion to ask directions. The battalion commander, a major, was just sitting down to lunch and invited his unexpected guest to join him. The simple but exquisitely cooked meal was accompanied by a vintage wine and served on spotless linen.[22]

During the last week of January Allen went out to Pershing's chateau headquarters at Chaumont for a final round of briefings and to talk with the growing number of senior officers he knew who had already joined the A.E.F., among them Generals Robert L. Bullard, Hunter Liggett, James G. Harbord, and Clarence Edwards. Bullard, gloomy over the Allies' chances, divided his time between Chaumont and his own nearby 1st Division headquarters. Liggett had just been chosen by Pershing to command the First Corps as soon as enough divisions were combat-ready. Harbord, Allen's successor as Chief of Constabulary, had become Pershing's chief of staff. Edwards, once head of the Bureau of Insular Affairs, commanded the 26th National Guard Division.[23]

Having his future division commanders stop over for a week at Chaumont served an additional purpose for Pershing. It gave him a chance for a final evaluation of each man's fitness for command before he brought his unit overseas. Chiefly because of their lack of physical vigor but for various other reasons as well, Pershing rejected over half of the first batch of generals sent him by the War Department.[24] Allen passed muster.

Two who did not pass were Major Generals J. Franklin Bell and Leonard Wood. By then, General Bell was a sick man and showed it. Despite his personal fondness for Bell, Pershing asked the War Department not to send him back with the 77th. Heartbroken, Bell returned to the United States. Less than a year later he died of diabetes.[25] Pershing claimed to have doubts about Wood's physical fitness as well (he limped slightly as a result of an old brain-tumor operation), but his real reasons for rejecting Wood were quite different. Wood was not only healthy, but he had political friends who agreed with his contentions that the war effort was being mismanaged in Washington. Some of them also believed he was the best man to run the A.E.F. Given command of the 89th National Army Division at Fort Riley, Kansas, and faced with the same kinds of problems as Allen and Bell, Wood had not endeared himself to the Administration by publicly complaining about the shortage of equipment and supplies. On his way to France, he had stopped in London. In conferences with British leaders, he pointedly criticized the failure of the American high command to heed Allied advice and made no secret of his desire to have Pershing's job. And, when he returned from France, Wood added to his unpopularity in the War Department by testifying against its policies before the Senate Committee on Military Affairs. Pershing would not tolerate such an obstreperous subordinate. President Wilson and Secretary Baker backed him up. In May, 1918, as Wood's division embarked at New York, he was notified of his relief from command. Despite an outcry from Rooseveltian Republicans and personal pleas from Wood himself, Wilson and Baker refused to change their decision. Wood stayed in the United States for the duration, commanding the

Western Department.[26] A famous political cartoon of the era commented ironically on Wilson's treatment of both Wood and Roosevelt. It showed these two disappointed gentlemen consoling each other over the caption: "Well, 'he kept *us* out of war.'"[27]

While Allen came under Pershing's scrutiny at Chaumont, a team of War Department inspectors descended on Camp Travis. In the two months since Allen's departure the problems of the 90th Division had grown more serious. "Since the division was organized," reported the inspectors, "it has been greatly depleted by transfers of enlisted personnel." The transfers had "seriously interfered with the progress in training" and "tended to weaken" the division's *esprit de corps*. As for equipment, almost everything was in short supply. Although the division had all of its authorized number of bayonets, only sixty-five per cent of its rifles had been issued. There were "practically no canteen covers, cartridge belts, haversacks or pistol belts on hand." The same was true of signal equipment. Even worse, there were "no rolling kitchens, water wagons, ration carts, water carts, combat carts, medical carts, spring wagons and motor vehicles. . . ." With these exceptions, the inspectors said blandly, "the division has nearly 100% of equipment. . . ." They concluded:

> . . . all has been accomplished which could reasonably be expected under existing conditions. In some cases the training is more advanced than could be expected. There is still lacking that accuracy and attention to details . . . which mark disciplined troops, and subordinate officers have not yet acquired that complete confidence in themselves . . . to make them efficient commanders. It cannot be stated definitely . . . when the division will be ready to take the field. It will never advance beyond its present state . . . if its personnel . . . is continually to be changed and depleted. If it is filled to war strength and furnished complete equipment . . . , it will in a short time become an efficient organization.[28]

Although the needed equipment continued to trickle in, the War Department ignored the recommendation to bring Allen's division up to strength. It continued to lose men to other units at the rate of about 100 a day.[29] When Allen returned to Camp Travis on March 1, the 90th was understrength by about forty per cent. He protested to Pershing and the War Department.[30] Thereafter, the influx of recruits about balanced the losses by transfer, but new men arriving every day made a shambles of the training schedule.[31] The turnover among officer personnel was almost as rapid. Among the new arrivals was Lieutenant Henry T. Allen, Jr. He became his father's aide-de-camp.[32]

By the end of April, the 90th Division still had only 15,000 men. Then, around midnight on May 7, orders arrived from the War Department. The division would sail for France in mid-June![33] Recruits from several Midwestern states began pouring in to Camp Travis. Training went on fifteen hours a day, seven days a week. Within a month, Allen had 25,000 officers and men ready to leave for the port of embarkation. There were still serious equipment shortages, and half the enlisted personnel had received only four weeks' instruction, but there were plans to take care of these problems overseas.[34]

During the spring of 1918, at the height of the last desperate German offensive, the first of the National Army divisions began to join the A.E.F. Landing in late June and early July, the 90th was the eighth of these in order of arrival and the twenty-second American division to reach France.[35]

From the ports of Cherbourg and Le Havre it was a thirty-hour trip in boxcars, the famous French "*8 chevaux ou 40 hommes*," to the training area northeast of Dijon, where 400 square miles of rolling plateau between the Seine and Saône valleys had been set aside for the division's use. Allen established his headquarters near the center of this area, at Aignay-le-Duc. His irreverent troops immediately named it "Agnes the Duck."[36] Allen's artillery brigade, even less ready for combat than the rest of the division because of the shortage of guns and ammunition at Camp Travis, went to a separate training area in the south of France near Bordeaux.[37]

Although military censorship forbade disclosing the division's location, Allen got around this problem very neatly when he wrote Dora. "Not far from where we are," he told her, "Caesar had his big battle with Vercingetorix."[38] Too busy or perhaps too ignorant of history, the censor let the letter pass. Except for this tidbit of military information, it contained only the kind of news an anxious wife and mother would be waiting to hear. In his usual good health and high spirits, Allen reassured her about two of the three other men in the family as well.

Joe Viner, in France since his release from duty at West Point that February and proudly wearing his new major's leaves, had driven over from the A.E.F.'s Staff School at Langres to welcome his father-in-law. Although a student at the two-month course at Langres, Joe also had the honor of commanding the first and, as yet, the only tank battalion in the American Army. Evidently back in Pershing's favor, he was "looking thoroughly well."

Harry, "thin, but apparently very healthy," was still aide-de-camp.

Recently promoted to captain, he also worked in the intelligence section of the division staff. The two jobs kept him hopping.[39]

Having his son at his side was obviously Allen's wish, but in a military atmosphere it was sometimes awkward for both of them and always hell on Harry. His father went to great lengths to avoid being accused of nepotism. Once when he had given his son a particularly unpleasant task, Harry asked him, "Are you telling me to do this because you are my father or because you are my commanding officer?" "Because I'm both," growled the senior Allen. The other officers of the division took their cue from the general and gave his son no special consideration. In fact, with all the dirty jobs that came his way it sometimes seemed to Harry that just the opposite was the case. The chief of staff, in particular, was always finding things for him to do. Once, after the division had entered the line, he ordered Captain Allen to take a motorcycle and locate the forward elements of the attacking battalions. All radio and telephone contact with them had been lost, and a fog was closing in. With visions of getting lost himself, the captain innocently inquired as to how he could tell when he reached the front lines. "By which way the bullets are coming at you," replied the colonel in a tone calculated to make young Allen feel like a slightly retarded recruit.[40]

As soon as the 90th had settled into its new areas, many of the field-grade officers left to go to the school at Langres. The rest of the division began an intensive period of unit training. Every man had already more or less learned his own job. Officers and men now practiced their diverse skills in unison. As squads and platoons gained in proficiency, the weekly tactical exercises grew in complexity and size. Platoons came together as companies, companies merged into battalions, and battalions maneuvered side by side or supported each other under the eyes of their regimental commanders. Concurrently, there was also a number of special terrain exercises for Allen, his two brigade commanders, and their three staffs to work on. For these problems Allen used only token numbers of troops so as not to interfere with the other training. Within a month he and his senior officers had practiced putting the division through an approach march, an attack, the organization of a defensive position, a passage of lines, and a continuation of the attack.[41] The A.E.F.'s training agenda evidently did not include practice for a withdrawal or a retreat. Allen was well satisfied with the division's progress even though he knew his men needed more time before they would be completely prepared for combat.[42] Everyone else, in the words of the British "Tommy," was already "jolly well fed oop with training." [43] The 90th had originally been scheduled to receive three more months of it after arriving in France.[44] The division was needed too badly in the line to be permitted that luxury.

In mid-July, following the collapse of the German spring offensive, Marshal Foch, Commander in Chief of the Allied armies, launched a counterattack along the Marne. Eight American divisions participated in this drive, which gradually widened and gained momentum until it became a general advance all along the western front. To help sustain it, more American divisions were needed. On August 15, 1918, Allen's headquarters issued Field Order No. 1, directing the division to move by train to a still secret "new area." [45]

The 90th entered combat in a quiet sector, relieving the battle-tested 1st Division along a nine-kilometer front. The area, immediately west of the Moselle River and north of Toul, had been the scene of savage fighting between the French and Germans in 1915. Since then, the opposing lines had stabilized, facing a wide no man's land scarred with old trenches and bristling with barbed wire and mine fields. The relief began on August 19. Brigadier General Joseph P. O'Neil, with two regiments of three battalions each in his 179th Brigade, moved his troops into the left half of the division's sector. The similarly organized 180th Brigade, commanded by Brigadier General William H. Johnston, occupied the right half of the line. Since the 90th's artillery was still detached and undergoing training, fire support for both infantry brigades was provided by the guns of a reserve division. By August 24, all units were in place and the relief was complete [46]—one day less than a year after Allen had arrived at Camp Travis to take command of a unit then existing only on paper.

Activity along the division's front during the next eighteen days consisted only of reconnaissance patrolling and exchanges of artillery fire. For the first few nights there were also frequent jittery outbursts of rifle and machine-gun fire until the new men in the trenches got over their habit of seeing German assault waves forming in the flickering shadows cast by every parachute flare. Although the front seemed quiet, a few kilometers to the rear the scene was very different. In the woods, in quarries, haystacks, barns, or any spot hidden from the German airplanes overhead, vast quantities of men, supplies, and equipment were being gathered.[47] The American First Army was about to make its fighting debut under the personal command of General Pershing.

His objective was to cut off a German salient into the Allied lines at St. Mihiel. Three French divisions would hit the nose of the salient and keep the Germans fixed in place while ten more divisions (nine American and one French) attacked along both flanks. The two flanks would swing like double doors to close a trap behind St. Mihiel. The mission of the 90th Division was to act as the hinge for the swinging door of the main attack.[48]

At five A.M. on September 12, after a night of steady rain and a four-hour artillery preparation, the men of Allen's two brigades "went over the top" and joined an advancing wave of khaki stretching to the western horizon and beyond. Under a rolling barrage they picked their way in the gathering light through the battered maze of no man's land and assaulted the positions the Germans had held against the French for three years. In the zone of the 90th's attack, the units on both flanks reached and secured their objectives ahead of schedule and without excessive casualties. The battalions in the center had a much more difficult time of it. Several were disorganized by heavy German artillery fire as they left their own trenches, and most took heavy losses trying to get through the lethal streams of machine-gun bullets lacing the enemy barbed wire. The well-camouflaged and protected German machineguns had to be silenced one by one. Nine hours later, all of Allen's units had reached their initial objectives.[49] Pershing's other divisions had been equally successful. For three more days all pushed forward relentlessly. Sixteen thousand German prisoners were caught in the trap. Of this number, fourteen officers and 650 men surrendered to the 90th Division.[50]

With the St. Mihiel salient eliminated and his battle lines shortened and straightened, Pershing began shuffling more divisions into position west of Verdun in preparation for the coming battle of the Meuse-Argonne. At first, the 90th took no direct part in this operation. It merely held the line it had gained by September 15–16 and extended its flanks to take over more ground from several of the units being withdrawn from the St. Mihiel sector. During this period, Allen had his men stretched thinly across a front of twelve kilometers. Under constant and heavy artillery bombardment, their combat activities were restricted to local patrols and raids to harass the Germans and capture prisoners. When the Meuse-Argonne offensive began on September 26, the divisions remaining in the St. Mihiel sector were given the mission of making a demonstration attack to deceive the Germans as to the true location of Pershing's main effort. The 90th's "attack" bore all the earmarks of a real one, complete with a long artillery preparation, the noisy arrival and massing of a tank battalion (commanded by Joe Viner), and an assault against the first line of the enemy positions. Then, as the Germans struck back viciously with artillery, gas, and counterattacks, Allen had to order a withdrawal.[51] That the demonstration had successfully accomplished Pershing's purpose could not have been much comfort to Allen's exhausted men when they returned to their own trenches and counted up their dead, wounded, or missing comrades.

In little more than a month of combat, the 90th Division had already suffered over 5,000 casualties, of whom 524 had been killed and 445 severely wounded. The rest were either lightly wounded, gassed, missing, or captured.[52] These losses bothered Allen more than he cared to admit openly to Pershing. When he wrote to the A.E.F. commander on September 30 to bring him up to date on how the "Tough 'Ombres" were doing, Allen covered his anguish by adopting the confident, almost bantering tone of the successful combat leader:

> They [the Germans] would be glad to call it even and go in for a gentleman's agreement if I would let them alone. . . .
>
> Our experiences here have been wonderful for the development of the Division, even if our casualties have been considerable, but I know we have hustled the Boches to the limit.[53]

But to his wife, Allen said, "I will never be able to take back to Texas and Oklahoma as many of their sons as I had hoped." [54]

On October 8, another division came into the line to relieve the 90th. Two days later, in two long files, Allen's troops trudged back down the road to Toul. At the end of it they hoped to find a bed, a bath, hot meals, and a few nights' sleep away from the sound of the guns. But, even before the last unit had pulled into the staging area west of the city, the first men to arrive were already on trucks heading for the Meuse-Argonne sector. Closing into the rain-soaked Blercourt area west of Verdun on October 16, the division finally had a chance for a brief rest.[55]

The battle of the Meuse-Argonne was by then well into its second phase. The first had ended late in September when the American offensive stalled after several days of spectacular gains. After a massive artillery preparation, the second phase began on October 4. Several fresh divisions joined the attack. This time the defenders were ready. The battle became a giant meat grinder, using up the best men each side had to throw against the other. The Americans continued to advance, but the line moved forward slowly and unevenly. For the Germans, under increasing Allied pressure all along the western front, the

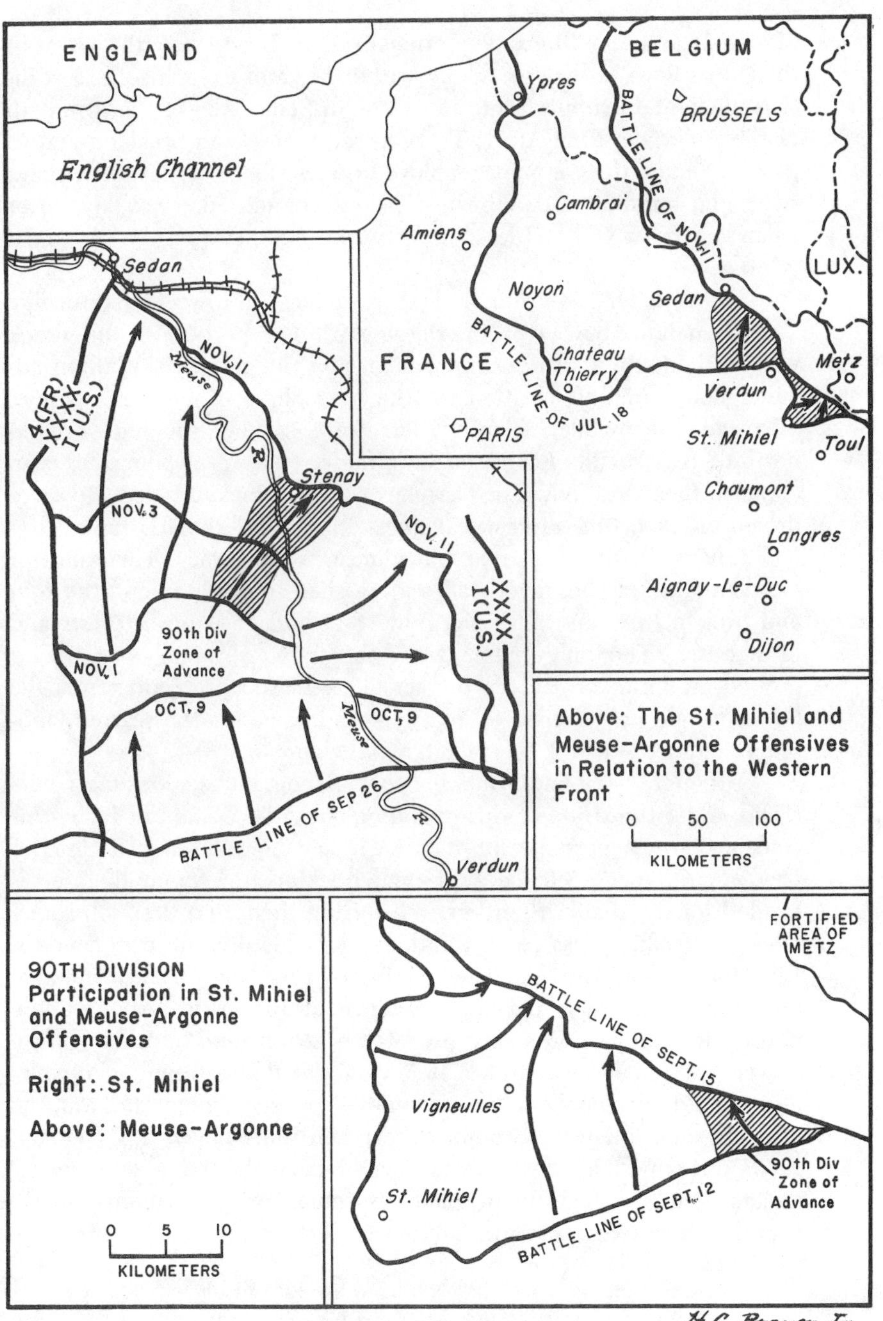

Northern France

Meuse-Argonne had become a crucial sector. It was now the hinge of their own lines as they gradually withdrew from French soil. In addition, their main supply route ran through Sedan, directly in the path of the American First Army. To keep the hinge from breaking and to protect Sedan, the Germans employed no less than forty-two divisions, twice the number of American divisions committed.[56] Six days after Allen's men arrived at Blercourt, it was their turn to enter the meat grinder.

The 90th Division took its first objective, the town of Bantheville and the heights beyond it, on October 23. The purpose of the attack was to eliminate a small enemy salient and put the division in an advantageous jump-off position for the next phase of the First Army's offensive. Meanwhile, Allen's orders were to hold the high ground north of Bantheville. For eight days, under constant shelling, his men clung to their positions. The Germans counterattacked twice and were driven off each time after advancing within hand-grenade range.[57]

Life in the division's rear was almost as dangerous. Thousands of German shells arched overhead and crashed to earth among the torn and broken trees and piles of rubble that had once been forests and farmhouses. The only refuge from the flying shrapnel was underground, in a bunker. Even a bunker offered scant protection from the Germans' gas as it seeped in invisible tendrils across the scarred landscape and settled into every crater and depression.[58]

Although Allen had sympathy for his men, any senior officer who failed under the strain of this pounding could be certain of facing his cold anger in a personal interview. Those who still showed signs of weakness or incompetence after one "bucking up" found themselves headed for the rear with orders transferring them to a desk job somewhere.[59] Pershing was equally ruthless with his division commanders. Like him, what Allen expected of his officers was physical courage and endurance, their personal presence at the critical spot on the battlefield, and an intelligent use of the terrain and supporting firepower when making an attack. Believing also that extreme aggressiveness would ultimately reduce casualties by shortening the war, he told his subordinates: "Ground once taken must never be given up. . . ."[60] Having already relieved several colonels and a good many majors, Allen reluctantly decided his senior brigade commander, a friend of many years, would have to go, too:

> . . . this morning . . . [he] had no knowledge of his left regiment and was just about as vague as usual. After writing specific tasks for each of his regiments I returned . . . and made official request for his relief.[61]

By the time Allen brought himself to take this step, the entire First Army was once again moving forward in the attack. The third phase of the Meuse-Argonne offensive began on November 1. In the next eleven days there was little time for drastic changes. The brigade commander kept his job.

Within forty-eight hours the Germans on Allen's front had begun to withdraw across the Meuse. On November 3, his men met only light resistance as they advanced to the bluffs overlooking the river. All the bridges were destroyed.

As the 90th prepared to force a crossing, the Germans dug in on the opposite heights and kept up a continual harassing fire on anything moving in the valley floor below.[62] Allen ordered his artillery commander, a colonel, to make a personal reconnaissance on horseback with him along the front to try to pinpoint accurately the enemy artillery positions from which this fire came. As the two men rode side by side, a German barrage caught them in the open. When the fire lifted, the colonel had disappeared. Shaken but unscathed, Allen returned alone to his command post. His companion's shattered body was found the next day, half-buried in a shell crater.[63]

The enemy fire continued without interruption for the next six days. In spite of it, the division's engineers managed to repair one span across the Meuse and put in several foot bridges. On November 9, the crossing began. Both brigades soon reached the far bank, only to be met by more artillery and machine-gun fire placed with deadly accuracy across every route leading away from the river. It took another day of bitter fighting to establish a secure bridgehead.[64] Then, at 7:20 A.M. on November 11, word came that an armistice had been signed and all fighting would cease at eleven o'clock that morning. The message from Pershing's headquarters stressed that this was "an armistice only, not a peace." There was to be no relaxation of vigilance: "The troops must be prepared any moment for further operations." Allen's men dug in and waited to see if the war was really over. There was little excitement or jubilation in the ranks.[65] Having seen 4,000 more of their comrades killed or wounded in the last three weeks,[66] perhaps they shared their commanding general's feeling, expressed in a letter to Pershing ten days after the armistice began:

> . . . I have come over to remain to the end, regardless of how many months or years may be required to finish the work properly. Under no circumstances would I want to return home without planting my hob-nailed boots on German soil.[67]

Almost immediately, this wish came true, though only for the 90th Division and not for Allen. On November 24, after a farewell ceremony that cost him "many a pang," he parted company with the "Tough 'Ombres." He remained in France to take command of the three divisions and 90,000 men of the Eighth Corps while his old unit headed for occupation duty in Germany as part of the newly created Third Army. As a guarantee against German violation of the armistice pending negotiation of a peace treaty, four Allied armies marched into the Rhineland on December 1, 1918.[68]

Both these assignments, command of a corps for Allen and occupation duty for his division, were indicative of Pershing's high regard for their past performance. Although the 90th had been given only prosaic, unspectacular missions, it had accomplished them well. Pershing told Allen his division was "one of the very best." Lieutenant General Hunter Liggett, commanding the First Army, of which the 90th had been a part, called it "as good and dependable as any division in the army." [69] It is therefore rather surprising to find a disparaging appraisal from another senior officer in the A.E.F., Lieutenant General Robert L. Bullard.

His book, *Fighting Generals*, published in 1944, contains biographical sketches of seven major generals who commanded divisions during World War I. After reviewing Allen's earlier career, Bullard said:

> With all his experience in organization and training of troops he should have been an expert at both. It must be noted with surprise . . . that his division . . . was not started to France until June. . . . Divisions generally were forwarded to France as soon as they were deemed sufficiently trained. Unquestionably Allen's division was slow. . . . This is surprising, not understandable, for Allen had within him qualities that won acceptance, liking, and even enthusiasm for him as a leader.[70]

Bullard then summarized the 90th Division's achievements in the battles of St. Mihiel and Meuse-Argonne:

> In its very first fight [St. Mihiel] Allen's 90th Division had done well. Still it is to be remembered that this was against third or fourth class German troops, not their best. . . .[71]
>
> . . . as the American attack opened November 1st, the Germans were already withdrawing, but fighting a rear guard action. On November 1st and 2nd, Allen's division drove ahead. . . .
>
> The 90th Division was surprised on November 3rd to find almost no opposition to their front. . . . So the rest of [its] . . . advance up to the

day of the Armistice . . . amounted practically to a pursuit, without fighting of any consequence.[72]

It would be well to know something about Bullard and his relationship with Allen before examining the truth and fairness of these passages. The two men had known each other as cadets at West Point and, though their paths later crossed several times in the Philippines and in Washington, they had not served together until World War I. Even then, Allen was never directly under Bullard's command. In army parlance, Bullard stayed "close to the flagpole" on troop duty for most of his career while Allen had the more glamorous assignments.[73] The lack of correspondence between them in Allen's papers indicates they were never close friends. A thin, almost ascetic-looking man, Bullard commanded the first American division to reach France and enter the line. He then became, successively, commanding general of the Third Corps and the Second Army.[74] Americans who knew him called him "indomitable." The French called him "a daring leader" and a "master of his profession."[75]

Bullard's comments about the 90th Division being "slow" to reach the combat zone imply that Allen failed to train his men as rapidly and as well as he should have. The fact that Bullard's own 1st Division had been in France for a year and fighting for eight months when the 90th arrived may have colored his judgment. If so, the comparison was grossly unfair. The 1st Division had been a token force, assembled from existing regular army units and sent over as quickly as possible after the United States declaration of war to bolster Allied morale.[76] It is more likely Bullard meant to compare Allen's unit with the other National Army divisions, all of which had similar personnel problems and equipment shortages. As we have seen, the 90th was the eighth National Army division to sail, and all eight landed in France within a two-month period beginning in mid-April of 1918. It appears that the priority of sailing for these units was determined primarily by their relative proximity to the port of embarkation and the availability of rail transport and shipping. The level of training reached was also a factor in the determination, but, for each unit, this level was more dependent on the date when replacements stopped coming and going in large numbers (thus allowing instruction to proceed without interruption) than on any significant differences between divisions in the quality of the training itself. The first seven National Army divisions to go were trained at camps on the East Coast or Midwest. All were brought up to strength and left alone to finish their training as soon as or sooner than Allen's division.[77] The final refutation of Bullard's criticism of the 90th's slowness is the fact that only one of the National Army divisions preceding the "Tough 'Ombres" to France actually entered active combat before they did.[78]

It is true that, at the start of the battle of St. Mihiel, Allen's men faced "third or fourth class German troops, not their best." The 90th Division's official history admits it. But it also points out that the Germans kept better troops in reserve for offensive operations and counterattacks. After the battle began, they threw a first class division between the 90th and the unit on its left flank.[79] The hinge held.

As for the division's advance "without fighting of any consequence" in the last phase of the Meuse-Argonne offensive, perhaps it looked that way from Bullard's distant perspective as an army commander on another front. The Germans were in fact fighting only a "rear guard action," as he says, but they still put up enough resistance to make casualties of 4,000 of Allen's men. The pursuit to the Meuse and across was hardly a pleasant country stroll.

The best way to put Bullard's remarks in perspective is to compare the battle statistics of the 90th with those of the other twenty-eight American divisions (ten of them National Army) that actually saw combat. Of these twenty-nine divisions, Allen's was the twentieth to arrive in France.[80] Only thirteen divisions spent more time in the line than the 90th. It stood fourteenth overall in the number of prisoners captured and fifteenth in the amount of ground gained. Only two National Army units could claim to stand higher than the "Tough 'Ombres" in both the latter two categories. Allen's casualties may have been high, but they were even higher in fifteen other divisions.[81]

When Bullard wrote *Fighting Generals* he should have known these facts. Yet, while acknowledging Allen's likable personal qualities, he chose to disparage his achievements as a combat leader. There are some clues to Bullard's motives in his book. Clearly, like Lockett, he resented some of Allen's earlier assignments and thought him too much of a politician and a playboy. Bullard, however, was no plodding nonentity. As a successful three-star general he can hardly have been very jealous of Allen's own wartime rise to two-star rank. The contrast in their careers after the war may thus be the main reason for Bullard's sour portrayal of Allen. Bullard went home to take command of the Eastern Department in an army going through a painful demobilization and returning to the doldrums of peacetime.[82] Allen stayed on in Europe to take what was probably the most interesting, potentially one of the most important, and certainly the most glamorous assignment in the postwar army.

CHAPTER X

Exactly the Right Man

Major General Henry T. Allen was among the spectators who crowded into the Hall of Mirrors to watch the signing of the Treaty of Versailles on June 28, 1919.[1] By then he was almost certain of Pershing's reasons for keeping him on in Europe, in successive command of three different corps, while loaded troopships sailed for home every week and the repeatedly reorganized A.E.F. shrank to a mere ten divisions.[2] Allen had long suspected Pershing intended to put him in command of the American occupation force in the Rhineland if the terms of the peace settlement included a provision for the continuation of the four-power occupation.[3]

Annexed to the Treaty of Versailles was the Rhineland Agreement, a document establishing just that—the maintenance on German soil of the armies of France, Great Britain, Belgium, and the United States for a period of up to fifteen years. Less than two weeks after the signing of the treaty, Allen took command of the American contingent at Coblenz, no longer called the Third United States Army but newly designated as the American Forces in Germany (A.F.G.).[4]

His new command consisted of five divisions totaling approximately 110,000 men, the still-formidable residue of an occupation army more than twice that size at the start of the armistice period seven months earlier.[5] By October, however, when the A.E.F. had been completely withdrawn from Europe, the A.F.G. was reduced to a force of less than 10,000, close to its intended peacetime strength.[6] Pershing sailed to the United States with all but the remnants of his wartime command. Before he left, he wrote Allen a personal letter of advice on how to maintain "harmonious relations" with the Allies and particularly the French. Although Allen would soon be taking his orders not from Pershing but directly from the War Department, he was going to have to deal with the same problems of inter-Allied co-ordination and co-operation that had so often strained Pershing's relations with the prickly French. Pershing said to Allen, "in dealing with the French it is essential to avoid magnifying questions of minor importance. My good wishes for your complete success impel me to give you this advice." [7]

Soon after Pershing's arrival in the United States, he wrote a letter to Dora Allen expressing his confidence in her husband's "complete success" in the Rhineland:

> . . . He is exactly the right man in the right place. . . . I have no notion there will be any change for a long time unless he himself should indicate a desire for it. . . .[8]

Pershing was right. Almost all of Allen's experiences, official and personal, in thirty-seven years of military service seemed to have combined to make him "exactly the right man" for command of the A.F.G. Knowing her husband too well to believe he would ever "indicate a desire" to be relieved from such an assignment, Dora decided to join him. She arrived in October to find a reception fit for a general's wife and a home on Coblenz's tree-lined *Rhein Anlagen* that she happily described as "most palatial." [9] She was immediately swept into a social whirl that must have made her the envy of Europe's lesser royalty. High-ranking Americans and foreigners, kings and dukes, generals, statesmen, ambassadors, businessmen, and private citizens, all came to discuss official matters with her husband, to be honored by a ceremonial parade or an inspection of his troops, or simply to enjoy the marvelous scenery and delightful wines of the region.[10] Envious Americans were soon calling the A.F.G. "Allen's kingdom on the Rhine." Wags gave another meaning to the initials A.F.G. Since Captain Henry T. Allen, Jr., remained in his father's command and Lieutenant Colonel and Mrs. Frank Andrews joined it in September of 1920, many said the three letters stood for "Allen's Family in Germany." [11]

As pleasant as the family and social life was for Dora in Coblenz and necessary as the elaborate protocol and ceremonies were for her husband in maintaining harmonious relations with the Allies, Allen and the A.F.G. served an infinitely more important function. They were the visible symbol of the United States's continuing determination to stand by its wartime allies against Germany and of America's interest in the postwar problems of Europe. Although the A.F.G. was

Commanding General, American Forces in Germany. (Photograph courtesy of Col. Henry T. Allen, Jr.)

smaller in size and occupied less territory than any of the three other armies in the Rhineland, Allen was able to exercise an influence far out of proportion to the size of his command by virtue of the power of the nation he represented.

If both Allen's role and the issues in which he became involved are to be understood, the story must first be told of how the United States came to have an occupation army in Germany at all, since American leaders had neither foreseen that possibility during the war nor desired it after the armistice ended. In essence, it is the story of the conflicting war aims of the victors and of the compromise settlement, not wholly satisfactory to any of them, that eventually became the peace treaty.

Since the Germans had occupied part of northern France for two and one-half years following the Franco-Prussian War of 1870–71, there was nothing particularly startling or unusual to the nations of Europe in the idea *per se* of the victors imposing a military occupation after the Great War of 1914–18. The French, however, seem to have had plans from very early in the war for something more than a tit for a historical tat. They first revealed their postwar intentions toward the Rhineland in secret negotiations in 1916 with their floundering Russian ally. In exchange for certain French concessions, the Czar readily agreed to detaching the Rhineland from Germany and setting it up as an independent state.[12] For the French, living in the shadow of Germany's greater economic strength and larger population and haunted by feelings of insecurity born of two German invasions in the span of forty-four years, the prospect of a Rhenish state made good sense both militarily and psychologically. Aside from its obvious advantage to France in balancing the Franco-German power equation, there was also some slight historical justification for an autonomous Rhineland. Separatist sentiment had existed there for more than a century, ever since most of the area had been placed under Prussian control by the Congress of Vienna. The relatively liberal political traditions and predominantly Catholic faith of the Rhinelanders had made them even more restive in a Reich unified and dominated after 1871 by an ultraconservative, Protestant Prussia. Although such centrifugal tendencies were extremely weak compared with the counteracting bonds of a common race, language, and culture, some French leaders thought that if the Rhineland became another Luxemburg or Holland it would provide the best guarantee of the future peace of Europe—even if this chunk of German territory had to be amputated by French bayonets.[13]

During the war the French had tried in vain to interest the British in separating the Rhineland from Germany. Foreign Minister Lord Balfour dismissed the proposal as a "wild project" and at first did not bother to inform Prime Minister Lloyd George about it.[14] Although British leaders did not share their French counterparts' obsession with territorial security, they had had their own war aims, designed to cripple Germany as a naval and colonial competitor. The British government became even less receptive to the idea of an independent Rhineland after the secret French proposal became public knowledge. The new Bolshevik masters of Russia, having taken their nation out of the war, published the year-old agreement with France as part of their campaign to discredit the Czarist regime and "Western Imperialism" in general.[15]

By late 1917, the entire question of war aims had become a sensitive political issue. The European belligerents all faced the need to offer their people some hope for tangible rewards to offset the seemingly endless sacrifice, while at the same time having to counter a growing tide of pacifist dissent and general war weariness. This dissent expressed itself in the idea that nothing could justify a continuation of the fighting. To many it seemed as if the Allies would lose whatever claim they had to moral superiority if the Central Powers were crushingly defeated and then forced to submit to a harsh and vindictive peace.[16]

Such feelings were by no means confined to European pacifists. Traditionally hostile to the militarism and diplomatic machinations of the Old World and insulated by 3,000 miles of ocean from the very real problems of national security of which these supposed evils were a natural result, a large segment of the American population, while neither war-weary nor pacifist, was also becoming increasingly skeptical of the war aims of the Allies. Their spokesman was Woodrow Wilson, and the Fourteen Points were his answer to the problem of achieving a just and lasting peace. Couched in broad and idealistic generalities, Wilson's points were received less enthusiastically by the governments to whom they were addressed than by the masses under them.[17]

The creation of a Rhenish state would, of course, have been contrary to Wilson's great principle of the "self-determination of peoples." For this reason, despite the Bolshevik revelation of French intentions toward the Rhineland, it appears that Washington, like London, did not give the postwar fate of the area any serious thought until the last month of the war. Not even the possibility that the French might seek a prolonged occupation of the Rhineland seems to have been considered.[18] Thus, despite British and American objections to an occupation when the French formally proposed one at the beginning of the armistice negotiations in October, 1918, Washington and London were unprepared to offer any other plan that would as effectively guarantee Allied security during the armistice period. In addition, neither government clearly recognized French intentions to convert this "temporary" measure into a long-term provision of the peace settlement. Both Wilson and Lloyd George were maneuvered into a commitment neither had foreseen or wanted and from which they could not extricate themselves without appearing to desert their wartime partner.[19]

The success of French diplomacy during the armistice negotiations was enhanced by the obscurity of Germany's internal situation in the fall of 1918. No outside observer realized the extent of that nation's growing social and political demoralization, still hidden behind a menacing military façade. Few would have predicted the imminent abdication of the Kaiser or the revolutionary overthrow of the caretaker government he left behind. Although by late October the German armies were being fôrced back all along the western front, they were far from beaten. Nor had they yielded an inch of German territory. Nevertheless, the tide was running visibly in the Allies' favor, and some generals (among them Pershing) wanted to press for a clear-cut military victory.[20] At the very least, many felt, the Germans had to be convinced of their actual defeat.

When the German armistice delegation arrived at Marshal Foch's headquarters on November 8, they read for the first time the Allies' terms for an end to the fighting. Among the conditions were these relating to the Rhineland: (1) Evacuation of all German military forces from the west bank of the Rhine and a neutral zone on the east bank averaging fifty kilometers in width; (2) The maintenance of Allied occupation troops on the west bank and within three bridgehead enclaves on the east bank, each having a thirty-kilometer radius, across from the cities of Mainz, Coblenz, and Cologne; (3) Nothing to be removed from the territory on the left bank; all factories, railroads, and other facilities to be left intact.[21]

At 5 A.M. on November 11, the armistice was signed. The Allies granted few of the numerous German requests for softening its conditions. Six days later, under the overall command of Marshal Foch, more than 800,000 French, British, Belgian, and American soldiers resumed their advance, following the retreating German armies closely as they withdrew through Belgium and Luxemburg. On December 1, the first Allied columns entered Germany.[22]

In the winter and spring of 1919, while Allen shifted from one corps to another in what remained of the A.E.F. and General Joseph T. Dickman's Third Army settled into the routine of occupation duty around Coblenz, the statesmen of the Allied and Associated Powers met in Paris to work out the terms of the settlement that would supersede the armistice. By early April, the general outline of the peace treaty had emerged. Germany was going to lose all its colonies and considerable border territory. Its army and navy would be reduced in size to those of a third-rate power. The Allies, particularly France, were to be paid enormous reparations, though the amount and duration of the payments were still unspecified. With regard to the question of the Rhineland, the pattern of negotiation of the previous fall had repeated itself. As adamant as ever on the need for an occupation for their own military security, the French now had an additional argument to justify keeping troops in the Rhineland—their presence would serve to guarantee German reparations payments.[23] As before, Wilson and Lloyd George objected to an occupation, but, once again, they and their advisors could offer Clemenceau no acceptable alternatives. Wilson would consent neither to a permanent occupation nor to one of indefinite length. However, when Clemenceau proposed a treaty committing the United States and Britain to aid France if she were ever again attacked by Germany in exchange for a fifteen-year time limit on the occupation, the President accepted the bargain—as long as it might be terminated earlier if Germany met her obligations under the peace treaty.

Generals Pershing and Tasker Bliss advised Wilson against American participation in such an occupation. Nevertheless, as long as an occupation was inevitable, the President had several cogent reasons for keeping at least a small contingent on the Rhine. It would be a reassuring symbol of America's interest in French security and a hostage against a future German invasion. Perhaps of equal importance to Wilson was the hope that an American presence in the Rhineland might frustrate French attempts to separate it from Germany.[24]

The next problem was the creation of the political machinery to administer the occupation. Here again the French and the Americans were in basic disagreement. Clemenceau and his military advisors saw no reason to replace Foch's headquarters as the supreme representative of the Allied and Associated Powers in the occupied territory or to change the relationship between him and the military governors of the four zones. Since the occupation would be maintained by military forces, the existing arrangement seemed simple and logical.[25] The French reckoned without Wilson's well-justified suspicions of their motives toward the Rhineland and the traditional American distrust of all things military.

In late May, there was an attempted separatist coup in the French-occupied zone of the Rhineland. With the connivance and support of two French generals, a Dr. Hans Dorten proclaimed a Rhenish Republic. Dorten's "republic" quickly collapsed for lack of popular support.[26] The coup came at the very time the American delegation in Paris was casting about for a proposal to counter the French plan to maintain Foch's headquarters in overall command of the occupied territory after the peace settlement. At American and British insistence, an inter-allied Rhineland commission had already been set up under the Supreme Economic Council to oversee nonmilitary affairs in the Rhineland. Although Foch had bitterly fought this dilution of his powers, the commission was generally successful in the last months of the armistice period in blocking moves by the French intended solely to benefit themselves in the civil and economic spheres. The American representative on the commission was Pierrepont B. Noyes, a liberal-minded businessman and a close friend of two of Wilson's economic advisors.[27] Commissioner Noyes, disturbed by his firsthand observation of French machinations in the Rhineland and distrusting military men on principle, came up with the solution Wilson was looking for. On May 27, he submitted a memorandum to the President that envisioned an occupation with "as few troops as possible" and proposed "complete self government for the territory," with the exception of a "Civil Commission with powers: (a) to make regulations or change old ones whenever German law or actions . . . threaten the carrying out of treaty terms [or] . . . the comfort or security of troops; (b) to authorize the army to take control under martial law, either in danger spots or throughout the territory, whenever conditions seem to the commission to make this necessary."[28]

Wilson was delighted with Noyes's plan, Foch was outraged, and Clemenceau, embarrassed by the Dorten episode and faced with a sudden British attempt to back out of the occupation agreement completely, was in a difficult bargaining position. Before Wilson had a chance to become infected with British faintheartedness and to mollify his suspicions, Clemenceau quickly agreed to the idea of a civil commission. Lloyd George reluctantly fell into line. Negotiations proceeded on the basis of Noyes's proposal and, on June 16, the Allies initialled the Rhineland Agreement.[29]

The agreement provided for a four-member civilian body, with a Frenchman as chairman, to be known as the Inter-Allied Rhineland High Commission (I.R.H.C.). Upon ratification of the peace treaty by all the signatories, Foch's headquarters would transfer its governmental functions to the High Commission and become responsible only for the military planning and co-ordination necessary to meet the contingency of a future resumption of hostilities.[30]

When the terms of the Treaty of Versailles were announced, German opinion, both public and official, was vehemently opposed to signing. But, on June 28, 1919, with the Allied blockade still crippling the German economy, with the Allied armies on the Rhine standing by their guns and ready to march again, and with German forces already partially disarmed and demobilized, the government in Berlin had no real choice except to sign.[31]

By the time of Allen's arrival in Coblenz in July, almost half of the 2,500 square miles originally allotted for the American zone of occupation had already been turned over to the French because of the partial withdrawal of the U.S. Third Army. When this withdrawal was complete in September, the American zone had shrunk to less than one-third its former size. Allen still had responsibility for most of the bridgehead and for a slightly larger area on the west bank, but that was all. There were no major industrial plants or large cities in the American zone. Coblenz, the largest town, had a population of 65,000.[32] Immediately to the north of the Americans were the British, with their bridgehead at Cologne. North of the British zone was the Belgian, occupying a triangle of land bounded by the Rhine, the Belgian and Dutch borders, and a line running roughly from Aachen to Düsseldorf. Everything south of Coblenz was occupied by the French, who had their own bridgehead across from Mainz.[33]

The 12,000 square miles under Allied control comprised only six and one-half per cent of Germany's land area in 1919, but the 7,000,000 inhabitants of the Rhineland represented almost eleven per cent of the nation's population. More than two-thirds of the occupied territory belonged to the largest German state, Prussia. The remaining one-third, corresponding roughly with the French zone, contained the Saar district, plus the Bavarian Palatinate and segments or enclaves of several smaller German states.[34] Dominating for 250 miles one or both banks of Europe's greatest commercial artery and bordering on the city of Frankfurt in the south and the Ruhr industrial basin in the north, the Allied Occupation Zone represented a potent military, political, and economic sanction against Germany.

Having taken the Fourteen Points at face value at the time of the armistice, the Germans bitterly resented both the "trick" played on them at Versailles and its most visible result, the Rhineland occupation. Although President Wilson's assent to American participation in it was something of a trick on the American public as well, the reaction in the United States was not entirely negative. Only dimly aware of the underlying diplomatic struggle at Versailles and of Wilson's compromises in the face of the French obsession with their own security, most Americans had assumed the occupation would end when the armistice did. Some greeted the news with great satisfaction, for nothing else would as conclusively demonstrate to the German people their defeat and the continuing solidarity of the Allies against them.[35] On the other hand, the idea of United States troops remaining on European soil in peacetime made most Americans decidedly uneasy. It seemed a dangerous precedent to set. The bland reassurances of the Administration that the Rhineland occupation did not really constitute a foreign entanglement were not very convincing, especially when conservatives and isolationists could also point to the presence of American soldiers in Russia and Italy as evidence that President Wilson intended to commit the nation to a permanent role as a world policeman.[36] Doubts about the wisdom of participating in the occupation were, of course, part of the larger American debate over ratification of the Treaty of Versailles and joining the League of Nations. In his eagerness to "sell" the treaty and the league to Congress and the American public, Wilson was for a long time less than candid about what he had agreed to in the Rhineland. For several months after the bare fact of continuing American participation became known, the wildest rumors as to the size and permanence of the contingent at Coblenz were allowed to circulate without comment or clarification from Washington. Depending on which newspaper a man read and when, he might have expected the occupation force to be an army of 200,000, a mere regiment as an honor guard for the flag, or something intermediate in size, perhaps a division or a corps.[37] Although the decision as to the actual strength of the A.F.G. was made shortly after the Germans signed at Versailles, the number of troops, along with the specific terms of the Rhineland Agreement, officially remained a secret to the American public until late August. By that time the details of the agreement and the total strength of the four occupation armies (totaling 151,000 men and 6,500 officers) had been published in foreign sources and were known in the United States.[38] The announcement of an A.F.G. less than 10,000 strong was greeted with considerable relief by both Wilson's supporters and his growing number of critics. Token or not, however, the army on the Rhine represented a new and uncomfortable departure in American foreign policy whose usefulness and very existence would need continual justification to those who wanted to "bring the boys home."

Allen understood very well the basic American hostility to the mission he had been given, not only from a lifetime of study of American history, but also from his personal correspondence. It had always been wide and varied, but now that he was the nation's chief military representative in Europe it was astonishingly so.[39] Whatever else these letters contained (and Allen was deluged by flattery, appeals for money or favors, and countless requests for his personal or official hospitality at Coblenz), the ones from Americans frequently contained some variation on this theme:

> I enclose . . . the extract from the Declaration of Independence which the [N.Y.] *Sun* is now keeping standing at the head of their editorial column. We used to hear words to that effect on July 4 quite frequently, but I suppose the Declaration of Independence along with the Constitution, has been superseded by the "League of Notions." [40]

Allen invariably answered such comments in the following vein:

> . . . the fact remains that fighting continues in many places throughout Europe. . . . The League of Nations, regardless of whether it will embroil the United States in European brawls, will appeal to many people as a helpful means for diminishing warfare. . . .
>
> From this Central European point . . . I can pretty well keep abreast of world politics. As a result the greed and selfishness of different states are shown up with increasing force. I am confirmed in the thought that selfishness and disregard of others dominates the policy of all nations—unless it be our own.[41]

Believing in the necessity for United States participation in the Rhineland occupation but aware that he and his soldiers could stay on in Coblenz only at the sufferance of their doubting countrymen, Allen set out to make the A.F.G. into such a model of military perfection that its prestige alone might justify its existence, at least among those Americans who took pride in "showing Europe a thing or two." Given the material Allen had to work with in the fall of 1919, his goal seemed almost impossible. Except for his staff and the senior troop commanders, the A.F.G. was no longer composed of combat veterans, but of soldiers just out of basic training who had been enlisted specifically for occupation duty.

The army's drive to recruit these men began in June, 1919, shortly after Washington's first public acknowledgement that American troops would remain on the Rhine. With the final size of the A.F.G. then anybody's guess, the War Department settled on a figure of 50,000 for planning purposes. The army had no difficulty filling this quota. Since the fathers and older brothers of many of the young men who signed up were returning veterans of the A.E.F., occupation duty gave these eager new volunteers an unexpected chance to do their patriotic share.[42] When the A.F.G. turned out to be smaller than anticipated, only one-fifth of these men were sent to Coblenz, beginning in August. Almost another 10,000 went into the so-called Silesian Brigade, earmarked to help supervise the plebiscites required in Silesia by the Treaty of Versailles. In October, pending ratification of the treaty, the Silesian Brigade was also shipped to Coblenz, to remain there in readiness until orders came to move into Silesia. Since the treaty was defeated in the U.S. Senate, those orders never came. The Silesian Brigade became part of the A.F.G., making Allen's command more than twice as large as originally intended.

He organized it into two brigades, each with an infantry regiment and a machine-gun battalion. One brigade also had an artillery battalion and a cavalry detachment. The other included a company of engineers and various other smaller service and supply units. On an organizational chart this force looked fairly impressive. The reports on Allen's desk told a different story. The venereal disease and court-martial rates were soaring, the dress was slovenly, and military courtesy practically nonexistent among these callow, unseasoned youths, many of whom had seemingly enlisted for no other reason than to prove their manhood and who equated toughness with a lack of discipline.[43]

Allen soon showed them the difference. The A.F.G began what amounted to a second cycle of basic training. Gone was the old routine (a carryover from the armistice period) of a half-day for training and a half-day for play. Passes and leaves suddenly became a reward to be earned instead of a right to be expected. The new schedule included eight hours a day of marching, shooting, and practice maneuvers, with inspections on weekends and alert drills at any hour of the day or night. Allen took seriously the plans worked out by Marshal Foch's headquarters for the co-ordinated defense of the occupation zones, both from external attack and from uprisings within. American troops periodically practiced their part in these plans.[44] Perfectionist that he was, Allen kept his staff officers even busier. Among those whose ability to plan, supervise, and report pleased him were two lieutenant colonels whose names would be well known a generation later: Jonathan M. Wainwright and Brehon Somervell.[45]

But Allen wanted more than a competent force of field soldiers who could be relied on in a military crisis; the A.F.G. also had to shine as a ceremonial unit. The generals of the four occupying armies and their military and civilian superiors spent a lot of time visiting each others' zones. Whether the visit was official or strictly social (most often it was both), it called for a parade, the presentation of medals, and other manifestations of military pomp and circumstance. From his long experience as an attaché, Allen knew how much store his European counterparts set by such martial displays, and he was determined to surpass them at their own game. When a battalion of his men lined up at present arms, so even and straight were the lines that a bullet fired down each rank could have shot off the nose of every man in it.[46] In addition to parading in Coblenz, detachments of the A.F.G. participated in ceremonies in other occupation zones and in the Allied capitals.

By the spring of 1920, the A.F.G. had improved so much in every respect Allen decided it was time to show it off a little. He requested a formal inspection by officials of the War Department. Secretary Baker sent his regrets, but Chief of Staff Peyton C. March and Inspector General John L. Chamberlain decided to visit Coblenz.[47] Both generals found minor deficiencies in Allen's command, but overall they were impressed by what they saw and highly complimentary in their reports.[48] The few remaining flaws in the A.F.G.'s training, discipline, and administrative procedures were quickly corrected to the War Department's satisfaction. Thereafter, Allen heard nothing but praise of his troops from Americans and foreigners alike. Several European countries sent teams of officers to the American zone to observe and learn from his methods.[49] Even the dour Bullard, who visited Coblenz in 1922, was admiring: "The American forces in Europe became the most spick-and-span, the most highly polished and burnished soldiers that the government of the United States ever had."[50]

Once Allen's model army reached this plateau of perfection, he shortened the number of hours devoted each week to military subjects and, at the direction of the War Department, began an intensive program of educational and vocational training. Soldiers desiring to improve their basic educational qualifications could attend unit schools offering courses, each lasting seven weeks, in reading, spelling, arithmetic, penmanship, history, geography, and civics, all at the grammar school level. Several thousand men voluntarily attended these classes, while the 500 illiterates in the A.F.G. were required to go. There was also a six-month General and Commercial School in Coblenz with professional civilian instructors who prepared their students for college, better paying civilian jobs, or higher positions in the army. This school offered higher level versions of many of the courses taught in the units, plus such subjects as physics, geometry, bookkeeping, stenography, auditing, typewriting, and commercial law. Finally, there were the Service Schools, Ordnance, Signal Corps, Engineer, and so forth. These, while teaching the mechanical and technical skills needed within the A.F.G., also made potentially more useful citizens of their students by training many a mechanic, radio repairman, or architectural draftsman.[51] Always a believer in the nonmilitary benefits of military training, Allen said of his program in Coblenz:

> If our people could clearly see the results accomplished in the domain of physical culture, without mentioning the great value of inculcating order, discipline and hygiene in our young men or the important assets given [them] by primary education and vocational training, I am sure we would have many converts to the principle [of universal military training]. In my opinion all our responsible thoughtful officers keep foremost in their minds the improvement in the soldier with a view to making him a better citizen and therefore a greater asset to the government when his term ends.[52]

Valuable and important as the A.F.G. may have been in maintaining the military prestige of the United States in the eyes of Europeans and in making better citizens out of its soldiers, these benefits were merely byproducts of Allen's accomplishment of his primary mission: to represent and safeguard his nation's military interests in the Rhineland.

For six months after taking command in Coblenz, he was, in fact, also responsible for the supervision of civil affairs in the American zone, just as his predecessors during the armistice period had been. The I.R.H.C. set up by the Rhineland Agreement had already established its headquarters in Coblenz by the fall of 1919 and begun drafting its initial ordinances, but, until the Treaty of Versailles went into effect, the commission was without formal power. Its French chairman was Paul Tirard, a close friend and former subordinate of Marshal Foch's. Sir Harold Stuart and Baron Rolin-Jacquemyns represented Britain and Belgium respectively. As we have noted, Pierrepont Noyes represented the United States. The ordinances these four gentlemen and their staffs were drawing up would become the highest law of the Rhineland when the I.R.H.C. assumed Foch's governmental responsibilities.[53] The commission was scheduled to begin its official life on January 10, 1920, the date set for the deposit of ratifications by the signatories of the treaty. By mid-November all except the United States had already ratified. On November 19, after a bitter five-month debate, the U.S. Senate rejected the treaty. The consternation in Coblenz was almost as great as in Washington. Although Wilson's supporters still hoped to get the treaty through the Senate, its eventual passage was by no means assured, even with reservations. At best, ratification might be delayed many months. America's partners in the Rhineland tried to decide whether to go ahead and convene the High Commission on January 10, regardless of what happened in Washington. Since France, Britain, and Belgium were now at peace with Germany while the United States remained technically at war, the commission's ordinances and the Rhineland Agreement itself would be without legal force in the American zone. Under these circumstances, it was doubtful whether it would even be proper for Noyes to attend the commission's meetings. His active participation in its future deliberations seemed entirely out of the question.[54]

After several weeks of waiting in vain for instructions from Washington, Allen asked his legal advisors to recommend a solution to the problem. The experts came up with several courses of action, all equally legalistic and impractical.[55] From the germ of an idea suggested by an assistant to the British Commissioner and seconded by Noyes, Allen developed a way out of the impasse himself.

His plan was quite simple. To achieve administrative uniformity throughout the Rhineland and present a united front to the German population, Allen proposed to publish the ordinances of the I.R.H.C. in the American zone as the orders of his own headquarters. Noyes would sit as an "observer" on the commission and act as liaison between that body and Allen's headquarters.[56] Even though the American would have no vote, so glad was Chairman Tirard at the prospect of not losing his participation entirely that he told Noyes his views would "have the same weight as heretofore."[57]

Believing he still had Noyes's support for his solution, Allen cabled the proposal through the American Ambassador in Paris to Secretary of State Robert E. Lansing on January 2.[58] Noyes, however, had changed his mind about the wisdom of continuing military rule in the American zone. A week after Lansing received Allen's message, he also had a cable direct from Noyes suggesting that Allen's headquarters "remain quiescent" and the United States government agree to the direct promulgation of the High Commission's ordinances in the American zone.[59] Lansing accepted Allen's plan as offering a greater degree of control over any policies the commission might adopt. The strong desire of the other occupying powers to preserve the appearance of quadripartite unanimity *vis-à-vis* the Germans would give Allen what amounted almost to a veto power, for he could always refuse to adopt and publish any ordinances not in consonance with American interests. With a typical lack of urgency, however, the State Department's reply with Lansing's decision did not reach Coblenz until several days after the High Commission met on January 10.[60] Rather than risk damaging the commission's prestige at the outset, Allen assumed Lansing had accepted his plan and on his own responsibility published the I.R.H.C.'s first three ordinances on the same day they were promulgated in the other occupation zones.[61]

These three documents formed the basic law of the occupation from then on and provided the substructure for all subsequent enactments by the commission. They also raised doubts in Noyes's mind (and among many Germans as well) that the High Commission intended to abide by the relatively liberal spirit of the Rhineland Agreement.

That agreement, based closely on Noyes's original memorandum to President Wilson, defined the jurisdiction of the High Commission in very general terms and failed to enumerate the specific powers it would have. In view of the disputes that later arose over the extent of these powers, the most important clause of the agreement was Article Three, which stated: "The High Commission shall have the power to issue ordinances so far as may be necessary for securing the maintenance, safety, and requirements of the Allied and Associated forces." It had been Noyes's intent that such powers would be used only in the most limited ways. The High Commission was to interfere with or override the existing German political, administrative, and legal structure only when absolutely necessary.[62] Such were not the views of the French and the Belgians. They intended to endow the High Commission with any and all powers not expressly forbidden by the Rhineland Agreement. There was, of course, more than a conflict between the Anglo-Saxon and continental philosophies of government involved here. Having suffered the most at the hands of the Germans and acutely conscious of their lack of territorial security, the French and the Belgians wanted the harshest possible occupation and one that would neutralize the Rhineland for as long as possible as a factor in Germany's economic and military strength. The British and the Americans, on the other hand, fearing no invasion and desiring to restore their trade with the continent, wanted a mild occupation that would promote rather than hinder German economic and political recovery. The latter's goal could only be achieved by the fullest possible integration of the civil and economic affairs of the Rhineland with the rest of Germany.[63] But, with a Frenchman chairing the High Commission and with American participation limited to observation, the general tone of the initial ordinances should have surprised no one.

The first ordinance defined the legislative powers of the commission, the second outlined the conditions under which the occupation authorities could intervene in the German judicial system, and the third dealt with rules governing public meetings and freedom of expression in the press. The commission gave itself both direct powers (since its ordinances automatically became the highest law in the Rhineland and it could also annul court decisions) and indirect ones (through its ability to nullify German laws contrary to its own pronouncements and to issue "instructions" to German civil agencies). There was no attempt at a separation of powers within the commission; the same men performed executive, legislative, and judicial functions. And, since they represented the victors, there could naturally be no responsibility to the people of the occupied territory. Legally, the commission was bound only by the precedents of international law, the Rhineland Agreement, and its own enactments. Inevitably, however, its members were also responsive to the often conflicting political goals of their respective home governments.[64] This tension between what was legal and what was politically expedient was to lead to much inter-Allied friction.

Before such frictions developed, the Germans pointed out some even more fundamental contradictions in the legal basis of the occupation itself. The initial ordinances of the High Commission were met by an outburst of criticism in the German press and an official protest from Berlin. In a note to the Supreme Council on January 12, the German government stated that these new laws violated in several important ways the principle of minimum interference in German affairs established by the Rhineland Agreement. First, the High Commission had given itself the power to review and approve German laws before they went into effect in the Rhineland (instead of allowing such laws to go into operation automatically and then vetoing them if necessary). Next, German violators of the commission's ordinances were to be prosecuted in the military courts of the occupiers instead of in German civil courts. And, finally, the civilian representatives of the commission at the district and municipal levels were to have not just a liaison function but were to retain certain of the administrative and executive powers of their military government predecessors.[65] The Allies rejected these complaints, and the "civil" period of the occupation thus began on a note of discord.

By the winter of 1920, Pierrepont Noyes was a very unhappy man. He had seen the Rhineland Agreement, largely his own conception, rejected by the U.S. Senate and bent and twisted by the French and Belgians to serve their own purposes. Instead of being an equal member of the High Commission and the chief representative of American interests in the Rhineland, he was reduced to the status of a mere observer in a subsidiary role to Allen, who remained the supreme authority in the American zone. Noyes's relationship with Allen through the last half of 1919 had been amicable, but, after the unexpected reversal of their roles, it became increasingly strained. They were able to agree on such matters as the complete replacement of Allen's civil affairs officers at the local level by Noyes's men and the publication by Allen's headquarters of a code of instructions and regulations based on the commission's new ordinances, but there were also a number of quarrels between them, some of them quite petty.[66] Of the two, Allen was the better diplomat. Noyes disliked military methods and distrusted French motives—and too often showed it. Allen understood and sympathized with the emotions and fears of the French, though he did not always condone their harsh actions. As a result, he was much more inclined than Noyes to be co-operative with and conciliatory toward the commission and its policies, preferring to preserve for important occasions what little leverage he possessed by (as Pershing had advised him) not making an issue out of every minor disagreement. "There must be teamwork in the High Commission," Allen said to his staff; "outsiders should never know of the differences that may arise there." [67] Thus, to Noyes, Allen seemed to be "pro-French" and, because of this, "a secret disbeliever in the High Commission." [68] In the first half of 1920, a number of factors combined to isolate and estrange Noyes further, not only from Allen and the High Commission but also from his superiors in Washington.

It was a long, bitter winter, with shortages of fuel and food in countries on both sides of the Rhine. Germany, not yet fully recovered from the effects of the blockade, was plagued by inflation, strikes, and a general economic and political dislocation. German reparations payments began to lag, particularly shipments of coal to France. In that country pressure for sterner enforcement of the treaty caused the downfall of one government and obligated its successor to threaten the Germans with force, including an occupation of the Ruhr, to insure the coal deliveries.

Simultaneously, in order to bolster their own weak economic position and apply further pressure on Germany, the French attempted numerous encroachments on "both the word and letter of the Rhineland Agreement." [69] With the support of Sir Harold Stuart, Noyes succeeded in blocking some of these moves (for example, the French demand for control of all Rhine navigation [70]), but in so doing he made himself extremely unpopular with Tirard. Without consulting Allen, Noyes soon was urging Washington to withdraw American forces from an occupation that was only contributing to German economic ruin and serving as a cloak for a French takeover of the Rhineland. Then, on March 6, he submitted his resignation. "It is impossible," he said, "that the occupation with French forces can be as tolerable a burden as the President had hoped. . . ." [71] Before acting on Noyes's resignation, Washington sought the opinions of Allen, Ambassador Hugh C. Wallace in Paris, and Commissioner Ellis L. Dresel in Berlin, as to whether the situation was as bad as Noyes pictured it. None of the three felt American withdrawal from the occupation was called for; all believed its continuation would have a mitigating effect on the current tensions.[72] To Secretary of War Baker, Allen said of Noyes's recommendations:

> . . . the chief suggestions contained in Mr. Noyes' cable were not considered opportune either by the British High Commissioner, with whom he had been working in close relations, nor by myself. American participation in the High Commission and in the Rhine holding involve such complex matters that recommendations bearing on them should be considered most seriously before being forwarded. A change at present would be considered a grievous blow by France, who is beginning to recognize her coming isolation.[73]

Meanwhile, on March 13, 1920, plagued by deepening popular resentment over food shortages, inflation, reparations, disarmament, territorial losses, and the occupation, the government of German President Friedrich Ebert was nearly toppled by a right-wing coup. Dissident elements in the German army took control of Berlin and set up a short-lived government under Wolfgang Kapp. Although Ebert was soon restored to full power by a nation-wide general strike called in his support, a Communist revolt broke out in the Ruhr in the strike's aftermath. Since most of the Ruhr basin lay within the neutral zone on the east bank of the Rhine, the Ebert government was prevented by treaty from sending in troops to put down the uprising.[74] For two weeks, while the Germans kept asking for a temporary waiver of the limits of the neutral zone, the French tried unsuccessfully to use the situation to get their allies to agree to an occupation of the Ruhr. Finally, on April 2, Berlin acted unilaterally and sent its units against the Communist rebels. Four days later, in retaliation for this treaty violation, the French occupied Frankfurt, in the neutral zone opposite the Mainz bridgehead.[75] Before doing so, they announced the decision had been unanimously approved by the High Commission. That was not true. To correct the impression of Allied unanimity, Noyes issued a statement to the press disassociating himself from the action of the French. Since Washington said nothing publicly concerning the occupation of Frankfurt, Noyes's statement "was the only positive evidence of the U.S. attitude."[76] The French press reacted with references to the American "desertion" of their cause.[77]

Within a month German troops had left the Ruhr after restoring order. Negotiations looking toward the French evacuation of Frankfurt were planned. The immediate crisis was over, but Noyes saw others coming. Having recently recommended complete American withdrawal from the occupation, he suddenly reversed himself and began advocating an activist policy. "The general direction of the now hopelessly mixed European settlement will be, with temporary ups and downs, steadily downward toward disaster until the U.S. ratifies [the treaty] and takes the lead," he said.[78] On April 22, after the treaty's second defeat in the Senate, he sent a message to the State Department urging ratification, "reservations, mild reservations, [or] no reservations. . . ."[79]

A month later, Noyes received a cable from Washington directing him to "wind up the Commissionership" and turn over as much of his staff to Allen as he needed "temporarily."[80] Noyes's outspoken opposition to the French and his strained relations with the A.F.G. commander undoubtedly contributed to this decision, but the main reason for Noyes's recall was probably his desire for decisive American action in the Rhineland. He wanted the United States to take the lead or get out. Washington was not prepared to do either, though Noyes seems to have assumed that his own relief meant the latter. In a press interview he gave the impression that American representation on the I.R.H.C. would soon be ended.[81] He was mistaken. Allen was appointed to fill his position on the commission.

Washington was not yet ready to disentangle itself from its commitment to a four-power occupation, though Noyes's recall did signify a decision that the United States must play a less active role in European affairs. That, of course, was a foregone conclusion after the second defeat of the treaty in the Senate. Despite his undercutting of Noyes by criticism, Allen had not been maneuvering to take over his job.[82] In fact, he thought his replacement of Noyes ironic:

> We . . . were largely responsible for a civil commission here and it hardly seems consistent to put a military man [in]. . . . Presumably they do not consider me a soldier.[83]

During this period of transition, Allen wrote a series of letters expressing his feelings about Allied policy toward the Rhineland and his own role. At the time of Noyes's relief, Allen sent Secretary Baker an analysis of France's motives for the recent occupation of Frankfurt. It was "largely due," he said,

> . . . to excessive fear of Germany and to the belief, temporary at least, that she was deserted by both England and the United States and that she must act alone while the relative strength conditions permitted such action. . . .[84]

Allen went on to say that while it was "not always easy to understand or agree with the views of our Allies, we can at least have respect for them and endeavor by a sympathetic attitude to counsel and possibly modify them." But, he warned, an effort by England or the United States "to bolster up France so that she may successfully compete as a great State with Germany must fail in the end. . . ." The French simply did not have the resources or the manpower to maintain such a status. The Germans knew this and were acting accordingly:

> . . . Germany has little respect for the . . . prowess of France nor does she show . . . the spirit the latter thinks should be displayed by a conquered state. . . . This attitude is excessively painful to their pride and till now has prevented such economic agreements as would have been advantageous to both sides and for the welfare of all.[85]

After having sat on the High Commission for two months, Allen sent another assessment to Baker:

> It has developed that our representation [here] supports a more civil and conciliatory policy than do at least two of the countries. . . . Such an attitude especially from a military man does not fail to have a restraining effect—at times urgently needed. . . . Although technically at war, I am sure we have the most *civil* administration of any in the several zones. The German representatives here . . . lose no opportunity to declare that they hope our Government maintains troops on the Rhine as long as any country does. . . . They know that when we go, the French will move in.[86]

Allen saw the seeds of another war in France's tragic shortsightedness. To his friend Leonard Wood, recently defeated in his bid for the Republican presidential nomination but still a contender for a cabinet position if his party won in 1920, he wrote:

> France would prefer to forego her trade advantage with Germany and accept the consequent further injury to her present unfortunate financial status if by so doing she could delay Germany's rehabilitation. Naturally I see France's view point, but feel that in the end her policy is a mistaken one and that she is sowing dragon's teeth.[87]

In the summer of 1920, Washington's policy toward the Rhineland appears to have drifted into one of following the line of least resistance. Despite some discussion in Congress and the press of the desirability of reducing or withdrawing altogether the troop contingent at Coblenz, the strength of the A.F.G. remained approximately 15,000 for the rest of the year. The difficult decisions about its future status and Allen's would have to await the outcome of the November election.[88]

Although that election was supposed to have been a "solemn referendum" on the treaty and the League of Nations, what to do about the A.F.G. was not a major issue in the campaign. The only specific mention of it by either candidate came from the Republican hopeful, Warren G. Harding. Though Harding was not noted for his brilliant insight into the problems and issues of the day, he was heavily favored to win on a tide of national disenchantment with eight years of Wilsonian "internationalism." Until late in the campaign, on the recommendation of his political advisors, Harding contented himself with vague campaign promises and policy statements as he sat and rocked on the front porch of his home in Marion, Ohio. As one tough old Republican "pol" put it: "Keep Warren at home. Don't let him make any speeches. If he goes out on tour somebody's sure to ask him questions, and Warren's just the sort of damned fool that will try to answer them."[89] Harding finally took to the hustings in October, preaching a confused mixture of nationalism and internationalism. After one of his speeches someone in the crowd asked him what he intended to do about the "boys over in Germany yet." Replied Harding: "They haven't any business there, and just as soon as we have formal peace we can be sure they will be coming home, as they ought to come." In practically the next breath he also said he would be satisfied with the Treaty of Versailles with reservations instead of a separate peace treaty with Germany.[90] Democrats and Republican internationalists were quick to point out the contradiction of a policy that looked toward the eventual ratification of a treaty while simultaneously promising the nullification of one of its key provisions. Harding said no more on the subject of the A.F.G. during the campaign.[91] Although his promise to "bring the boys home" was significant evidence of his own beliefs and future intentions, it is doubtful whether the statement affected the November ballot totals very much. What votes it may have cost Harding among those who still wanted an activist foreign policy (or merely the punishment of Germany), were probably balanced by a gain in support from Southerners and German-Americans, two groups having special reasons for wanting to disassociate the United States from the Rhineland occupation by the fall of 1920.

Following the Frankfurt occupation the previous April, the German government had begun a concerted propaganda campaign to discredit French conduct in the Rhineland. What attracted the most international attention was the German charge that the French had deliberately stationed large numbers of "half-civilized" Negro colonial troops in their zone in an attempt to brutalize and humiliate the white German population. Pamphlets printed in Germany and widely distributed in many languages luridly described this so-called "Black Horror on the Rhine." If the pamphlets were to be believed, murder, rape, and molestation were the daily lot of the hapless Rhinelanders. The German charges were picked up and repeated, without investigation, by Francophobe writers and newspapers in many countries. By June, so many Americans from the South and Midwest had written letters of protest to Washington that, at President Wilson's request, Secretary of State Bainbridge Colby cabled Allen in Coblenz and Ambassador Wallace in Paris and asked them for the truth in the matter.[92] Both men reported that, though there were many French colonial troops on the Rhine, their number did not far exceed their ratio in the French Army as a whole and that most were not actually negroid but dark-skinned North Africans. Furthermore, black or not, their disciplinary record was not as bad as pictured in the German press.[93] Allen's and Wallace's reports might have had a calming effect on the "Black Horror" issue during the election campaign, but they were not released until early 1921. In the meantime, the German propaganda went largely unrefuted in the United States, causing a former assistant secretary of state to write the President, "continued occupation of Germany in conjunction with these beasts in French uniform is equivalent to an approval by the United States of the inhuman policy." [94]

In the four months between Harding's election and inauguration, a lame-duck President Wilson did everything in his power to leave a diplomatic situation that would force the new administration to act decisively with respect to American representation in Europe. The American observers with the League of Nations and the Reparations Commission were recalled, as was the American representative on the Council of Allied Ambassadors.[95] Continued participation on these bodies would thus be entirely Harding's decision. As for Allen and his command, Wilson made no change except to order a reduction to the originally planned strength level of 6,500 by the end of May, 1921, evidently reasoning that a complete withdrawal from Coblenz would make it even more difficult for his successor to obtain senate acceptance of the Treaty of Versailles. Failing in that forlorn hope, Harding might still find the question of the continued existence of the occupation army a useful bargaining point in separate peace negotiations with Germany.[96]

Despite the earlier ambiguity of Harding's position on European affairs, the outline of a definite policy began to emerge in the spring of 1921, and it was rather surprisingly internationalist in spirit. On March 9, Secretary of War John Weeks announced there were no immediate plans to bring home the rest of the A.F.G.[97] Harding, in his first message to Congress, stated he would strive for disarmament and an "association of nations." On May 6, Secretary of State Charles E. Hughes returned the American observers to their posts with the Council of Ambassadors and the Reparations Commission. The announcements with regard to the A.F.G. and the Reparations Commission were correctly interpreted by the Allies as evidence of the United States's renewed willingness to pursue a hard line against Germany, then seriously in default on reparations and somewhat embarrassed by the gradual international realization of the shrill exaggerations of the "Black Horror" propaganda campaign.[98] Paradoxically, while feelings in Washington warmed toward the Allies and cooled toward Germany, just the opposite had occurred in Coblenz.

Throughout the course of the occupation, relations at all levels between the forces in the American and British zones had remained close and cordial. Sharing a common heritage and similar views as to their purpose for being in the Rhineland, the representatives of the two nations almost invariably supported each other's positions, both on the High Commission and in their military dealings with their continental partners.[99] America's relations in the Rhineland with the French, their Belgian alter-egos, and the Germans followed a much more complex and subtly varied pattern.

Even during the armistice phase of the occupation there were cracks in the edifice of Franco-American solidarity. Pershing's well-known disputes with Foch did not end on November 11, 1918. That winter the two generals fought over such issues as Foch's intention to assign French units to each of the other occupying armies.[100] To prevent Foch from placing French troops under General Dickman's command, Pershing had to agree that the French should take control of part of the Coblenz bridgehead. Within Dickman's headquarters there were lingering resentment at this compromise and an increasing dismay at French high-handedness in dealing with the German population.[101] As far as the French were concerned, the entire Third Army, from its commander on down, was too "pro-German." Dickman was suspect because of his very name and looks. In appearance he was the image of a fat, Teutonic burgher. Although Pershing went so far as to have his family background investigated to prove Dickman had no German connections (he was of Dutch descent), the subtle French campaign against him eventually won out.[102] In the interests of harmony, Pershing replaced Dickman with General Hunter Liggett, a man whose name conjured up nothing but visions of an English country squire. Liggett arrived in Coblenz in early May, 1919. Within a month, after his refusal to permit separatist activity in the American zone during the Dorten coup, Liggett was also *persona non grata* with the French.[103]

At a lower level, the basic cause of friction was French resentment of the mild American attitude toward the civilian population. After years of wartime propaganda in which each side pictured the other as cruel and inhuman monsters, neither the men of the Third Army nor their unwilling hosts quite knew what to expect when the occupation began. No serious incidents marred its first weeks. As the tension eased, the Americans found most Rhinelanders to be decent, orderly, hard-working, obedient, and eager to please. They, in turn, discovered many likable qualities in these good-natured and free-spending khaki-clad men.[104] To the French it often must have seemed the Americans liked their recent enemy better than they did their ally. Nevertheless, some ill feelings between Germans and Americans always remained.

Some of the irritants were constants, inherent in any postwar occupation. The rules against fraternization, long enforced more strictly in the American zone than elsewhere, were intended to minimize incidents and the venereal disease rate, but to many Rhinelanders they seemed only a haughty attempt to demonstrate American superiority over them.[105] Despite the vigilance of the military police, V.D. remained a major health problem for both sides. In addition, the army had taken over the best hotels, restaurants, and private homes. During the armistice period at least, many troops were billeted with German families. Among a soldiery with free time and plenty of money (by local standards) to spend on the beverages denied by Prohibition to their relatives back home, there were inevitable ugly incidents. The German press noted these with disdain, citing them as proof of the general boorishness of Americans.[106]

Other factors contributing to German-American tensions in the Rhineland were simply reflections of the prevailing economic and political problems of Europe as a whole. An example was the shortage of food in the first two winters of the occupation. No one starved in the American zone, but the sight of well-fed soldiers and their overflowing garbage pails full of edible morsels set more than the Germans' stomachs to growling. A program begun by Noyes and continued by Allen to feed more than 10,000 children with food provided by Herbert Hoover's civilian relief organization only partially offset German resentment.[107] The final determinant of German attitudes toward their American "guests" was the apparent degree of their government's acquiescence in the many French attempts to make the occupation as harsh as possible. Bitterness against the United States reached its highest peak in the spring of 1919 with the announcement of the treaty terms. There was another outburst of anti-American criticism a year later at the time of the Frankfurt occupation, though Noyes's statement dissociating himself from the actions of his colleagues on the High Commission quickly brought praise for his sense of justice from several German newspapers.[108] Allen's debunking of the "Black Horror" campaign led to a number of editorials questioning his fairness and objectivity.[109] In general, when the barometer of Franco-American relations read "fair" in the Rhineland, the corresponding reading on the German-American dial said "stormy"—and vice versa.

On the personal and social level, Allen got along very well with the French military and members of the High Commission. After Dickman and Liggett, he was welcomed as a man who understood more than just the language of his Gallic allies. At the conference or the dinner table he was adept at saying the right things at the right time. His son's marriage, in February, 1921, to Mademoiselle Juliette du Souzy produced many smiles of satisfaction among her countrymen. Harry and Juliette had met in the winter of 1918–19, when his father's 8th Corps was headquartered at Montigny sur Aube, near her father's chateau.[110] Although the protocol surrounding the marriage was as intricately prescribed as the steps of a minuet and caused Allen to grumble privately that he felt like a "damn fool" going through such a rigmarole, he was extremely fond of his new daughter-in-law.[111] Sharing the family's love of horses, she was a picture of feminine grace riding sidesaddle. Beautiful and vivacious, she became the crown princess of Allen's "Kingdom on the Rhine."

An observer of the international cast who enjoyed the glittering social life in Coblenz would never have guessed at the official discords it concealed. As long as Noyes remained on the commission, the French tended to blame him for the policy differences that arose, and they often turned to Allen in the hope of finding a friendly mediator. Although he succeeded in changing Noyes's mind on occasion, Allen was seldom totally sympathetic to the French. Even during Noyes's tenure, Allen had his own difficulties with them. Usually the disputes were quite trivial, but they epitomized an underlying difference in French and American attitudes toward the goals and purposes of the Rhineland occupation. One example was Allen's objection to the French practice of allowing their soldiers to wear bayonets on their belts when on pass. What the French did in their own area was their own business, but he refused to let them wear bayonets in the American zone unless they were on duty. To give soldiers roaming the streets a weapon of any kind was to Allen's mind not only an invitation to incidents but also a needlessly harsh reminder to the Rhinelanders who their masters were.[112] Another example was the disagreement over methods of administering civilian relief. Although in the American zone the food supplied by the Hoover Commission came through army channels, it was served in German churches and schools by German and American civilian personnel. The French units in the Coblenz bridgehead were willing to participate in this program, but their commander insisted on using soldiers to serve the food to drive home the point to the recipients that the French were not only their masters but their benefactors.[113]

After Allen assumed Noyes's responsibilities, it was not long before he found himself embroiled in the same kinds of disputes that had made his predecessor so unpopular with the French. Like Noyes, he was occasionally able to block some particularly objectionable French move. Unlike him, he never mentioned his objections in public and seldom flaunted his victories, which perhaps accounted for the continuing inter-Allied harmony on the social level in Coblenz. In Allen's first fourteen months as American Observer on the High Commission, he achieved some notable successes as a diplomat. Most of them had the effect of moderating French policy toward the Rhineland and calming international tensions.

In July, 1920, German police arrested Dr. Dorten in the French zone and spirited him into unoccupied territory, where he was to be tried by the national authorities for his separatist activities. Dorten's arrest was a clear violation of the Rhineland Agreement and the ordinances of the I.R.H.C. Under pressure from his government to take swift retaliatory action, commission chairman Tirard proposed to take extralegal measures against two Wiesbaden officials suspected of complicity in Dorten's abduction. Opposing their suspension from office and expulsion from occupied territory without a hearing but realizing the difficulty of Tirard's position, Allen negotiated a solution to the crisis. Through the Berlin government's highest representative in the Rhineland, *Reichskommissar* von Starck, he obtained an official apology and the release of Dr. Dorten. The French dropped their charges against the Wiesbaden officials.[114]

Von Starck, a master at finding ways to stymie French ambitions, was high on Tirard's list of undesirable Germans. In the winter of 1921, at the height of the tension of the first reparations crisis and after more than a year of putting up with von Starck's bureaucratic obstructionism, Tirard resolved to abolish the Reichskommissar's position. Allen and the new British Commissioner, Arnold Robertson, objected to this as an obvious attempt to remove a major obstacle to French penetration and control of the Rhineland. They could only delay von Starck's ouster, but they thwarted Tirard's real ambition. With the approval of the Council of Ambassadors, von Starck was merely replaced by another official, Prince von Hatzfeld-Wildenburg.[115]

A third area in which Allen was able to exercise a moderating influence was in the troublesome matter of the Allied-imposed customs border between the occupied territory and the rest of Germany. This was a one-way barrier to trade, rigged in such a way as to allow the Allies to flood the occupation zones and goods-starved Germany with their own products, while pricing competing German wares out of the market in the Rhineland. The arrangement benefited the French and Belgians the most, the British to a considerable extent, and the Americans hardly at all. This "Hole in the West" had been discontinued after the armistice period, only to be reinstated in the reparations crisis of March, 1921. Allen's objections on the commission to the customs border only delayed its reimposition by a few months,[116] but his continuing opposition to its unfairness may well have been a factor in its final elimination later that summer. In August, Allen attended an inter-Allied conference in Paris. Although there only as an advisor to the American observer, Ambassador George Harvey, Allen was asked for his views on the customs problem by Lloyd George, who by then had decided to break with the French on this issue and was looking for support for his position. Before Allen had obtained State Department permission to speak, the French agreed to abolish the customs line in exchange for a British concession on another matter. Even so, he was convinced that the sudden reasonableness of the Briand government was partly induced by fear of what he would say.[117]

Not that Allen was blindly "pro-German" in his opposition to the French. Although by the end of 1921 the original nonfraternization rules were so long forgotten that one out of every twenty of Allen's soldiers had married a German woman, his own relations with the Rhinelanders were restricted to the coolly correct transaction of official business with their appointed or elected representatives.[118] His report on the "Black Horror" charges was evidence of his objectivity, to the French if not to the Germans. And, when American and German interests conflicted, Allen could be just as imperious as Foch or Tirard, though he was usually more subtle in getting his way. A perfect example was the way he handled the "Bergdoll affair."

Grover Cleveland Bergdoll was a convicted American draft-dodger of German descent who had escaped confinement in the United States and fled to Germany after the war. In the fall of 1920, army criminal investigators under Allen's command learned that Bergdoll was living in the neutral zone. In an excess of enthusiasm and without Allen's knowledge or consent, they entered the zone and attempted to capture him. Bergdoll escaped, but in the melee the agents fired several shots and wounded a German girl. The two agents were arrested by the German police, tried, convicted, and sentenced to prison. This was a kind of Dorten case in reverse, only it was not so easily resolved by Allen. The Baden state government, in whose territory the incident occurred, was determined to go through with the trial. No apologies from Allen or pressure by him on the Berlin government could free the two men beforehand. The case aroused a storm of newspaper protest in the United States over this "outrageous" treatment of American citizens, but the German press was just as adamant in pointing out that German sovereignty had been violated. Although Allen recognized the legality of the German position, he refused to accept the explanations from Berlin that the national government could not interfere with a state's judicial procedures. In impressing on the German Foreign Minister that the release of the prisoners was "urgent," Allen's implication was clear: he might be forced to side with the French on the High Commission more often in the future. That velvet-sheathed threat secured the freedom of the two agents after they had served only a few days of their sentence. Allen handled all the negotiations in the Bergdoll case himself, by-passing the State Department's commissioner in Berlin, Ellis Dresel.[119]

Dresel was soon to be replaced by a full-fledged ambassador. In August, 1921, Germany and the United States could anticipate resuming normal diplomatic relations after signing a separate treaty of peace. The treaty provided for the continuation of the A.F.G. at Coblenz. Curiously, both the Germans and the French appeared to welcome that fact. Despite all the irritants of the American presence in the Rhineland, most Germans had come to realize that the A.F.G.'s withdrawal would leave them even more at the mercy of their traditional enemies. And, for all of Allen's obstinacy, the French still valued his command as a pledge for their security and a symbol of Franco-American solidarity.[120]

Nevertheless, since the United States and Germany were finally at peace and the President's own campaign promise to "bring the boys home" was still unfulfilled a year after he made it, the maintenance of an occupation army on the Rhine became increasingly difficult for the Administration to justify. In October, 1921, the War Department announced a reduction in the size of the A.F.G. to 5,600 men.[121] Although long expected, the news caused many solemn faces in Coblenz.

Allen's reaction was that the reduction would diminish American prestige and give him even less leverage in his dealings with Foch and

Tirard. Soon, in fact, the marshal was pressing him to allow French troops to take over most of the rest of the American zone.[122] Those of Allen's men who were leaving were no less disappointed than their commander, but for entirely different reasons. Not only had the A.F.G. become a model army, but Coblenz had been developed into a veritable vacation resort.

To complement the A.F.G.'s system of educational and vocational training, Allen had instituted a comprehensive athletic and recreational program, modeled on the one set up by the A.E.F. in the spring of 1919 but going far beyond it in the variety of attractions offered. Teams and leagues had been organized in baseball, football, basketball, boxing, and track. In the latter sport, there were even inter-Allied meets, at which the Yanks usually won most of the trophies. In Coblenz, the Y.M.C.A., Y.W.C.A., Red Cross, Salvation Army, and American Legion maintained offices and recreational facilities. There were clubs for enlisted men, N.C.O.'s, and, of course, the officers. Troupes of professional actors and musicians came from the United States to put on performances. The A.F.G. even had its own newspaper, *The Amaroc News.* And, old cavalryman that he was, Allen saw to it there were enough horses to form several polo teams, put on fox hunts and steeplechases, and establish a racing club with its own beautifully landscaped clubhouse and one-mile track.[123] Everyone in the Allen family except Dora and Juliette played polo, and Allen himself often joined the A.F.G. team to participate in matches against the Allies.[124] The sight of a gray-headed general in his sixties holding his own on the field against captains and lieutenants half his age brought the ultimate in sophisticated praise from one French spectator: "*Très chic!*"[125] Even if most of Allen's soldiers never tasted the patrician pleasures of polo and horse racing, they would never see another duty station as enjoyable as Coblenz. Not surprisingly, the A.F.G.'s re-enlistment rate was the highest in the army—another reason why the strength of Allen's force had consistently remained above the levels originally planned by the War Department.

For Allen and the troops remaining after the fall of 1921, Coblenz was as pleasant a place as ever, though some of the recreational facilities had to be closed down for lack of personnel to run them. Despite Allen's fears, the troop reduction did not seem to have much adverse impact on his effectiveness on the High Commission. He could still speak with full authority for the United States before Chairman Tirard. Allen's difficulties with that gentleman continued. When several of

Allen in His Favorite Pose. (Photograph courtesy of Col. Henry T. Allen, Jr.)

Foch's subordinates in the French zone openly violated an I.R.H.C. ordinance, Tirard's lack of response drew this comment from Allen:

> . . . In plain language, we [the I.R.H.C.] were violating our own ordinances and failing to admit it, much less punish our officials when they were wrong. . . . Political conditions in France make heavy demands on Tirard which he must satisfy, and in consequence his position is at times most difficult. . . . Fortunately we are able to indulge in talks [about our disagreements] and yet separate in a most friendly manner.[126]

In the winter of 1921–22, Allen had two more disagreements with Tirard that probably caused them to separate from their talks in less than a "most friendly manner." The first came over Tirard's reaction to the arrest of another Rhenish separatist, Joseph Smeets, by the German authorities. Smeets had been conducting a vicious propaganda campaign in the Rhineland against several government leaders in Berlin. When his attacks on them descended to personal libel, they ordered him arrested. Although Smeets was undoubtedly guilty and his arrest was perfectly proper under existing German law and occupation statutes, there were obvious political overtones to the case reminiscent of the Dorten episode. Tirard demanded Smeets's release, saying his guilt would be judged "politically" by the High Commission. Allen and his British counterpart, Arnold Robertson, refused to acquiesce in this judicial usurpation by the commission. After unsuccessfully attempting to exclude Allen from the commission's deliberations on the issue, Tirard finally agreed to let the German courts try the case. But then, after Smeets was convicted, Tirard insisted on nullifying the decision despite Allen's vehement protests. Allen called the commission's handling of the Smeets affair "its least worthy act." [127] Meanwhile he was at odds with Tirard on another issue, what to do about a threatened railway strike in the Rhineland. To insure the continuation of logistical support for the occupation armies, the French wanted to declare martial law and seize control of the railroads. Fearing that once the French took control they would never relinquish it, Allen said he would refuse to publish the declaration of martial law in the American zone. When the strike began he then used his authority under an existing I.R.H.C. ordinance to draft those workers essential for the continued operation of the railroads in his zone. Tirard had no choice but to follow suit for the rest of the occupied territory. The strike soon ended and the railroads resumed normal operations, still under German control.[128]

From these examples it would appear that Allen's ability to exercise a restraining influence on the French in the Rhineland was as strong as ever. In his dealings with the High Commission that was true, but in the military sphere it was not. During this same period the strength of the A.F.G. was reduced to a mere 1,000 men, and more and more French units moved into what was nominally still the American zone. Although these units were under Allen's command and he could theoretically force their commanders to abide by his rules, he was helpless to change their mental attitudes, much less those of their men.[129] For Germans living in the Coblenz area, the occupation had become much less bearable by mid-1922.

Had it not been for the Washington Disarmament Conference, the entire A.F.G. would probably have been brought home in the fall of 1921. Because President Harding hoped the French would agree to significant naval limitations, to maintain American representation on the Rhine a while longer served a useful purpose. The complete withdrawal of the A.F.G. before the conference might have made the French less willing to make concessions, since it could only have increased their growing fear of diplomatic isolation and their obsession with military security.[130] In March of 1922, however, Secretary of War Weeks announced that the rest of Allen's command was coming home. Harding and Weeks had made the decision in order to head off a congressional move to cut the size and cost of the army. They had not consulted Secretary of State Hughes before making the announcement. When Hughes pointed out that the A.F.G. might still be a useful lever in the pending negotiations over the inter-Allied distribution of the German-paid occupation costs, Harding agreed to postpone the recall decision until June.[131] In the meantime he received numerous requests to keep at least a token force in Europe, including cables from several congressmen and General J. G. Harbord, Pershing's Deputy Chief of Staff, all three of whom were then visiting Coblenz.[132] When Harding met in June with Weeks and Hughes, the latter was prepared with a staff study justifying the continuation of the A.F.G. It had been prepared by a friend of Allen's in the State Department, partly from information supplied by Allen's headquarters. The study made three important points. First, the other occupying powers and the Germans had all requested that the A.F.G. remain. Second, if peace in Europe was to be preserved, French policy in the Rhineland had to be restrained (all of the examples of Noyes's and Allen's restraining influence on the I.R.H.C. were listed). And, third, if the French resorted to force to achieve their goals in the Rhineland, American trade interests would suffer.[133] Evidently presented with no convincing counterarguments, Harding decided to leave 1,000 men on the Rhine for the time being.[134] The *New York Times* probably expressed his reasons: "If the Americans can perform a service to the world by postponing . . . [the A.F.G.'s] departure, it would be a pity to insist upon the order of recall." [135]

Nevertheless, the summer and fall of 1922 were months of anticlimax for Allen. It was obvious to everyone that his government was only waiting for the right psychological moment to bring the occupation to an end. The social life at Coblenz was as glittering as ever, but the formalities had a somewhat hollow ring. These were lonely months for him as well. Harry and Juliette and Frank and Jeanette were still with him, but Dora had been gone almost continuously for more than a year. Always close to her brothers and sisters, she had spent part of the time with Roy, then living in England and bedridden with a prolonged illness. Dora also went back to the States to stay with an ailing Dasha in Cincinnati, who, with Joe, had settled there after Viner resigned his commission to take a well-paying position with the chemical firm of old family friends, the Wiborgs.[136] Joe's resignation saddened Allen, but he had to admit there was probably more challenge for his energetic son-in-law in his new job than in most assignments in the postwar army.[137] Allen was beginning to look forward to the end of his own career. On his next birthday, April 13, 1923, he would reach mandatory retirement age. After his sixty-second birthday he had ruefully written his friend Harbord, "What a terrible age for an advocate of chloroform for soldiers at 50." [138] But, before he went "out to pasture," Allen was to have one last important chance to exercise a moderating influence on the troubled course of the Rhineland occupation.

The most serious postwar crisis in Europe began in the fall of 1922. Germany was again unable or unwilling to meet its reparations debts, and there was fresh talk of a French occupation of the Ruhr. As the tension increased, Secretary Hughes first warned the French that such a move would be a "great danger to future peace," and then, on January 8, 1923, flatly told their ambassador in Washington that an occupation of the Ruhr would mean the withdrawal of the A.F.G.[139] By then, the French had already determined to have their way. On January 7, Allen was notified that French troops were beginning to concentrate in the Rhineland. On January 10, twenty-four hours after the Reparations Commission had declared Germany in "willful default" on its deliveries of coal, the French announced they were marching into the Ruhr to take over the mines. The same day, Harding, Weeks, and Hughes met at the White House, where a statement was soon released that the A.F.G. was coming home.[140] After Hughes's threat, the President could hardly have acted otherwise, but the timing of the announcement was the clearest possible sign of American displeasure at the French course of action. While official Paris tried to shrug off the American decision as one that had long been made, the French press was less diplomatic: "To our friends and allies who came to fight on French soil, hail! To the occupiers of the Rhine who helped to frustrate the fruits of victory, good-bye!" [141] German reaction was mixed, pleased at the dramatic nature of the American protest but aware that it "would make the accomplishment of the criminal aims of our oppressors easier." [142]

Even as the A.F.G. began to pack, Allen had one last card to play. On January 11, acting on a hint from Tirard that French Premier Poincaré was still in a mood to negotiate on the Ruhr, Allen called for a meeting of the High Commission to discuss the possibility of starting Franco-German talks.[143] This action, taken on his own responsibility, was immediately followed by an explanatory cable to Hughes: "The seriousness of the situation . . . and the way in which the High Commission is connected with the new occupation . . . indicate a usefulness of an expression from that source." [144] Three days later, after a complaint from Poincaré that the American general's actions were "inappropriate," Hughes cabled Allen to mind his own business. The situation was too "delicate," said Hughes, for any move "without explicit instructions from the Department." [145] In his thirty months as an observer on the High Commission, those were almost the only really explicit instructions Allen ever received from Washington.[146] He replied to Hughes by expressing his "deep regret that my intentions should have annoyed you." [147]

On January 24, 1923, the Stars and Stripes were lowered from the centuries-old fortress of Ehrenbreitstein across the river from Coblenz, and the remaining troops of the 8th Infantry Regiment marched through the city to board their train at the station. Allen noted the "genuine sorrow depicted on the faces of both allies and Germans." [148] The French took over the city three days later. On February 7, after a ceremonial burial at sea of "Aleck J. Corkscrew," the troop-, wife-, baby-, dog-, horse-, and furniture-laden *St. Mihiel* returned the A.F.G. from Europe to the Land of Prohibition.[149]

Allen was not at all certain Washington had meant for him to come home also. The White House announcement of January 10 had said only that the A.F.G. was being withdrawn and nothing about ending American participation on the High Commission. Unofficially he had been told there was a chance he might stay.[150] On February 1, word came he was to withdraw from the commission. He said his farewells to its members five days later. Each of them replied with a speech of his own. All were highly complimentary, even eulogistic. Tirard too seemed genuinely sorry to see him go:

> It is unnecessary to dwell upon the military merits of General Allen. . . . I wish rather to express for my part my opinion of the diplomat and the man. [Here Tirard reminded his listeners that it was Allen who found the way to continue American representation on the commission after the United States failure to ratify the Versailles treaty.] It is thanks to him that for three years . . . no difficulty has arisen from the special situation of the American troops. . . . Our relations have been of the best.
>
> As for the man, I will express what you all feel; every time that he has taken his place among us we have been impressed by his high mindedness and the perfect impartiality of his judgments. . . .[151]

Allen landed in New York on March 3. On the way home he put the finishing editorial touches on his diary of the occupation, dictated daily to a stenographer for the past three and one-half years. Since December of 1921 Allen had had a contract with the Houghton Mifflin Company to publish it as soon as possible after his retirement.[152]

When the ship docked Allen was handed this note from Secretary Hughes:

> It has been of inestimable value to have the benefit of your mature judgment and opinion regarding the important developments that have transpired in the Rhineland and I deeply appreciate the manner in which, through your comprehensive reports, you have kept the Department in touch with the situation.
>
> Permit me, in addition, to express my pride and satisfaction in having had, as the Department's representative in Coblenz, an official of your high qualities and distinction, and also my thanks . . . for the manner in which you have maintained at all times the honor and prestige of the United States.[153]

Newspaper comment on Allen's return was generally complimentary though cursory. Symbolic in its brevity of the nation's real lack of interest was this eighteen-line editorial in the *New York World:*

> Gen. Henry Allen . . . is returning to America after a most extraordinary adventure.

> He has been the commander of an army occupying the territory of a vanquished foe, of the first American army which ever performed this duty on European soil. He commanded a force stationed in the very heart of the most complicated diplomatic tangle, amid the most ancient and bitter hatreds. His legal status was at all times doubtful and irregular. Yet from beginning to end his administration has been a triumph of common sense, of honesty and of decency. He has left Europe with the applause of allies whom our Government has officially deserted and with the tearful regrets of the people whom we overcame. When he arrives home he should not fail of recognition from the Nation to whose good name he has added so much.[154]

In the weeks following his arrival in the United States Allen was assigned to the War Department to finish his report on the occupation. Meanwhile, he also gave a number of unofficial speeches and interviews about his experiences in the Rhineland, stressing the past and future value for world peace of America's disinterested participation in the affairs of Europe.[155] He was politely received, but few of his listeners shared the urgency of his convictions. Although just as disillusioned with the peace settlement as their former allies and enemies, most Americans thought they could afford to ignore the postwar problems it had caused. It has often been said that the Treaty of Versailles would have been more enduring had it been either harsher or milder, but, given the conflicting war aims and philosophies of the victors, its unfortunate blend of the two qualities was perhaps inevitable. The Rhineland occupation was a microcosm of the peace settlement as a whole.

It must have seemed to many of Allen's listeners that, for all of his attempts at moderation and his ability to restrain the worst passions of the French and Germans, all he had done was to postpone the confrontation in the Ruhr and make it more violent when it did come. In honesty, Allen could not claim any lasting success for American policy in the Rhineland, but he could say and did for the rest of his life that the proper response to the nation's failure in Europe was not to quit the role of moderator but to keep on trying.

Soon he was able to speak his mind without the restraints imposed by his uniform. On April 12, 1923, he was retired from the United States Army at an impressive mounted review at the base of the Washington Monument.[156] At the age of sixty-four he had completed forty-one years of distinguished military service to his country, and as a private citizen he still had much to give.

CHAPTER XI

The Last Battlefield

In retirement, Allen became a man of many causes, contributing his services or the use of his name to dozens of philanthropic organizations, groups promoting international understanding, and do-gooders of practically every other stripe. For example, among the positions he accepted were the presidency of the Washington chapter of the English Speaking Union, the vice-presidency of the American Olympic Association, the chairmanship of the board of directors of the American-German Student Exchange, membership on the Committee on Foreign Relations of the U.S. Chamber of Commerce, trustee of Peekskill Military Academy, and managing director (fund raiser) for Lincoln Memorial University, the latter an impecunious institution devoted to the betterment of the backward mountain people of East Tennessee.[1]

Such causes in any case were surely innocuous enough. Behind Allen's affiliation with several of them, however, lay a strongly held conviction that was to involve him in many other activities of a more controversial nature. He believed there was still much that Americans could do to help ease the tensions of Europe, even if their government no longer seemed interested in playing an active mediating role abroad. However well intentioned his efforts, what embroiled him in controversy was the fact that few Americans were as genuinely interested in European affairs as he and even fewer agreed with his diagnosis of Europe's postwar ills or with most of his prescriptions for a cure. In his own mind France's economic warfare against Germany was perhaps the gravest threat of all to a world still struggling toward a real peace in the spring of 1923:

It is astonishing to find such an anti-German sentiment here in Washington four years after the war. It seems that ninety per cent of the people one meets favor the present French advance. They do not measure the extent to which it may go, nor do they visualize the direct injuries to the states involved and to Europe, and therefore less directly to us.[2]

A trip to Europe that June gave Allen his first opportunity as a civilian to work on a "cure" for Europe's troubles. The ostensible reason for his visit was to help make arrangements for the next year's Olympics, but with the French still holding the Ruhr and fomenting Rhenish separatism, Germany gripped by a ruinous inflation and on the brink of economic chaos, and the entire European atmosphere poisonous with hatred, talk of games made Allen feel uncomfortably like a Nero in a burning Rome. Interested in promoting international cooperation on a higher level than sports, he had conceived a plan for a permanent settlement of the Rhineland problem and wanted to discuss it unofficially with Colonel House, then in London.[3] The plan envisioned a joint attempt by the American and British governments to obtain French and German agreement to a change in the political status of the Rhineland. The area would remain a part of the Reich but would be removed from the domination of Prussia and become a new German state, perhaps with special economic ties with France. Allen foresaw objections to such an idea by both France and Germany, since it represented a major concession by the latter and yet did not fulfill the former's maximum goal of a totally independent Rhenish state. Nevertheless, he believed his plan might offer the basis for an acceptable compromise, especially if both the United States and Great Britain lent it their support. Encouraged by House, Allen presented his proposal to Secretary Hughes in Washington on July 23. Hughes was noncommittal, saying Allen's plan was "nothing new." Allen insisted that it was, since it involved a negotiated settlement and not an imposed one, and said that his talks in Europe had convinced him it might work. He followed up the interview with a memorandum to Hughes of what had been said.[4] When several weeks passed without any discernible indication that the State Department was pursuing his proposal through diplomatic channels, Allen decided to force the issue. On August 16, 1923, in a speech at a symposium on the European situation at Williams College, he combined an assertion of the United States's moral obligation to take a more active role in settling the European crisis with a hint that he had a plan for its solution already under consideration in Washington. Newspapers in Boston and New

York quickly picked up the hint and printed speculative stories as to what the deails of the "Allen Plan" might be.[5]

Although Allen's remarks at Williams brought him a letter of congratulations for speaking out from John Foster Dulles, then a lawyer with a New York firm,[6] the reaction of the State and War departments was entirely negative. In a telegram sent on August 17, Secretary Hughes rebuked Allen:

> Your statement is disquieting because [it] . . . excites curiosity without accomplishing any good. . . . When you made this suggestion I told you that I did not regard it as essentially new and that my understanding was that Germany would not agree to it. You believed that she would. . . . I took immediate steps to ascertain authoritatively the attitude of the German government . . . and found it absolutely opposed. . . . In as much as you have stimulated inquiry as to the nature of your proposal and I am unwilling that it should be supposed that a remedy is available in your hands, I propose to make public informally exactly what your proposal was. . . .[7]

As Hughes had promised, newspaper articles soon appeared deflating the so-called "Allen Plan." [8] The War Department took a little longer to react, but, on September 6, Allen received a letter from the Adjutant General's Office. There had been "considerable criticism in the press" of his recent speeches, said the Adjutant General, and since Allen could not "divest himself of his character as a public official," he was directed to delete from his future "public utterances" any "remarks which might cause criticism of the government." [9] To which Allen replied by defending his statements as factual and nonpartisan and denouncing as "untrue and incorrect" any deduction that he intended to criticize his government. However, he promised to be more careful in the future.[10]

When Allen had a luncheon meeting with Secretary of War John Weeks and tried to explain his position, the Secretary made it clear to him that the Administration did not appreciate his meddling in affairs of state.[11] Rebuffed but not chastened, Allen simply channeled more of his energy into another of his causes. This was a program he had helped organize the previous April to provide food and other basic necessities for those European children who were the innocent victims of the economic crisis brought on by what he considered the blind folly of their elders. The organizers of the Committee for Central European Relief had not originally intended that only German children would receive such aid since the virtual standstill in the Ruhr was having an adverse impact on the economies of all of Germany's neighbors,[12] but, during Allen's trip to Europe in June, he had apparently found that French leaders were not interested in American charity. He talked at length with the still vigorous Clemenceau, no longer in power, but Allen was able to have only a brief and unsatisfactory informal interview with President Millerand.[13] Thus, after Allen's return from Europe in July, the Committee for Central European Relief evolved into the American Committee for the Relief of German Children. Allen became its chairman. In the next year, he raised more than $3,000,000, most of which was funneled through a Quaker organization, the American Friends Service Committee, to provide one meal a day to hundreds of thousands of children, primarily in the Ruhr and Rhineland area.[14]

The relief committee drew protests from Francophiles who felt the Germans' woes were a well-earned reward for their recalcitrance on repatriations. One particularly vociferous critic of Allen's fund-raising activities was Owen Wister, the well known author of *The Virginian* and a close friend of Theodore Roosevelt's. In an open letter to Allen, Wister expressed his "amazement that a man who wore his country's uniform during the war should now take up arms for the starving German babies while German profiteers wax fat [on the inflation]." [15] Allen retorted he did not "give a German mark" for what Owen Wister thought. "This movement," he said, "is one in which the peace of the world is directly concerned," and added, "our boys did not make war on babies." [16]

The hostility of men such as Wister bothered Allen very little. More disturbing to him was his growing unpopularity in the higher circles of the French and American governments. The publication of his diary of the occupation, entitled *My Rhineland Journal,* in November, 1923, did nothing to improve Franco-American relations. Despite a review of Allen's manuscript by the State Department that resulted in the deletion of many politically sensitive passages,[17] the book was still an exposé of the differences in Allied policy toward the Rhineland. As such it brought the author more than one angry letter from Frenchmen who had once considered him a friend.[18] A translated edition of Allen's *Journal* soon appeared in Germany, where its unflattering description of French methods and motives became a potent anti-French propaganda weapon.[19] It was useless for Allen to protest that, although he considered certain French policies unwise, he had nothing but sympathy for the French people and their leaders.[20] In March of 1924, shortly before Allen's scheduled return to Europe in company with the U.S. Olympic delegation, Ambassador to France Myron T. Herrick notified the State Department that in his opinion Allen would not be welcome in that country.[21] The Olympic delegation left without him.

By the summer of 1924, when the end of the Ruhr and reparations crises were in sight as a result of international acceptance of the Dawes Plan, Allen began to close down the operations of his German relief committee and look around for other useful ways to occupy his time. There were plenty of controversial or unpopular causes left for him to join.

Long a believer in the League of Nations and an advocate of American participation in it, he soon became a member of the League of Nations Non-Partisan Council, a group devoted to "educating" the American people into accepting fully their international obligations.[22] He also joined several other organizations with similar purposes, such as the Committee on Educational Publicity in the Interests of World Peace and the World Alliance for International Friendship Through the Churches.[23] Although he took a gloomy view of man's ability to live at peace with his neighbor ("as long as there be one woman and two men on earth, fighting will be more or less normal" [24]), he began to make speeches advocating controlled disarmament as a way of limiting the destructiveness of war.[25] By 1928 he was actively involved in an unsuccessful campaign to have the drafters of the Kellogg-Briand Pact add effective punitive sanctions to their vaguely worded renunciation of "aggressive war." [26]

As an adjunct to all these various activities Allen began to write newspaper editorials. From time to time, beginning in August of 1924, he submitted articles on the issues of the day to the Cosmos Newspaper Syndicate. This organization, which claimed among its contributors more than fifty prominent Americans, including Bernard Baruch, Ida M. Tarbell, and William Allen White, sold their articles to as many as forty different independent newspapers having a combined circulation of approximately 4,000,000. Despite the quality of its stable of authors, the Cosmos Syndicate never quite succeeded as a business venture. Allen was seldom paid in full or on time for the articles he wrote on disarmament, "delegalizing" war, and half a dozen other pieces dealing with European current events.[27] Nor did he make much money from his other writing efforts. Although he received some profit from the sales of *My Rhineland Journal,* he never got a cent from his next and historically far more important book. That work, entitled *The Rhineland Occupation,* was published in 1927, but only after Allen offered to waive all royalties in order to overcome the Bobbs-Merrill Company's reluctance to risk a low-selling loss. Bobbs-Merrill gauged the market for the book correctly. Despite kind reviews agreeing with the publisher's blurb that "no war library of more than three volumes can be complete without it," fewer than 1,000 copies of *The Rhineland Occupation* were sold.[28] But Allen could at least take pride in having satisfied an aspiration, expressed in his diary long ago when he was an attaché in Russia, " of doing something in a literary way before my end arrives." [29]

On the same page he had written, "By nature I am better fitted for a man of action than for a writer," [30] and that had certainly been a prophetic self-appraisal. Nor, a third of a century later, was he through with a life of action. For Allen the last battlefield was politics.

The decision to throw his hat in the ring probably startled many of his friends. Knowing his contempt for the compromising and glad-handing of the political process, they must have had great difficulty picturing a dignified Henry Allen consorting in smoke-filled rooms, much less kissing babies. He did neither and for most of his retirement never really took seriously the possibility of reaching high elective office, but, from 1924 onward, there was a presidential bee buzzing ever more loudly in his bonnet. Ambitious, well known in business, government, and academic circles if not by the general public, and holding strong opinions about the misguided foreign policy of the "ins," it was perhaps inevitable for Allen to be tempted to try for the White House, especially when men whose political expertise he respected murmured that seductive suggestion in his ear. Other generals before him (most recently Leonard Wood [31]) had succumbed to the temptation in similar circumstances.

The first murmur came from Colonel House on October 11, 1923. Allen's reaction was to scoff at the idea of himself as President.[32] He seems to have put it out of his mind until the following February, when he received a letter from a long-time friend, Judge Robert S. Marx of the Ohio Superior Court. After reviewing the political handicaps of all the announced Democratic candidates, Marx said:

> [The convention] . . . must turn to a man who is untainted and untouched by political scandals; to a man who is in no sense a politician; to a man who is above all a patriot, who has made a record as an executive and an administrator; who has high ideals of public service and national honor; who has deep human sympathy for the oppressed of all Nations and for all races and who believes in cooperation to achieve International good-will and Peace. To my mind, there is no man in America who meets these qualifications so perfectly as you. . . .

Probably, thoughts such as these have been very foreign from your mind but no man can refuse a call to the Presidency. I am not asking whether you would make a canvass for the nomination or even that you permit your friends to do so, I only desire to know whether your political affiliations are such that you could conscientiously accept a Democratic nomination, and, if so, I am convinced there are enough others to do the active work.[33]

This time Allen was more interested, though unwilling to declare himself a candidate or take any other overt action on his own behalf.[34] Marx undertook to sound out House on the possibility of Allen's nomination, and he also wrote to a friend who was a rising star in the Democratic Party, Franklin Delano Roosevelt. House replied that he was by then committed to William G. McAdoo, but in the event of a deadlock at the convention between his man and New York Governor Alfred E. Smith, the other major candidate, House said he would be "more than content" to see the deadlock broken by Allen's nomination.[35] Roosevelt, a backer of Smith, was more noncommittal. Allen's candidacy was a "brand new thought" to him and though Roosevelt "liked him immensely" and believed he "would command respect and admiration for the splendid work he has done," his nomination might present some problems. "Lots of the more progressive element will be afraid of the 'man on horseback,'" said F.D.R., reminding Marx that "several times the Democrats have chosen a leading general and have gone down to serious defeat." But Roosevelt was too canny to rule out any possibility. Telling Marx to "write me again and keep me advised," he closed by saying:

It would not be a bad idea to throw a feather into the air by getting something about General Allen's possibility for the nomination in the newspapers—then see which way the wind blows.[36]

Taking any answer but outright rejection of his suggestion by House and Roosevelt as encouraging, Marx wrote Allen that he would quietly begin to push his candidacy through a "small committee" of Allen's "close personal friends." [37]

On June 24, 1924, the badly divided Democratic Party met in New York City to select its candidates. McAdoo had the support of the southern and far western states; Smith's strength was in the East and Midwest. The contest dragged on for an incredible 103 ballots. When it was over on July 10, neither man had won. The weary delegates finally selected John W. Davis, a lawyer and a former Ambassador to Great Britain, as their presidential nominee. To please the farm bloc,

Nebraska's Governor Charles W. Bryan and brother of the former Secretary of State was chosen as Davis' running mate.[38] Of his efforts behind the scenes Marx wrote to Allen:

> I have no regrets over "our campaign." I did the best and all that could be done up to the point when I and all my friends were convinced that further endeavor would be both undignified and useless and that the nomination for either the Presidency or Vice Presidency this time is a doubtful and empty honor. . . .
>
> Throughout my presentation of your name and availability to those who *counted* . . . I was careful to put the matter [so] that you were heightened and not lessened in their esteem. The result is that your position is higher than ever in the judgment of such men as Roosevelt-Baker-Baruch-Brennan-Wise-Morganthau, etc., and if you care to support Davis I think in the event of victory these leaders would look with favor upon you as a Cabinet or other important officer.[39]

Ignoring a suggestion from another source that he run with Senator Robert M. La Follette on the Progressive Party ticket,[40] Allen took Marx's hint and worked to build support for Davis. Too badly divided by the convention ordeal, the Democrats were hardly in the race. One potential campaign contributor disgustedly returned Allen's letter touting Davis' merits with the word "BUNK!" written with a red crayon in large letters across the page.[41] On election day President Coolidge received almost twice as many votes as Davis and nearly four times as many as La Follette.[42]

For the next three years Allen was content to leave politics to the professionals, although it is probable that many of the activities on his extremely busy schedule were at least partly motivated by a desire to keep his name and qualifications in the minds of the powers of the Democratic Party. Even if this was so he could hardly have been accused of trying to build himself a popular image, for most of the principles he stood for were hardly likely to achieve that. Nevertheless, beginning in the fall of 1927, in contrast to his experience prior to the last nominating convention, Allen heard his name increasingly mentioned in public as a possible candidate.[43] He had a number of private meetings concerned with campaign strategy and the wording of the planks in the Democratic platform with Colonel Daniel C. Roper, McAdoo's former campaign manager.[44] Once again Judge Marx encouraged Allen to run, as did another Ohio friend of long standing, Frank Wiborg. Wiborg sent him a check for $500 to help with his campaign expenses and passed along some advice he had gleaned from Democratic leaders: since Governor Smith was certain of the nomination this time, Allen would be well advised to try for second place on the ticket.[45] Despite his uncertainty that the Kentucky delegation would even back him as its favorite son at the convention,[46] Allen finally decided to enter the race. He hired as his campaign manager Colonel John Noonan, a glib political huckster who might have passed for the double of William Jennings Bryan with his florid features and bald pate surrounded by a halo of curly hair.[47] Together, Allen and Noonan mapped out their strategy. The campaign would be dignified, short, and simple, because neither time nor funds permitted anything else.[48] Although Allen approved the wording of the announcement of his candidacy before it went to the newspapers on June 11, he must have made a wry face over it. Noonan had taken the bare facts of Allen's life and shaped them into a capsule biography that slighted his genuine accomplishments in a lifetime of varied and important public service in order to portray him as the perfect running mate of Governor Smith. Smith was Roman Catholic. Allen, an agnostic for most of his adult life, suddenly became a Baptist again, "and therefore would appeal to the ultra-Protestant Group." Smith favored repeal of Prohibition. Noonan stretched Allen's temperate drinking habits into the statement: "He is a lifelong advocate of temperance and believes in the strict enforcement of the eighteenth amendment." Smith was a Yankee and a city slicker. It had been a long time since anyone had called Allen a "Reb" or a rube. But, because of his rural origins, he was "thoroughly familiar with the science of agriculture," and, being a "Southerner from a border state," he could "swing Kentucky and Tennessee into line behind the Democrats, and . . . hold in line the solid South." [49]

The rest of Allen's two-week campaign consisted of several more press releases rounding out the picture of his qualifications and a series of letters and telephone calls to influential Democrats asking for their support at the impending convention.[50]

The convention began in Houston on June 26. Allen arrived with "no delusions" about his chances.[51] As expected, Smith easily won the presidential nomination despite Southern objections to his religion, Tammany connections, and opposition to Prohibition.[52] There were three candidates for the vice-presidential nomination: Allen, Senator Joe T. Robinson of Arkansas, and Senator Alben W. Barkley of Kentucky. (Allen had not won the undivided support of his home state's delegation.) Colonel L. B. Musgrove of Alabama put Allen's name before the convention. If the speech was flowery, at least Musgrove described Allen's life and achievements more recognizably than had some of Noonan's campaign rhetoric.[53]

It was all over on the first ballot. Allen's very real qualifications for the position he sought were not the ones needed to balance the Democratic ticket, and neither Smith nor the convention delegates were taken in by his other claims. When the votes were counted, Senator Robinson had 1,032, Allen had 21, and Senator Barkley had 9.[54]

Between the convention and election day, Allen worked loyally for the party by organizing a Democratic Veterans' Committee to proselyte the "soldier vote," despite the misgivings of some of his friends (among them former Secretary of War, Newton D. Baker) that such an organization might become a permanent political pressure group.[55] With Herbert Hoover's victory in November, Allen must have been glad to have done with yet another losing cause. But, for the first time in many years, he then had almost nothing of any importance to do. He became a full-time country squire.

Three years before, in December of 1925, he had purchased an estate called Charmian eighty miles north of Washington on the Maryland-Pennsylvania border.[56] He intended Charmian to be a family retreat from the Washington summers and had already invested a lot of money in it for remodeling and improvements, but Dora had spent more time there than he. It was a home fit for a monarch in exile, and it suited Allen perfectly once he finally decided there were no more battles to fight. Situated on twenty-four acres of wooded Blue Ridge mountainside, the enormous twelve-bedroom central manor house commanded a magnificent view. On the grounds there were two comfortable guest cottages, a swimming pool, a riding ring, a six-car garage with stables beneath, and an enormous playroom in the loft above for noisy grandchildren on rainy days. The whole complex was surrounded by several acres of lawn and beautifully tended gardens and was approached by a winding, tree-lined drive. Harry and Juliette Allen, living at Fort Myer in Virginia, brought their children often for visits. The Viners were still in Cincinnati, and the Andrews' assignments sometimes took them away from the Washington area, but both couples came to Charmian whenever they could. Henry and Dora stayed there from the first green of spring to the last red and gold of fall, returning occasionally even on snowy winter weekends from their Washington apartment at Stoneleigh Court.[57] Allen allowed himself plenty of time for enjoying the pleasures of riding, reading, and playing with his grandchildren, but he also worked several hours each day. Just keeping up with his correspondence and cataloging his lifetime

Charmian, Allen's Estate near Washington. (Photograph courtesy of Mrs. William S. Culbertson)

collection of papers filled much of the time, and he was still writing for publication as well. *Current History* printed an article of his on Marshal Foch in 1929, and another, on the Philippines, in 1930. Many of his views were still controversial. In September, 1929, after announcement of the forthcoming French evacuation of the Rhineland five years ahead of the treaty's time limit, the *New York Herald Tribune* printed an article by Allen critical of France's postwar policies toward Germany. Several readers responded angrily. "Rather than sowing the seeds of discord between France and Germany and France and the United States," said one, "General Allen would do better to confine his energies to cementing true and lasting friendship between these three great nations." [58]

Besides his writing there were business matters to look after. In addition to investments in the United States, he still owned property in the Philippines and had also bought stock in several large German corporations after his retirement. With careful management these investments had grown into a sizeable estate that brought the family comfortably through the crash of 1929.[59] And, however busy or controversial, he was, as always, the perfect host in his own home and in constant demand as the guest of others.

On a pleasant late August afternoon, while chatting over tea on the porch of the nearby summer home of Rudolf Leitner, the First Secretary of the German Embassy, Henry Allen died instantly of a stroke.[60] He was seventy-one.

On September 3, 1930, he was buried on a steep hillside in Arlington National Cemetery overlooking Washington and the Potomac River. Many officers with whom Allen served are buried close by, among them Frank Andrews, killed as a four-star general in a plane crash early in World War II. Other loved ones are near as well. Jeannette Andrews is with Frank; Juliette Allen with Harry. Dora lies beside her husband. On the back of Allen's plain, chest-high marble tombstone is a large bronze plaque, so weathered it is difficult to see its details. If the visitor bends close he can make out a handsome man in uniform, unmistakably Allen, surrounded by children and a mother with their arms outstretched in gestures of supplication and gratitude. Beneath this tableau is the inscription, "In Grateful Commemoration of the Noble Service Rendered to the Suffering Children of Germany by Major General Henry Tureman Allen, 1924."

The visitor, knowing little of Allen, might wonder at the incongruity of such a memorial to a man most of whose life was devoted to the profession of war and who was pleased to be called the "Iron *Comandante.*" Those who knew him better realize there is no incongruity at all. Not only in Germany, but long before in Cuba and the Philippines, Henry Allen had shown that, for all his soldier's toughness, he was above all else a man of compassion for the suffering that war brings to people.

Epilogue

Iron-hard soldier and compassionate victor, a man of action with the mind of a scholar, equally at home in the drawing rooms of Europe and the wilds of Alaska, Henry Allen *was* an unusual and complex man. Ambitious and egotistical, he never lost sight of his own interests, often to the detriment of the happiness of his family and frequently to the great annoyance of others. He always had difficulty understanding why anyone should oppose him. For every acquaintance who thought him gracious and charming, there was another who saw him as cold and arrogant. Many people admired and respected him, but he was not always a lovable figure. More to the point, however, is the question: what did Allen accomplish with his life that was of lasting importance?

Although most of his military assignments were extremely interesting and of more than routine importance at the time, three stand out as being of true historical significance: his exploration of Alaska in 1885, his work with the Philippine Constabulary from 1901 to 1907, and his dual position after World War I as commanding general of the American Forces in Germany and observer on the Inter-Allied Rhineland High Commission.

Allen's Alaskan venture remained little known and resulted in no wave of settlement such as that which followed the earlier Lewis and Clark exploration of the climatically more hospitable Northwest. Nevertheless, his accomplishment has rightly been called one of "the great explorations of North America." Few explorers have done more in less time and with such meager resources. Later, larger, and better equipped expeditions gradually refined and added to Allen's data, but they were to find his work a solid foundation on which they could build.[1] Such a useful fate is the hope of every explorer. Allen's hope was realized.

The Philippine Constabulary is still in existence. For many years it remained largely as Allen left it, though many of its American officers resigned during World War I and none have served in it since Philippine independence.[2] Despite the criticism of the constabulary in Allen's day, time has vindicated his basic conception of its organization and purpose and shown the value of its peace-keeping work.

Allen's influence on the course of history in the Rhineland is more difficult to measure, but there can be little doubt that he made his influence felt. His ability to partially restrain the French probably kept tensions in the Rhineland from rising even higher during his years in Coblenz. It is also possible that his very success at frustrating French ambitions only served to intensify them and thus contributed to the bitterness of the Ruhr crisis when it finally came.[3] What is indisputable is that Allen represented the military and political interests of the United States as he understood them with dignity, honesty, and honor.

Allen's activities on behalf of international co-operation and understanding after his retirement were also of more than passing importance in the nation's history. He was right in his analysis of the tragic consequences of the French Rhineland policy. One historian has recently called the Ruhr crisis the "seedbed of World War II." [4] Had Allen lived to see the holocaust unleashed by the bitterness of the German people, he could ruefully have said to his critics, "I told you so." To rouse his countrymen from their apathy toward Europe's problems and to soften the hearts of Europeans towards each other were Allen's twin goals. That he failed with the limited means at his disposal does not detract from the remarkable clarity of his vision. Better known and more powerful statesmen also failed to find a way to lasting peace.

Since Allen published four books and several dozen magazine and newspaper articles and gave countless speeches over the course of his lifetime, his importance as a writer and thinker must also be assessed. Typically diffuse and wide ranging, his literary and intellectual endeavors defy any other classification than eclectic. Although gifted with considerable insight into the military and political problems of the era and capable of original thought, he was not a man to develop a consistent personal philosophy in either of those two spheres. In fact, he was in many ways the intellectual disciple of Leonard Wood and Theodore Roosevelt up to the end of World War I and a "Wilsonian" thereafter. Perhaps the most that can be said is that Allen was an intelligent and articulate commentator to whom men listened with respect if not always agreement. Much of what he wrote for publication remains of value to scholars interested in the men and issues of his day. Of even more importance to the historian is the collection of personal and official papers he left.

Was Allen's career an unusual one for a military professional? The answer to that question may be as important historically as any of his specific accomplishments. In terms of his narrowly professional education at West Point and earliest assignments, he began his military service typically enough. But, soon thereafter, his interests, personality, and political connections led him into one of the most unusual military careers that any American officer ever had. Army officers have always been expected to be generalists capable of handling a wide variety of assignments, but Allen was the military generalist *par excellence*. Although officers such as Wood, Bliss, and Pershing had career patterns similar to Allen's in many respects, and responsibilities often far greater than his, none of them could match the diversity of his experiences. Many of Allen's army contemporaries were envious of him, but others regarded him with scorn or even distrust. He did not fully conform to the pattern.[5] His assignments frequently took him to the controversial or ill-defined borderline of civil-military relations, where the carefully prescribed code of his profession did not always provide the surest guide for action. He often made his own rules. A lifetime of success in dealing with such experiences helps to explain his retirement activities, despite an army saying that goes: "The best service a retired general can perform is to turn in his tongue along with his suit." [6] Seeing Allen's name constantly in print, Pershing could growl:

> His egoism seems to have gotten the better of him,—an outcome which I have always more or less feared and it is a pity too. . . . It shows the fatal consequences of military men trying to dip into civil affairs. . . .[7]

But Allen was only being a little more "civilian" and a little less "military" than he had been all his life.

And yet, if his career was rather atypical for a professional officer, in another sense it startlingly paralleled the history of the institution and the nation he served and loved. When Allen entered the army it was a tiny organization with little influence and less prestige, physically isolated from the rest of American society and intellectually stagnant. When he retired forty-one years and three wars later, the army was once again in a postwar cycle of neglect, but it had become both a more professional force than he had known as a young lieutenant and one capable of exercising, for good or ill, a much more influential part in the nation's life. With the army's help—whether by exploration and conquest, pacification and civil works, hemispheric intervention, coalition warfare on a global scale, or the peacetime occupation of foreign soil—the United States had become a world power. Henry Tureman Allen was there at every step along the way.

Appendix

Preferment, Promotion and Professionalism [1]

The increasing professionalism of the army during the course of Allen's career has been alluded to several times in the text. Among the more important aspects of this professionalization were the development of: (1) an effective general staff; (2) service schools at the postgraduate level to continue the education of officers throughout their careers; (3) a variety of service journals providing technical information and vehicles for the discussion of wider military issues; and (4) fairer and more rational personnel policies. Except for the service schools (none of which Allen attended), all of these developments directly influenced his career. Since the text explains Allen's role in the early history of the general staff and also illustrates the way in which the service journals served as a forum for his ideas on army reform, the purpose of this appendix is to analyze Allen's experiences in relation to the army's promotion and assignment policies.

Promotions and desirable assignments for an officer in any army have always depended on more than mere professional competence. The successful officer must also have a certain amount of luck, or, to put it more bluntly, be in the "right place at the right time" or know the "right people." In the personnel system of a truly professional army, however, ability as a selection factor must far outweigh luck and influence, even if the two latter can never be eliminated entirely. In the army Allen entered in 1882, ability had very little to do with the importance of an officer's assignments or the rapidity of his advances in rank—at least in peacetime.

Up to the rank of colonel, promotions in the peacetime regular army were based on a system of strict seniority. Selection of general officers was, with the consent of the Senate, a presidential prerogative, but even Presidents usually followed the dictates of seniority. Only occasionally was a relatively junior officer with an outstanding record and/or the right connections rewarded with a general's star. Throughout Allen's career these policies remained in force, but within this general framework many changes were made that had the effect of screening out the most unfit officers and making promotions more equitable for the rest, even if Allen's fondest hope—accelerated advancement below the rank of general for the exceptionally able—was not adopted by the army until long after his death.

Prior to 1890, officers normally served in the same regiment for most of their careers. Promotions came within the regiment as its senior officers died or retired. Retirement at the age of sixty-four had been made mandatory in 1882, but even if this reform eliminated many superannuated colonels it still left a lot of frustrated lieutenants of forty and captains of fifty. In 1890 the army adopted a system of promotion by branches, with each branch allocated a certain strength in each grade. The most senior officer of a given rank was promoted whenever a vacancy in the next higher grade occurred anywhere in his branch. All this accomplished was to average out the waiting time and eliminate the most glaring inequities of the older system. For example, a captain in one regiment no longer had to wait fifteen years for his colonel to retire before he could move up a notch, while a captain in another regiment might be promoted in five years if he was lucky enough to have a colonel who died before reaching retirement. However, the new system introduced another inequity. There were soon disparities in the rate of promotion among the various branches. This occurred because some branches (generally those represented by a chief in the War Department) were more successful than others in persuading Congress to authorize increases in their officer strength. Thus, promotion in the cavalry (which had no congressionally authorized chief until 1920) was much slower than in branches such as the artillery and engineers whose chiefs were powers in Washington. Besides the morale problem among the officers in the less favored arms, the branch system of promotion had another unhealthy effect on the army. Every time one chief pried an increased officer authorization for his branch out of Congress, his counterparts in the War Department felt obligated to follow suit. The result was that the number of officers in some branches was out of proportion to what it should have been considering the size of the army as a whole.

In 1920 the army dropped promotion by branch and adopted its present method, known as the "single list system." Promotions are distributed equitably to all eligible officers, regardless of branch, whenever vacancies occur. Not until 1950 was the strict seniority rule modified. Since that year the army has been able to promote up to ten per cent of the ablest officers in any grade below the rank of colonel more rapidly than their fellows. Such a system was advocated by Allen as early as 1905, although he proposed accelerated advancement for as many as fifty per cent of all such officers (see p. 147 for a quotation from Allen's "Notes on Promotion" taken from the *Journal of the Military Service Institute*). In Allen's day, however, all that officers in the peacetime army could do was ruefully agree with one another that "promotion's very slow."

With the avenues of promotion in peacetime thus constricted, it was perhaps natural for able and ambitious officers to seek the most glamorous or important assignments for which they were eligible as an alternative way of satisfying their craving for prestige and distinction. In this kind of competition seniority hardly mattered, ability counted for much, and influence counted even more. Allen's maneuvering for the attaché position in Russia is an excellent example of the practice. Such techniques were less and less successful for him as the years went by. This may have been partly due to the retirement of his earliest patrons, Generals Drum and Miles, and, later, the declining political fortunes of such friends as Theodore Roosevelt, Leonard Wood, and William H. Taft, but there was also a growing revulsion within the army itself against the use of political influence. Many officers were coming to feel that such practices were "nonprofessional" and compromised their corporate integrity. Chief of Staff Young appears to have reacted in this way to Allen's 1903 "campaign" to obtain the governorship of the Moro Province and have his constabulary general's rank made permanent.

There were other indicators of the army's growing determination to stop outside meddling in its assignment and promotion practices. After 1890 officers below the rank of lieutenant colonel had to pass a rigorous examination before they could be promoted. A simultaneous step toward a more professional officer corps was the requirement that each officer's superior periodically render a formal, written efficiency report on him. The institution of these policies was intended to give the Adjutant General's Office a file on each officer that accurately reflected his professional and personal strengths and weaknesses as well as his potential for promotion and aptitude for special assignments. However, efficiency reports required a generation of modification and improvement before they gained acceptance in the army as effective tools of personnel management. The series of reports in Allen's ACP File runs from 1890 to 1916. Their brevity and superficiality would make it difficult for anyone who did not know Allen well to form a true picture of his abilities. This helps explain Allen's continuing attempts to use influence to bolster his chances. The practice remained so widespread that in 1905 President Roosevelt issued an executive order to the effect that henceforth such attempts would result in an unfavorable notice on the officer's record. Roosevelt's order was only partially effective (as witness, for example, Pershing's promotion in 1906), but at least it created an atmosphere increasingly inhospitable to the blatant abuse of patronage and influence. Taft had to reckon with that atmosphere in deciding whether to make Allen a general again in 1912.

Although advancement in the regular army was very slow in peacetime, wartime expansion increased the rate of promotion by creating additional vacancies in all officer grades. Between 1898 and 1902 Congress twice raised the strength of the regular army and did so again in 1916. However, there were even faster ways outside of regular army channels for an officer to be promoted in wartime because of the need for a temporary fighting force vastly larger in size than the permanent peacetime establishment. In the Spanish-American War and Philippine Insurrection, as in the Mexican and Civil wars, state volunteer units provided most of the extra man power. Although most of the officers in these units were commissioned directly from civilian life, a certain number of regular officers were permitted to apply for volunteer commissions. This gave each volunteer unit a cadre of experienced professionals, and it also gave such officers a chance to serve for the duration in a higher rank than they might otherwise aspire to, but for this very reason the volunteer system was rife with the evils of political influence. Long frustrated and desperate for a chance to prove themselves worthy of higher command, officers like Allen were only too willing to ask their powerful friends for help in obtaining such positions. The War Department attempted to regulate the number of volunteer commissions and the assignments of the officers who received them, but with the governors and the congressional delegates of every state clamoring for the release of as many regulars as possible, the pressures and confusion in the Adjutant General's Office can be easily imagined. This was the main reason why the volunteer system was discarded in World War I. National army units supplemented the Regular Army, and all aspects of the expansion were completely under Federal control. There were very few "political generals" in World War I. Most regular army officers received temporary appointments to higher rank in the National Army, but the War Department alone decided who got what. Allen's major generalship was a national army appointment until 1920, when it became his permanent regular army rank. Despite the glacial slowness of the army's promotion system, it finally rewarded Allen as he deserved.

Abbreviations Used in the Notes

AFG: American Forces in Germany

AG: Adjutant General of the U.S. Army.

AGO: Adjutant General's Office.

Allen ACP File: National Archives, Record Group 94, Box 1000, Appointment Commission and Promotion File on Allen, Henry T., Adjutant General's Office.

Allen Papers: Library of Congress, Manuscript Division, Henry T. Allen Papers.

Correspondence Relating: United States War Department. *Correspondence Relating to the War with Spain and Conditions Growing out of Same, Including the Insurrection in the Philippine Islands and the China Relief Expedition, Between the Adjutant General of the Army and Military Commanders in the United States, Cuba, Puerto Rico, China, and the Philippine Islands, from April 15, 1898 to July 30, 1902,* 2 vols. Washington: Government Printing Office, 1902.

Courts-Martial in the Philippine Islands: 57th Congress, 2nd Session, Senate Document 213 (Serial 10735). *Trials or Courts-Martial in the Philippine Islands in Consequence of Certain Instructions.*

Cullum's Register: Cullum's Biographical Register of the Officers and Graduates of the U.S. Military Academy, 9 vols. Various editors and publishers.

11th Cavalry, "Report": "Narrative Report of the 11th Cavalry in Mexico," June 8, 1916, in files of Office, Chief of Military History, Washington, D.C.

FRUS: United States, Department of State. *Foreign Relations of the United States.* Washington: Government Printing Office, various years.

L/Reg., USMA, 1877, AGO: National Archives, Record Group 94, Letter Register, United States Military Academy, 1877, No. 546, Adjutant General's Office.

MC: Microcopy.

OCMH: Office, Chief of Military History, Washington, D.C.

Pershing, "Report": John J. Pershing, "Report of Operation, Punitive Expedition," National Archives, Record Group 94, File No. 2480591, Trunk 141, Adjutant General's Office.

Relief Commission Report: United States, War Department. *Report on Operations of the United States Relief Commission in Europe.* Washington: Government Printing Office, 1914.

RG: Record Group.

R.P.C.: United States, War Department. *Report of the Philippine Commission.* Washington: Government Printing Office, various years.

USMA: United States Military Academy.

Notes

Preface and Acknowledgments

1. Henry T. Allen, *My Rhineland Journal* (Boston: Houghton Mifflin Co., 1923); Henry T. Allen, *The Rhineland Occupation* (Indianapolis: Bobbs-Merrill Co., 1927).

2. Robert L. Bullard, *Fighting Generals* (Ann Arbor, Mich.: J. W. Edwards Co., 1944), pp. 87–95; Harris E. Starr, ed., *Dictionary of American Biography* (New York: Charles Scribner's Sons, 1944), XXI, 22–23.

Chapter I

1. John A. Richards, *A History of Bath County, Kentucky* (Yuma, Ariz.: Southwest Printers, 1961), pp. 3, 42–43.

2. Henry T. Allen, "Allen," *Register of the Kentucky State Historical Society*, XXVIII, No. 82 (Jan., 1930), 86; Richards, *History of Bath County*, pp. 38, 41.

3. V. B. Young, *An Outline History of Bath County, 1811–1876, An address delivered July 4, 1876* (Owingsville, Ky.: Printcraft, 1946), p. 6.

4. Henry T. Allen, Jr., interview, Washington, D.C., Jun. 15, 1964.

5. Richards, *History of Bath County*, p. 361.

6. U.S., Department of Commerce, Bureau of the Census, "Eighth Census of the United States, 1860: Kentucky, Free Inhabitants," II, 69–75.

7. Letterhead, Henry T. Allen to Secretary of War, Dec. 18, 1876, National Archives, Record Group 94, Letter Register, United States Military Academy, 1877, No. 546, Adjutant General's Office. Source hereafter cited as: L/Reg., USMA, 1877, AGO.

8. Bureau of the Census, "Eighth Census, 1860: Kentucky, Slaves," I, 81, and "Eighth Census, 1860: Kentucky Free Inhabitants," II, 69.

9. Henry T. Allen, Jr., interview, Washington, D.C., Apr. 1, 1970. Col. Allen's recollection of his father's home corresponds in all essential respects to a house pointed out to the author as the original Allen home by Mr. Clark Ramey of Sharpsburg on July 9, 1970.

10. Obituary notice, Susan S. Allen, newspaper unknown, Apr. 16, 1885, Library of Congress, Manuscript Division, Box 5, Allen Papers, hereafter cited as: Allen Papers.

11. Allen interview, 1964.

12. Richards, *History of Bath County*, p. 570.
13. Allen interview, 1970.
14. Bureau of the Census, "Ninth Census, 1870: Kentucky," II, 92.
15. Richards, *History of Bath County*, p. 484.
16. Bureau of the Census, "Ninth Census, 1870: Kentucky," II, 92.
17. Young, *Outline History*, pp. 15–16, 31.
18. Allen interview, 1964.
19. Richards, *History of Bath County*, pp. 389, 580.
20. *Ibid.*, pp. 128, 362.
21. Allen interview, 1970. The author's search for 1873–76 attendance records for these two secondary schools proved fruitless. The records of Georgetown College indicate that Allen entered there in September, 1876.
22. Allen interview, 1964. See Orlando E. Huddle, "A History of Georgetown College" (M.A. thesis, University of Kentucky, 1930), pp. 72, 151, 154.
23. Bath County, Ky., "Will Book F," p. 223, County Court House, Owingsville, Ky.
24. Allen, "Allen," p. 83; information on William C. Allen from "Chronology of the Aztec Club, 1928," p. 42, in possession of J. Conway Hunt, Washington, D.C.
25. Don Rickey, Jr., *Forty Miles a Day on Beans and Hay* (Norman, Okla.: University of Oklahoma Press, 1963), p. 27.
26. L/Reg., USMA, 1877, AGO, H.T.A. to Sec. War, Dec. 18, 1876.
27. Sherman Goodpaster, Jr., interview, Owingsville, Ky., Jul. 9, 1970. Mr. Goodpaster is Charles Goodpaster's grandson.
28. L/Reg., 1877, AGO, J.B.C. to Sec. War, Jul. 5, 1877.
29. *Ibid.*, H.T.A./J.W.A. to Sec. War, Jul. 17, 1877.
30. Hugh T. Reed, *Cadet Life at West Point* (Chicago: Hugh T. Reed, 1896), appendix, pp. vi, ix.
31. Allen Papers, diplomas, Peekskill Military Academy, Jun. 20, 1878, Box 43.
32. Reed, *Cadet Life*, appendix, p. xv.
33. The occupations of the fathers of 5,486 cadets admitted during period of 1842 to 1899 were tabulated. Of the 151 occupations listed, those which fall obviously in the middle to upper-class category comprised more than two-thirds of the total.

Middle/Upper Class Occupations		Other	
Businessmen	31 %	Employees/Laborers	3.6%
Professional Men	20.5%	Farmers/Planters	21.4%
Military Officers	8.0%	Miscellaneous	3.0%
Politics/Civil Officials	4.4%	Unknown/No Occupation	4.1%
Clergymen	2.3%		
Educators	1.7%		

United States Military Academy, *The Centennial of the United States Military Academy at West Point, New York, 1802–1902* (Washington: Government Printing Office, 1904), pp. 482–83.

34. Allen Papers, H.T.A. to Jennie Dora Johnston, Nov. 27, 1886, Box 5.

CHAPTER II

1. Printed in Joseph P. Farley, *West Point in the Early Sixties* (Troy, N.Y.: Pafraets Book Company, 1902), pp. 181–94.

2. Description based on Hugh T. Reed, *Cadet Life at West Point* (Chicago: Hugh T. Reed, 1896), pp. 42–43. The starting date for Allen's entrance examinations is from United States Military Academy, "Staff Records," X, 448, USMA Archives, West Point, N.Y.

3. Reed's account of the candidate's first brush with cadet upper-classmen has been lightly paraphrased. See his *Cadet Life,* pp. 42–43.

4. United States Military Academy, *Official Register of Officers and Cadets, 1879* (West Point, N.Y.: USMA, 1879), p. 19.

5. Thomas J. Fleming, *West Point* (New York: William Morrow and Co., Inc., 1969), p. 249; Stephen E. Ambrose, *Duty, Honor, Country: A History of West Point* (Baltimore: The Johns Hopkins Press, 1966), pp. 226–37.

6. Henry T. Allen, Jr., interview, Washington, D.C., April 1, 1970; USMA, *Register of Graduates, 1963* (West Point, N.Y.: West Point Alumni Foundation, Inc., 1963), pp. 273–74.

7. USMA, *Official Register, 1879,* p. 19.

8. A cadet slang word best translated as "a love of fun and general hell-raising."

9. Robert L. Bullard, *Fighting Generals* (Ann Arbor, Mich.: J. W. Edwards Co., 1944), p. 87.

10. USMA, "Register of Delinquencies, 1877–1882," pp. 263, 466, 555, 579, USMA Archives.

11. John L. Chamberlain, "Cadet Reminiscences" (ms. in Rare Book Room, USMA Library), p. 2.

12. USMA, *Official Register, 1882,* p. 10.

13. Bullard, *Fighting Generals,* p. 87.

14. USMA, *Official Register, 1881,* p. 9, and *Official Register, 1882,* p. 9.

15. Bullard, *Fighting Generals,* p. 87.

16. *Ibid.*

17. Ambrose, *Duty, Honor, Country,* pp. 73–76, 87–91.

18. *Ibid.,* pp. 91–104.

19. In its first one hundred years, the academy's graduates totaled

4,214. Of the 2,371 who returned to civilian life, two-thirds were engaged in the following occupations:

Farmers/Planters	9.7%	State Militia Officers	6.7%
Civil Engineers	9.7%	Professors/Teachers	5.7%
Attorneys	8.5%	Merchants	5.2%
Authors	7.5%	Corporation Presidents	3.7%
U.S. Civil Officers	7.2%	State Officers	3.3%

In addition there were 46 college or university presidents, 24 members of Congress, 20 clergymen, 16 state governors, 14 physicians, 2 Presidents (counting Jefferson Davis for the Confederacy), and 1 bishop. USMA, *Centennial*, pp. 483–84.

20. Ambrose, *Duty, Honor, Country*, pp. 201–203.

21. Fleming, *West Point*, p. 235.

22. *Ibid.*, p. 232.

23. USMA, *Regulations, 1880* (West Point, N.Y.: USMA, 1880), p. 264.

24. Reed, *Cadet Life*, pp. 111–12. USMA, *Regulations, 1880*, p. 364.

25. Reed, *Cadet Life*, pp. 114–17.

26. Fleming, *West Point*, p. 242.

27. *Ibid.*, p. 236. Ambrose, *Duty, Honor, Country*, pp. 204–205.

28. *Ibid.*, pp. 204–206.

29. USMA, *Centennial*, pp. 387–88.

30. *Ibid.*, pp. 389–415.

31. In reality, the professors, by virtue of their tenure and powerful connections, usually had their way on important issues, whether or not related to the curriculum. Ambrose, *Duty, Honor, Country*, p. 202.

32. Fleming, *West Point*, pp. 233–34.

33. In 1876, the size of the Regular Army was set at 27,442. It remained at or below this level until the Spanish-American War. Maurice Matloff, ed., *American Military History*, Army Historical Series (Washington: Government Printing Office, 1969), p. 282.

34. Ambrose, *Duty, Honor, Country*, pp. 211–18.

35. *The New York Times*, Jun. 10, 1882, p. 8, "Revels at West Point." Interviews by the author with Allen's and Drum's descendants have not established how and when Allen became acquainted with the Drum family. It was a close relationship, and although Allen did not marry Miss Drum, her father was his "patron" during his tenure as Adjutant General, as subsequent chapters show.

36. *Ibid.*, June 13, 1882, p. 8, "Soldiers of the Republic."

37. *Ibid.*, "The Cadets at Dinner."

38. Farley, *West Point in the Early Sixties*, pp. 195–99.

39. U.S., Department of War, AGO, *General Orders, 1882* (Washing-

ton: Government Printing Office, 1883), General Orders No. 75, Jul. 11, 1882. Allen's oath of office, dated July 29, 1882, is in "Allen, Henry T.," Appointment, Commission and Promotion File, National Archives, RG 94, Box 1000, AGO. Source hereafter cited as: Allen ACP File.

40. Don Rickey, Jr., *Forty Miles a Day on Beans and Hay* (Norman, Okla.: University of Oklahoma Press, 1963), p. 224.

41. U.S., Department of War, *Report of the Secretary of War, 1882* (Washington: Government Printing Office, 1882), I, 94–95.

42. Allen, interview, 1964.

43. Allen ACP File, "Military Record."

44. War Department, *Report of the Secretary of War, 1882,* I, 89, 92.

45. U.S., Department of War, *Official Army Register, 1882* (Washington: Adjutant General's Office, 1882), p. 54; Post Returns, Fort Keogh, Mont., Sept., Oct., 1882, National Archives, RG 94, Microcopy 617, Roll 572, "Returns from U.S. Military Posts, 1800–1916," AGO.

46. Rickey, *Forty Miles a Day,* pp. 50–61.

47. Robert W. Frazer, *Forts of the Old West* (Norman, Okla.: University of Oklahoma Press, 1965), p. 82.

48. U.S., Department of War, Quartermaster General's Office, *Outline Description of Military Posts in the United States and Alaska* (Washington: Government Printing Office, 1904), pp. 225–28; Post Returns, Fort Keogh, Oct., 1882–May, 1884.

49. War Department, *Report of the Secretary of War, 1882,* I, 36.

50. Rickey, *Forty Miles a Day,* p. 51.

51. Allen ACP File, H.T.A. to J. S. Williams, Dec. 20, 1882.

52. Allen ACP File, AGO Memo, Jan. 25, 1883, attached to letter, H.T.A. to J.S.W., Dec. 20, 1882. Lacking even a rudimentary knowledge of arctic conditions and techniques, Garlington also failed to reach Greely. Theodore Powell, *The Long Rescue* (Garden City, N.Y.: Doubleday and Co., Inc., 1960), pp. 95–96.

53. This was common practice, engaged in by many army officers who had powerful friends. For a discussion of the practice, and of army assignment and promotion policies in general in Allen's day, see the Appendix.

54. Rickey, *Forty Miles a Day,* p. 90, n.

55. Post Returns, Fort Keogh, Dec., 1882–Apr., 1883; Register of Letters Sent, Fort Keogh, 1883, National Archives, RG 393, pp. 1–89.

56. U.S. Army, Department of Dakota, *General Orders, 1883,* No. 11, Apr. 20, 1883, Box 3, RG 393.

57. Description of the terrain in the river valley is from William E. Strong, *A Trip to the Yellowstone National Park in July, August and September, 1875* (Norman, Oklahoma: University of Oklahoma Press, 1968), pp. 146–47, and War Department, *Report of the Secretary of War, 1883,* I, 206–207.

58. Allen's Diary, 1884, p. 9, Box 1, and H.T.A. to Dora Johnston Allen, Apr. 10, 1888, Box 5, Allen Papers.

59. Allen Papers, Allen's Diary, 1884, pp. 6, 37, Box 1.

60. *Ibid.*, p. 14.

61. Post Return, Fort Keogh, Sept., 1883.

62. Allen Papers, H.T.A. to Dora Johnston Allen, Jul. 10, 1888, Box 5.

63. *Ibid.*, H.T.A. to Dora Johnston, Jun. 1, 1884; Oct. 8, 1884.

64. Col. and Mrs. Joseph W. Viner, interview, Virginia Beach, Va., May 31, 1970. Mrs. Viner is Allen's daughter. Also: Allen Papers, newspaper clipping, date and newspaper unknown, with 1887 material in Box 5.

65. Edward Arpee, *Lake Forest, Illinois—History and Reminiscences* (Chicago, Illinois: R. R. Donnelly and Sons Co., 1964), p. 95; Herma N. Clark, *The Elegant Eighties—When Chicago Was Young* (Chicago, Ill.: A. C. McClung and Co., 1941), p. 34.

66. Allen Papers, newspaper clipping, date and newspaper unknown, 1887 material, Box 5; Arpee, *Lake Forest*, pp. 62, 83, 94–95. The Lake Forest home stood for 60 years; from 1900 to 1930 it became a hotel, the famous Deer Path Inn.

67. Arpee, *Lake Forest*, p. 95; Viner interview, 1970.

68. Hiram M. Chittenden, *The Yellowstone National Park*, ed. Richard A. Bartlett (Norman, Okla.: University of Oklahoma Press, 1964), p. 93 and fn. Although the park had been open since 1872, free of any serious Indian threat since 1877, and already visited by many thousands of tourists and numerous scientific expeditions (see pp. 83–108; also U.S., Department of Interior, *Report of the Secretary of the Interior, 1882*, II, 1001–1002) the opening of the N.P.R.R. seems to account for the unusually large number of important people who came there in 1883.

69. Allen Papers, H.T.A. to D.J., Jun. 1, 1884, Box 5.

70. *Ibid.*, H.T.A. to D.J., Ash Wednesday, 1884.

71. *Ibid.* He habitually set aside three hours a day for "reading and study." Allen interview, 1970.

72. Regimental Return, 2nd Cavalry Regiment, May 1884, National Archives, RG 94, Box 92, "Regular Army Organization Returns, 1879–1892," AGO.

73. Allen Papers, Allen's Diary, 1884, pp. 1–24, Box 1.

74. Allen Papers, H.T.A. to D.J., June 1, 1884, Box 5. Allen referred to Rice by his Civil War brevet rank of lieutenant colonel.

75. *Ibid.*, pp. 23–45.

76. *Ibid.*, pp. 46–51.

77. Allen, interview, 1964.

78. Allen Papers, Allen's Diary, 1884, pp. 52–55, Box 1.

79. *Ibid.*, p. 55.

Chapter III

1. Allen Papers, H.T.A. to D.J., Oct. 8, 1884, Box 5.

2. *Ibid.*, Allen's Diary, 1884, pp. 55–59, Box 1.

3. *Ibid.*, H.T.A. to D.J., Oct. 8, 1884, Box 5. For more on Schwatka and his report see p. 43, and p. 287, n. 55.

4. *Ibid.*, Allen's Diary, 1884, pp. 60–82, Box 1.

5. Bruce Grant, *American Forts, Yesterday and Today* (New York: E. P. Dutton and Co., 1965), pp. 347–48.

6. Allen Papers, Allen's Diary, 1884, pp. 75–82, Box 1; H.T.A. to D.J., Oct. 17, 1884, Box 5.

7. *Ibid.*, Allen's Diary, 1884, pp. 86–87, Box 1.

8. *Ibid.*, pp. 87–103.

9. *Ibid.*, H.T.A. to D.J., Jan. 10, 1885, Box 5.

10. Alfred H. Brooks, *Blazing Alaska's Trails* (Caldwell, Idaho: Published jointly by the University of Alaska and the Arctic Institute of North America, 1953), p. 253. The company that organized the ice-shipping venture grossed nearly a half million dollars in the 1850's.

11. *Ibid.*, pp. 245–46.

12. *Ibid.*, pp. 243–45.

13. Valarie K. Stubbs, "U.S. Troops in Alaska, 1867–77," *Military Collector and Historian*, XII (Spring, 1960), 6–8.

14. Brooks, *Blazing Alaska's Trails*, p. 267. Four years later, Allen estimated Sitka's population to be under one thousand, including Indians.

15. *Ibid.*, p. 245.

16. *Ibid.*, pp. 273–74.

17. Frederick Schwatka, *Report of a Military Reconnaissance in Alaska Made in 1884* (Washington: Government Printing Office, 1885), p. 121.

18. *Ibid.*, p. 119.

19. Frederick Schwatka, *A Summer in Alaska* (St. Louis, Mo.: J. W. Henry, 1893), p. 11. This account was more widely read than his official report and created a flurry of public interest in Alaska.

20. Allen ACP File, telegram, General J. Pope to General P. H. Sheridan, Jan. 22, 1885. Miles and Sheridan communicated through Pope, the intermediate commander, whose headquarters (Division of the Pacific) was in San Francisco.

21. *Ibid.*, Sheridan to Pope, Jan. 24, 26, 1885.

22. Allen Papers, Allen's Diary, 1884, pp. 104–109, Box 1. Payment of illiterate Indian guides by check in the wilds of Alaska seems incongruous, but the record of disbursements is shown inside the front cover of his 1885 diary (Jan. 28–Jul. 28).

23. Henry T. Allen, *Report of an Expedition to the Copper, Tanana and Koyukuk Rivers in the Territory of Alaska in the Year 1885* (Washington: Government Printing Office, 1887), pp. 10–12.

24. *Ibid.*, p. 32.
25. *Ibid.*, pp. 31–33.
26. *Ibid.*, p. 34.
27. *Ibid.*, pp. 35–41.
28. *Ibid.*, pp. 14, 41–46, 164.
29. *Ibid.*, p. 47.
30. *Ibid.*, pp. 48–50.
31. *Ibid.*, pp. 50–58.
32. *Ibid.*, p. 59.
33. *Ibid.* There is also a "Mt. Tillman" named in Allen's report and plotted on his map which does not show on modern maps. The explanation for this mystery is found in *The National Geographic,* XIII (May, 1902), pp. 181–82. From certain points in the river valley, part of Mount Sanford appears to be a separate and distinct peak, and this is what Allen called "Mt. Tillman." His mistake was not discovered until the Copper River was more accurately surveyed sixteen years later.
34. Allen, *Report of an Expedition,* p. 65.
35. *Ibid.*, pp. 66–67.
36. *Ibid.*, pp. 68–79.
37. *Ibid.*, pp. 80–87.
38. *Ibid.*, p. 89.
39. *Ibid.*
40. *Ibid.*, p. 95.
41. Allen also gave a tributary of the Koyukuk a native version of his own name: Allenkakat. Neither name stuck. Fickett's river is now named the John, and Allen's the Alatna. Morgan B. Sherwood, *Exploration of Alaska, 1865–1900* (New Haven: Yale University Press, 1965), pp. 114–15.
42. Allen, *Report of an Expedition,* pp. 97–109.
43. *Ibid.*, p. 109.
44. *Ibid.*, pp. 109–13.
45. Allen Papers, Allen's Diary, 1885 (No. 3), Box 1.
46. *Ibid.*, p. 5. Obituary notice, Mrs. Susan S. Allen, newspaper unknown, Apr. 16, 1885, Box 5.
47. *Ibid.*, Allen's Diary, 1885 (No. 3), pp. 10–11, Box 1.
48. *Ibid.*, N. A. Miles to H.T.A., Oct. 24, 1885, Box 5. This was the beginning of a continuing personal correspondence between the two. One of Miles' early letters to Allen includes this revealing statement: "My friends from the Atlantic to the Pacific have taken a warm interest in my promotion. If your friends from Kentucky and the South were so inclined they could render very great assistance." N.A.M. to H.T.A., March 6, 1886. For Miles' evaluation of Allen's accomplishments in Alaska, see Nelson A. Miles, *Serving the Republic* (New York: Harper and Brothers, 1911), pp. 213–14.
49. Allen Papers, H.T.A. to D.J., Nov. 1, 1885, Box 5.
50. *Ibid.*, H.T.A. to D.J., Dec. 21, 1885.

51. Allen ACP File, Memo, Attending Surgeon to AG, Dec. 18, 1885.

52. See n. 33 on p. 286.

53. Allen, *Report of an Expedition,* pp. 142–44.

54. Allen Papers, P. M. Lindeman to W. H. Dall, forwarded to H.T.A., Dec. 14, 1885; L. R. Scidmore to H.T.A., Dec. 20, 1886, Box 5.

55. Sherwood, *Exploration of Alaska,* p. 115. On the next page he adds, "Schwatka's trip was like a schoolboy's excursion in comparison." Although Allen had nothing to do with the discovery or mapping of Mount McKinley, it was originally known to Alaskan Americans as "Mt. Allen," in honor of him. See Allen Papers, "Our Highest Mountain," *The Baltimore Sun,* date and page unknown, Box 5.

56. Allen ACP File, H.T.A. to AG, May 10, 1886.

57. *Ibid.,* AG to H.T.A., May 28, 1886.

Chapter IV

1. Allen interview, 1970.
2. See pp. 68, 71, 72–73.
3. Allen Papers, H.T.A. to D.J., Jul. 11, 1886, Box 5.
4. *Ibid.,* H.T.A. to D.J., Jul. 27, 1886.
5. *Ibid.*
6. *Ibid.,* H.T.A. to D.J., Aug. 9, 1886, Box 5.
7. *Ibid.,* H.T.A. to D.J., Oct. 8, 1884.
8. *Ibid.,* quoted in H.T.A. to D.J., Aug. 29, 1886.
9. *Ibid.*
10. *Ibid.,* H.T.A. to D.J., Sept. 9, 1886, Box 5.
11. *Ibid.,* H.T.A. to D.J., Sept. 20, 29, 1886.
12. *Ibid.,* H.T.A. to D.J., Oct. 10, 1886.
13. *Ibid.,* H.T.A. to D.J., Dec. 10, 1886.
14. *Ibid.,* H.T.A. to D.J., Dec. 28, 1886.
15. *Ibid.,* H.T.A. to D.J., Jan. 16, 1887.
16. *Ibid.,* D.J. to H.T.A., Feb. 1, 1887.
17. *Ibid.,* H.T.A. to D.J., Feb. 27; Apr. 23; May 2, 1887.
18. *Ibid.,* quoted in H.T.A. to D.J., Mar. 3, 1887.
19. *Ibid.,* H.T.A. to D.J., Mar. 24, 1887.
20. *Ibid.,* H.T.A. to D.J., Mar. 26, 1887.
21. *Ibid.,* H.T.A. to D.J., May 13, 20, 1887.
22. *Ibid.,* H.T.A. to D.J., May 23, 1887.
23. *Ibid.,* H.T.A. to D.J., Jan. 16, 26; Feb. 1, 14; Mar. 3; May 2, 25; Jun. 3, 1887.
24. *Ibid.,* Special Orders 153, Jul. 5, 1887, Headquarters of the Army, AGO.
25. *Ibid.,* H.T.A. to D.J., Jun. 27, 1887.

26. *Ibid.*, marriage certificate, Jul. 12, 1887; *The Chicago Herald*, Jul. 17, 1887, p. 3.

27. Allen Papers, H.T.A. to D.J., Mar. 24, 1887, Box 5. In Europe Dora did hire a French maid, Mina, who stayed with her for almost a year.

28. Dora Allen's Diary, 1887, Aug. 13–Sept. 15. The diary is in the possession of Col. H. T. Allen, Jr.

29. Isabel F. Hapgood, *Russian Rambles* (Boston: Houghton, Mifflin and Co., 1895), pp. 22–60.

30. Dora Allen's Diary, 1887, Sept. 18–20, 30; Oct. 1–7.

31. Allen, interview, 1964.

32. Dora Allen's Diary, 1887, Oct. 20; Nov. 24; Dec. 19.

33. Allen ACP File, H.T.A. to AG, Nov. 13, 1887.

34. H.T.A. to "Sister Jennie," Dec. 11, 1887. Letter in possession of Mrs. J. W. Viner.

35. Dora Allen's Diary, 1887, Dec. 25–30.

36. Allen ACP File, AG to H.T.A., Jan. 25, 1888. F. D. Holton to Asst. AG, Dept. of Columbia, Dec. 21, 1887, with attached endorsements and WD memos.

37. *Ibid.*, J. B. Beck to Sec. War, Feb. 7, 1888; Sec. War to J. B. Beck, Feb. 11, 1888; Allen Papers, M. R. Waite to H.T.A., Feb. 21, 1888, Box 5.

38. Allen, interview, 1964.

39. Allen Papers, H.T.A. to D.J.A., Apr. 5, 1888, Box 5. Until 1894 their combined income averaged about $800 per month, of which $125–$150 was Allen's army pay. For several years thereafter Dora's income was reduced by $150 a month because of labor unrest and unsettled economic conditions in Chicago. (See Allen's Diaries, esp. Feb.–Mar., 1894.) Henry's investment in Tom's ranch near Miles City never paid off. Tom eventually went bankrupt.

40. *Ibid.*, H.T.A. to D.J.A., Apr. 14, 1888, Box 5.

41. *Ibid.*, quoted in H.T.A. to D.J.A., Apr. 29, 1888.

42. *Ibid.* The least unpleasant translation for *cochon* is "suckling pig." Dora objected to Henry's use of it, but he persisted for several months.

43. *Ibid.*, H.T.A. to D.J.A., May 25, 27, 1888, Box 5.

44. *Ibid.*, H.T.A. to D.J.A., Jun. 1, 1888.

45. *Ibid.*, H.T.A. to D.J.A., June 6, 20; July 4, 1888.

46. *Ibid.*, H.T.A. to D.J.A., Jun. 13, 14, 16, 20, 29, 1888.

47. *Ibid.*, H.T.A. to D.J.A., Jun. 8, 14, 24, 1888.

48. *Ibid.*, H.T.A. to D.J.A., Jun. 29, 1888.

49. *Ibid.*, N.A.M. to H.T.A., Jun. 5, 1888.

50. *Ibid.*, H.T.A. to D.J.A., undated fragment (probably mid-Jun., 1888).

51. *Ibid.*, H.T.A. to D.J.A., Jun. 29, 1888.

52. *Ibid.*, H.T.A. to D.J.A., Jun. 23, 29; Jul. 4, 7, 15, 17, 20, 24; Aug. 4, 1888.

53. *Ibid.*, H.T.A. to D.J.A., Jul. 4, 10, 1888.

54. *Ibid.*, H.T.A. to D.J.A., Jul. 12, 1888.

55. *Ibid.*, H.T.A. to D.J.A., Jul. 15, 1888.

56. *Ibid.*, H.T.A. to D.J.A., Jul. 20, 1888.

57. *Ibid.*, H.T.A. to D.J.A., Jul. 24, 1888.

58. *Ibid.*, H.T.A. to D.J.A., Aug. 4, 1888.

59. *Ibid.*, H.T.A. to D.J.A., Aug. 10, 1888. Most of their original herd had died in the severe winter of '86–'87.

60. *Ibid.*, H.T.A. to D.J.A., Aug. 23, 1888.

61. Dora Allen, "Life and Times of the Allen Children, 1888–1898," ms. in possession of Mrs. J. W. Viner, p. 1.

62. Allen Papers, H.T.A. to D.J.A., Jul. 23, 1888, Box 5.

63. Description of quarters based on photographs in possession of Col. H. T. Allen, Jr.

64. Dora Allen, "Life and Times," p. 2.

65. Allen Papers, N.A.M. to H.T.A., Dec 29, 1888; Mar. 29, 1889, Box 5.

66. Elizabeth Bethel, "The Military Information Division: Origin of the Intelligence Division," *Military Affairs,* XI (Spring, 1947), 18–19. American military attachés had been sent abroad before, but such assignments were always temporary and intended to obtain specific information about a particular military force or operation, pp. 17–19. See also Bruce W. Bidwell, "History of the Military Intelligence Division, Department of the Army General Staff," I (draft ms. in files of Office, Chief of Military History, Department of the Army, Washington, D.C.), VI-1 to VI-9.

67. Allen Papers, J. B. Beck to Sec. War, Feb. 16, 1890; J. M. Wilson (Superintendent, USMA) to C. E. Smith, Feb. 12, 1890; L. Merrill (retired general who knew both Smith and Allen) to H.T.A., Feb. 20, 1890; C.E.S. to H.T.A., Feb. 20, 1890, all in Box 5. Allen ACP File, J. C. S. Blackburn to Sec. War, and R. C. Drum, Feb. 14, 1890; W. C. P. Breckenridge to Sec. War, Feb. 20, 1890.

68. Allen ACP File, R. C. Drum to Sec. War, Feb. 24, 1890.

69. Allen Papers, Sec. War to R. C. Drum, Feb. 28, 1890, Box 5. The four other officers selected as attachés in 1890 were all captains and majors. See Bidwell, "History of the Military Intelligence Division," p. VI-10. Their length of service averaged almost ten years per man more than Allen's.

70. Allen ACP File, AG to H.T.A., Mar. 29, 1890. That someone in the AG's office resented the favor being shown Allen is evident from a comment on an office memo attached to the above letter. The memo asked if Allen's instructions should be broadened to allow him greater freedom to obtain information. The comment was: "NO! He's just a plain *damned* attaché." At the time a Captain Ray was the only other officer available who could speak Russian. Allen Papers, R. Proctor to H.T.A., Jul. 22, 1903, Box 8.

71. Dora Allen, "Life and Times," pp. 4–6.

72. Allen ACP File, AG to H.T.A., Mar. 29, 1890.

73. Alfred Vagts, *The Military Attaché* (Princeton, N.J.: Princeton University Press, 1967), pp. 26–36.

74. Dora Allen, "Life and Times," pp. 6–43. These *dachas* could hardly be classed as "summer cottages," though that was Dora's phrase. The one at Terrioki had twelve rooms plus a kitchen and cook's room, stables, an ice house, tennis courts, and a summer pavilion. The rent was 650 rubles (about $340) for the summer. Other members of the diplomatic community lived nearby, while in St. Petersburg 100 people died of cholera each day. See Allen Papers, entries in Allen's Diary, Jul., 1894.

75. Many entries in Allen's diaries substantiate this. Any month picked at random from October to June would show the same general pattern of activity.

76. For example, at the request of the Department of Labor, in 1891–92, he worked on a report on labor conditions, wages, etc., in Russia. Allen Papers, Carrol D. Wright (Commissioner of Labor) to Sec. War, Aug. 13, 19, 1891; C.D.W. to H.T.A., Jul. 7, 1892, Box 5. Another example was a request from the American writer Poultney Bigelow for data from Napoleon's captured maps in the Russian archives. P.B. to H.T.A., Jan. 27, 1894.

77. From "Memorandum of Despatches Received from Lt. H. T. Allen, Military Attaché, U.S. Legation, St. Petersburg," National Archives, RG 165, War Department General Staff, Military Information Division. Many of the dispatches included books on military subjects in Russian or other European languages as well as clippings from military journals (usually with translations). Some of the other more interesting items sent: secret data on Russian military budgets (each winter) and a "supposed" copy of the Triple Alliance Agreement (sent on Sept. 5, 1893). Most of the material, however, was purely technical in nature.

78. See Allen Papers, the *Liste du Corps diplomatique accrédité auprès de la Cour impériale de Russie*, 1895, in Box 5.

79. Dora Allen, "Life and Times," pp. 9–29.

80. Allen Papers, H.T.A. to D.J.A., Nov. 17, 28; Dec. 7, 11, 25, 1893; Feb. 4, 1894, etc., Box 5.

81. Allen Papers, Allen's Diary, 1893, Sept. 3–15, Box 1.

82. *Ibid.*, Sept. 16.

83. *Ibid.*, 1894, Jan. 27.

84. The extent of his acquaintanceship with the society ladies of St. Petersburg is evident from the end pages of his 1895 diary. Listed there are the names of forty-seven countesses, baronesses, princesses, "mmes" and "mlles" on whom he paid farewell calls in one week before leaving Russia. The love notes are mentioned in Allen Papers, H.T.A. to D.J.A., Nov. 17, 1893, Box 5.

85. *Ibid.*, A.D.W. to C.R.B., Aug. 27, 1894.

86. *Ibid.*, Allen's Diary, 1894, Sept. 20; Oct. 2, Box 1.

87. *Ibid.*, Oct. 15, Nov. 16, 1894; Allen's Diary, 1895, Jan. 1, 2.

88. *Ibid.*, Allen's Diary, 1894, Sept. 6; Nov. 19.

89. *Ibid.*, Feb. 11.

90. Allen ACP File, H.T.A. to Sec. War, Dec. 9, 1890; AGO to H.T.A., Dec. 29, 1890. The scare ended on Dec. 29, with the ugly massacre of the Sioux at Wounded Knee.

91. Allen Papers, Allen's Diary, 1894, Sept. 28, 29, Box 1.

92. Henry T. Allen, "Instructions for Foot Combat in the Russian Army," II (Dec., 1889), 364–67 and "A Hundred Verst's Race," *Journal of the United States Cavalry Association*, VIII (Mar., 1895), 61–63; N. Zabudski, "Resistance of the Air for Great Velocities of Projectiles," trans. H. T. Allen, *Journal of the United States Artillery*, V (May, 1896), 369–75. The establishment of these unofficial service journals and others like them was one mark of the increasing professionalism of the American army as it emerged from its physical, social and intellectual isolation of the post-Civil War period. For a further discussion of this and other aspects of the army's professionalization at the turn of the century, see the Appendix.

93. Theodore Roosevelt, ed., *Hunting in Many Lands* (New York: Forest and Stream Publishing Co., 1895).

94. Allen Papers, T.R. to H.T.A., Aug. 27, 1894, Box 5.

95. Dora Allen, "Life and Times," pp. 44–45.

96. Allen Papers, Allen's Diary, 1895, Apr. 29, 30; May 14, 15, 25, Box 1.

97. *Ibid.*, Jun. 20, 21.

98. *Ibid.*, Jul. 1, 2, 8.

99. *Ibid.*, Sept. 13. For his report, see U.S., War Department, Military Information Division, *The Military System of Sweden* (Washington: Government Printing Office, 1896).

100. Allen Papers, Allen's Diary, 1895, Sept. 17–Oct. 5, Box 1.

101. *Ibid.*, Oct. 8–12.

102. Allen ACP File, efficiency report on Allen by Col. G. H. Huntt, CO 2d Cav. Regt., Jan., 1892. The system of rendering formal written efficiency reports on a periodic basis was begun by the War Department in 1890 and is another example of the professionalization of the army. See the Appendix for an analysis of the strengths and weaknesses of the new system as it evolved and its impact on the course of Allen's career.

103. Dora Allen, "Life and Times," pp. 48–52; Allen Papers, Allen's Diaries, 1895, Oct. 19–Dec. 31; 1896, Jan. 1–Feb. 28, Box 1.

104. *Ibid.*, H.T.A. to G. D. Ruggles, May 2; H.T.A. to D.J.A., May 3; A.D.W. to H.T.A., May 6, 1897, Box 6. Dora Allen, "Life and Times," pp. 52–53.

105. Nelson A. Miles, *Serving the Republic* (New York: Harper and Brothers, 1911), pp. 262–65.

106. Allen Papers, Allen's Diary, 1897, Aug. 10–11, Box 1.

107. *Ibid.*, H.T.A. to J.D.J., Sept. 20, 1886, Box 5.

108. *Ibid.*, Allen's Diary, 1897, Aug. 10–11, Box 1.

109. *Ibid.*, Sept. 11–Oct. 27. A "Memorandum of Despatches Received" also exists in RG 165 for Allen's tour as attaché in Berlin. From July 1897 to May, 1898, he submitted 128 dispatches, an average of one every two or three days. It appears he submitted nothing particularly remarkable; only the usual kinds of military books, samples of materiel, technical data, articles, clippings, and translations.

110. Allen Papers, H.T.A. to N.A.M., Mar. 22; N.A.M. to H.T.A., Apr. 1, 1898, Box 6.

111. *Ibid.*, H.T.A. to D.J.A., Apr. 21, 1898.

112. *Ibid.*, H.T.A. to C.E.S., May 9; Telegram, AGO to H.T.A., May 17, 1898.

113. Dora Allen, "Life and Times," p. 56.

CHAPTER V

1. Dora Allen, "Life and Times of the Allen Children, 1888–1898," ms. in possession of Mrs. J. W. Viner, p. 57.

2. Allen Papers, Allen's Diary, 1898, May 27, Box 1.

3. *Ibid.*, May 29.

4. *Ibid.*, May 28; June 2–6.

5. Henry T. Allen, "Mounted Cavalry in the Santiago Campaign," *Journal of the United States Cavalry Association*, XII (Dec., 1899), 365.

6. Frank B. Freidel, *The Splendid Little War* (Boston: Little, Brown and Co., 1958); H. Wayne Morgan, *America's Road to Empire: The War with Spain and Overseas Expansion* (New York: John Wiley, 1965). Chapter 15 of Maurice Matloff, ed., *American Military History* (Washington: Government Printing Office, 1969), and chapter 13 of Russell F. Weigley, *History of the United States Army* (New York: The Macmillan Co., 1967) tell the same story more briefly.

7. Allen Papers, Allen's Diary, 1898, Jun. 7–14, Box 1.

8. Allen, "Mounted Cavalry," p. 361.

9. U.S., War Department, *Annual Reports* (Washington: Government Printing Office, 1898), I, Part 1, p. 73.

10. Allen, "Mounted Cavalry," p. 371.

11. Allen Papers, Allen's Diary, 1898, June 30–July 2, Box 1.

12. U.S., War Department, *Correspondence Relating to the War with Spain and Conditions Growing out of Same, Including the Insurrection in the Philippine Islands and the China Relief Expedition, Between the Adjutant General of the Army and Military Commanders in the United States, Cuba, Puerto Rico, China, and the Philippine Islands, from April 15, 1898*

to July 30, 1902, I (Washington: Government Printing Office, 1902), 79–81. Hereafter cited as: *Correspondence Relating.*

13. Allen, "Mounted Cavalry," pp. 368–69.

14. *Ibid.*, p. 369; Allen Papers, Allen's Diary, 1898, Jul. 10–16, Box 1.

15. Allen, "Mounted Cavalry," pp. 369–80.

16. Allen Papers, Allen's Diary, 1898, July 10, Box 1.

17. Dora Allen, "Life and Times," p. 57.

18. Allen Papers, Allen's Diary, 1898, Aug. 27–Oct. 29, Box 1; H.T.A. to D.J.A., Dec. 20, 1898, Box 6. The situation in regard to Allen's rank in 1898–99 was this: while in Cuba as a regular army lieutenant he was promoted to volunteer major in the Adjutant General's Corps, though he continued to command a troop of cavalry (a job that called for a captain). Later in the year he was promoted to regular army captain while still holding the higher volunteer commission. He remained a volunteer major until he left Atlanta. See the Appendix for a discussion of the difference between regular army, volunteer, and brevet promotions.

19. Despite a concerted effort to obtain a colonelcy for himself during the army reorganization, Allen arrived in Berlin as a regular army captain. For details of his "campaign plan" see Allen Papers, H.T.A. to D.J.A., Dec. 15, 16, 18, 1898, Box 6, and the ACP File series of letters, Feb. 25 to May 12, 1900, from Allen's friends in Kentucky and Congress to the Adjutant General, the Secretary of War, and the President.

20. Allen ACP File, H.T.A. to H.W.L., Jun. 26, 1899.

21. *Ibid.*, N.A.M. to President, Aug. 5, 1899. Other letters in this file on the same subject include: Frank Allen to President, Aug. 3; Frank Allen to Sec. War, Aug. 18; William Lindsay to President, Aug. 19; etc.

22. *Ibid.*, H.C.C. to H.T.A., Aug. 8, 1899.

23. *Ibid.*, H.T.A. to H.C.C., Sept. 30, 1899.

24. Allen Papers, T.R. to H.T.A., Sept. 20, 1899, Box 6.

25. *Ibid.*, Telegram, AGO to H.T.A., Aug. 24, 1899.

26. *Ibid.*, H.T.A. to D.J.A., Aug. 28, 30, 1899. Corbin became Adjutant General of the Army in February, 1898, having served continuously in the Department since 1880 and risen from major to brigadier general in that time. In the Allen Papers there are several friendly letters from Corbin of the "anything I can do for you" variety prior to 1898, but it appears Allen's frequent use of influence increasingly irritated him. The "plain damn attaché" comment (see p. 289, n. 70) in Allen's ACP File seems to be in Corbin's handwriting.

27. *Ibid.*, engraved steeplechase invitation, Oct. 10, 1899, with marginal note in Allen's handwriting; telegram, AGO to H.T.A., Oct. 26, 1899.

28. W. Cameron Forbes, *The Philippine Islands,* I (Boston: Houghton Mifflin Co., Inc., 1928), 50–60.

29. Leon Wolff, *Little Brown Brother* (London: Longmans Green and Co., 1961), p. 117.

30. Forbes, *The Philippine Islands,* I, 62–73.

31. *Ibid.,* pp. 73–75.

32. See Robert L. Beisner, *Twelve Against Empire: The Anti-Imperialists, 1898–1900* (New York: McGraw-Hill Co., 1968), for a study of a representative selection of the anti-imperialists and their varied motives. Beisner summarizes their objections under six headings: "constitutional, economic, moral, racial, political, and historical."

33. Wolff, *Little Brown Brother,* pp. 145–46.

34. Forbes, *The Philippine Islands,* I, 91.

35. *Ibid.,* pp. 92–94, 192; Matloff, *American Military History,* p. 337.

36. Allen Papers, H.T.A. to D.J.A., Nov. 11, 1899, Box 6.

37. *Ibid.,* H.T.A. to D.J.A., Dec. 5, 1899; Henry T. Allen, "Proposed Reorganization for our Central Staff," *Journal of the Military Service Institution of the United States,* XXVIII (Jul., 1900), 26–30. Allen's plan involved an expansion of the functions and authority of the Adjutant General's Office at the expense of the other bureaus and departments and resembled the organization of the Prussian General Staff. The reorganization effected by Secretary of War Elihu Root in 1903 bore no relation to Allen's ideas.

38. Allen Papers, H.T.A. to D.J.A., Dec. 31, 1899, Box 6; H.T.A. to D.J.A., Jan. 6, 8, 1900, Box 7. The other two battalions were commanded by Majors L. C. Andrews and J. C. Gilmore.

39. Matloff, *American Military History,* p. 338.

40. Forbes, *The Philippine Islands,* I, 4–6, 15.

41. *Ibid.,* pp. 93–101.

42. Joseph L. Schott, *The Ordeal of Samar* (New York: Bobbs-Merrill Co., Inc., 1964), pp. 15–18.

43. War Department, *Annual Reports,* 1900, I, Part 4, pp. 396–97.

44. Schott, *Ordeal of Samar,* pp. 4, 13–16.

45. Frederick Palmer, "Through the Hemp Country with General Kobbé," *Collier's Weekly,* XXV (Apr. 14, 1900), 10–11; Allen Papers, Allen's instructions from Kobbé, Jan. 27, 1900, Box 7.

46. Allen Papers, H.T.A. to D.J.A., Feb. 2, 1900; War Department, *Annual Reports,* 1901, I, Part 6, p. 69.

47. War Department, *Annual Reports,* 1900, I, Part 4, p. 397. Estimates of Samar's population varied; Allen used the figure from the last Spanish census, 237,000.

48. Palmer, "Through the Hemp Country," p. 10.

49. War Department, *Annual Reports,* 1901, I, Part 6, p. 70; Allen Papers, H.T.A. to D.J.A., Feb. 2, 1900, Box 7.

50. John M. Gates, "An Experiment in Benevolent Pacification: The U.S. Army in the Philippines, 1898–1902" (Ph.D. dissertation, Duke University, 1967), pp. iii–v, 65–81, 91–92; War Department, *Annual Reports,* 1901, I, Part 4, p. 90.

51. Matloff, *American Military History,* pp. 338–39. The final report of

General Otis is in War Department, *Annual Reports,* 1900, I, Part 4, pp. 199–561.

52. Wolff, *Little Brown Brother,* pp. 140–42; Gates, "Experiment in Benevolent Pacification," p. 262.

53. War Department, *Annual Reports,* 1901, I, Part 4, p. 90.

54. *Ibid.,* Part 6, p. 201, letter quoted, from Abrose Moxica to Major Gilmore, dated Mar. 9, 1901.

55. Gates, "Experiment in Benevolent Pacification," pp. 243–45. While recognizing that atrocities occurred, Gates maintains the stories about them were overemphasized and exaggerated at the time by the anti-imperialists and a sensation-seeking press and have thus tended to color subsequent accounts of the army's actions in the Philippines. He presents much evidence in support of his thesis that "benevolence, not severity, was the key to American victory."

56. See, for example, an extract from the *Washington Post,* Apr. 24, 1902, entitled "Torture of a Priest—Alleged Murder by American Soldiers at Bolo—A Water Cure Atrocity. . . ." and an open letter to President Roosevelt, July 23, 1902, signed by Charles F. Adams, Carl Schurz, Edwin B. Smith, and Herbert Welsh, both printed in 57th Congress, 2nd Session, Senate Document 213 (Serial 10735), *Trials or Courts-Martial in the Philippine Islands in Consequence of Certain Instructions,* pp. 92–96, 106–107. Hereafter cited as: *Courts-Martial in the Philippine Islands.*

57. Virginia W. Johnson, *The Unregimented General: A Biography of General Nelson A. Miles* (Boston: Houghton Mifflin Co., 1962), pp. 353–57.

58. *Courts-Martial in the Philippine Islands,* pp. 17–28, 48–62. This document contains a summary of the charges, proceedings, testimony, and findings of nine trials in the Philippines in 1902–03.

59. John R. M. Taylor, "The Philippine Insurrection Against the United States: A Compilation of Documents with Notes and Introduction," National Archives, RG 94, MC T143, pp. 18 HS, 52 HS, 57 HS, 83 HS. This long-suppressed and never-published official study of the Philippine Insurrection was written by Captain Taylor from official reports and thousands of captured insurgent documents, with which he was intimately familiar as a result of his duties with the Military Intelligence Division in Manila. Although it is not entirely free of a pro-American bias, it is one of the best histories of the insurrection yet written.

60. Schott, *Ordeal of Samar,* pp. 27–55; *Courts-Martial in the Philippine Islands,* p. 9.

61. *Courts-Martial in the Philippine Islands,* p. 2.

62. *Ibid.,* pp. 2–6, 43–48. A detailed account of the trials may be found in the same source on pp. 188–279.

63. Allen Papers, H.T.A. to W.H.T., Jan. 16, 1902, Box 7.

64. War Department, *Annual Reports,* 1901, I, Part 4, pp. 91–96.

65. *Ibid.,* pp. 351–63. Except on Samar and Batangas Province on

Luzon, where insurgent resistance continued into 1902, and on Mindanao, where it continued well after 1902, the Philippines were "pacified" by mid-1901.

66. *Ibid.*, pp. 258–59.

67. *Ibid.*, Part 5, pp. 30–87, 101–105, 109–12 ,130–32, 135–47, 169–99, 239–58, 266–96, 300–15, 346–400, 468–82; Part 6, pp. 23*–35*, 36–77, 78*–129*, 253–58, 266–93, 323–32, 352–416. Allen's reports and those of his subordinates are in Part 6 on pages marked *.

68. Allen Papers, F. C. Prescott to H.T.A., Nov. 15, 1900, Box. 7.

69. *Ibid.*, H.T.A. to D.J.A., Feb. 17, 1900.

70. *Ibid.*, H.T.A. to D.J.A., Mar. 17; April 25, 1900.

71. War Department, *Annual Reports,* 1901, I, Part 6, pp. 70–72.

72. Allen Papers, H.T.A. to D.J.A., Mar. 17, and to W.A.K., Mar. 24, 1900, Box 7.

73. War Department, *Annual Reports,* 1900, I, Part 4, p. 400. A year later there were fifty-five companies with a total strength of over 4,700 working throughout the Philippines.

74. *Ibid.*, I, Part 6, pp. 72–73; *Correspondence Relating,* p. 1168.

75. Allen Papers, H.T.A. to W.A.K., March 24, 1900, Box 7.

76. *Ibid.*, Proclamation, April 25, 1900.

77. War Department, *Annual Reports,* 1901, I, Part 6, pp. 69–77. Allen was criticized by General Otis for his too aggressive methods. By comparison with Murray's results on Leyte, the criticism may have seemed justified. With one battalion, Murray killed more than 800, while losing only seven killed and twenty-one wounded. The total killed by Allen was 500. However, this sort of simplistic statistical comparison overlooks many factors such as difference in terrain, relative strengths of the insurgents' men and weapons, etc. Moreover, there is no way of knowing whether Murray or Allen or both indulged in inflated "body counts." Part 4, p. 398, and Part 6, pp. 74–76.

78. Allen ACP File, examination, Jun. 22, 1900. At the time the examinations were being evaluated in Washington to determine who should get the promotion, Roosevelt put in a good word for Allen with General Corbin. To no avail. T.R. to H.C.C., Jul. 26, 1900.

79. Nothing ever came of any of the recommendations Allen received for brevet promotions. In January, 1901, Murray again put him in, this time for lieutenant colonel of Volunteers. In April, 1901, General R. P. Hughes, commanding the Department of the Visayas, recommended Allen for brigadier general of Volunteers. *Ibid.*, A.M. to AG, U.S. Army, Jan. 4, 1901; R.P.H. to AG, Division of the Philippines, Apr. 26, 1901.

80. War Department, *Annual Reports,* 1900, I, Part 4, p. 398.

81. *Ibid.*, Part 6, p. 24.

82. *Ibid.*, pp. 24–25.

83. Allen Papers, H.T.A. to D.J.A., Jul. 7, 12, 1900, Box 7.

84. *Ibid.*, H.T.A. to D.J.A., Aug. 1, 1900.

85. Allen ACP File, A. Murray to AG, U.S. Army, Jan. 4, 1901.

86. War Department, *Annual Reports*, 1901, I, Part 6, pp. 23–24.

87. *Ibid.*, p. 26.

88. *Ibid.*, pp. 24–34; Allen Papers, H.T.A. to D.J.A., Feb. 17, 1900, Box 7.

89. War Department, *Annual Reports*, 1901, I, Part 6, pp. 29–31.

90. Allen Papers, H.T.A. to D.J.A., Oct. 19; Nov. 11, 1900, Box 7. Allen's own nickname for himself (and his moustache) was "Joe Bush."

91. *Ibid.*, H.T.A. to D.J.A., Sept. 20, 1900.

92. *Ibid.*, H.T.A. to D.J.A., Oct. 2, 19, 27; Dec. 1, 1900. The manuscripts are in Box 40.

93. *Ibid.*, H.T.A. to D.J.A., Apr. 25, 1900, Box 7.

94. War Department, *Annual Reports*, 1901, I, Part 6, p. 64.

95. *Ibid.*, pp. 61–69, 78–124. Allen estimated that in reaching the real supporters of the rebellion the new policies increased the effectiveness of his own command "by at least 25 per cent." P. 80.

96. Allen Papers, General Orders No. 4, HQ 1st District, Dept. of the Visayas, Jan. 8, 1901, Box 7.

97. War Department, *Annual Reports*, 1901, I, Part 6, pp. 241–43.

98. *Ibid.*, pp. 132–60.

99. *Ibid.*, pp. 168, 172.

100. *Ibid.*, pp. 223–24.

101. *Ibid.*, p. 202.

102. Allen Papers, H.T.A. to D.J.A., Feb. 22, 24, 1901, Box 7. Allen was due to be mustered out as a volunteer major at the end of June and would again be a captain.

103. *Ibid.*, H.T.A. to R. P. Hughes, Jan. 16, 1901.

104. In November, 1898, while on convalescent leave, Allen had given a talk on his experiences in Cuba to the Cincinnati Chamber of Commerce, and Judge Taft sat beside him at the head table. Nothing had yet come of this chance meeting; the two men were merely distantly acquainted. *Ibid.*, H.T.A. to D.J.A., April 25, 1900.

105. Allen Papers, Dora Allen's Diary, 1901, May 3, 7, Box. 1.

106. *Ibid.*, Jan. 23.

107. Allen Papers, Special Orders No. 201, HQ Division of the Philippines, Jul. 31, 1901, Box 7, and H.T.A. to Caspar Whitney, Aug. 27, 1901.

108. *Ibid.*, H.T.A. to Caspar Whitney, Aug. 27, 1901.

Chapter VI

1. Harold H. Elarth, ed., *The Story of the Philippine Constabulary* (Los Angeles: Globe Printing Co., 1949), p. 21.

2. Leon Wolff, *Little Brown Brother* (London: Longmans, Green and Co., 1961), pp. 311–12.

3. *Ibid.*, p. 313.

4. William Howard Taft Papers, Elihu Root to Adna R. Chaffee, Feb. 26, 1901, Library of Congress, Manuscript Division, Series 21, Vol. II.

5. U.S., War Department, *Annual Reports* (Washington: Government Printing Office, 1901), I, Part 1, pp. 33, 63.

6. *Ibid.*, Part 8, p. 58. This is the *Report of the Philippine Commission*, hereafter cited as: *R.P.C.* (by part when appropriate, and year). See also: General Order No. 179, HQ, Division of the Philippines, July 20, 1901, National Archives, RG 350, File No. 1184.

7. War Department, *Annual Reports*, 1901, I, Part 1, pp. 63–65.

8. W. Cameron Forbes, *The Philippine Islands* (Boston: Houghton, Mifflin Co., 1928), I, 203–204, 240.

9. *R.P.C.*, 1901, pp. 58–59.

10. Forbes, *The Philippine Islands*, I, 228–29.

11. *Ibid.*

12. See pp. 131, 139.

13. War Department, *Annual Reports*, 1902, IX, 203–204.

14. The original appointees were Captains E. G. Curry, J. S. Garwood, W. L. Goldsborough, and W. C. Taylor. Elarth, *Story of the Philippine Constabulary*, pp. 151, 155–56, 179. Later Allen had as many as seven regular officers under his command. Two subsequent appointees, James G. Harbord and Henry H. Bandholtz, suceeded him as Chief of Constabulary and went on to become general officers in World War I. Forbes, *The Philippine Islands*, I, 204–205.

15. Victor Hurley, *Jungle Patrol: The Story of the Philippine Constabulary* (New York: E. P. Dutton and Co., 1938), p. 60; Forbes, *The Philippine Islands*, I, 204–206.

16. Forbes, *The Philippine Islands.* The pay of the enlisted men varied from 50 pesos a month for a first sergeant to 20 a month for a second-class private. War Department, *Annual Reports*, 1901, I, Part 10, p. 373. This part contains the laws and resolutions enacted by the Philippine Commission and will be hereafter cited as *Acts of the Philippine Commission.*

17. Allen Papers. Description of Allen's office is based on photographs in Box 44.

18. Hurley, *Jungle Patrol*, p. 62.

19. *R.P.C.*, 1903, Part 3, pp. 91–92; *Manila Times*, Aug. 19, 1902, p. 1.

20. *Manila Times*, Jan. 16, 1903, p. 1, and Jan. 26, 1903, p. 1.

21. *Ibid.*

22. Elarth, *Story of the Philippine Constabulary*, p. 23.

23. Quoted in George Y. Coats, "The Philippine Constabulary: 1901–1917" (Ph.D. dissertation, Ohio State University, 1968), p. 243, from a letter

from White to his father. Coats's history of the constabulary is an island-by-island account of its accomplishments, but contains very little information about Allen, organizational or administrative problems, or the constabulary's relationship with the army.

24. *Ibid.*, pp. 248–52.

25. *R.P.C.*, 1905, Part 3, p. 80; *Manila Times,* Sept. 14, 1904, p. 2.

26. See p. 139.

27. *R.P.C.*, 1901, p. 390.

28. Hurley, *Jungle Patrol,* pp. 92–93.

29. *Acts of the Philippine Commission,* p. 370. See also *R.P.C.*, 1901, pp. 77–81.

30. *R.P.C.*, 1903, Part 3, p. 46.

31. Allen Papers, H.T.A. to Senator A. J. Beveridge, Dec. 5, 1901, Box 7.

32. *R.P.C.*, 1902, Part 1, p. 180; 1903, Part 3, p. 49; 1904, Part 3, p. 1; 1906, Part 2, p. 198; 1907, Part 2, p. 267.

33. *Ibid.*, 1903, Part 3, p. 46.

34. Adna R. Chaffee to AG, July 30, 1901, National Archives, RG 350, File No. 1184. See also: *R.P.C.*, 1901, p. 389.

35. *R.P.C.*, 1901, p. 389; 1902, Part 1, p. 184; 1905, Part 3, pp. 37–38; 1907, Part 2, p. 269.

36. Elarth, *Story of the Philippine Constabulary,* p. 14.

37. John R. White, *Bullets and Bolos* (New York: The Century Co., 1928), pp. 35–36.

38. The entire passage is a paraphrase of an account (the newspaper quote is verbatim) in Forbes, *The Philippine Islands,* I, 222–23.

39. Taft Papers, W. H. Taft to Elihu Root, Oct. 14, Nov. 17, 1901; Nov. 22, 1902, Series 8, Philippine Commission Letterbook, 1900–03.

40. Henry F. Pringle, *The Life and Times of William Howard Taft* (New York: Farrar and Rinehart, Inc., 1939), I, 212–13; Allen Papers, W.H.T. to H.T.A., Dec. 24, 1902, Box 7.

41. For an example of the political capital Administration opponents tried to make of the instability on Samar in the fall of 1904, see p. 138.

42. War Department, *Annual Reports,* 1901, Part 6, pp. 84–87.

43. Allen Papers, H.T.A. to J. M. Crawford, Feb. 19, 1902, Box 7.

44. *Ibid.,* H.T.A. to T.R., Nov. 7, 1901.

45. See, for example: *ibid.,* H.T.A. to Simeon Spina (Secretary of Leyte), Feb. 17, 1902.

46. *Ibid.,* H.T.A. to D.J.A., Oct. 19, 1900.

47. *Ibid.,* H.T.A. to W.H.T., Jan. 16, 1902; H.T.A. to W.H.T., Oct. 17, 1904, Box 8.

48. For a discussion of the racial views of senior army officers see: Richard C. Brown, "Social Attitudes of American Generals: 1898–1940" (Ph.D. dissertation, University of Wisconsin, 1951), pp. 173–86. It would

be too much to call Allen a believer in racial equality; he merely had a higher opinion of the abilities and potential of Negroes (and Filipinos) than most of his army contemporaries.

49. MacArthur's views on keeping a strong army contingent in the Philippines have been mentioned above. For the similar views of his successors, see War Department, *Annual Reports,* 1903, III, 209–10; 1904, III, 205–206; 1905, III, 241–42.

50. Allen Papers, H.T.A. to H. C. Corbin, Feb. 1, 1902, Box 7.

51. War Department, *Annual Reports,* 1902, III, 134. By Oct., 1903, the figures were 15,500, 5,000, and 7,000; 1903, I, 32.

52. Allen Papers, H.T.A. to W.H.T., Jan. 31, 1902; H.T.A. to H.C.C., Feb. 1, 1902, Box 7.

53. *Ibid.,* H.T.A. to W.H.T., Jan. 27, 1902.

54. *Ibid.,* W.H.T. to H.T.A., Dec. 24, 1902.

55. *Ibid.,* H.T.A. to A. J. Beveridge, Feb. 14, 1902. See also H.T.A. to W.H.T., Feb. 7, 1902, for a similar statement.

56. *Ibid.,* H.T.A. to W.H.T., April 19, 1902; H.T.A. to H.C.C., May 9, 1902; H.T.A. to L.E.W., Oct. 1, 1902; H.T.A. to H.C.C., Nov. 4, 1902.

57. *Ibid.,* H.T.A to L.E.W., Oct. 1, 1902.

58. *Ibid.,* H.T.A. to W.H.T., Mar. 28; H.T.A. to L.E.W., Apr. 22, 1902.

59. See the Nov.–Dec., 1902 letters in the Index of Philippine Constabulary Correspondence, Philippine Commission and Bureau of Insular Affairs, National Archives, RG 350, Records of Bureau of Insular Affairs.

60. *R.P.C.,* 1902, Part 1, p. 32. War Department, *Annual Reports,* 1903; I, 33; III, 131, 221–23.

61. Coats, "The Philippine Constabulary," pp. 142–50, 287–92.

62. Allen Papers, H.T.A. to L.E.W., Dec. 23, 1902, Box 7.

63. "News of the Philippines," *Army and Navy Journal,* Nov. 15, 1902, p. 253.

64. Allen ACP File, quoted in *El Noticero de Manila,* Jan. 31, 1902, clipping.

65. Allen's record was not entirely clean on the matter of "water cures." At the time the various atrocity courts-martial were about to begin he wrote his friend Clarence Edwards, Chief of the Bureau of Insular Affairs: "You, as well as I, know that in bringing to a successful issue war measures out here, certain things will take place not intended by the higher authorities. . . . I have heard that under me, though against my orders, the 'water cure,' and other methods as bad . . . were adopted. . . ." Allen Papers, H.T.A. to C. R. Edwards, Apr. 18, 1902, Box 7.

66. *R.P.C.,* 1903, Part 3, p. 9.

67. War Department, *Annual Reports,* 1903, III, 144.

68. *R.P.C.,* 1903, Part 3, p. 9.

69. The Adjutant General's Office never considered Allen's constabulary tour as "troop duty." To the bureaucrats in Washington, he was on

"detached service." In addition, until 1904, Allen was not allowed credit for his temporary rank in the annual *Army Register.*

70. War Department, *Annual Reports,* 1903, I, 33; 1904, III, 205; 1905, III, 240.

71. D.J.A. to "Dear Girls" (her sisters), Sept. 26, 1901. Letter in possession of Mrs. J. W. Viner.

72. Allen, interview, 1964.

73. Allen ACP File, H.T.A. to T.R., Jun. 6, 1903.

74. *Ibid.,* S.B.M.Y. to T.R., Oct. 15, 1902. The President may have accepted Young's arguments in Allen's case, but he was not averse to promoting deserving captains to generalships. In 1906, John J. Pershing got his star for subduing the Lake Lanao Moros on Mindanao. See Thomas J. Fleming, "Pershing's Island War," American Heritage, XIX (Aug., 1969), 32–35, 101–104.

75. Allen ACP File, S.B.M.Y. to T.R., Oct. 15, 1903.

76. See in the Allen Papers, Allen's Diary for Dec., 1903, through Apr, 1904, Box 1, and in the Allen ACP File the series of cablegrams and letters, Feb. 17 through Apr. 8, 1904.

77. For Allen's reports see documents 2192, 2206, 2220, 2313 a-e, 2263, and 2434 a-f, all dated between Feb. 4 and Apr. 9, 1904, in the files of the War College Division, National Archives, RG 165, Records of the War Department General Staff. Copies of Allen's personal reports to Taft are in the 1904 material, Box 8, Allen Papers. No mention is made of Allen in the official report of the observer team: War Department, Military Information Division, *Reports of the Military Observers Attached to the Armies in Manchuria During the Russo-Japanese War* (Washington: Government Printing Office, 1906).

78. *R.P.C.,* 1904, Part 3, pp. 101–105.

79. *Ibid.,* 1902, Part 1, pp. 34, 182; 1905, Part 3, p. 32.

80. Computed by taking the total number of constabulary desertions between 1901 and 1907 (250) found in *R.P.C.,* 1907, Part 2, p. 268, and dividing it by the total of the strength figures found in each year's report. The army figure is from War Department, *Annual Reports,* 1907, I, 220.

81. *Ibid.,* 1903, Part 3, pp. 49–50.

82. *Ibid.,* 1904, Part 3, pp. 91–92.

83. Coats, "The Philippine Constabulary," pp. 188, 208–209.

84. *R.P.C.,* 1905, Part 3, p. 4.

85. *Ibid.,* pp. 28–29, 80, 90. *Manila Times,* Aug. 11, 1904, p. 1; Aug. 24, 1904, p. 1; Sept. 4, 1904, p. 2.

86. *Manila Times,* Aug. 17, 1904, p. 1; Nov. 28, 1904, p. 1; Dec. 23, 1904, p. 1. See also *New York Times,* Dec. 25, 1904, p. 4, and *R.P.C.,* 1905, Part 3, p. 90.

87. Forbes, *The Philippine Islands,* I, 150–51.

88. Allen Papers, L.E.W. to H.T.A., Dec. 27, 1904; H.T.A. to L.E.W., Dec. 31, 1904, both quoted in full in Allen's Diary, 1904, Box 1.

89. *Manila Times,* Feb. 17, 1905, p. 1; Feb. 20, p. 1; Mar. 9, 1905, p. 3. Also: Allen Papers, H.T.A. to W. C. Forbes (Wright's successor as Secretary of Commerce and Police), Mar. 5, 1905, Box 8.

90. *Manila Times,* Feb. 4, 1905, p. 1.

91. Allen Papers, H.T.A. to L.E.W., March 5, 1905, Box 8; H.T.A. to W.C.F., Mar. 5, 1905; Hurley, *Jungle Patrol,* p. 61.

92. *Manila Times,* Apr. 5, 1905, p. 1.

93. *R.P.C.*, 1905, Part 3, p. 30.

94. Allen Papers, H.T.A. to W.H.T., Dec. 29, 1906, Box 9.

95. *Ibid.*, H.T.A. to L.E.W., May 25, 1905, Box 8.

96. *R.P.C.*, 1905, Part 3, p. 90; 1906, Part 2, pp. 201, 227, 254–55. *Manila Times,* Dec. 6, 1906, p. 1; April 24, 1907, p. 2. Coats, "The Philippine Constabulary," pp. 347–48.

97. "Philippine Constabulary a Failure," *Army and Navy Journal,* Jun. 10, 1905, p. 1115. See also, Letter to Editor from "Observer," Jul. 15, 1905, pp. 1259–60; "Would Abolish Constabulary," *Manila Times,* Jun. 3, 1905, and on Jul. 7, 1905, translations of attacks on the constabulary by *La Democracia* and *El Renacimiento.*

98. *R.P.C.*, 1905, Part 3, p. 32.

99. Allen Papers, H.T.A. to W.H.T., Dec. 29, 1906, Box 9.

100. War Department, *Annual Reports,* 1905, III, 242.

101. *Ibid.*, 1906, Part 2, pp. 198–99.

102. Allen Papers, H.T.A. to W.H.T., Jan. 13, 1906; memo by H.T.A., Apr. 22, 1906; H.T.A. to D.J.A., May 21, 1906, Box 9. At this time he had investments in coal and timber in Kentucky as well as gold, coal, copper mines, and land in the Philippines. He estimated the net value of his assets at $35,000.

103. *Ibid.*, Allen's Diary, 1906, Mar. through May, Box 1.

104. *Ibid.*, H.T.A. to D.J.A., Dec. 13, 1906, Box 9.

105. *Ibid.*, W.H.T. to H.T.A., Nov. 21, 1906.

106. *Ibid.*, H.T.A. to J.F.B., Jan. 13, 1907.

107. Forbes, *The Philippine Islands,* I, 192–93, 227. The constabulary death figures include 30 American and 3 Filipino officers. By 1907, 25 per cent of the officers were native.

108. *R.P.C.*, 1902, Part 1, p. 180; 1905, Part 3, p. 36; 1907, Part 2, p. 268. Complete statistics for the years 1906 and 1907 are not found in *R.P.C.*, but are contained in the draft manuscript annual reports of the Chief of Constabulary (1906, p. 17; 1907, p. 14) in the National Archives, RG 350, Records of the Bureau of Insular Affairs. By fiat of the Amnesty Proclamation of July 4, 1902, there were no more *insurrectos;* only ladrones, etc. In existence less than a year at that time, the constabulary had already accounted for 400 of the former and 4,000 of the latter (killed, wounded,

or captured). By contrast, between February, 1899, and July, 1902, the army had killed, wounded, or captured approximately 35,000 insurgents.

109. Forbes, *The Philippine Islands,* I, 205–13; Coats, "The Philippine Constabulary," pp. 215–39.

110. Richard O'Connor, *Black Jack Pershing* (Garden City, N.Y.: Doubleday and Co., Inc., 1961), pp. 85–89.

111. Allen Papers, J.F.B. to H.T.A., Feb. 18, 1907, Box 9.

112. *Ibid.,* H.T.A. to J.F.B., March 29, 1907. There are numerous letters recommending Allen for promotion in Box 9. See, for example: Leonard Wood to AG, Apr. 13, 1907.

113. See pp. 72–73.

114. Allen Papers, J.F.B. to H.T.A., May 10, 1907, Box 9.

115. *Ibid.,* H.T.A. to D.J.A., Apr. 15, 1907.

CHAPTER VII

1. Henry T. Allen, "Notes on Promotion," *Journal of the Military Service Institution of the United States,* XXVII (Jul., 1905), 1–2. For a discussion of how the promotion system worked in Allen's day and his proposals for changing it, see the Appendix.

2. Allen Papers, Allen's Diary, 1907, Apr. 15–May 15, Box 1. The article appears to have been one of an anonymous series on this subject appearing in the *Journal of the United States Cavalry Association* in 1907–09. See below, n. 52.

3. Allen Papers, Allen's Diary, 1907, May 24–June 6, 1907, Box 1.

4. *Ibid.,* June 24–30.

5. U.S., Department of War, Quartermaster General's Office, *Outline Description of Military Posts in the United States and Alaska* (Washington: Government Printing Office, 1904), pp. 567–70; George S. Anderson, "Work of the Cavalry in Protecting the Yellowstone National Park," *Journal of the United States Cavalry Association,* X (Mar., 1897), 5–6.

6. Allen Papers, Allen's Diary, 1907, Jul. 1–17, Box 1.

7. Two of the troops departed the post in September, leaving Allen with five officers and eighty-four men. Post Returns, Fort Yellowstone, Jun.–Oct., 1907, National Archives, RG 94, MC 617, Roll 1480, "Returns from U.S. Military Posts, 1800–1916," AGO.

8. Allen Papers, Allen's Diary, 1907, Jul. 1, Box 1.

9. See pp. 134–35.

10. Anderson, "Cavalry in Yellowstone Park," pp. 5–6; letter to author from Horace M. Albright, Los Angeles, California (park superintendent from 1919 to 1929), Jun. 24, 1970; Richard A. Bartlett, "Five Ages of Yellowstone" (draft ms. history of the park), pp. 827–34. Dr. Bartlett, a leading historian of the park, has kindly permitted the author to use his ms. prior to its publication.

11. Anderson, "Cavalry in Yellowstone Park," pp. 6–10.

12. *Ibid.*

13. Report of Investigation of Desertions at Fort Yellowstone, HQ, Department of Dakota, Jan. 6, 1909, National Archives, RG 94, Box 5491, File No. 1432477/Folders B&D.

14. U.S., Department of Interior, *Report of the Secretary of the Interior,* 1907 (Washington, Government Printing Office, 1907), I, 552–54.

15. Allen Papers, H.T.A. to J.F.B., Aug. 11, 1907; Oct. 14, 1908, Box 9.

16. *Ibid.,* Allen's Diary, 1907, July 11–25, Box 1; J.F.B. to H.T.A., Nov. 25, 1907; S.B.M.Y. to Sec. Interior, Dec. 29, 1907, quoted in H.T.A. to AG, U.S. Army, Dec. 12, 1908, Box 9.

17. Bartlett, "Five Ages of Yellowstone," p. 863.

18. Allen Papers, J.F.B. to H.T.A., Aug. 16; W.H.T. to H.T.A., Sept. 11, 1907, Box 9.

19. Allen interview, 1964.

20. Allen Papers, Allen's Diary, 1907, Sept. 29, Box 1; L.W. to H.T.A., Feb. 17, 1908; W.C. to H.T.A., Feb. 17, 1908, Box 9.

21. *Ibid.,* J.F.B. to H.T.A., Aug. 16; Sept. 29; Nov. 25, 1907; H.T.A. to J.F.B., undated draft, Oct. 1907.

22. *Ibid.,* J.F.B. to H.T.A., Apr. 14, 1908.

23. *Ibid.*

24. Post Returns, Fort Yellowstone, May, 1908.

25. H. M. Albright to author, Jun. 24, 1970.

26. Hiram M. Chittenden, *The Yellowstone National Park,* ed. Richard A. Bartlett (Norman, Okla.: University of Oklahoma Press, 1964), pp. 128–40; interview with R. A. Bartlett, Washington, D.C., May 12, 1970.

27. H. M. Albright to author, Jun. 24, 1970.

28. Allen Papers, H.T.A. to J.F.B., Oct. 14, 1908, Box 9.

29. *Ibid.;* Allen interview, 1970; H.M.A. to author, Jun. 24, 1970.

30. H.M.A. to author, Jun. 24, 1970; Interior Department, *Report of the Secretary of the Interior,* 1908, I, 410–12; Jack E. Haynes, "Yellowstone Stage Holdups," *Brand Book,* ed. Elvon L. Howe (Denver: Arthur Zeuch Printing, 1952), VIII, 85–98.

31. Allen Papers, H.T.A. to J.F.B., Oct. 14, 1908, Box 9.

32. "Desertions at Fort Yellowstone," National Archives, RG 94, Box 5491, File No. 1432477/Folders B&D; Allen Papers, H.T.A. to Adjutant General, U.S. Army, Dec. 12, 1908, Box 9.

33. Allen Papers, C. G. Treat to H.T.A., Oct. 19, 1908.

34. *Ibid.,* Telegrams, H.T.A. to J.F.B., L.E.W., J.R.G., W.L., Oct. 21, 1908.

35. *Ibid.,* W.L. to H.T.A., Oct. 30, 1908.

36. Post Returns, Fort Yellowstone, Nov., 1908. Child eventually got the new wing on his hotel in 1913. H.M.A. to author, Jun. 24, 1970.

37. L.E.W. to H.T.A., Jan. 20, 1909, letter in possession of Col. H. T. Allen, Jr.

38. U.S., Department of War, *Annual Reports* (Washington: Government Printing Office, 1909), III, 117–18.

39. War Department, *Description of Military Posts,* pp. 208–11; War Department, *Annual Reports,* 1910, III, 129; Viner interview, 1970.

40. Viner interview, 1970.

41. Allen Papers, AG to H.T.A., Jan. 27, 1909, Box 9.

42. *Ibid.,* H.T.A. to D.J.A., May 26, 1909.

43. Allen interview, 1970.

44. Viner interview, 1970; Allen Papers, W.H.T. to H.T.A., Nov. 24, 1909, Box 9.

45. *Ibid.,* L.W. to H.T.A., Nov. 24, 1909.

46. *Ibid.,* A.M. to H.T.A., Nov. 30, 1909.

47. New York *Evening Post,* Dec. 16, 1909, p. 8.

48. Allen Papers, L.W. to H.T.A., Dec. 24, 1904, Box 8. See also pp. 96, 147–48, 153.

49. Hermann Hagedorn, *Leonard Wood: A Biography* (New York: Harper and Brothers, 1931), II, 116.

50. USMA, *Register of Graduates, 1963* (West Point, N.Y.: West Point Alumni Foundation, Inc., 1963), pp. 273–74; Wirt Robinson, ed., *Cullum's Biographical Register of the Officers and Graduates of the U.S. Military Academy,* Supplement (Saginaw, Mich.: Seeman and Peters, Printers, 1920), VI-A, 335. Hereafter cited as: *Cullum's Register.*

51. Allen Papers, H.T.A. to R. L. Patterson, Dec. 15, 1910, Box 9; Allen's Diaries, 1911; 1913, Box 2. See also documents 6363-1, Jan. 9, 1911; 6572-1, Apr. 24, 1911; 7545-16, Apr. 30, 1914, all in the War College Division files, National Archives, in RG 165. These are staff papers typical of the many Allen worked on.

52. See the anonymous series of articles on the need for a chief of cavalry in the quarterly issues of the *Journal of the United States Cavalry Association,* XVIII–XIX (Jul., 1907–Jan., 1909). Judging from its tone and literary style, the first of these articles was written by Allen. See p. 148.

53. Allen Papers, Allen's Diary, 1911, Jan. 2, Box 2. Congress finally authorized a chief of cavalry in 1920.

54. *Ibid.,* Jun.–Dec.; inspection schedule, Fort Riley, Kansas, *ca.* Oct., 1911, Box 10; list of officers to be called to testify, Office of the Chief of Staff, Dec. 30, 1911, National Archives, RG 94, Box 396, File No. 1863364.

55. Allen Papers, Allen's Diary, 1911, Jul.–Aug., Box 2.

56. *Ibid.,* Jan.–Jun.; "Horseshow" folder with 1912 material, Box 9.

57. *Ibid.,* H.T.A. to Rep. J. S. Sherley (D., Ky.), Feb. 29, 1912.

58. *Ibid.,* E.R. to H.T.A., Feb. 17, 1912; C. D. Hilles (Taft's Private Secretary) to H.T.A., Apr. 30, 1912; H.T.A. to Senator M. J. Foster, Dec. 3, 1912.

59. *Ibid.*

60. Richard O'Connor, *Black Jack Pershing* (Garden City, N.Y.: Doubleday and Co., Inc., 1961), p. 89.

61. Samuel P. Huntington, *The Soldier and the State: The Theory and Practice of Civil-Military Relations* (New York: Vintage Books, 1957), pp. 270–73, 279–80; Russell F. Weigley, *History of the United States Army* (New York: The Macmillan Co., 1967), pp. 328–29.

62. Otto L. Nelson, Jr., *National Security and the General Staff* (Washington: Infantry Journal Press, 1946), pp. 39–44; C. Joseph Bernardo and Eugene H. Bacon, *American Military Policy: Its Development since 1775* (Harrisburg, Pa.: The Military Service Publishing Co., 1957), pp. 290–91.

63. Bernardo and Bacon, *American Military Policy,* pp. 293–96; Weigley, *History of the United States Army,* pp. 322–23.

64. Weigley, *History of the United States Army,* pp. 323–27; Nelson, *National Security and the General Staff,* pp. 75–132.

65. Johnson Hagood, *The Services of Supply: A Memoir of the Great War* (Boston: Houghton Mifflin Company, 1927), p. 21; Hagedorn, *Leonard Wood,* II, 99–100; copy of War Department Memo, Office of the Chief of Staff, June 14, 1911, in file of War Department material, OCMH, Washington, D.C.

66. Elting E. Morrison, *Turmoil and Tradition: A Study of the Life and Times of Henry L. Stimson* (New York: Atheneum, 1964), pp. 120, 126; Hagedorn, *Leonard Wood,* II, 115–16.

67. Hagedorn, *Leonard Wood,* pp. 109–10; Weigley, *History of the United States Army,* pp. 335–40; John M. Palmer, *America in Arms: The Experience of the United States with Military Organization* (New Haven: Yale University Press, 1941), pp. 141–47.

68. Mabel E. Deutrich, *Struggle for Supremacy: The Career of General Fred C. Ainsworth* (Washington, D.C.: Public Affairs Press, 1962), p. 111; Hagedorn, *Leonard Wood,* II, 116.

69. Hagedorn, *Leonard Wood,* pp. 95–96; Deutrich, *Struggle for Supremacy,* pp. 105–11.

70. Deutrich, *Struggle for Supremacy,* pp. 88–104; Nelson, *National Security and the General Staff,* pp. 112–32.

71. Hagedorn, *Leonard Wood,* II, 97.

72. *Ibid.,* p. 108.

73. *Ibid.,* pp. 109–10.

74. *Ibid.,* pp. 120–21; Deutrich, *Struggle for Supremacy,* pp. 113–14, 119–20; Nelson, *National Security and the General Staff,* pp. 151–62.

75. Henry L. Stimson and McGeorge Bundy, *On Active Service in Peace and War* (New York: Harper and Brothers, 1948), pp. 34–36; Hagedorn, *Leonard Wood,* II, 122.

76. Hagedorn, *Leonard Wood,* p. 123; Deutrich, *Struggle for Su-*

premacy, pp. 123–24. Wood's four-year tenure ended in the summer of 1914.

77. Deutrich, *Struggle for Supremacy,* p. 126; Hagedorn, *Leonard Wood,* II, 124–25; Stimson and Bundy, *On Active Service,* p. 37.

78. See among the Allen Papers the series of letters, Feb. 2 to Mar. 16, 1912, Box 9, which indicate that Allen may have incurred the personal wrath of at least one of Wood's enemies, Representative Hay. At Wood's request, Allen organized a publicity campaign against Hay's proposal to cut the number of cavalry regiments by one-third in the interests of economy.

79. *Ibid.,* Allen's Diary, 1913, Jan. 1–Feb. 15, Box 2.

80. *Ibid.,* Mar. 4.

81. *Ibid.,* H.T.A. to D.J.A., Jun. 1, 1916, Box 10.

82. Allen ACP File, W.H.T. to H.T.A., Mar. 15, 1913; also H. L. Stimson to H.T.A., Mar. 1, 1913.

83. Viner interview, 1970; "Reorganization of Cavalry Division," National Archives, RG 165, War College Division, File No. 7545-16, April 30, 1914.

84. Hagedorn, *Leonard Wood,* II, 111, 126–27; Weigley, *History of the United States Army,* pp. 334–35; Morrison, *Turmoil and Tradition,* pp. 137–38.

85. Arthur S. Link, *Wilson the Diplomatist: A Look at his Major Foreign Policies* (Baltimore: The Johns Hopkins Press, 1957), pp. 17–24; Hagedorn, *Leonard Wood,* II, 134–35, 143–44.

86. Hagedorn, *Leonard Wood,* pp. 148–96.

87. Viner and Allen interviews, 1970; Allen Papers, Allen's Diary, 1914, Aug. 4, Box 2.

88. *Ibid.*

89. The *Washington Post,* Aug. 4, 1914, p. 1.

Chapter VIII

1. Allen Papers, Allen's Diary, 1914, Aug. 4, Box 2. The official report on the expedition is U.S., Department of War, *Report on Operations of the United States Relief Commission in Europe* (Washington: Government Printing Office, 1914), hereafter cited as *Relief Commission Report.* Hermann Hagedorn, *Leonard Wood: A Biography* (New York: Harper and Brothers, 1931), II, 148.

2. Allen Papers, Allen's Diary, 1914, Aug. 4–5, Box 2.

3. *Ibid.,* Aug. 6–8; roster of personnel assigned to commission with 1914 material in Box 10.

4. *Ibid.,* Allen's Diary, 1914, Aug. 8–17, Box 2; *Relief Commission Report,* pp. 2–3.

5. *Relief Commission Report,* pp. 27–28; Allen's Diary, 1914, Aug. 18–21, Box 2, Allen Papers; Herbert Hoover, *The Memoirs of Herbert Hoover:*

Years of Adventure, 1874–1920 (New York: The Macmillan Co., 1951), pp. 141–48.

6. *Relief Commission Report,* pp. 4–5.
7. Allen Papers, Allen's Diary, 1914, Aug. 23–24, Box 2.
8. *Ibid.*
9. *Ibid.*, Aug. 26–27.
10. *Ibid.*, Aug. 27.
11. *Ibid.*, Aug. 28–29.
12. *Ibid.*, Aug. 30–Sept. 3; Allen interview, 1970.
13. Allen Papers, Allen's Diary, 1914, Sept. 4–6, Box 2; Barbara W. Tuchman, *The Guns of August* (New York: The Macmillan Co., 1962), pp. 373–94.
14. Allen Papers, Allen's Diary, 1914, Sept. 6–14, Box 2.
15. Allen ACP File, copy of Cable 35, Breckenridge to Sec. War, Sept. 9, 1914; Allen Papers, Allen's Diary, 1914, Aug. 4–Sept. 6, Box 2.
16. Allen Papers, Allen's Diary, 1914, Sept. 17, Box 2.
17. *Ibid.*, Sept. 19–26.
18. *Ibid.*, Sept. 21.
19. *Relief Commission Report,* p. 1.
20. Allen Papers, H.T.A. to L.W., Oct. 14, 1914, Box 10.
21. H.T.A. to Sec. War, document 8997-1, Oct. 21, 1914, War College Division files, National Archives, RG 165.
22. *Ibid.*
23. *Ibid.*
24. *Ibid.*
25. *Ibid.*
26. *Ibid.*
27. Hagedorn, *Leonard Wood,* II, 149–57; Henry L. Stimson and McGeorge Bundy, *On Active Service in Peace and War* (New York: Harper and Brothers, 1948), pp. 86–87.
28. Hugh L. Scott, *Some Memories of a Soldier* (New York: The Century Co., 1928), pp. 544, 548.
29. Johnson Hagood, *The Services of Supply: A Memoir of the Great War* (Boston: Houghton Mifflin Co., 1927), pp. 22–24; Russell F. Weigley, *History of the United States Army* (New York: The Macmillan Co., 1967), pp. 244–46. Both Garrison and Breckenridge resigned in early 1916 because of Wilson's refusal to support their Continental Army plan.
30. Notification of date and subject of talk, Oct. 27, 1914, National Archives, RG 94, File No. 2223161. From the marginal notes on Allen's copy of his report to the Sec. War in the 1914 material, Box 10, Allen Papers, it appears he used this as his script.
31. Allen, Viner interviews, 1970.
32. John N. Albright, "The Secretary of War and the Colorado Coal Strike," draft ms. in files of OCMH, Washington, D.C., pp. 18–34.
33. Viner interview, 1970. The Viners were married in November, 1915.

34. *Ibid.; Cullum's Register,* III, 320; (1900), IV, 315; (1910), V, 292–94; (1920), VI-A, 274–75.

35. L. M. Garrison to President, May 6, 1914, Letterbook, item 77, National Archives, RG 107.

36. Albright, "Colorado Coal Strike," pp. 22–36.

37. Viner interview, 1970. See Allen Papers, invitations, programs, and press clippings, Box 10.

38. *Ibid.,* T.R. to H.T.A., Jun. 23, 1915. T.R.'s letters to other friends on this subject are in Elting E. Morison, ed., *The Letters of Theodore Roosevelt,* 8 vols. (Cambridge, Mass.: Harvard University Press, 1954), VIII, 947, 1089, 1164, 1189.

39. Allen Papers, L.W. to H.T.A., March 16; July 12; Dec. 30, 1915; Jan. 4, 1916; Box 10; Regimental Returns, 11th Cavalry, Feb.–Aug., 1915, National Archives, RG 94, MC 744, Roll 105. For Wood's role in the Plattsburg Movement, see Hagedorn, *Leonard Wood,* II, 158–69.

40. Allen ACP File, Allen's Efficiency Report, 1915.

41. *Ibid.,* 1916.

42. Allen Papers, H.T.A. to D.J.A. Mar. 16, 1916, Box 10.

43. Frederick Funston, "Annual Report of the Southern Department for Fiscal Year 1916," National Archives, RG 94, File No. 2432310, Trunk 141, AGO, pp. 21–33, hereafter cited as: Funston, "Report"; Harry A. Toulmin, Jr., *With Pershing in Mexico* (Harrisburg, Pa.: Military Service Publishing Co., 1935), pp. 29–43. The best eyewitness account of the raid and its aftermath is Frank Tompkins, *Chasing Villa: The Story Behind the Story of Pershing's Expedition into Mexico* (Harrisburg, Pa.: Military Service Publishing Co., 1943). A recent reinterpretation of Villa's motives is James A. Sandos, "German Involvement in Northern Mexico, 1915–1916: A New Look at the Columbus Raid," *The Hispanic American Historical Review,* L (Feb., 1970), 70–88. All of these accounts vary slightly as to details (times, numbers af casualties, etc.). When in doubt, the author has used the official version.

44. Vengeance and the desire to provoke intervention are given as Villa's motives in Samuel F. Bemis, *A Diplomatic History of the United States,* 3rd ed. (New York: Henry Holt and Co., 1950), pp. 550–51. Sandos, however, in "A New Look at the Columbus Raid," while accepting revenge as a motive, suggests that Villa was encouraged to make the raid by German agents in the United States and Mexico, one of whom was Villa's personal physician. Sandos' thesis is that Villa did not necessarily intend to provoke American intervention, but the Germans did, hoping to tie the United States down in a war with Mexico.

45. Funston, "Report," pp. 25–26.

46. Viner interview, 1970; Allen Papers, news clipping, Chattanooga *Daily Times,* Mar. 13, 1916, Box 10; Regimental Returns, 11th Cavalry, Mar. 1916, National Archives, RG 94; MC 744, Roll 105; "Narrative Report of the Operations of the 11th Cavalry in Mexico," p. 1. A copy of the latter docu-

ment, a report to General Pershing dated June 8, 1916, is in OCMH files in Washington, D.C., and is hereafter cited as: 11th Cavalry, "Report."

47. 11th Cavalry, "Report," March 16–17; Regimental Returns, 11th Cavalry, March 1916, National Archives, RG 94, MC 744, Roll 105.

48. U.S., Department of State, *Foreign Relations of the United States,* 1916 (Washington: Government Printing Office, 1916), p. 485. Hereafter cited as: *FRUS.*

49. *Ibid.,* p. 488.

50. John J. Pershing, "Report of Operation, Punitive Expedition," National Archives, RG 94, File no. 2480591, Trunk 141, AGO, p. 10. Hereafter cited as: Pershing, "Report."

51. *FRUS,* 1916, p. 493.

52. Howard F. Cline, *The United States and Mexico* (Cambridge, Mass.: Harvard University Press, 1953), pp. 175–77.

53. *Ibid.,* pp. 177–78; Richard O'Connor, *Black Jack Pershing* (Garden City, N.Y.: Doubleday, and Co., Inc., 1961), pp. 118–22, 134–35.

54. Robert S. Thomas and Inez V. Allen, "The Mexican Punitive Expedition under Brigadier General John J. Pershing, United States Army," draft ms. in OCMH files, Washington, D.C., pp. II-13, 14.

55. *Ibid.,* pp. II-17 to III-11; Tompkins, *Chasing Villa,* pp. 74–106.

56. O'Connor, *Black Jack Pershing,* pp. 133–45.

57. Pershing, "Report," pp. 11–12, 17–20.

58. Viner interview, 1970.

59. Thomas and Allen, "The Mexican Punitive Expedition," pp. III-23, 24; O'Connor, *Black Jack Pershing,* p. 125. Patton's flair for bizarre self-dramatization was well developed even then. On one occasion; according to O'Connor, he persuaded Pershing to let him use an automobile to go on a "foraging expedition." He returned with the bodies of two of Villa's bodyguards tied to the fenders "like slaughtered deer." P. 134.

60. Robert Dunn, "With Pershing's Cavalry," *Collier's Weekly,* XXXXI (Sept. 23, 1916), 8.

61. Allen Papers, H.T.A. to D.J.A., Apr. 2, 4, 1916, Box 10.

62. *Ibid.,* H.T.A. to D.J.A., Apr. 10, 1916.

63. *Ibid.,* H.T.A to D.J.A., Apr. 18, 1916.

64. *Ibid.,* H.T.A. to D.J.A., Apr. 21, 1916.

65. Pershing, "Report," pp. 18–19; Tompkins, *Chasing Villa,* pp. 158–60.

66. Tompkins, *Chasing Villa,* pp. 135–42; Pershing, "Report," pp. 21–33.

67. Tompkins, *Chasing Villa,* pp. 153–57; 11th Cavalry, "Report," entries for Apr. 13–15; Allen Papers, H.T.A. to D.J.A., Apr. 18, 1916, Box 10.

68. Thomas and Allen, "The Mexican Punitive Expedition," pp. IV-5, IV-10.

69. *Ibid.,* pp. V-3, 4; Pershing, "Report," p. 34 and Inclosure 18.

70. Pershing, "Report," pp. 23–31; Thomas and Allen, "The Mexican Punitive Expedition," p. IV-33.

71. Allen Papers, H.T.A. to D.J.A., May 5, 1916, Box 10. Diary of James L. Collins (then a lieutenant in Pershing's headquarters), 1916, Apr. 28, in Collins Papers in OCMH files.

72. Copies of Allen's reports as Inspector General are in Allen Papers, Box 32.

73. Pershing, "Report," pp. 32–33.

74. In Pershing's papers there are only a half dozen letters from Allen prior to 1916, all written after 1914 and mostly army "shop talk." See Pershing Papers, Box 9, Library of Congress, Manuscript Division.

75. James G. Harbord, *The American Army in France* (Boston: Little, Brown and Co., 1936), p. 33. Pershing lost his level head at least twice during the expedition. Frustrated and angry, he recommended war with Mexico to General Funston after the encounters at Parral and Carrizal. Pershing Papers, J.J.P. to F.F., Apr. 18; Jun. 22, 1916, Box 372.

76. Harbord, *The American Army in France,* pp. 110–12.

77. *Ibid.,* p. 136.

78. Allen Papers, Allen interview, 1970; H.T.A. to D.J.A., Aug. 20, 1916, Box 10.

79. Allen ACP File, Allen's Efficiency Report, 1916.

80. Allen Papers, H.T.A. to D.J.A., May 23; Jun. 23; 1916, Box 10.

81. Viner interview, 1970.

82. *Cullum's Register* (1920), VI-A, 274–75.

83. Allen Papers, H.T.A. to D.J.A., July 1, 1916, Box 10; Regimental Returns, 11th Cavalry, July–Aug., 1916, National Archives, RG 94, MC 744, Roll 105.

84. Thomas and Allen, "The Mexican Punitive Expedition," pp. IV-34, 35.

85. Allen Papers, copy of telegram, June 12, 1916, Box 10. Among others it was sent to: General Scott (Chief of Staff); Generals Funston and Wood; General Macomb (President of the War College); Senators Luke Lea (D., Tenn.), Ollie James and J. W. Beckham (D., Ky.); Henry Breckenridge (former Asst. Secretary of War), J. C. Scofield (Chief Clerk of the War Department), and former President Roosevelt.

86. *Ibid.,* see letters (Jun.–Aug., 1916) from men listed above.

87. *Ibid.,* T.R. to H.T.A., Jun. 26, 1916.

88. *Ibid.,* H.T.A. to D.J.A., Aug. 6; Oct. 25, 1916.

89. *Ibid.,* H.T.A. to D.J.A., Aug. 23; Oct. 15, 1916.

90. *Ibid.,* H.T.A. to D.J.A., Jul. 1; Oct. 25; Nov. 11, 1916; Regimental Returns, 11th Cavalry, Oct., 1916, National Archives, RG 94, MC 744, Roll 105; O'Connor, *Black Jack Pershing,* p. 124.

91. Viner interview, 1970.

92. Ray S. Baker, *Woodrow Wilson, Life and Letters* (Garden City,

N.Y.: Doubleday and Co., Inc., 1937), VI, 79–82; *FRUS*, 1916, pp. 604–605, and 1917, pp. 916–38.

93. O'Connor, *Black Jack Pershing*, pp. 138–40; Weigley, *History of the U.S. Army*, pp. 350–52.

94. Henry S. Commager, ed., *Documents of American History*, 6th ed. (New York: Appleton-Century-Crofts, 1958), II, 310.

95. Pershing Papers, J.J.P. to H.T.A., March 10, 1917, Box 9.

Chapter IX

1. Pershing Papers, H.T.A. to J.J.P., May 16, 1917, Box 9, Library of Congress, Manuscript Division.

2. *Ibid.*, J.J.P. to H.T.A., May 18, 1917.

3. Hugh L. Scott, *Some Memories of a Soldier* (New York: The Century Co., 1928), pp. 561–62.

4. Allen Papers, Allen's Diary, 1917, May–Aug., Box 2.

5. George Wythe, *A History of the 90th Division* (San Antonio: The De Vinne Press, 1920), pp. 3–4.

6. Marvin A. Kreidberg and Merton G. Henry, *History of Military Mobilization in the United States Army, 1775–1945* (Washington: Government Printing Office, 1955), p. 222.

7. *Ibid.*, p. 241.

8. *Ibid.*, pp. 244–46.

9. *Ibid.*, p. 298. In the spring of 1918, this figure was revised upward to eighty divisions in response to the deteriorating military situation on the western front (pp. 302–304). A total of forty-two divisions actually reached France before November, 1918, of which twenty-nine participated in combat. Leonard P. Ayres, *The War with Germany: A Statistical Summary* (Washington: Government Printing Office, 1919), p. 33. See p. 214.

10. Ayres, *The War with Germany*, pp. 16–17, 26–28.

11. Wythe, *History of the 90th Division*, pp. 6–7.

12. *Ibid.*, pp. 6, 8; Pershing Papers, H.T.A. to J.J.P., Mar. 20, 1918, Box 9.

13. Wythe, *History of the 90th Division*, pp. 7–9. For a description of the difficulties with equipment shortages in the national army divisions, see Hermann Hagedorn, *Leonard Wood: A Biography* (New York: Harper and Brothers, 1931), II, 242–48. The official account of this problem is in Kreidberg and Henry, *History of Military Mobilization*, pp. 318–24.

14. Pershing Papers, H.T.A. to J.J.P., Oct. 8, 1917, Box 9.

15. Wythe, *History of the 90th Division*, p. 8; Richard O'Connor, *Black Jack Pershing* (Garden City, N.Y.: Doubleday and Co., Inc., 1961), p. 219.

16. Allen Papers, Allen's Diary, 1917, Nov. 22, Box 2.

17. *Ibid.*, Nov. 25–Dec. 3; Viner interview, 1970. The position of Chief

of Staff changed hands no less than seven times in the year after United States's entry in the war. Biddle held the job twice in the absence of Scott's successor, General Tasker H. Bliss, who was frequently in Europe conferring with Allied leaders. On March 4, 1918, General Peyton C. March became Chief of Staff. He held the position for the duration. Kreidberg and Henry, *History of Military Mobilization,* pp. 215–16.

18. Allen Papers, Allen's Diary, 1917, Dec. 4–20, Box 2.

19. War Department, Historical Section, Army War College, *Order of Battle of the United States Land Forces in the World War: American Expeditionary Forces—Divisions* (Washington: Government Printing Office, 1931), p. 299.

20. Allen Papers, Allen's Diary, 1917, Dec. 20, Box 2.

21. *Ibid.,* 1917–1918, Dec. 20–Jan. 5.

22. *Ibid.,* 1918, Jan. 9–19.

23. *Ibid.,* Jan. 22–28; O'Connor, *Black Jack Pershing,* p. 219. Both Bullard and Liggett became army commanders as the American Expeditionary Forces expanded in the fall of 1918.

24. O'Connor, *Black Jack Pershing;* Edward M. Coffman, *The War to End All Wars* (New York: Oxford University Press, 1968), p. 142; James C. Harbord, *The American Army in France, 1917–1919* (Boston: Little, Brown and Co., 1936), pp. 193–95.

25. Harbord, *The American Army in France;* O'Connor, *Black Jack Pershing,* pp. 220–22.

26. O'Connor, *Black Jack Pershing;* Harbord, *American Army in France,* 193–94; Hagedorn, *Leonard Wood,* II, 242–51, 267–94.

27. Hagedorn, *Leonard Wood,* p. 316.

28. Report of Inspection of 90th Division to the AG, Jan. 22, 1918, National Archives, RG 120, World War I Organization Records, 90th Division Historical File, Box 13.

29. William H. Johnston (acting division commander in Allen's absence) to John F. Morrison (Inspector General of the Army), Feb. 9, 1918, National Archives, RG 120, 90th Division Historical File, Box 2.

30. Pershing Papers, H.T.A. to J.J.P., March 1, 20, 1918, Box 9.

31. War Department, *Order of Battle,* p. 411; Monthly Training Progress Reports, Dec., 1917 to May, 1918, National Archives, RG 120, 90th Division Historical File, Box 13.

32. Wythe, *History of the 90th Division,* p. 3. Allen had several other aides, among them Sidney W. Fish, son of New York socialite Stuyvesant Fish.

33. Telegram, AG to Commanding General, 90th Division, 10:15 P.M., May 7, 1918, National Archives, RG 120, 90th Division Historical File, Box 3.

34. War Department, *Order of Battle,* p. 411; Wythe, *History of the 90th Division,* pp. 8–9.

35. Ayres, *Statistical Summary,* p. 33; Wythe, *History of the 90th Division,* p. 15.

36. Allen interview, 1970; Wythe, *History of the 90th Division,* pp. 14–15.

37. Wythe, *History of the 90th Division.* When the war began, the American Army had enough artillery for ten per cent of the forces it eventually mobilized. Because of tooling and manufacturing difficulties in the United States, American units were equipped with guns of French and British manufacture once they arrived in Europe. These guns were built from raw materials and component parts supplied by the United States. Much the same procedure was followed for trucks, tanks, and airplanes, though a higher percentage of these machines used by the A.E.F. were of American manufacture. Ayres, *Statistical Summary,* pp. 73–92.

38. Allen Papers, H.T.A. to D.J.A., July 12, 1918, Box 11.

39. *Ibid.* Frank Andrews, promoted to lieutenant colonel and transferred to the Signal Corps, was at this time stationed in California taking pilot training. After receiving his wings, he remained in the United States as a flight instructor for the duration. *Cullum's Register* VI B, 1247.

40. Allen interview, 1970.

41. Wythe, *History of the 90th Division,* pp. 15–17.

42. Allen Papers, H.T.A. to D.J.A., Aug. 12, 27, 1918, Box 11.

43. Wythe, *History of the 90th Division,* p. 17.

44. Report of the Inspection of the 90th Division, June 6–13, 1918, National Archives, RG 120, 90th Division Historical File, Box 16.

45. Wythe, *History of the 90th Division,* p. 17.

46. *Ibid.,* pp. 21–24. General Johnston left within a few days to take command of the 91st Division. Brigadier General Ulysses G. McAlexander replaced him. The 90th Division's artillery brigade completed its training in October but did not join its parent until after the armistice. The 90th Division thus fought all its battles with "borrowed" artillery support.

47. *Ibid.,* pp. 24–32.

48. *Ibid.,* pp. 32–33; John J. Pershing, *My Experiences in the World War,* 2 vols. (New York: Frederick A. Stokes Co., 1931), II, 259–66; Harvey A. De Weerd, *President Wilson Fights His War: World War I and the American Intervention* (New York: The Macmillan Co., 1968), pp. 330–35.

49. Wythe, *History of the 90th Division,* pp. 38–48.

50. "Brief History of the 90th Division," National Archives, RG 120, 90th Division Historical File, Box 1, p. 2; De Weerd, *Wilson Fights His War,* pp. 336–37.

51. De Weerd, *Wilson Fights His War,* pp. 339–44; Viner interview, 1970; Coffman, *The War to End All Wars,* pp. 229–306; Wythe, *History of the 90th Division,* pp. 63–73.

52. Wythe, *History of the 90th Division,* p. 199. Sources vary on the 90th's casualties. Wythe gives a total of 5,484 for all operations in the St.

Mihiel sector and a grand total of 9,710 as of Nov. 11, 1918. Ayres's *Statistical Summary,* p. 117, gives the latter figure as 7,277. However, the difference is almost exactly accounted for in the numbers given by Wythe for those gassed, missing, or captured, which probably were not included in Ayres's tabulation, labeled "dead and wounded."

53. Pershing Papers, H.T.A. to J.J.P., Sept. 30, 1918, Box 9.

54. Allen Papers, H.T.A. to D.J.A., Sept. 29, 1918, Box 11.

55. Wythe, *History of the 90th Division,* pp. 73–76.

56. *Ibid.,* pp. 77–86; Coffman, *War to End All Wars,* pp. 321–35; De Weerd, *Wilson Fights His War,* pp. 348–54.

57. Wythe, *History of the 90th Division,* pp. 88–94.

58. *Ibid.,* pp. 94–98.

59. Allen interview, 1970.

60. Pershing Papers, Memorandum: "For Commanders of all grades," attached to H.T.A. to J.J.P., Oct. 17, 1918, Box 9. Of Pershing's ruthlessness with his officers, Bullard said, "He is looking for results. He intends to have them. He will sacrifice any man who does not bring them." Coffman, *War to End All Wars,* p. 142.

61. Allen Papers, Allen's Diary, 1918, Nov. 4, Box 2; see also Oct. 26.

62. Wythe, *History of the 90th Division,* pp. 101–17.

63. Allen Papers, Allen's Diary, 1918, Nov. 4–6, Box 2.

64. Wythe, *History of the 90th Division,* pp. 117–29.

65. *Ibid.,* pp. 130–31.

66. *Ibid.,* p. 199.

67. Pershing Papers, H.T.A. to J.J.P., Nov. 21, 1918, Box 9.

68. *Ibid.,* H.T.A. to D.J.A., Nov. 29, 1918, Box 11. Wythe, *History of the 90th Division,* pp. xv, 180–82.

69. Wythe, *History of the 90th Division,* p. xvi.

70. Robert L. Bullard, *Fighting Generals* (Ann Arbor, Mich.: J. W. Edwards, 1944), p. 91.

71. *Ibid.,* p. 92.

72. *Ibid.*

73. *Cullum's Register* (1890), III, 390; (1900), IV, 408; (1910), V, 374–75; (1920), VI-A, 402–403.

74. *Ibid.,* p. 403.

75. Frederick Palmer, *Newton D. Baker: America at War,* 2 vols. (New York: Dodd, Mead and Co., 1931), II, 363; George S. Viereck, ed., *As They Saw Us* (Garden City, N.Y.: Doubleday, Doran and Co., Inc., 1929), pp. 84, 137.

76. Pershing, *Experiences,* I, 70–94; De Weerd, *Wilson Fights His War,* p. 216.

77. War Department, *Order of Battle,* pp. 299, 311, 349, 361, 403, 431.

78. Ayres, *Statistical Summary,* p. 331.

79. Wythe, *History of the 90th Division,* pp. 47–50.

80. Ayres, *Statistical Summary*, p. 33. Above on p. 204, it was stated that the 90th Division was the twenty-second division to reach Europe. Two of the divisions arriving ahead of the 90th became training depot units and did nothing but provide replacements to other divisions.

81. *Ibid.*, pp. 114–17.

82. *Cullum's Register* (1930), VIII, 225. Bullard retired in 1925.

Chapter X

1. Allen Papers, H.T.A. to D.J.A., Jun. 29, 1919, Box 11.

2. Robert S. Thomas, "The United States Army, 1914–1923" (draft ms. in OCMH files, Washington, D.C.), Part 3, pp. XX-17 to XX-24, contains a good account of the A.E.F.'s demobilization. The corps Allen commanded were the 8th, 9th, and 7th, in that order, from November 24, 1918, to May 24, 1919. His chief of staff for several months at 8th Corps was Colonel George C. Marshall. Allen described him as "brilliant." Allen Papers, Allen's Diary, 1919, Jan. 4, Box 2.

3. Allen Papers, H.T.A. to D.J.A., June 8, 14, 29, 1919, Box 11.

4. Henry T. Allen, *My Rhineland Journal* (Boston: Houghton Mifflin Co., 1929), pp. 6–11.

5. *Ibid.*, p. 9; Thomas, "U.S. Army," Part 3, p. XIX-36.

6. Thomas, "U.S. Army," Part 3, p. XIX-37. Relying on Pershing's "best judgment," Wilson accepted an agreement between the A.E.F. commander and Marshal Foch that the A.F.G. would be gradually reduced to a permanent strength of 6,500. Pershing Papers, Pershing's Diary, Jun. 27, 30, 1919, Box 4. For the reasons why the A.F.G.'s strength never stabilized at this figure, see pp. 226, 236, 244–45.

7. Pershing Papers, J.J.P. to H.T.A., Aug. 26, 1919, Box 9.

8. *Ibid.*, J.J.P. to D.J.A., Sept. 14, 1919.

9. Allen Papers, D.J.A. to G. (probably her sister Gertrude), Oct. 16, 1919, Box 11.

10. Both Allen's published diary and his papers are full of details about the constant stream of celebrities visiting Coblenz. See, for example, his *Rhineland Journal*, pp. 39, 61.

11. Allen interview, 1964.

12. Jere C. King, *Foch versus Clemenceau: France and German Dismemberment, 1918–19* (Cambridge, Mass.: Harvard University Press, 1960), p. 12.

13. *Ibid.*, pp. 3–11; United States Army, *American Military Government of Occupied Germany, 1918–20*, 4 vols. (Washington: Government Printing Office, 1943), I, 291–96. An earlier edition of this report was published in Coblenz in 1921 and is included in the Allen Papers, Boxes 59–62.

14. David Lloyd George, *The Truth about the Peace Treaties*, 2 vols. (London: V. Gollancz, Ltd., 1938), I, 384; W. M. Jordan, *Great Britain,*

France and the German Problem, 1918–1939 (London: Oxford University Press, 1943), pp. 170–72.

15. Keith L. Nelson, "The First American Military Occupation of Germany, 1918–1923" (Ph.D. dissertation, University of California, Berkeley, 1965), pp. 9, 13.

16. Arno J. Mayer, *Political Origins of the New Diplomacy, 1917–1918* (New Haven: Yale University Press, 1959), pp. 313–28.

17. *Ibid.*, pp. 329–67.

18. Nelson, "First American Military Occupation," p. 9.

19. *Ibid.*, pp. 14–15.

20. *Ibid.*, J.J.P. to E. M. House, Oct. 30, 1918, cited, p. 29.

21. Louis L. Snyder, ed., *Documents of German History* (New Brunswick, N.J.: Rutgers University Press, 1958), pp. 368–69.

22. Thomas, "U.S. Army," Part 3, pp. XIX-14 to XIX-21.

23. Philip M. Burnett, *Reparations at the Paris Peace Conference from the Standpoint of the American Delegation*, 2 vols. (New York: Columbia University Press, 1940), I, 94–95; Nelson's "First American Military Occupation," pp. 112–54, contains an excellent discussion of the French security demands and the complex and interrelated negotiations over reparations and the Rhineland.

24. *Ibid.*, pp. 131–41, 153.

25. *Ibid.*, p. 155.

26. King, *Foch vs. Clemenceau*, pp. 75–78; Pierrepont B. Noyes, *While Europe Waits for Peace* (New York: The Macmillan Co., 1921), pp. 51–57.

27. Nelson, "First American Military Occupation," pp. 160–70.

28. *Ibid.*, pp. 171–74. The quoted material is from Noyes's diary, Jun. 12, 1919. Nelson has had access to Noyes's papers in possession of the family at Oneida, N.Y.

29. *Ibid.*, pp. 174–76, 186–94.

30. Henry Allen, *The Rhineland Occupation* (Indianapolis: Bobbs-Merrill Co., 1927), pp. 116–18. The text of the Rhineland Agreement is printed on pp. 299–305.

31. Arno J. Mayer, *Politics and Diplomacy of Peacemaking: Containment and Counterrevolution at Versailles, 1918–1919* (London: Weidenfeld and Nicolson, 1968), pp. 767–812; S. William Halperin, *Germany Tried Democracy: A Political History of the Reich from 1918 to 1933* (New York: W. W. Norton and Co., 1965), pp. 148–53.

32. U.S. Army, *American Military Government*, I, 1–23, 34–35.

33. Allen, *Rhineland Occupation*, p. 30.

34. U.S. Army, *American Military Government*, I, 1–23.

35. "Future Relations with Germany," *Literary Digest*, LXII (July 5, 1919), 21–24.

36. U.S., Congress, *Congressional Record,* First Session, LV (Sept. 24, 1919), 5849; *Nation,* CIX (Sept. 6, 1919), 323.

37. *New York Times,* Jun. 17, 1919, p. 20; *Boston Evening Transcript,* Jun. 26, 1919, p. 2.

38. Nelson, "First American Military Occupation," pp. 204–206, 234.

39. Of the twenty-four boxes of correspondence in the Allen Papers, thirteen contain letters dating from the occupation period.

40. Allen Papers, Stuyvesant Fish to H.T.A., July 8, 1919, Box 11. The wealthy banker and railroad magnate Fish was the father of one of Allen's wartime aides.

41. *Ibid.,* H.T.A. to S. Fish, Aug. 19, 1919.

42. *New York Times,* Jun. 17, 1919, p. 20.

43. Pershing Papers, H.T.A. to J.J.P., Sept. 23; Oct. 19, 1919, Box 9; Allen Papers, H.T.A. to Peyton C. March, Dec. 20, 1919, Box 11. Organization of the A.F.G. is in Thomas, "U.S. Army," Part 3, pp. XIX-37 to XIX-38.

44. Thomas, "U.S. Army," Part 3, pp. XIX-39 to XIX-41; Allen, *Rhineland Occupation,* pp. 136–37; *Review of the American Forces in Germany* (Coblenz: James G. Adams, 1921), p. 19. The latter item, published under A.F.G. auspices, is an unofficial summary of its organization and activities similar to a yearbook. *Review of A.F.G.* is in the possession of the family of Col. H. T. Allen, Jr.

45. *Review of A.F.G.,* pp. 19, 25; Allen interview, 1970. In World War II, Somervell became Chief of the Army Service Forces, responsible for all army logistics.

46. Perhaps a slight exaggeration, but see the photographs of Allen's troops in perfect ceremonial formation in Allen Papers, Box 68.

47. *Ibid.,* H.T.A. to Peyton C. March, Dec. 20, 1919, Box 11; P. C. March to H.T.A., May 11, 1920, Box 12; John L. Chamberlain to H.T.A., May 19, 1920, Box 13.

48. *Ibid.,* P. C. March to H.T.A., Jun. 17, 1920; Memorandum, "Inspection of Command," J. L. Chamberlain to H.T.A., Jul. 10, 1920; Newton D. Baker to H.T.A., Jul. 12, 1920.

49. *Ibid.,* H.T.A. to J.J.P., Sept. 12, 1921, Box 18; H.T.A. to J. G. Harbord, Oct. 7, 1921, Box 14.

50. Robert L. Bullard, *Fighting Generals* (Ann Arbor, Mich.: J. W. Edwards Co., 1944), p. 93.

51. *Review of A.F.G.,* pp. 35–41.

52. Allen Papers, H.T.A. to Senator J. C. W. Beckham, Feb. 12, 1920, Box 12.

53. Allen, *Rhineland Occupation,* pp. 81–85, 116–23.

54. *Ibid.,* pp. 119–21.

55. Allen Papers, H.T.A. to J.J.P., Jan. 17, 1920, Box 12.

56. Allen, *Rhineland Occupation,* pp. 121–22; Nelson, "First American Military Occupation," pp. 260–62.

57. *Ibid.*, Noyes's Diary, Jan. 24, 1920, quoted, p. 262.

58. Allen, *Rhineland Occupation*, p. 121.

59. P.B.N. to R.E.L., Jan. 9, 1920, National Archives, RG 59, Records of the Department of State, File 763.72119/8585.

60. Allen, *Rhineland Journal*, pp. 68–71.

61. *Ibid.*

62. Ernst Fraenkel, *Military Occupation and the Rule of Law: Occupation Government in the Rhineland, 1918–1923* (New York: Oxford University Press, 1944), pp. 190–91.

63. *Ibid.*, pp. 194–97.

64. *Ibid.*, pp. 81–91, 197.

65. Von Lersner to Clemenceau, Jan. 12, 1920, National Archives, RG 256, Records of the Department of State, File 185.1711/132.

66. U.S. Army, A.F.G., Assistant Chief of Staff, G-2, *American Representation in Occupied Germany, 1920–21*, 2 vols. (Coblenz, 1922), II, 11, 24–30; Pierrepont B. Noyes, *A Goodly Heritage* (New York: Rinehart, 1958), pp. 255–56.

67. Allen, *Rhineland Journal*, pp. 122–23, 400, 482–83.

68. Nelson, "First American Military Occupation," Noyes's Diary, Feb. 9, 1920, quoted, p. 262.

69. *Ibid.*, pp. 264–65. Quote is from letter, cited by Nelson, P.B.N. to Colonel David Stone (Allen's assistant with the I.R.H.C.), Feb. 6, 1920.

70. *Ibid.*, p. 265.

71. P.B.N. to Acting Secretary of State, Mar. 6, 1920, in U.S., Department of State, *FRUS, 1920* II, 296.

72. H. C. Wallace to Bainbridge Colby, Mar. 19, 1920; E. L. Dresel to B. Colby, Mar. 23; Apr. 2, 1920, all in the National Archives, RG 59, Records of the Department of State, File nos. 862t.01/9/14/28.

73. Allen Papers, H.T.A. to N.D.B., Mar. 29, 1920, Box 12.

74. Halperin, *Germany Tried Democracy*, pp. 168–88; Koppel S. Pinson, *Modern Germany: Its History and Civilization* (New York: The Macmillan Co., 1961), pp. 407–10.

75. Allen, *Rhineland Occupation*, pp. 168–69.

76. Nelson, "First American Military Occupation," Noyes's Diary, Apr. 18, 28, 1920, quoted, p. 271.

77. *Ibid.*

78. *Ibid.*, p. 273.

79. P.B.N. to B.C., April 23, 1920, National Archives, RG 59, Records of the Department of State, File 763.72119.

80. Nelson, "First American Military Occupation," Noyes's Diary, May 23, 1920, quoted, p. 274.

81. Allen, *Rhineland Journal*, p. 122.

82. Allen Papers, H.T.A. to Ellis L. Dresel, Jun. 4, 1920, Box 13.

83. *Ibid.*, H.T.A. to Hunter Liggett, Jun. 14, 1920.

84. *Ibid.*, H.T.A. to N.D.B., May 25, 1920.

85. *Ibid.*

86. *Ibid.*, H.T.A. to N.D.B., Aug. 10, 1920, Box 14.

87. *Ibid.*, H.T.A. to L.W., Sept. 14, 1920. During the summer and fall of 1920 Allen began to hear from mutual friends that if Wood became Harding's Secretary of War he (Allen) was Wood's choice for Chief of Staff. However, the subject was never mentioned in the correspondence between the two generals. See: H.T.A. to L.W., Jun. 21, 1920, Box 13; and H.T.A. to F. Wiborg, Aug. 20, 1920; W. H. Harts to H.T.A., Oct. 11, 1920; and H.T.A. to L.W., Oct. 22, 1920, Box 14.

88. Nelson, "First American Military Occupation," pp. 280–83.

89. William E. Leuchtenburg, *The Perils of Prosperity, 1914–32* (Chicago: University of Chicago Press, 1958), p. 88.

90. *New York Times,* Oct. 8, 1920, pp. 1–2.

91. Thomas A. Bailey, *Woodrow Wilson and the Great Betrayal* (New York: The Macmillan Co., 1945), pp. 327–31.

92. Keith L. Nelson, "The 'Black Horror on the Rhine': Race as a Factor in Post World War I Diplomacy," *The Journal of Modern History,* XLII (Dec., 1970), 614–17.

93. *Ibid.*, p. 617. Allen's report is printed in his *Rhineland Occupation,* pp. 319–22.

94. Nelson, "First American Military Occupation," Dudley F. Malone to Woodrow Wilson, Oct. 18, 1920, quoted, p. 289.

95. *Ibid.*, pp. 290–91.

96. *Ibid.*, pp. 291–92. Yet, by the end of 1921, the A.F.G.'s strength was still 465 officers and 8,245 men. Allen, *Rhineland Occupation,* p. 130.

97. *New York Times,* March 9, 1921, p. 2.

98. Nelson, "First American Military Occupation," pp. 295–99.

99. See, for example, Allen's comments on British-American co-operation in his *Rhineland Journal,* pp. 20, 93; and in his *Rhineland Occupation,* p. 153. He got on less well personally with Arnold Robertson, Sir Harold Stuart's successor as commissioner.

100. Thomas, "U.S. Army," Part 3, pp. XIX-16 to XIX-18.

101. Nelson, "First American Military Occupation," pp. 63–69.

102. *Ibid.*, p. 68.

103. Pierrepont B. Noyes, *While Europe Waits for Peace* (New York: The Macmillan Co., 1921), pp. 51–57; Hunter Liggett, *Commanding an American Army: Recollections of the World War* (Boston: Houghton Mifflin Co., 1925), pp. 142–44.

104. Allen, *Rhineland Occupation,* pp. 24–27; Nelson, "First American Military Occupation," pp. 51–53, 75, 85.

105. Nelson, "First American Military Occupation," p. 83.

106. *Ibid.*, pp. 100–103; U.S. Army, *American Military Government,* III, 292–300.

107. Allen, *Rhineland Journal,* p. 137.

108. Noyes's report to Department of State, Mar. 16, 1921, National Archives, RG 59, Records of the Department of State, File No. 862t.01/245.

109. Allen, *Rhineland Occupation,* p. 322.

110. Allen interview, 1970.

111. Allen Papers, H.T.A. to J. C. Montgomery, Jan. 13, 1921, Box 16.

112. Allen interview, 1970. For other examples of French military displays in the American zone, see Allen Papers, H.T.A. to J.J.P., Jul. 28; Aug. 9, 1919, Box 11.

113. Allen Papers, H.T.A. to P. Tirard, Sept. 24, 1920; H.T.A. to T. Bliss, Oct. 9, 1920, Box 14.

114. Allen, *Rhineland Journal,* pp. 135–37; Allen, *Rhineland Occupation,* p. 218; Fraenkel, *Military Occupation and the Rule of Law,* p. 117.

115. H.T.A. to Charles E. Hughes, May 17; June 23, 1921, National Archives, RG 59, Records of the Department of State, File Nos. 862t.01/279/303; Allen, *Rhineland Journal,* pp. 186, 223.

116. Allen, *Rhineland Journal,* pp. 188–91; Nelson, "First American Military Occupation," pp. 252–54, 343–44; Allen, *Rhineland Occupation,* pp. 204–10.

117. Allen Papers, H.T.A. to D.J.A., Aug. 10, 1921, Box 18; Allen, *Rhineland Journal,* pp. 235–44.

118. U.S. Army, *American Representation in Occupied Germany,* II, 49. For examples of Allen's dealings with German officials, see his *Rhineland Journal,* pp. 122, 373–74.

119. *Ibid.,* pp. 178, 182, 192–95; U.S. Army, *American Representation in Occupied Germany,* I, 102–13.

120. Allen, *Rhineland Journal,* p. 291; Nelson, "First American Military Occupation," pp. 350–51.

121. *New York Times,* Oct. 23, 1921, p. 9.

122. Allen Papers, H.T.A. to J.J.P., Sept. 12; Nov. 20, 1921, Box 18; Allen, *Rhineland Journal,* pp. 331–32.

123. *Review of A.F.G.,* pp. 15, 315–430.

124. Allen interview, 1970.

125. Allen Papers, N. E. Margetts to H.T.A., Jun. 21, 1920, Box 13.

126. Allen, *Rhineland Journal,* pp. 268–69. In his *Military Occupation and the Rule of Law,* p. 158, Fraenkel comments on the unfortunate consequences of the occasional tendency of the I.R.H.C. to violate its own ordinances: "It was of little help that in average cases the occupation authorities observed the law satisfactorily. . . . One big case . . . overshadows the wisest application of the law in 1000 small cases."

127. Allen, *Rhineland Occupation,* pp. 325–32; H.T.A. to C. E. Hughes, Oct. 2, 1922, National Archives, RG 59, Records of the Department of State, File No. 862t.01/458; U.S. Army, *American Representation in Occupied Germany, 1922–23,* pp. 156–61; Allen, *Rhineland Journal,* pp. 284–86, 291.

128. Allen, *Rhineland Journal,* pp. 297–300.

129. *Ibid.,* pp. 385, 391.

130. Nelson, "First American Military Occupation," pp. 312–14.

131. *Ibid.,* pp. 321–23.

132. Allen Papers, J. G. Harbord to H.T.A., April 21, 1922, Box 19; May 29, 1922, Box 20; Allen's Diary, 1922, April 17; May 18, 21, Box 3.

133. Memorandum to C. E. Hughes from William Phillips, May 27, 1922, National Archives, RG 59, Records of the Department of State, File no. 862t. 01/412. Phillips, the former Ambassador to Belgium and a supporter of the A.F.G., had become Undersecretary of State. For the source of much of Phillips' information, see Allen Papers, Manton Davis (Allen's legal advisor on the I.R.H.C.) to W.P., Apr. 13, 1922, Box 19.

134. C. E. Hughes to A. B. Houghton (U.S. Ambassador to Berlin), Jun. 3, 1922, in *FRUS: 1922,* II, 218.

135. *New York Times,* May 5, 1922, p. 16.

136. Allen, Viner interviews, 1970.

137. Allen Papers, J. W. Viner to F. B. Wiborg, Jan. 6, 1920; H.T.A. to F. B. Wiborg, Feb. 1, 1920, Box 12.

138. *Ibid.,* H.T.A. to J. G. Harbord, Jun. 19, 1921, Box 17.

139. Memorandums by Hughes of conversations with Ambassador Jusserand, Dec. 14, 1922, in *FRUS: 1922,* II, 187; and Jan. 8, 1923 in *FRUS: 1923,* II, 47.

140. Allen, *Rhineland Journal,* p. 507; Nelson, "First American Military Occupation," p. 414.

141. "End of Our Watch on the Rhine," *Literary Digest,* LXXVI (Feb. 17, 1923), 22.

142. A. B. Houghton to C. E. Hughes, Jan. 29, 1923, National Archives, RG 59, Records of the Department of State, File no. 862t.01/618.

143. Allen, *Journal,* pp. 514–15.

144. *FRUS: 1923,* II, 51, H.T.A. to C.E.H., Jan. 12, 1923.

145. *Ibid.,* p. 52; Nelson, "First American Military Occupation," pp. 421–22.

146. In his introduction to *The Rhineland Occupation,* Allen said: "Neither the State Department nor the War Department saw fit to burden its representative with matters of policy; but as there was no adverse criticism of the frequent reports of his acts and decisions as they occurred, it must be assumed that both were satisfied." Underlings in both departments kept Allen informed as best they could (one confided to him that no one in Washington was expert enough on European affairs to advise him) but Allen received only a few vaguely worded answers to his bi-weekly reports from the Secretaries of State and War. See Allen's *Rhineland Journal,* pp. 321, 331, 362. Typical of the information and guidance he did receive are: Allen Papers, W. Phillips to H.T.A., Jun. 3; Jul. 26; Aug. 23; Sept. 3; Dec. 2, 1923; J. G. Harbord to H.T.A., Sept. 18, 1922; and J. W. Weeks to H.T.A., Dec. 16, 1922, all in Box 20.

147. H.T.A. to C.E.H., Jan. 18, 1923, National Archives, RG 59, Records of the Department of State, File no. 862t.01/657.

148. Allen, *Rhineland Journal*, pp. 537–38.

149. *New York Times*, Jan. 26, 1923, p. 3; and Feb. 8, 1923, pp. 1, 10.

150. Allen Papers, W. Phillips to H.T.A., Dec. 2, 1922, Box 20.

151. Allen, *Rhineland Occupation*, pp. 334–35.

152. Allen Papers, Ferris Greenslet to H.T.A., Dec. 24, 1921, Box 18; Allen, *Rhineland Occupation*, p. 245.

153. Allen, *Rhineland Occupation*, p. 245.

154. Allen Papers, "The Return of General Allen," *New York World*, Feb. 23, 1923, clipping in Box 21. See Nelson, "First American Military Occupation," pp. 418–20, for a discussion of newspaper comment on the A.F.G.'s withdrawal.

155. See the numerous speaking invitations, programs, lecture notes, etc., in the Allen Papers, March, 1923, folder, Box 21, and April and May folders, Box 22.

156. *Ibid.*, Telegrams and letters of commendation in April, 1923, folder. Collection of newspaper clippings and photographs of General Allen's retirement in possession of the family of Col. H. T. Allen, Jr.

Chapter XI

1. Allen Papers, Allen's Diary, 1923, Apr. 17; Jun. 25, Box 4; Charles A. Robinson to H.T.A., Apr. 27, 1923, Box 22; John Daniels to H.T.A., Jan. 5, 1925, Box 23; John H. Hammond to H.T.A., Jan. 20, 1926, Box 23; Anna Selig to H.T.A., March 14, 1927, Box 24.

2. *Ibid.*, H.T.A. to L. Hollingsworth Wood, Apr. 10, 1923, Box 22.

3. *Ibid.*, Allen's Diary, 1923, Jul. 2, 6, Box 4.

4. *Ibid.*, Jul. 23, 24; H.T.A. to C. E. Hughes, Jul. 24; C.E.H. to H.T.A., Jul. 26, Box 22.

5. *Ibid.*, Allen's Diary, 1923, Aug. 16, 17, Box 4.

6. *Ibid.*, J.F.D. to H.T.A., Aug. 18, 1923, Box 22.

7. *Ibid.*, C.E.H. to H.T.A., Aug. 17, 1923.

8. *Washington Star*, Aug. 18, p. 7; *New York Times*, Aug. 19, p. 6; also Allen Papers, undated clipping from *Washington Post*, Box 22.

9. Allen Papers, AG to H.T.A., Sept. 6, 1923.

10. *Ibid.*

11. *Ibid.*, Allen's Diary, 1923, Sept. 9, Box 4.

12. *Ibid.*, H.T.A. to Irving T. Bush, Apr. 23, Box 22.

13. *Ibid.*, Allen's Diary, 1923, Jun. 26, Box 4.

14. *Ibid.*, Wilbur K. Thomas to H.T.A., Oct. 21, 1924, Box 22.

15. *Boston Evening Globe*, Feb. 25, 1924, p. 12.

16. *Ibid.*

17. See in the Allen Papers the series of letters between H.T.A. and

Roger L. Scaife and H.T.A. and Newton Feussle from March through May, 1923, in Boxes 21 and 22. Excerpts from Allen's *Rhineland Journal* were also printed in *Collier's*. Henry T. Allen, "What I Saw on the Rhine," *Collier's*, LXXII (Oct. 6, 1923), 5–6, and (Oct. 13, 1923), 16.

18. Allen Papers, J. C. Taufflieie to H.T.A., undated but probably *ca.* late 1923, and undated fragment from Paul Tirard to H.T.A., Box 22. Although Tirard was upset by what Allen had revealed in his *Rhineland Journal*, he evidently bore no personal grudge. His *La France sur le Rhin: douze années d'occupation rhénane* (Paris: Plon, 1930), pp. 219–20, contains a flattering description of Allen's accomplishments in Coblenz.

19. Allen Papers, Le Vert Coleman to H.T.A., Sept. 2, 1924, Box 22; Keith L. Nelson, "First American Military Occupation, 1918–1935" (Ph.D. dissertation, University of California, Berkeley, 1965), p. 432. Five thousand copies of Allen's *Rhineland Journal* were sold in the German edition as against sales of less than 4,000 in the United States. Allen Papers, F. Greenslet to H.T.A., Oct. 22, 1924, Box 22.

20. Allen Papers, H.T.A. to M. T. Herrick, Mar. 10, 1924.

21. *Ibid.*, Allen's Diary, 1924, Mar. 6, Box 4; Nelson, "First American Military Occupation," p. 431.

22. Allen Papers, William H. Short to H.T.A., Sept. 26, 1924, Box 22. In early 1919, Allen had written to Pershing to say that he endorsed the League of Nations "even to the limit of World Government." Pershing Papers, H.T.A. to J.J.P., Feb. 24, 1919, Box 9.

23. Typical of Allen's correspondence with these organizations are: Allen Papers, Fred B. Smith to H.T.A., Oct. 18, 1927; and George G. Battle to H.T.A., Oct. 18, 1927, Box 24.

24. *Ibid.*, H.T.A. to Stuyvesant Fish, Aug. 19, 1919, Box 11.

25. *Ibid.*, undated *New York Times* clipping, *ca.* May, 1926, Box 23; Gretchen D. Cunningham to H.T.A., Apr. 4, 1928, Box 24.

26. *Ibid.*, *New York Times* clipping, Jul. 1, 1928.

27. See *ibid.* the series of letters between H.T.A. and Herbert S. Houston from August 12, 1924 to May 8, 1929, in Boxes 22 through 25.

28. See *ibid.* the series of letters between H.T.A. and D. L. Chambers, and H.T.A. and Anne Johnston from May 25, 1926, to February 10, 1928, in Boxes 23 and 24.

29. *Ibid.*, Allen's Diary, 1894, Sept. 28, 29, Box 1.

30. *Ibid.*

31. Wood's unsuccessful campaign for the 1920 Republican Presidential nomination is described in Hermann Hagedorn, *Leonard Wood: A Biography*, 2 vols. (New York: Harper and Brothers, 1931), II, 331–359.

32. Allen Papers, Allen's Diary, 1923, Oct. 11, Box 4.

33. *Ibid.*, R.S.M. to H.T.A., Feb. 25, 1924, Box 25.

34. *Ibid.*, H.T.A. to R.S.M., Mar. 10, 1924, Box 22; Allen's Diary, 1924, Mar. 6, 9, 11, 30; Apr. 10, Box 4.

35. *Ibid.*, E.M.H. to R.S.M., Mar. 23, 1924, Box 22.

36. *Ibid.*, F.D.R. to R.S.M., Mar. 31, 1924.

37. *Ibid.*, R.S.M. to H.T.A., Mar. 27; Apr. 11, 1924.

38. Arthur S. Link and William B. Catton, *American Epoch: A History of the United States since the 1890's*, 2nd ed. (New York: Alfred A. Knopf, 1963), pp. 320–21.

39. Allen Papers, R.S.M. to H.T.A., Jul. 10, 1924, Box 22.

40. *Ibid.*, H. D. Kissinger to H.T.A., Jul. 12, 1924.

41. *Ibid.*, H.T.A. to E. K. Howe, Oct. 21, 1924.

42. Link and Catton, *American Epoch*, p. 322.

43. See, for example, in Allen Papers, Mrs. J. W. Nicholson (President of National Woman's Democratic Law Enforcement League) to H.T.A., Aug. 15, 1927, Box 24.

44. *Ibid.*, Allen's Diary, 1927, Aug. 21; Nov. 9, 22, Box 4.

45. *Ibid.*, F. B. Wiborg to H.T.A., Mar. 14, 19, 1928, Box 24.

46. *Ibid.*, Allen's Diary, 1928, Feb. 5 to Mar. 18, Box 4.

47. Allen interview, 1964. Newspaper photograph of Allen and Noonan, together with a group of Democratic coworkers, in *New York Herald Tribune*, Aug. 14, 1928, p. 9.

48. See the office memos between H.T.A. and Noonan and their correspondence with potential backers and contributors to Allen's campaign, Allen Papers, May–Jun., 1928, Box 24.

49. *Ibid.*, press release, and clippings from the *New York Times* and *Washington Post*, all dated Jun. 11, 1928.

50. *Ibid.*, additional press releases, form letters, and mailing list.

51. *Ibid.*, H.T.A. to Wade Cooper, Jun. 28, 1928.

52. Link and Catton, *American Epoch*, p. 361.

53. Copy of nominating speech in possession of the family of Colonel H. T. Allen, Jr.

54. Allen Papers, clippings, newspaper unidentified, Jul. 5, 1928, Box 24.

55. Allen Papers, *New York Herald Tribune*, Aug. 14, 1928, p. 9. N.D.B. to H.T.A., Sept. 14, 1928, Box 24.

56. *Ibid.*, N. F. Keller to H.T.A., Dec. 8, 1925, Box 23.

57. Allen, Viner interviews, 1970.

58. Henry T. Allen, "Marshal Foch's Achievements as a Military Commander," *Current History*, XXX (Aug., 1924), 797–810; "The Philippines; America's Duty to Retain Control," *Current History*, XXXII (May, 1930), 277–83; *New York Herald Tribune*, Sept. 1, 1929, Sec. III, p. 1, and Sept. 8, 1929, Sec. II, p. 11.

59. Allen interview, 1964.

60. *Ibid.*, obituary in the *Washington Post*, Aug. 30, 1930, p. 1.

Epilogue

1. Morgan B. Sherwood, *Exploration of Alaska, 1865–1900* (New Haven, Conn.: Yale University Press, 1965), pp. 115–17.

2. Harold H. Elarth, ed., *The Story of the Philippine Constabulary* (Los Angeles: Globe Printing Co., 1949), pp. 98–139.

3. Keith L. Nelson, "The First American Military Occupation of Germany, 1918–1935" (Ph.D. dissertation, University of California, Berkeley, 1965), p. 436.

4. Royal J. Schmidt, *Versailles and the Ruhr: Seedbed of World War II* (The Hague: Martinus Nijhoff, 1968).

5. Morris Janowitz, *The Professional Soldier: A Social and Political Portrait* (New York: The Free Press, 1965), pp. 215–55, contains a thorough discussion of the traditional military code of honor, self-image, and attitude toward politics.

6. *Ibid.*, p. 388.

7. Pershing Papers, J.J.P. to Robert C. Davis, Feb. 6, 1924, Box 58.

APPENDIX

1. The appendix is based on Henry T. Allen, "Notes on Promotion"; Malin Craig, Jr., "History of the Officer Efficiency Report System, 1775–1917," draft ms. in files of OCMH, Washington, D.C.; Jay B. Durst, "Promotion and Assignment in the U.S. Army: An Historical Survey of the System of Efficiency Evaluation," draft ms., OCMH; File 210.2, Officers' Promotion Systems, OCMH; Samuel P. Huntington, *The Soldier and the State: The Theory and Politics of Civil Military Relations* (Cambridge, Mass.: Harvard University Press, 1957), pp. 222–54; Morris Janowitz, *The Professional Soldier* (New York: The Free Press, 1965), pp. 54–172; Maurice Matloff, ed., *American Military History*, Army Historical Series, OCMH (Washington: Government Printing Office, 1969), pp. 287–90.

Bibliography

A. Primary Sources

1. Published Public Documents

Allen, Henry T. "Atnatanas; Natives of Copper River, Alaska," *Annual Report of the Board of Regents of the Smithsonian Institution for the Year Ending June 30, 1886*, pp. 258–66. Washington: Government Printing Office, 1889.

——. *Cavalry Notes*. Washington: Government Printing Office, 1911.

——. *Report of an Expedition to the Copper, Tanana, and Koyukuk Rivers in the Territory of Alaska in the Year 1885*. Washington: Government Printing Office, 1887.

——. *The Military System of Sweden*. Washington: Government Printing Office, 1896.

Ayres, Leonard P. *The War with Germany: A Statistical Summary*. Washington: Government Printing Office, 1919.

Glenn, Edwin F. and W. R. Abercrombie. *Reports of Explorations in the Territory of Alaska, 1898*. Washington: Government Printing Office, 1899.

Heitman, Francis B. *Historical Register and Dictionary of the United States Army From Its Organization Sept. 29, 1789 to March 2, 1903*. Washington: Government Printing Office, 1903.

Kreidberg, Marvin A. and Merton G. Henry. *History of Military Mobilization in the United States Army*. Washington: Government Printing Office, 1955.

Philippine Commission. *Reports of the Philippine Commission to the President*. Washington: Government Printing Office, 1901–1907.

Philippine Constabulary. *Manual for Philippine Constabulary*. Manila: Bureau of Printing, 1915.

Schwatka, Frederick. *Report of a Military Reconnaissance in Alaska Made in 1883*. Washington: Government Printing Office, 1885.

Taft, William H. *Special Report to the President on the Philippines, January 28, 1908*. Washington: Government Printing Office, 1919.

United States, Army, American Expeditionary Forces, General Staff, G-2, *Press Review*. N.p., 1917–19.

United States, Army, American Forces in Germany, Assistant Chief of Staff, G-2. *American Representation in Occupied Germany, 1920–23*, 4 vols. Coblenz, 1923.

United States, Congress, House of Representatives. *Bibliographical Directory of the American Congress, 1774–1961*. Washington: Government Printing Office, 1961.

——. *Conditions in the Philippine Islands: Report of the Special Mission to the Philippine Islands to the Secretary of War*. Washington: Government Printing Office, 1922.

United States, Congress, Senate, Committee on Military Affairs. *Compilation of Narratives of Explorations of Alaska*. Washington: Government Printing Office, 1900.

——. *Hearings Before the Committee on the Philippines*. Washington: Government Printing Office, 1902.

——. *Trials or Courts-Martial in the Philippine Islands in Consequence of Certain Instructions*. Washington: Government Printing Office, 1902.

United States, Interior Department. *Annual Report of the Secretary of the Interior*. Washington: Government Printing Office (for years 1882–83, 1907–09).

United States Military Academy. *Official Register of Officers and Cadets*. West Point, N.Y.: USMA (for years 1879–1882).

——. *Register of Graduates, 1963*. West Point Alumni Association, Inc., 1963.

——. *Regulations*, 1880. West Point, N.Y.: USMA, 1880.

——. *The Centennial of the United States Military Academy at West Point, New York, 1802–1902*. Washington: Government Printing Office, 1904.

United States, State Department. *Papers Relating to the Foreign Relations of the United States*. Washington: Government Printing Office (for years 1916–1923).

United States, War Department. *American Military Government of Occupied Germany, 1918–1920*, 4 vols. Washington: Government Printing Office, 1943.

——. *Annual Report of the Secretary of War*. Washington: Government Printing Office (for years 1879–1923).

——. *Annual Report of the Superintendent, USMA*. Washington: Government Printing Office (for years 1878–1882, 1888–1889).

——. *Correspondence Relating to the War with Spain and Conditions Growing out of Same, Including the Insurrection in the Philippine Islands and the China Relief Expedition, Between the Adjutant General of the Army and Military Commanders in the United States, Cuba, Puerto Rico, China, and the Philippine Islands, from April 15, 1898 to July 30, 1902*, 2 vols. Washington: Government Printing Office, 1902.

——. *Report of the Military Governor of the Philippine Islands, 1899–1900*, 3 vols. Washington: Government Printing Office, 1900.

——. *Report on Operations of the United States Relief Commission in Europe*. Washington: Government Printing Office, 1914.

United States, War Department, Adjutant General's Office. *General Orders, 1882*. Washington: Government Printing Office, 1883.

——. *Official Army Register*. Washington: Government Printing Office (for years 1882–1923).

United States, War Department, Army War College Historical Section. *Order of Battle of the United States Land Forces in the World War: American Expeditionary Forces—Divisions*. Washington: Government Printing Office, 1931.

United States, War Department, Battle Monuments Commission. *90th Division Summary of Operations in the World War*. Washington: Government Printing Office, 1944.

United States, War Department, Military Information Division. *Reports of Military Observers Attached to the Armies in Manchuria During the Russo-Japanese War*. Washington: Government Printing Office, 1906.

United States, War Department, Quartermaster General's Office. *Outline Description of Military Posts in the United States and Alaska*. Washington: Government Printing Office, 1904.

2. Official Public Records

Bath County, Kentucky, "Will Book F." County Courthouse, Owingsville, Ky.

General Headquarters, Allied Expeditionary Forces, G-3 Map Room, *Divisional History Charts (1919)*. Office, Chief of Military History, Washington, D.C.

"Narrative Report of the Operations of the 11th Cavalry in Mexico." In files of Office, Chief of Military History, Washington, D.C.

National Archives, Record Group 48: General Records of the Department of the Interior. Records Relating to National Parks and Monuments, 1872–1915.

——, Record Group 59: General Records of the Department of State. Diplomatic Correspondence, 1789–1906; Despatches, 1789–1906; The Role of American Forces in Germany (AFG) as a Moderating Influence in Franco-German Relations, 1920–1923; Records Relating to Internal Affairs of Germany, 1910–1929.

——, Record Group 79: Records of the National Park Service. General Correspondence, 1907–1925.

——, Record Group 94: Records of the Adjutant General's Office. Records of the "Book Period," 1800–1889; Records of the "Record Card Period," 1890–1917; Decimal Files, 1917–1935; Rolls, Returns and Other Records of the Regular and Volunteer Armies, 1789–1912; Reports Made by Officers, 1895–1917; Records Relating to the United States Military Academy, 1803–1917; History of the Philippine Insurrection.

——, Record Group 107: Records of the Office of the Secretary of War. Correspondence, 1890–1914.

——, Record Group 108: Records of the Headquarters of the Army. Records, 1827–1903.

——, Record Group 111: Records of the Office of the Chief Signal Officer. Photographs, 1861–1923.

——, Record Group 120: Records of the American Expeditionary Forces, 1917–1921. Records of the Services of Supply and of Troop Organizations, 1912–1922; Records of American Forces in Germany, 1919–1923, G-2 Reference and Historical File.

——, Record Group 126: Records of the Division of Territories and Island Possessions. General Files of the Bureau of Insular Affairs, 1898–1939; Other Records of the Bureau of Insular Affairs, 1899–1937.

——, Record Group 165: Records of the War Department General Staff. Records of the Office of the Chief of Staff, 1903–1921; Records of the Army War College, 1903–1919.

——, Record Group 256: Records of the American Commission to Negotiate Peace.

——, Record Group 393: Records of the United States Army Continental Commands, 1821–1920.

Officer Promotion Systems, File 210.2, Office, Chief of Military History, Washington, D.C.

United States, Department of Commerce, Bureau of the Census. "Eighth Census of the United States, 1860: Kentucky, Free Inhabitants," II.

——. "Eighth Census of the United States, 1860: Kentucky, Slaves," I.

United States Military Academy. "Register of Delinquencies, 1877–1882." USMA Archives, West Point, N.Y.

——. "Staff Records," X. USMA Archives, West Point, N.Y.

3. *Books and Articles*

Allen, Henry T. "Allen," *Register of the Kentucky State Historical Society*, XXVIII. Frankfort, Ky.: The State Journal Co., Jan., 1930.

——. "Effect of Germany's Industrial Condition." *Annals of the American Academy of Political Science*, CXIV (Jul., 1924), 7–9.

——. "A Hundred Versts Race." *Journal of the United States Cavalry Association*, VIII (Mar., 1895), 61–63.

——. "Instructions for Foot Combat in the Russian Army. *Journal of the United States Cavalry Association*, II (Dec., 1889), 364–67.

——. "Marshal Foch's Achievements as a Military Commander." *Current History*, XXX (Aug., 1929), 797–810.

——. *Mein Rheinland-Tagebuch*. Berlin: R. Hobbing, 1924.

——. "Mounted Cavalry in the Santiago Campaign." *Journal of the United States Cavalry Association,* XII (Dec., 1899), 357–71.

——. *My Rhineland Journal.* Boston: Houghton Mifflin Co., 1923.

——. "Notes on Promotion." *Journal of the Military Service Institution of the United States,* XXXVII (Jul., 1905), 1–7.

——. "The Philippines: America's Duty to Retain Control." *Current History,* XXXII (May, 1930), 277–83.

——. "Possibility of Disarmament—Necessity for United States Cooperation." *Annals of the American Academy of Political Science,* CXX (Jul., 1925), 65–66.

——. "Present Franco-German Situation." *Annals of the American Academy of Political Science,* CXXVI (Jul., 1926), 15–18.

——. "Proposed Reorganization for our Central Staff," *Journal of the Military Service Institution of the United States,* XXVII (Jul., 1900), 26–30.

——. *The Rhineland Occupation.* Indianapolis: Bobbs-Merrill Co., 1927.

——. "Saddles." *Journal of the United States Army Cavalry Association,* XIX (Jul., 1908), 185–87.

——. "We Must not Secede from the World." *Survey,* LII (Aug. 1, 1924), 487–89.

——. "What I Saw on the Rhine." *Collier's,* LXXII (Oct. 6, 1923), 5–6, and (Oct. 13, 1923), 16.

——. "Wolf Hunting in Russia." *Hunting in Many Lands,* ed. Theodore Roosevelt. New York: Forest and Stream Publishing Co., 1895, pp. 151–186.

Bullard, Robert L. *Personalities and Reminiscences of the War.* Garden City, N.Y.: Doubleday, Page and Co., 1925.

Commager, Henry S., ed. *Documents of American History,* 6th ed. New York: Appleton-Century-Crofts, 1928, II.

Dickman, Joseph T. *The Great Crusade: A Narrative of the World War.* New York: D. Appleton and Co., 1927.

Hagood, Johnson. *The Services of Supply: A Memoir of the Great War.* Boston: Houghton Mifflin Co., 1927.

Hoover, Herbert. *The Memoirs of Herbert Hoover: Years of Adventure, 1874–1920.* New York: The Macmillan Co., 1951.

Liggett, Hunter. *Commanding an American Army: Recollections of the World War.* Boston: Houghton Mifflin Co., 1925.

Miles, Nelson A. *Serving the Republic.* New York: Harper and Brothers, 1911.

Morison, Elting E., ed. *The Letters of Theodore Roosevelt,* 8 vols. Cambridge, Mass.: Harvard University Press, 1954.

Noyes, Pierrepont B. *A Goodly Heritage.* New York: Rinehart, 1958.

Pershing, John J. *My Experiences in the World War,* 2 vols. New York: Frederick A. Stokes Co., 1931.

Root, Elihu. *The Military and Colonial Policy of the United States, Addresses and Reports.* Cambridge, Mass.: Harvard University Press, 1916.

Scott, Hugh L. *Some Memories of a Soldier.* New York: The Century Co., 1928.

Stimson, Henry L., and McGeorge Bundy. *On Active Service in Peace and War.* New York: Harper and Brothers, 1948.

Strong, William E. *A Trip to the Yellowstone National Park in July, August and September, 1875,* ed. R. A. Bartlett. Norman, Okla.: University of Oklahoma Press, 1968.

White, Andrew D. *Autobiography of Andrew Dickson White.* New York: The Century Co., 1905.

Zabudski, N. "Resistance of the Air for Great Velocities of Projectiles," trans. H. T. Allen. *Journal of the United States Artillery,* V (May, 1896), 396–75.

4. *Unpublished Personal Papers, Correspondence, and Interviews*

Allen, Dora. "Life and Times of the Allen Children, 1888–1898." Ms. in possession of Mrs. J. W. Viner, Virginia Beach, Va.

Allen, Henry T. Papers. Library of Congress, Manuscript Division.

Baker, Newton D. Papers. Library of Congress, Manuscript Division.

Bliss, Tasker H. Papers. Library of Congress, Manuscript Division.

Collins, James L. Papers. Office, Chief of Military History, Washington, D.C.

Chamberlain, J. L. "Cadet Reminiscences of J. L. Chamberlain, USMA 1880." Ms. in Rare Book Room, USMA Library.

Forbes, William C. Journals (1904–07). Library of Congress, Manuscript Division.

Garrison, Lindley M. Papers. Princeton University Library, Princeton, N.J.

Harbord, James G. Papers. Library of Congress, Manuscript Division.

Hughes, Charles E. Papers. Library of Congress, Manuscript Division.

Morgan, G. H. "Diary of G. H. Morgan, USMA, 1880." Ms. in Rare Book Room, USMA Library.

Pershing, John J. Papers. Library of Congress, Manuscript Division.

Taft, William H. Papers. Library of Congress, Manuscript Division.

Wilcox, C. D. "Recollections of C. D. Wilcox, USMA 1885." Ms. in Rare Book Room, USMA Library.

Wood, Leonard. Papers. Library of Congress, Manuscript Division.

Correspondence and/or interviews *re* General Allen between the author and the following:

Mr. Horace M. Albright, Los Angeles, Calif.

Col. Henry T. Allen, Jr., Washington, D.C.

Dr. Richard A. Bartlett, Tallahassee, Fla.

Gen. J. Lawton Collins, Washington, D.C.

Gen. J. K. Crain, Washington, D.C.

Mr. Lander Crockett, Sharpsburg, Ky.
Mrs. William S. Culbertson, Washington, D.C.
Mr. Sherman Goodpaster, Owingsville, Ky.
Maj. Gen. Guy V. Henry, Washington, D.C.
Gen. John L. Hines, Washington, D.C.
Brig. Gen. Willard A. Holbrook, Washington, D.C.
Mr. J. Conway Hunt, Washington, D.C.
Maj. Gen. John L. Millikin, Washington, D.C.
Mr. Clark Ramey, Sharpsburg, Ky.
Col. and Mrs. Joseph W. Viner, Virginia Beach, Va.

5. *Maps*

Alaska and Adjoining Territory, 1/3,168,000. U.S. Coast and Geodetic Survey, 1884.

General Chart of Alaska, 1/3,600,000. U.S. Coast and Geodetic Survey, 1890.

United States, Army, Map Service. *Alaska,* 1:250,000, Series Q501.

United States, Geological Survey. *Maps and Descriptions of Routes of Exploration in Alaska in 1898, with General Information concerning the Territory.* Washington: U.S. Geological Survey, 1899.

B. SECONDARY WORKS

1. *Published Materials*

Ambrose, Stephen E. *Duty, Honor, Country: A History of West Point.* Baltimore: The Johns Hopkins Press, 1966.

Anderson, George S. "Work of the Cavalry in Protecting Yellowstone National Park," *Journal of the United States Cavalry Association,* X (Mar., 1897), 3–10.

Andrist, Ralph K. *The Long Death: The Last Days of the Plains Indians.* New York: Macmillan, 1962.

Anonymous (probably Henry T. Allen). "Chief of Cavalry." *Journal of the United States Cavalry Association,* XVIII (Jul., 1907), 158–62.

Anonymous. "Chief of Cavalry." *Journal of the United States Cavalry Association,* XVIII (Jan., 1908), 555–56, 564–66.

Anonymous. "Chief of Cavalry." *Journal of the United States Cavalry Association,* XIX (Jan., 1909), 703–704.

Arpee, Edward. *Lake Forest, Illinois—History and Reminiscences.* Chicago: R. R. Donnelly and Sons Co., 1964.

Baclagon, Uldarico S. *Philippine Campaigns.* Manila: Graphic House, 1952.

Bailey, Thomas A. *A Diplomatic History of the American People,* 7th ed. New York: Appleton-Century-Crofts, 1964.

——. *Woodrow Wilson and the Great Betrayal.* New York: The Macmillan Co., 1945.

Baker, Ray S. *Woodrow Wilson, Life and Letters.* Garden City, N.Y.: Doubleday and Co., Inc., 1936, VI.

Bartlett, Richard A. "Will Anyone Come Here for Pleasure?" *The American West,* VI (Sept., 1969), 10–16.

Beale, Howard K. *Theodore Roosevelt and the Rise of America to World Power.* Baltimore: Johns Hopkins Press, 1956.

Beisner, Robert L. *Twelve Against Empire: The Anti-Imperialists, 1898–1900.* New York: McGraw-Hill Co., 1968.

Bell, William G. "Society and Journal of the Mounted Arm." *Armor Magazine,* LXVII (Mar.–Apr., 1958), 4–9.

Bemis, Samuel F. *A Diplomatic History of the United States,* 3rd ed. New York: Henry Holt and Co., 1950.

Berthoff, Rowland T. "Taft and MacArthur, 1900: A Study of Civil Military Relations." *World Politics,* V (1953), 196–213.

Bethel, Elizabeth. "The Military Intelligence Division: Origin of the Intelligence Division," *Military Affairs,* XI (Spring, 1947), 17–24.

Brooks, Alfred Hulse. *Blazing Alaska's Trails.* Caldwell, Idaho: Published jointly by the University of Alaska and the Arctic Institute of North America, 1953.

Brooks, Sidney. *America and Germany, 1918–1925.* New York: The Macmillan Co., 1925.

Bullard, Robert L. *Fighting Generals.* Ann Arbor, Mich.: J. W. Edwards Co., 1944.

Burnett, Philip M. *Reparations at the Paris Peace Conference from the Standpoint of the American Delegation,* 2 vols. New York: Columbia University Press, 1940.

Cantwell, R. "Ultimate Confrontation." *Sports Illustrated,* XXX (Mar. 24, 1969), 66–70.

Caswell, John E. *Arctic Frontiers: United States Explorations in the Far North.* Norman, Okla.: University of Oklahoma Press, 1955.

Cavioli, Frank J. *West Point and the Presidency; the American Voter's Attitude toward the Military Elite.* New York: St. John's University Press, 1962.

Chittenden, Hiram M. *The Yellowstone National Park,* ed., R. A. Bartlett. Norman, Okla.: University of Oklahoma Press, 1964.

Clark, Herma N. *The Elegant Eighties—When Chicago Was Young.* Chicago: McClung and Co., 1941.

Cline, Howard F. *The United States and Mexico.* Cambridge, Mass.: Harvard University Press, 1953.

Coffman, Edward M. *The Hilt of the Sword—The Career of Peyton C. March.* Madison, Wis.: University of Wisconsin Press, 1966.

——. *The War to End All Wars.* New York: Oxford University Press, 1968.

Cramer, Clarence H. *Newton D. Baker, a Biography*. Cleveland: World Publishing Co., 1961.

Cullum's Biographical Register of the Officers and Graduates of the U.S. Military Academy, 9 vols. Various editors and publishers.

DeConde, Alexander. *A History of American Foreign Policy*. New York: Charles Scribner's Sons, 1963.

Deutrich, Mabel E. *Struggle for Supremacy: The Career of General Fred C. Ainsworth*. Washington: Public Affairs Press, 1962.

DeWeerd, Harvey A. *President Wilson Fights his War: World War I and the American Intervention*. New York: The Macmillan Co., 1968.

Disque, Brice P. "Chief of Cavalry," *Journal of the United States Cavalry Association*, XVIII (Apr., 1908), 779.

Downey, Fairfax, *Indian-Fighting Army*. New York: Charles Scribner's Sons, 1944.

Dunn, Robert. "With Pershing's Cavalry," *Collier's Weekly*, XXXI (Sept. 23, 1916), 7–9.

Ekirch, Arthur A. *The Civilian and the Military*. New York: Oxford University Press, 1956.

Elarth, Harold H., ed. *The Story of the Philippine Constabulary*. Los Angeles: Globe Printing Company, 1949.

Eliot, C. B. *The Philippines to the End of the Military Regime*. Indianapolis: The Bobbs-Merrill Company, 1917.

"End of Our Watch on the Rhine," *Literary Digest*, LXXVI (Feb. 17, 1923), 22.

Farley, Joseph P. *West Point in the Early Sixties*. Troy, N.Y.: Pafraets Book Co., 1902.

Finer, Samuel E. *The Man on Horseback; the Role of the Military in Politics*. New York: Frederick A. Praeger, Inc., 1962.

Fleming, Thomas J. "Pershing's Island War," *American Heritage*, XIX (Aug., 1968), 32–35, 101–104.

——. *West Point*. New York: William Morrow and Co., Inc., 1969.

Forbes, W. Cameron. *The Philippine Islands*, 2 vols. Boston: Houghton Mifflin Co., 1928.

Fraenkel, Ernst. *Military Occupation and the Rule of Law: Occupation Government in the Rhineland, 1918–1923*. New York: Oxford University Press, 1944.

Frazer, Robert W. *Forts of the Old West*. Norman, Okla.: University of Oklahoma Press, 1965.

Freidel, Frank B. *The Splendid Little War*. Boston: Little, Brown and Co., 1958.

Fuller, John F. C. *Decisive Battles: Their Influence Upon History and Civilization*. New York: Charles Scribner's Sons, 1940.

"Future Relations with Germany," *Literary Digest*, LXII (Jul. 5, 1919), 21–24.

"Geographic Notes," *National Geographic*, XIII (May, 1902), 181–82.

Glad, Betty. *Charles Evans Hughes and the Illusion of Innocence; A Study in American Diplomacy.* Urbana, Ill.: University of Illinois Press, 1966.

Grant, Bruce. *American Forts, Yesterday and Today.* New York: E. P. Dutton and Co., 1965.

Grenville, John A. S., and George B. Young. *Politics, Strategy and American Diplomacy: Studies in Foreign Policy 1873–1917.* New Haven: Yale University Press, 1966.

Grunder, G. A., and W. E. Livezey. *The Philippines and the United States.* Norman, Okla.: University of Oklahoma Press, 1951.

Hagedorn, Hermann. *Leonard Wood: A Biography,* 2 vols. New York: Harper and Brothers, 1931.

Halperin, S. William. *Germany Tried Democracy: A Political History of the Reich from 1918 to 1933.* New York: W. W. Norton and Co., 1965.

Hapgood, Isabel F. *Russian Rambles.* Boston: Houghton Mifflin Co., 1895.

Harbord, James G. *The American Army in France.* Boston: Little, Brown and Co., 1936.

Haynes, Jack E. "Yellowstone Stage Holdups," *Brand Book,* ed. Elvon L. Howe. Denver: Arthur Zeuch Printing, 1952, pp. 85–98.

Herr, John K., and Edward S. Wallace. *The Story of the U.S. Cavalry.* Boston: Little, Brown and Co., 1953.

Hicks, John D. *Republican Ascendancy, 1921–1933.* New York: Harper and Row, 1960.

Holborn, Hajo. *American Military Government: Its Organization and Policies.* Washington: Infantry Journal Press, 1947.

Hopkins, J. A. H., and M. Alexander. *Machine-Gun Diplomacy.* New York: Lewis Copeland Co., 1928.

Huntington, Samuel P. *The Soldier and the State: The Theory and Politics of Civil Military Relations.* Cambridge, Mass.: Harvard University Press, 1957.

Hurley, Victor. *Jungle Patrol.* New York: E. P. Dutton and Co., Inc., 1938.

Janowitz, Morris. *The Professional Soldier: A Social and Political Portrait.* New York: The Free Press, 1965.

Jenks, J. W. "The Philippine Constabulary and Its Chief," *Review of Reviews,* XXVI (Oct., 1902), 436–38.

Jessup, Philip C. *Elihu Root.* Hamden, Conn.: Archon Books, 1964.

Johnson, Virginia W. *The Unregimented General—A Biography of Nelson A. Miles.* Boston: Houghton Mifflin Co., 1962.

Jordan, W. M. *Great Britain, France and the German Problem, 1918–1939.* London: Oxford University Press, 1943.

King, Jere C. *Foch versus Clemenceau: France and German Dismemberment, 1918–19.* Cambridge, Mass.: Harvard University Press, 1960.

Leuchtenburg, William E. *The Perils of Prosperity, 1914–32.* Chicago: University of Chicago Press, 1958.

Lininger, C. *The Best War at the Time.* New York: Robert Speller & Sons, Publishers, Inc., 1964.

Link, Arthur S., and William B. Catton. *American Epoch: A History of the United States since the 1890's*, 2nd ed. New York: Alfred A. Knopf, 1963.

Link, Arthur S. *Wilson the Diplomatist: A Look at his Major Foreign Policies.* Baltimore: The Johns Hopkins Press, 1957.

Lloyd George, David. *The Truth About the Peace Treaties*, 2 vols. London: V. Gollancz, Ltd., 1938.

Marshall, S. L. A., and the editors of American Heritage. *The American Heritage History of World War I.* New York: American Heritage Publishing Co., 1964.

Mason, Herbert M. *The Great Pursuit.* New York: Random House, 1970.

Matloff, Maurice, ed. *American Military History*, Army Historical Series, Office, Chief of Military History. Washington: Government Printing Office, 1969.

May, Ernest R. *Imperial Democracy.* New York: Harcourt, Brace and World, 1961.

Mayer, Arno J. *Political Origins of the New Diplomacy, 1917–1918.* New Haven: Yale University Press, 1959.

——. *Politics and Diplomacy of Peacemaking: Containment and Counter-revolution at Versailles, 1918–1919.* London: Weidenfeld and Nicolson, 1968.

Millis, Walter, ed. *American Military Thought.* Indianapolis: Bobbs-Merrill, 1966.

Millis, Walter. *The Martial Spirit: A Study of Our War with Spain.* Cambridge, Mass.: Harvard University Press, 1931.

Moore, Edmund A. *A Catholic Runs for President, the Campaign of 1928.* New York: Ronald Press Co., 1956.

Morgan, H. Wayne. *America's Road to Empire: The War with Spain and Overseas Expansion.* America in Crisis series, ed., Robert A. Divine. New York: John Wiley and Sons, Inc., 1965.

Morison, Elting E. *Turmoil and Tradition: A Study of the Life and Times of Henry L. Stimson.* New York: Atheneum, 1964.

National Park Service. *Soldier and Brave: Military and Indian Affairs in the Trans-Mississippi West, Including a Guide to Historic Sites and Landmarks.* New York: Harper and Row, 1963.

Nelson, Keith L. "The 'Black Horror on the Rhine': Race as a Factor in Post World War I Diplomacy." *The Journal of Modern History*, XLII (Dec., 1970), 606–27.

Nelson, Otto L., Jr. *National Security and the General Staff.* Washington: Infantry Journal Press, 1946.

Nichols, Jeannette P. *Alaska, A History Under United States Rule.* Cleveland, Ohio: Arthur H. Clark Co., 1924.

Nowak, Karl F. *Germany's Road to Ruin*, tr. E. W. Dickes. New York: The Macmillan Co., 1932.

——. *Kaiser and Chancellor,* tr. E. W. Dickes. New York: The Macmillan Co., 1930.

Noyes, Pierrepont B. *While Europe Waits for Peace.* New York: The Macmillan Co., 1921.

O'Connor, Richard. *Black Jack Pershing.* Garden City, N.Y.: Doubleday and Co., Inc., 1961.

Palmer, Frederick. *Bliss, Peacemaker: The Life and Letters of General Tasker Howard Bliss.* New York: Dodd, Mead and Co., 1934.

——. *Newton D. Baker: America at War,* 2 vols. New York: Dodd, Mead and Co., 1931.

——. "Through the Hemp Country with General Kobbé," *Collier's Weekly,* XXV (Apr. 14, 1900), 10–11.

Palmer, John M. *America in Arms: The Experience of the United States with Military Organization.* New Haven: Yale University Press, 1941.

Pier, Arthur S. *American Apostles to the Philippines.* Boston: The Beacon Press, 1950.

Pinson, Koppel S. *Modern Germany: Its History and Civilization.* New York: The Macmillan Co., 1961.

Pogue, Forrest C. *George C. Marshall, Education of a General (1880–1939).* New York: Viking Press, 1963.

Powell, Theodore. *The Long Rescue.* Garden City, N.Y.: Doubleday and Co., Inc., 1960.

Pratt, Julius W. *America's Colonial Experiment.* New York: Prentice-Hall, 1950.

——. *Challenge and Rejection: The United States and World Leadership, 1900–1921.* New York: The Macmillan Co., 1967.

——. *The Expansionists of 1898.* Baltimore: Johns Hopkins Press, 1936.

Perkins, Whitney T. *The Denial of Empire: The United States and Its Dependencies.* Leyden: A. W. Sythoff, 1962.

Pringle, Henry F. *The Life and Times of William Howard Taft,* 2 vols. New York: Farrar and Rinehart, 1939.

——. *Theodore Roosevelt.* New York: Harcourt, Brace and Co., 1931.

Ranson, Edward. "Nelson A. Miles as Commanding General, 1895–1903," *Military Affairs,* XXIX (Winter, 1965–66), 179–200.

Reed, Hugh T. *Cadet Life at West Point.* Chicago: Hugh T. Reed, 1896.

Review of the American Forces in Germany. Coblenz: James G. Adams, 1921.

Richards, John A. *A History of Bath County, Kentucky.* Yuma, Ariz.: Southwest Printers, 1961.

Rickey, Don, Jr. *Forty Miles a Day on Beans and Hay.* Norman, Okla.: University of Oklahoma Press, 1963.

Sandos, James A. "German Involvement in Northern Mexico, 1915–1916: A New Look at the Columbus Raid," *The Hispanic American Historical Review,* L (Feb., 1970), 70–88.

Seton-Watson, Hugh. *The Decline of Imperial Russia, 1855–1914.* New York: Frederick A. Praeger, Inc., 1952.

Schmidt, Royal J. *Versailles and the Ruhr: Seedbed of World War II.* The Hague: Martinus Nijhoff, 1968.

Schott, Joseph L. *The Ordeal of Samar.* New York: Bobbs-Merrill Co., Inc., 1964.

Schwatka, Frederick. *A Summer in Alaska.* St. Louis, Mo.: J. W. Henry, 1893.

Sexton, William T. *Soldiers in the Sun.* Harrisburg, Pa.: Military Service Publishing Co., 1939.

Sherwood, Morgan B. *Exploration of Alaska, 1865–1900.* New Haven: Yale University Press, 1965.

Slosson, Preston W. *The Great Crusade and After, 1914–1928.* New York: The Macmillan Co., 1939.

Smythe, Donald. *Guerilla Warrior: The Early Life of John J. Pershing.* New York: Charles Scribner's Sons, 1973.

Spaulding, Thomas M. "Allen, Henry Tureman," *Dictionary of American Biography,* Harris E. Starr, ed., XXI, Supplement One. New York: Charles Scribner's Sons, 1944, pp. 22–23.

Stallings, Laurence. *The Doughboys: The Story of the AEF, 1917–1918.* New York: Harper and Row, 1963.

Stubbs, Valarie K. "U.S. Troops in Alaska, 1867–77," *Military Collector and Historian,* XII (Spring, 1960), 6–8.

Tardieu, André. *France and America.* Boston: Houghton Mifflin Co., 1927.

Tirard, Paul. *La France sur le Rhin: douze années d'occupation rhenane.* Paris: Plon, 1930.

Tompkins, Frank. *Chasing Villa: The Story Behind the Story of Pershing's Expedition into Mexico.* Harrisburg, Pa.: Military Service Publishing Co., 1934.

Toulman, Harry A., Jr. *With Pershing in Mexico.* Harrisburg, Pa.: The Military Service Publishing Co., 1935.

Vagts, Alfred. *The Military Attaché.* Princeton, N.J.: Princeton University Press, 1967.

Viereck, George S., ed. *As They Saw Us.* Garden City, N.Y.: Doubleday, Doran and Co., Inc., 1929.

Weigley, Russell F. *History of the United States Army.* New York: The Macmillan Co., 1967.

White, John R. *Bullets and Bolos.* New York: The Century Co., 1928.

White, Leonard D. *The Republican Era: A Study in Administrative History, 1869–1901.* New York: The Macmillan Co., 1958.

Wolff, Leon. *Little Brown Brother: How the United States Purchased and Pacified the Philippine Islands at the Century's Turn.* Garden City, N.Y.: Doubleday and Co., Inc., 1961.

Wythe, George. *A History of the 90th Division.* San Antonio, Texas: The De Vinne Press, 1920.

Young, V. B. *An Outline History of Bath County, 1811–1876; An Address Delivered July 4, 1876.* Owingsville. Ky.: Printcraft, 1946.

2. Unpublished Materials

Albright, John M. "A Vignette of Imperialism: The 11th Cavalry in the Philippines, 1901–1904." Draft ms. in files of Office, Chief of Military History, Washington, D.C.

——. "The Secretary of War and the Colorado Coal Strike." Draft ms. in files of Office, Chief of Military History, Washington, D.C.

Bartlett, Richard A. "The Five Ages of Yellowstone." Draft ms. history of Yellowstone National Park.

Bidwell, Bruce W. "History of the Military Intelligence Division, Department of the Army General Staff." Draft ms. in files of Office, Chief of Military History, Washington, D.C.

Brown, Richard C. "The Social Attitudes of American Generals, 1898–1930." Ph.D. dissertation, University of Wisconsin, 1951.

"Chronology of the Aztec Club" in possession of J. Conway Hunt, Washington, D.C.

Coats, George Y. "The Philippine Constabulary, 1901–1917." Ph.D. dissertation, Ohio State University, 1968.

Craig, Malin, Jr. "History of the Officer Efficiency Report System, 1775–1917." Draft ms. in files of Office, Chief of Military History, Washington, D.C., 1953.

Durst, Jay B. "Promotion and Assignment in the U.S. Army: An Historical Survey of the System of Efficiency Evaluation." Draft ms. in files of Office, Chief of Military History, Washington, D.C., 1955.

Foss, Peter J. "Power and Prominence Through Publicity: A Study of the Publicity Campaigns of General Leonard Wood." M.A. thesis, University of Wisconsin, 1968.

Gates, John M. "An Experiment in Benevolent Pacification: The U.S. Army in the Philippines, 1898–1902." Ph.D. dissertation, Duke University, 1967.

Hewes, James E. "Organization and Management of the Department of the Army, 1942–1962." Draft ms. in files of Office, Chief of Military History, Washington, D.C., 1971.

Huddle, Orlando E. "A History of Georgetown College." M.A. thesis, University of Kentucky, 1930.

Kerr, Mitchell W., "Dollars, Sense, and Politics," draft ms. history of U.S. foreign policy after World War I, Chapter XVIII.

Nelson, Keith L. "The First American Military Occupation of Germany, 1918–1923." Ph.D. dissertation, University of California, Berkeley, 1965.

Thomas, Robert S., and Inez V. Allen. "The Mexican Punitive Expedition under Brigadier General John J. Pershing, United States Army." Draft ms. in files of Office, Chief of Military History, Washington, D.C., 1954.

Thomas, Robert S. "The United States Army, 1914–1923." Draft ms. in files of Office, Chief of Military History, Washington, D.C., no date.

Index

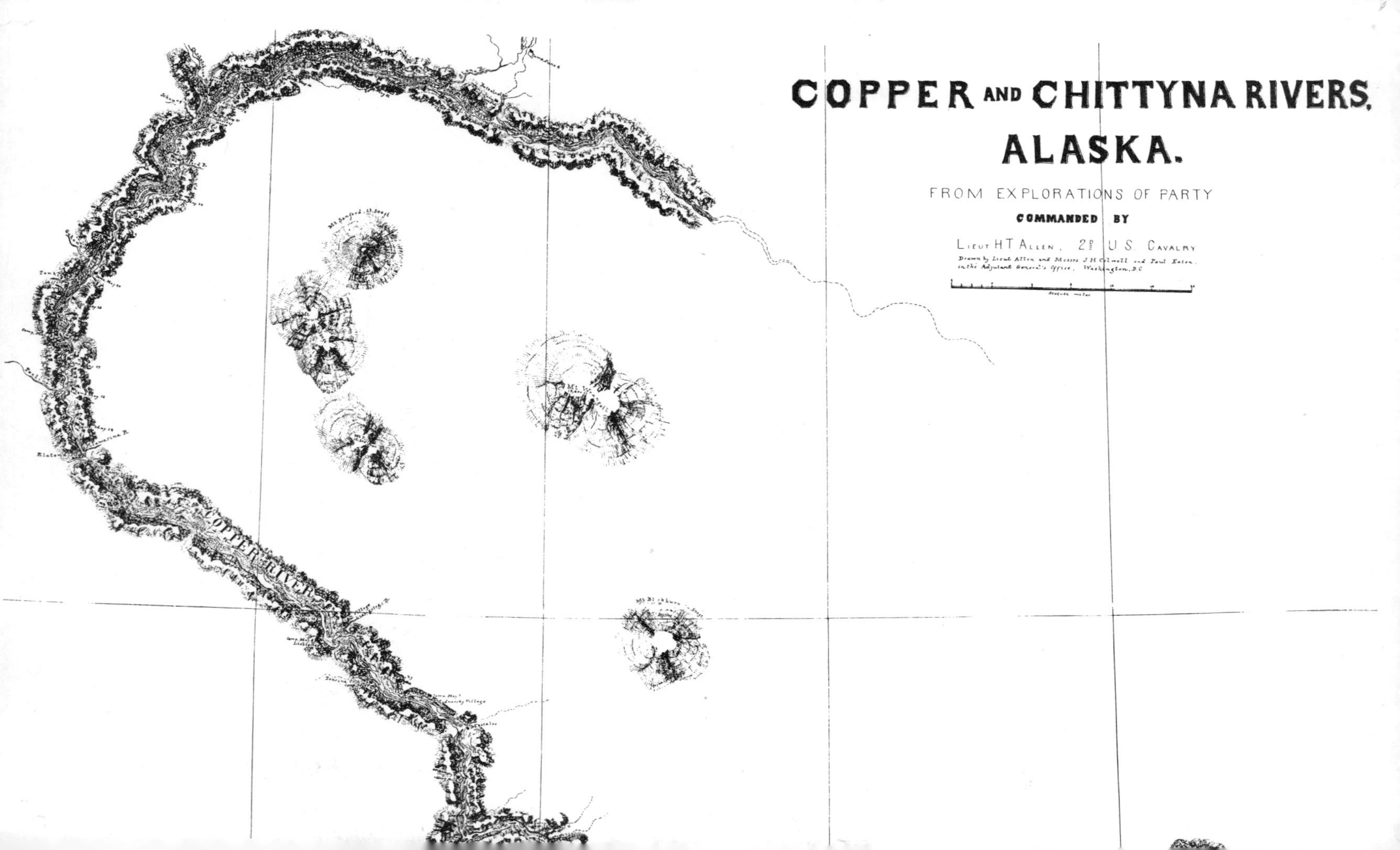
COPPER AND CHITTYNA RIVERS,
ALASKA.
FROM EXPLORATIONS OF PARTY
COMMANDED BY
LIEUT H T ALLEN, 2D U.S. CAVALRY
Drawn by Lieut Allen and Messrs J H Colwell and Paul Eaton, in the Adjutant General's Office, Washington, D.C.
Statute miles
COPPER RIVER